RABBI, MYSTIC, OR IMPOSTOR?

THE LITTMAN LIBRARY OF
JEWISH CIVILIZATION

Life Patron
Colette Littman

Dedicated to the memory of
Louis Thomas Sidney Littman
*who founded the Littman Library for the love of God
and as an act of charity in memory of his father*
Joseph Aaron Littman
and to the memory of
Robert Joseph Littman
who continued what his father Louis had begun
יהא זכרם ברוך

'*Get wisdom, get understanding:
Forsake her not and she shall preserve thee*'

prov. 4:5

*The Littman Library of Jewish Civilization is a registered UK charity
Registered charity no. 1000784*

RABBI, MYSTIC, OR IMPOSTOR?

The Eighteenth-Century Ba'al Shem of London

MICHAL ORON

Translated by
EDWARD LEVIN

London
The Littman Library of Jewish Civilization
in association with Liverpool University Press

The Littman Library of Jewish Civilization
Registered office: 14th floor, 33 Cavendish Square, London WIG 0PW

in association with Liverpool University Press
4 Cambridge Street, Liverpool L69 7ZU, UK
www.liverpooluniversitypress.co.uk/littman
Managing Editor: Connie Webber

Distributed in North America by Longleaf Services
116 S Boundary St, Chapel Hill, NY 27514, USA

First published in Hebrew 2002 © Bialik Institute, Jerusalem
English translation © The Littman Library of Jewish Civilization 2020
Introduction to the English edition © Todd M. Endelman 2020
First published in paperback 2025

All rights reserved.
No part of this publication may be reproduced,
stored in a retrieval system, or transmitted, in any form or by
any means, without the prior permission in writing of
the Littman Library of Jewish Civilization

This book is sold subject to the condition that it shall not, by way
of trade or otherwise, be lent, re-sold, hired out or otherwise circulated
without the publisher's prior consent in any form of binding or cover
other than that in which it is published and without a similar condition
including this condition being imposed on the subsequent purchaser

Catalogue records for this book are available from the
British Library and the Library of Congress
ISBN 978-1-835539-99-6

Publishing co-ordinator: Janet Moth
Copy-editing: Connie Webber, Philippa Claiden, Agi Erdos, Janet Moth
Proof-reading: Philippa Claiden
Index: Sarah Ereira
Designed and typeset by Pete Russell, Faringdon, Oxon.

The manufacturer's authorised representative in the EU for product safety is:
Easy Access System Europe, Mustamäe tee 50, 10621 Tallinn, Estonia https://
easproject.com (gpsr.requests@easproject.com)

This book is dedicated, in appreciation and love,
to the memory of
Rela and Professor Shalom Perelman
to the memory of
Sonia and Dr Louis Marks
my beloved London friends
and
to my best friend
Professor Chava Turniansky
who has been a compassionate companion and
forthright adviser over many years,

but above all I dedicate it to the memory of my life partner
Hanoch Bartov
who, as cultural attaché at the Israeli embassy,
fostered my interest in London and encouraged me in my writing.
He later closely followed the translation of this work,
but passed away while it was still being edited

PREFACE AND ACKNOWLEDGEMENTS

SAMUEL FALK's biography, as it emerges from his diary and from the diary of his factotum Zevi Hirsch of Kalisz, is living testimony to Jewish magic, and an important source for the study of its role in and influence on both the Jewish and Christian cultures of his time.

The picture of Falk's life that this book paints on the basis of many and diverse sources is that of a unique individual who, on the one hand, has almost vanished from Jewish historiography, in which he is mentioned (if at all) as the 'Ba'al Shem of London', or as a *ba'al shed* (possessor of/possessed by a demon rather than a wonder-worker), but who on the other hand was appreciated, and even held in great esteem, in the writings of the Freemasons and in research about them. In these works Falk is called 'Dr Falk' or 'Dr Falkon'.

The present volume contains an annotated edition of two diaries: the diary of Samuel Falk and that of his factotum Zevi Hirsch of Kalisz. A short sentence in Gershom Scholem's article on 'The Sabbatian Movement in Poland' aroused my curiosity. Scholem refers to two famous *ba'alei shem* who led somewhat colourful lives in the mid-eighteenth century: Moses David of Podhajce and Samuel Falk, who was known as 'Doctor Falk, the Ba'al Shem of London'.[1]

In my search for additional details about Dr Falk I came across two diaries, one written by Falk himself and the other by his factotum. Deciphering the two manuscripts proved to be a lengthy and arduous task. Both are written in Hebrew (which was not the vernacular of either author), and they are replete with spelling mistakes and the insertion of words from other languages. The numerous erasures by the two diarists raised additional obstacles to understanding the texts. Despite all these dif-ficulties, as the work of deciphering advanced and I uncovered the sources and documents relating to Falk's life I realized that the two diaries and the accompanying material that I had found during the course of my research present a fascinating story of the life of a charismatic individual who succeeded, by the force of his personality, in influencing both Jews and Christians and arousing their esteem.

This study would not have been possible without the support and aid of my friends and colleagues who encouraged me during the many years I devoted to this topic, and who graciously helped with their comments and references to sources of which

[1] Scholem, 'The Sabbatian Movement in Poland' (Heb.), III.

I was unaware. My friend Professor Chava Turniansky laboured together with me in deciphering the words in Yiddish. Her important comments and constant support helped me to overcome the obstacles and crises that arose during the course of the research. Professors Yehuda Liebes and Moshe Idel supported this study from the outset, and their comments and advice contributed to its completion. My friend Professor Ada Rapoport-Albert was always at my side offering practical assistance in my search for the original manuscripts, and also aided me in deciphering the place names written in the diaries, with numerous mistakes, in Hebrew transliteration of the English.

I wish to give special thanks to Hugh Alexander of the British Public Record Office (now The National Archives) for his assistance in photocopying Falk's original will. It is also my pleasure to thank the staff of the Institute of Microfilmed Hebrew Manuscripts of the National Library of Israel, and the staff of the Gershom Scholem Library and its director, my friend Dr Etti Liebes, who willingly and patiently assisted me. My thanks to the editor of the Hebrew edition, Shmuel Ram, and to Ms Geula Cohen, whose involvement in the book continued during the years of its gestation and who, like a good midwife, devotedly ensured that the birth would be smooth and swift.

I wish to extend my thanks to the School of Jewish Studies of Tel Aviv University, which contributed to financing the research and to its publication in Hebrew. The Secretary of the School of Jewish Studies, Gideon Spiegal, who followed the study from its inception, urged me to publish it.

My heartfelt thanks to Urit Wertheim-Eliraz, who took an interest in the book from its earliest days, and to all the staff of the Bialik Institute publishing house, who made me feel at home during the many years of joint work.

Special thanks to my friends Arela and Professor Shalom Perlman and Hannah and Professor Yisrael Levine for their many years of loyal friendship and help.

And last but not least, thanks to my teacher and friend Hanoch Bartov, who died before this English translation was published. He was both discerning and sensitive, and he supported me in reading, researching, and comprehending.

M.O.

CONTENTS

List of Plates	x
Note on Transliteration and Conventions Used in the Text	xi
Translator's Note	xiii
Note on the Editing of the Diaries	xvi
Introduction to the English Edition TODD M. ENDELMAN	1

INTRODUCTION

I	A Brief History of *Ba'alei Shem*	15
II	A Biography of Samuel Falk	28
III	Falk's Activities According to the Diary of Zevi Hirsch	35
IV	Samuel Falk as Seen by Jacob Emden	44
V	Samuel Falk and the Freemasons	49
VI	The Diaries and Their Research	62

THE DIARIES

The Diary of Zevi Hirsch of Kalisz	69
The Diary of Samuel Falk	165

APPENDICES

A.	People Featuring Prominently in the Diaries	243
B.	Falk's Dreams	248
C.	The Letter of Sussman Shesnowzi to His Son	251
D.	The Letter of Jacob Emden	261
E.	Falk's Library	265
F.	Falk's Will	273

Glossary	283
Bibliography	287
Index	297

PLATES

between pages 164 and 165

1. Hayim Samuel Jacob Falk, the Ba'al Shem of London. Portrait attributed to Philip James de Loutherbourg
2. Falk's tombstone in the United Synagogue's Alderney Road Cemetery, London
3. Inscription on a plaque affixed to Falk's tombstone
4. An extract from Falk's will
5. A page from the diary of Zevi Hirsch of Kalisz
6. A page from the diary of Samuel Falk
7. Tombstone of Theodor Stephan de Stein von Neuhoff, briefly king of Corsica
8. Stone commemorating leaders of the London Jewish community buried in the United Synagogue's Alderney Road Cemetery, London

NOTE ON TRANSLITERATION AND CONVENTIONS USED IN THE TEXT

❦

THE TRANSLITERATION of Hebrew in this book reflects consideration of the type of book it is, in terms of its content, purpose, and readership. The system adopted therefore reflects a broad approach to transcription, rather than the narrower approaches found in the *Encyclopaedia Judaica* or other systems developed for text-based or linguistic studies. The aim has been to reflect the pronunciation prescribed for modern Hebrew, rather than the spelling or Hebrew word structure, and to do so using conventions that are generally familiar to the English-speaking reader.

In accordance with this approach, no attempt is made to indicate the distinctions between *alef* and *ayin*, *tet* and *taf*, *kaf* and *kuf*, *sin* and *samekh*, since these are not relevant to pronunciation; likewise, the *dagesh* is not indicated except where it affects pronunciation. Following the principle of using conventions familiar to the majority of readers, however, transcriptions that are well established have been retained even when they are not fully consistent with the transliteration system adopted. On similar grounds, the *tsadi* is rendered by 'tz' in such familiar words as barmitzvah. Likewise, the distinction between *ḥet* and *khaf* has been retained, using *ḥ* for the former and *kh* for the latter; the associated forms are generally familiar to readers, even if the distinction is not actually borne out in pronunciation, and for the same reason the final *heh* is indicated too. As in Hebrew, no capital letters are used, except that an initial capital has been retained in transliterating titles of published works (for example, *Shulḥan arukh*).

Since no distinction is made between *alef* and *ayin*, they are indicated by an apostrophe only in intervocalic positions where a failure to do so could lead an English-speaking reader to pronounce the vowel-cluster as a diphthong—as, for example, in *ha'ir*—or otherwise mispronounce the word. An apostrophe is also used, for the same reason, to disambiguate the pronunciation of other English vowel clusters, as for example in *mizbe'aḥ*.

The *sheva na* is indicated by an *e*—*perikat ol*, *reshut*—except, again, when established convention dictates otherwise.

The *yod* is represented by *i* when it occurs as a vowel (*bereshit*), by *y* when it occurs as a consonant (*yesodot*), and by *yi* when it occurs as both (*yisra'el*).

Names have generally been left in their familiar forms, even when this is inconsistent with the overall system.

Citations from the books of Psalms and Daniel follow the numbering system used in the Hebrew; readers used to certain English translations, such as the Authorized or Revised Versions, may find that the verse numbers differ slightly. Similarly, in citing Mishnah *Pirkei avot* (*Ethics of the Fathers*), the numbering system that appears in the Travers Herford edition has been used in preference to alternative systems. Unless specified otherwise, the English versions of scriptural and rabbinic texts have been provided by the translator. References in the footnotes to FD and ZHD are to Falk's diary and Zevi Hirsch's diary respectively.

TRANSLATOR'S NOTE

HEBREW TEXTS of religious or quasi-religious content are usually written in a style all their own. Their vocabulary draws heavily upon words and phrases from classic Judaic works, whether written in Hebrew or Aramaic; they assume familiarity with traditional sources and concepts from the corpus of Jewish religious literature that might well be beyond the cultural experience of the target audience of the translation. Various techniques employed by these texts require special treatment, for example, flowery, often exaggerated language that cannot be literally rendered in another language; the use of wordplay, with the need for extra explanation and transliterated reference to the original Hebrew; numerology (*gematriyot*), based on the numerical value of each Hebrew letter (from *alef* = 1 to *taf* = 400), that often requires extensive explication.

Nor should we forget that, for a period extending over millennia, Hebrew was not a language in common usage. There was no standard form of the language, and every group or individual with occasion to speak or write in it was forced to devise linguistic solutions in order to communicate. The differing levels of Hebrew employed by Zevi Hirsch and Falk are neither rabbinic Hebrew, nor that of the *maskilim* (advocates of the Jewish Enlightenment) a century later as the language made its first tentative steps to the modern language with which we are familiar today.

All of these issues are compounded in texts that touch upon kabbalah. Despite some current efforts to turn it into an element of pop culture or a New Age universal panacea, this mystic discipline is, by definition, a mystery to the uninitiated.

In addition to these questions—which are the daily fare of Judaica translators—this study of the 'eighteenth-century Ba'al Shem of London' presented its translator with singular difficulties. The heart of the book consists of two diaries, one by Samuel Falk and the other by his factotum, Zevi Hirsch of Kalisz. Neither man could claim Hebrew as his mother tongue: Zevi Hirsch was most familiar with Yiddish, as was Falk. Nor was the Hebrew of their time well suited to the demands made on it by the material in these two diaries. On the one hand, as a personal document each diary reported on the full range of mundane, everyday experience, for much of which no words existed in Hebrew. On the other, accounts of the sublime were not lacking: Falk fancied himself a kabbalist and delved into esoterica, while his factotum attempted to describe some of these obscure practices. Their attempts to encompass pedestrian topics, such as Zevi Hirsch's accounts of the items of clothing he purchased or Falk's recipes, together with the secrets for which mystics claim no language is adequate, produced a text that, at best, requires great effort to understand even for native Hebrew speakers, and certainly for me, as I sought to render it into a different cultural milieu. Oftentimes words, or even entire passages, remained unintelligible even to Professor Oron, despite her heroic efforts to decipher these texts. In general, the poor Hebrew—even by eighteenth-century standards—of both diaries presented me with another quandary. I tried to make the English smoother than the original Hebrew and allow the content to shine through, but I felt uncomfortable putting it into flowing language, as I would for a translation from standard Hebrew.

In addition to these shared difficulties, each diary raised specific translation issues. As Marsha Schuchard notes, Zevi Hirsch was 'semi-literate'.[1] This country boy, whose native tongue was Yiddish, attempted to write a diary in Hebrew—and also to describe his master's mystical practices. Zevi Hirsch's diary is replete with grammatical mistakes and misspellings; these were fully annotated in the Hebrew edition but have been omitted here because of their irrelevance for English-speaking readers. His use of run-on sentences, too, is excessive. At times, his use of terminology with specific associations is obviously inappropriate, and reveals his lack of proper understanding of the original concept, such as his entry for Monday, 10 Iyar, in which a horse that fell and was wounded is described as 'just as if dead, *killed on the road*'.[2] The latter phrase is reminiscent of the biblical case of the victim of an unsolved murder that imposes a heavy responsibility on the elders of the town nearest to the corpse, who must then engage in a special ritual,[3] an association that obviously is inappropriate for a simple accident involving an animal.

Samuel Falk, a self-proclaimed kabbalist, was neither a mainstream practitioner nor a rabbinic scholar. His knowledge of Hebrew was far from perfect, and mistakes in grammar and spelling are not uncommon. On the other hand, some of his attempts to create new forms to answer his needs are fascinating, such as his use of the word *tsaḥtsaḥut* instead of the standard *tsiḥtsu'aḥ* for 'polishing';[4] but the reader interested in further study of points of this sort is referred to the Hebrew edition.

Altering, or omitting, content is generally understood to fall beyond the purview of the translator, one of whose goals should be fidelity to the original. Samuel Falk's diary, however, was terra incognita in this respect: rather than the rare word or phrase in an obscure source for which ellipsis is necessary I was faced instead with entire passages in the diary, of kabbalistic content, that were untranslatable, some owing to their impenetrable nature, others because the explanations required would be unwieldy. Indeed, in one place Falk copied what he had written earlier, and candidly admitted 'and I know not its meaning'![5] In practice, Professor Oron and I adopted

---

[1] Schuchard, 'Dr. Samuel Jacob Falk: A Sabbatian Adventurer', 11.   [2] ZHD, fo. 22b.
[3] Deut. 21: 1 ff. See Aaron Halevi of Barcelona, *Sefer haḥinukh*, trans. Wengrow, Commandment 530.
[4] FD, fo. 31a; entry for 25 Sivan 5519/20 June 1759.
[5] FD, fo. 33b; entry for 26 Shevat 5539/12 Feb. 1779.

the opposite approach in regard to the kabbalistic passages in Falk's diary: since the majority were untranslatable, we chose those that could be rendered into English to exemplify Falk's mystical techniques, and these have been explained to the extent possible.

Special attention was paid in the Hebrew edition to Falk's numerous transliterations, and most were explained in the notes at their first appearance. Some of his transliterations were quite accurate even by modern academic standards, while others can be charitably described as approximate; yet others reflect his Ashkenazi pronunciation of Hebrew (for example, the letter *taf* pronounced like the letter *s*). Falk's writing is marked by the widespread importing of words from a range of European languages, at times in combination with Hebrew or Yiddish words. In a broader sense, they offer a fascinating view of this European Jew making a life for himself in a new country, making use of all the cultural tools at his disposal. Professor Oron devoted considerable effort and copious glosses to explaining these non-Hebrew expressions whenever possible. In translating the diaries for an English reader it seemed less necessary to comment on the terms and spellings used in the Hebrew original, so in general the translation uses the English equivalent without further explanation.

A few technical issues should be mentioned here. The diaries, especially the kabbalistic passages in Falk's diary, make copious use of Hebrew terms and manipulations of biblical verses. Wherever possible, I rendered them in English translation. If some sense of the Hebrew was needed, the words appear in italics in transliteration. If even transliteration would have proven unwieldy, as in Falk's third- and fourth-order numerological exercises and other numerical reductions, the actual Hebrew is given, with translation when appropriate.

Both Zevi Hirsch and Falk date diary entries, and refer to past events, by the Jewish calendar. This was problematic for three reasons: (1) in the Jewish calendar a day extends from nightfall to nightfall, and there is some confusion as to which Gregorian day a given date or day of the week corresponds; (2) some of Falk's dates are probably erroneous, with internal inconsistencies between dates; (3) some entries are not in the proper chronological order. Where it was not possible to solve these problems, their existence is noted.

In the interests of fluency, some of the flowery or pious expressions common in religious Hebrew prose have been omitted from this translation.

A final note: the late David Louvish was the first to attempt the daunting task of translating the Hirsch and Falk diaries. After he had completed his initial translation Professor Oron added more material and explanatory notes. Unfortunately illness, followed by Louvish's untimely death, prevented him from completing the project, and I was asked to step into his shoes. David Louvish's translation provided the basis without which I could not have embarked on this task.

E.L.

NOTE ON THE EDITING OF THE DIARIES

It cannot be denied that editing the translated texts of the diaries and Michal Oron's copious learned notes on them has been a huge challenge. Quite a number of factors have contributed to the difficulty. Firstly, as Edward Levin has pointed out in his Translator's Note, the texts of the diaries are very difficult: neither Zevi Hirsch of Kalisz nor Samuel Falk was fluent in Hebrew, and neither seems to have had a secular education; both factors meant that their texts were often difficult to follow. They are stylistically inconsistent and often lack clear structure: material—even where it has a date attached—is presented out of order. Words are missing, sentences are unfinished, terms are not clearly defined, sums don't add up. Above all, the texts are full of esoteric material, which means that by definition they are difficult to understand. Our goal, I felt, was to make this material accessible to the English reader. Edward Levin had done a masterly job in rendering the obscure original texts into English—a task that required considerable knowledge of biblical sources as well as of kabbalistic terminology—but having the text in English was not in itself enough. His translation of the diaries was faithful to the original, but because the original was obscure the resultant text often remained obscure. Even where the underlying meaning was clear, one's attention was so distracted by inconsistencies—in the spelling of personal names and place names, in whether numbers were presented in words or in numerals, in the representation of units of measurement—that it was difficult to follow the storyline.

As Edward says in his Translator's Note, altering or omitting content falls beyond the purview of the translator, one of whose goals should be fidelity to the original. Editors, however, take a different view: they aim to produce a text that readers will be able to follow and understand easily, without being distracted by infelicities, inconsistencies, and a plethora of square brackets to indicate conjunctions, prepositions, and so forth that have been added by the translator to make the text comprehensible. Normally such editorial work is done in close consultation with the author. Here there were two problems to face: the original authors—that is, Zevi Hirsch and Samuel Falk—had been dead for years and could not be consulted. Professor Oron, who became by default their representative on Earth, was not very comfortable in English, and therefore had difficulty responding to the many questions that arose in the course of editing. Moreover her scholarly specialization is the language of Hebrew mystical literature, whereas the questions that arose in trying to make the text accessible related to a whole host of other areas.

Progress was further hampered by the deterioration in Professor Oron's health, which meant that she had neither the time nor the inclination to deal with such matters, and the decline in the health of her life partner, Hanoch Bartov, a writer of renown and a former cultural attaché at the Israeli embassy in London, who had helped solve some of the problems that arose during the protracted process of translation, but was unable to help with the problems that arose in editing. Sadly, he passed away while the editorial work was still ongoing. But it was actually much earlier that Professor Oron, faced with dozens of pages of editorial queries in English, said that she understood what I was trying to do, trusted my skills as an editor, and would accept my judgement. I in turn accepted her trust and persevered, even though I had not undertaken a project of quite such a nature in my thirty-odd years of copy-editing academic books.

It was a daunting task: the book was originally written for a Hebrew-speaking readership primarily interested in the philological aspects of the diaries as a work of literature. An English-speaking readership, I felt, was likely to be interested primarily in what the protagonists did and thought—where they went, who they met, how they lived, and other facets of life in eighteenth-century England, as well as the nature of the mystical activity in which they engaged—rather than in the language they used. This difference in focus had to be borne in mind in preparing the English edition. Three of my editorial colleagues at Littman—Philippa Claiden, Agi Erdos, and Janet Moth—helped me in this, each contributing according to her own area of specialization.

Supplementary information added to the lemmata by the editorial team is presented within square brackets, to make it clear which comments were in the original Hebrew edition and which have been added. Where text has remained incomprehensible, that has been indicated too, so that readers are aware that the lack of clarity has persisted despite our best efforts. Civil equivalents have generally been provided for the Hebrew dates used by the diarists, at least enough to provide a general orientation; in the case of Zevi Hirsch, they have been converted according to the Julian calendar (daytime) as the entire period covered by his diary precedes England's adoption of the Gregorian calendar. This information was not given at all in the Hebrew edition.

As I worked on the diaries, I often found myself distracted by linguistic glosses that were of no relevance to the narrative. The translator had retained quite a lot of such comments, but I increasingly felt that other English-speaking readers trying to follow the narrative would also find them a hindrance. Accordingly, and with Professor Oron's agreement, I have for the most part just used the appropriate English word without marking its derivation. Similarly, I have omitted comments relating to the form of the Hebrew text rather than its content—whether a particular phrase was written above the line, or whether it was crossed through and then rewritten, or whether it had actually been deleted and then editorially reconstructed—on the grounds that most English-speaking readers will be satisfied with how Professor Oron as a scholar has interpreted the text.

Another distracting feature of the original text was the diarists' inconsistency in the representation of numbers. In English there are standard conventions for when one uses numerals and when one uses words, so to minimize distractions I have imposed order. The same is true with regard to sums of money, which figure significantly in both diaries. Both diarists were foreigners in England and not well schooled in arithmetic—even simple calculations were often wrong—and used a bewildering variety of ways to record their transactions. In the interests of consistency I have as far as possible imposed the standard pre-decimal conventions of representing pounds, shillings, and pence in the form £5. 10s. 5d., and order has similarly been imposed on the representation of weights and measures. Place names, often misspelled, have been corrected silently. In referring to members of Falk's circle and other Jews with whom he was in contact I have used the names by which he and Zevi Hirsch referred to them rather than the anglicized forms found in the literature: thus, 'Tuvyah' and 'Shimon', not 'Tobias' and 'Simeon'; simply, this approach seemed more consistent with the authors' characters and lifestyle. Finally, no indication has been given of odd words apparently missing unless their absence makes the text incomprehensible, in which case a parenthetical [?] has been inserted. To sum up, the editorial practices adopted here are similar to those I would apply to any text to obtain a smooth reading.

Quite a few of Falk's esoteric manipulations of texts remained incomprehensible despite Edward Levin's best efforts; the more straightforward ones have been retained so that interested readers can get a sense of what he was doing, while others have been omitted and summarized in the lemmata. Where text has been omitted, the extent of the omission is indicated in the lemmata with reference to the line numbers of the Hebrew edition.

I trust that the sort of editorial interventions I have outlined here will help readers become familiar with the amazing world that Michal Oron has brought to light.

C.W.

INTRODUCTION TO THE ENGLISH EDITION

TODD M. ENDELMAN

MICHAL ORON'S account of Samuel Falk, the Ba'al Shem of London, complicates the conventional characterization of eighteenth-century Britain as the birthplace of the modern—the cradle of toleration, reason, liberty, science, and enlightenment.[1] In this reading of the century, rational religion and Enlightenment science discredited magic, superstition, prophecy, and wonders, along with ghosts, spirits, demons, and the like. Falk's career as a wonder-worker in London, from the early 1740s to 1782, suggests that the picture was more complex. Specifically, it suggests that, however triumphant Enlightenment ideas were in Georgian Britain, they did not succeed in uprooting and banishing faith in the occult. Well-born Christians and wealthy Jews alike turned to Falk to answer questions and solve problems that resisted conventional approaches. While never prominent in synagogue and communal affairs, Falk did not labour in obscurity. He was well known in occult and theosophical circles and enjoyed the support of leading Jewish families. Visitors to London with theosophical interests often sought him out and later recounted their meetings in memoirs and travelogues. In time he prospered, and at his death in 1782 he was a wealthy man.

Falk was a charismatic religious figure, a *ba'al shem* (literally, a master of the name), whose authority flowed from his virtuosity in employing divine names for magical ends rather than from his expertise in understanding and expounding Jewish law. While *ba'alei shem* (the plural) were, by definition, exceptional individuals, they were also familiar figures—at least in Jewish communities in eastern Europe, where kabbalah (the Jewish mystical tradition) was deeply entrenched among the learned and informed the beliefs and practices of the common folk. Drawing on esoteric, mystical knowledge, they performed various and sundry magical acts, including healing the sick, revealing lost treasures, writing amulets to combat demons and diseases, conjuring angels and spirits, and transforming base into precious metals. As a rule, they were not communally supported officeholders but freelance virtuosi who lived on the fees they received for their services. Their stature in a community or a region depended on how well they fulfilled the expectations they aroused.

---

[1] For example, Roy Porter, *Enlightenment: Britain and the Creation of the Modern World* (London, 2000).

In London, by contrast, a Jewish wonder-working kabbalist like Falk was a novelty. London was the westernmost outpost of European Jewry in the eighteenth century (with the exception, of course, of the tiny settlements in the New World). It was a new community, having been established only in the second half of the seventeenth century, known neither for its piety nor its learning. Its population, which numbered between 5,000 and 10,000 during Falk's residence there, was drawn from immigrants or the children of immigrants from central Europe. Unlike most European Jewish communities, London Jewry was a voluntary community, with no formal, state-sanctioned authority over Jews who lived there. The British state, unlike tutelary, absolutist states on the Continent, took little interest most of the time in what Jews did—that is, the trades they pursued; the synagogues, schools, and charities they established; the rites they practised (or neglected, as often was the case); where they lived, whom they married, and with whom they mixed. The state did not limit the number of Jews who settled in Britain nor impose taxes or duties on them as Jews. Jews who were born there were citizens, their legal status similar to that of other Britons who were not members of the Church of England.

Because London Jewry lacked well-established religious institutions and because communal authority and control were weak, secularization was more advanced there than it was in other European Jewish communities. Regular synagogue attendance and strict observance of the dietary laws and of the laws of sabbath and festival rest were more uncommon than common by the second half of the century. Knowledge of Hebrew and sacred texts was confined to small circles of traditionalists, whose influence on the community as a whole was insubstantial. There was no yeshiva (academy for the study of Talmud and legal codes), for example, during Falk's residence in London. As a rule, pious, learned Jews were unlikely to settle in London or anywhere else in Britain. The overwhelming majority of the newcomers were simple, largely penniless petty traders who were seeking to improve their lot in a society where state intervention and regulation were weak. They were seeking relief from the day-to-day harassment and occupational and residential restrictions that embittered the lives of most Jews in the German states. Among the newcomers were some whose past transgressions, either against the law of the land or against communal authority, had prompted them to restart their lives where their personal histories were unknown or irrelevant.

Falk's journey to London was both typical and atypical of the wave of immigration that contributed to the expansion of London Jewry in the Georgian period. Born in Podhajce (then in Poland, now in Ukraine) at the start of the century, Falk moved to Fürth in northern Bavaria as a young man. Both Podhajce and Fürth were hotbeds of Sabbatianism and Frankism, and his contact with sectarians in those towns undoubtedly fired his mystical interests. He then led a more or less peripatetic existence until the early 1740s, wandering in Germany from place to place, supporting himself and his family as a *ba'al shem*. In Cassel he was reported to have cured the court Jew's daughter of epilepsy using kabbalistic talismans alone. At times he enjoyed the patronage of Christian aristocrats whose fascination with the esoteric and the uncanny led them to seek knowledge in the mysteries and secrets of the Jews—that is, in kabbalah. While Christian interest in Jewish esoterica went back to at least the fifteenth century, in the eighteenth century it became 'a fad' in central and western Europe, extending way beyond the confines of an erudite elite.[2] Falk, like other eighteenth-century adventurers such as Giacomo Casanova (1725–98) and Count Alessandro di Cagliostro (1743-95), exploited aristocratic interest in alchemy, the occult, and ancient, non-Christian sources of knowledge, both to support himself and to further his alchemical experiments. In the 1730s he spent several years on the estate of Baron von Donop in Geilberg in Schleswig-Holstein, and later was hosted by Count Alexander Leopold Anton von Rantzow (1681–1747) at his castle in Braunschweig. (The count's son left a detailed account of Falk's activities, which Oron cites at length.[3]) On occasion he was forced to change his residence when his rites and experiments aroused the ire and fear of the authorities. In Westphalia he was once sentenced to burn as a sorcerer, while in Cologne he was expelled by the archbishop elector. He was banished from several German states, according to Rantzow's *Mémoires*, because he 'performed things that were above the prodigies that one can relate'.[4]

Around 1740 Falk made his way to The Hague, where he was able to operate more freely, and there gained the patronage of the banker Tobias Boas (1696–1782), to whom Falk refers as 'Tuvyah', perhaps the wealthiest Ashkenazi Jew in the Netherlands. Boas was the dominant figure in The Hague community, a traditional Jew who supported Jewish scholarship and who, apparently, was a votary of kabbalah. Falk's connection with the Boas family was critical to his career. Whether Boas encouraged his move to London is not known, but it was Boas who undoubtedly provided him with an introduction to the Amsterdam-born merchant banker Aaron Goldsmid (1715–82), who settled in London in 1763 and became Falk's wealthiest and most influential supporter there. The Boas and Goldsmid families did business with each other, and the latter contributed unwittingly to the collapse of the Boas bank in 1792, when Abraham Goldsmid (1756–1810) persuaded Abraham Boas (1728–98) and his brother Simeon (1730–95) to loan the Prince of Wales and his brothers the duke of Clarence and the duke of York 350,000 guilders (which they failed to repay).[5] The Boases were also close to the Prager family of Amsterdam, colonial merchants and financial

---

[2] Paweł Maciejko, *The Mixed Multitude: Jacob Frank and the Frankist Movement, 1755–1816* (Philadelphia, 2011), 221. [3] *Mémoires du Comte de Rantzow* (Amsterdam, 1762).
[4] Quoted in Raphael Patai, *The Jewish Alchemists: A History and Source Book* (Princeton, 1994), 456.
[5] Robert Huish, *Memoirs of George the Fourth*, 2 vols. (London, 1831), ii. 137; *The Correspondence of George, Prince of Wales, 1770–1812*, ed. Arthur Aspinall, 8 vols. (London, 1963–71), ii. 49.

speculators who established a branch in London in 1752.[6] The head of the Prager firm in London, Yehiel Prager (d. 1788), who was known as Israel Levin Salomons outside the Jewish community, was linked to the Goldsmid family through the marriage of his daughter Jessie (1767–1836) to Benjamin Goldsmid (1755–1808).[7] Prager also became a patron of Falk. One other possible link between Falk and the Goldsmids of London is that the Amsterdam (and later London) Goldsmids knew of Falk from his miraculous cure of the young woman with epilepsy in Cassel, where several members of the family served as court Jews to the Landgrave of Hesse-Cassel. Whatever the details, Falk's ties to Boas helped open doors for him in London.

Nonetheless, Falk's earliest years in London were difficult. As the diary of Zevi Hirsch of Kalisz, his factotum at the time, reveals, he only fed and clothed his household—his long-suffering wife, her son Gedaliah (from a previous marriage), and Zevi Hirsch himself—with much difficulty. He was forced repeatedly to pawn household goods (lamps, tablecloths, napkins, bowls), personal belongings (shirts, watches, rings, his hat), and ritual objects (a Torah mantle and curtain for the ark in his private synagogue), as well as objects that he used in his mystic rituals (a silver egg, seven gold stars, three pairs of candlesticks). What is striking about his recourse to pawnbrokers is that those whom Zevi Hirsch mentions by name in his diary appear to be Christians, not Jews. This is surprising because there was no shortage of Jewish pawnbrokers in the area where he lived. Only when he needed to pawn Hebrew books did he turn to a Jewish pawnbroker. I would guess that he avoided Jewish pawnbrokers when he could to prevent word of his hand-to-mouth existence spreading among Jews.

Falk's difficulties were, to a large extent, of his own making. According to Zevi Hirsch, he was irresponsible in money matters (a habitual problem for many in Georgian London). For example, in 1747 he purchased a lottery ticket for £10. 2*s*. 0*d*. at a time when, in Zevi Hirsch's words, 'there really was no bread in the house'. The next month he was unable to take delivery of a wooden chest, built to his own specifications for use in his occult rites, because he lacked the £13 that he owed the Christian workman who had made it. When it was finally delivered several months later, Zevi Hirsch commented, as he often did in reference to Falk's extravagance, 'This, too, is for nothing.' He used the same phrase in condemning Falk's expenditure of £8 to entertain guests at Purim that year. When Passover arrived, the situation was grim: there were no candlesticks in his private synagogue, just a lamp, and there was only one Torah scroll, which lacked a mantle and silver ornaments—'a great disgrace', in Zevi Hirsch's words.

[6] For evidence of the link between the Boas and Prager families, see Gedalia Yogev, *Diamonds and Coral: Anglo-Dutch Jews and Eighteenth-Century Trade* (Leicester, 1978), 307 n. 14.

[7] Albert M. Hyamson, 'An Anglo-Jewish Family', *Transactions of the Jewish Historical Society of England*, 17 (1953), 1–10.

Although Zevi Hirsch viewed his master's reckless spending with despair, Falk's extravagance was not purposeless. Falk was a charismatic religious virtuoso whose success rested on the willingness of others to stand in awe of him and acknowledge his power over unseen forces. He needed to radiate confidence, authority, and, of course, mystery. If we accept this, then we can understand why he strove to avoid the appearance of vulnerability, poverty, and weakness. Acting the role of generous host on Jewish holidays complemented and advertised his mystical virtuosity and power. Several Christian accounts of his activities noted the visual impression he made. Rantzow described his appearance, for example, as 'very noble and grand',[8] while the German historian Johann Wilhelm von Archenholz (1741–1812), in an account written around 1780 when Falk was no longer struggling to establish himself, noted that he occupied 'a splendidly decorated big house' (in Wellclose Square).[9]

We do not know where Falk resided when he first settled in London. In September 1747, Zevi Hirsch records that he moved to a house in Prescot Street, which is east of the City of London and north-east of the Tower. His new residence was in the heart of London's Jewish settlement—the easternmost wards of the City of London, Houndsditch, Spitalfields, Whitechapel, and Goodman's Fields. This was well before prosperous Jewish merchants and bankers in the area began migrating westward, and rich and poor lived in close proximity to each other, including Falk's wealthy patrons: Aaron Goldsmid, Aaron Hart, Lyon de Symons, and Israel Levin Salomons. Prescot Street was also convenient to London Bridge, where, in one of the houses and shops that lined the bridge itself and often jutted out over the water, Falk maintained a chamber for the performance of mystical rites, many of which Zevi Hirsch recorded in detail. It is not clear, however, how long Falk continued to rent rooms here. The houses and shops on the bridge were removed between 1758 and 1762, and none of the London newspapers, which covered their removal and the dislocation of the occupants, mentions Falk.[10] Falk's own diary, whose entries date from the 1760s and 1770s, says nothing about a workshop on the Thames.

Falk's reputation grew, at least among cognoscenti of the occult, and with prosperity he eventually moved his household to the grander address of Wellclose Square, south-east of Prescot Street, but within the same general locale. The square, a favourite of well-to-do Jews, was laid out in the late seventeenth century and was a smart location in the Georgian period. Here he remained until his death in 1782.

Despite Falk's residence in the midst of London Jewry and his connections to leading communal figures, he seems to have held himself aloof from the life of the community and maintained a low profile overall. For example, in the agitation surrounding repeal of the Jew Bill of 1753, in which extravagant accusations about Jewish

---

[8] Quoted in Patai, *The Jewish Alchemists*, 455.   [9] Quoted ibid. 462.
[10] For this and other information about the sites of Falk's activities I am deeply indebted to Stephen Massil, whose knowledge of Falk's environs has been invaluable.

chicanery and aggression circulated, pamphleteers and publicists never mentioned his name. His name is also absent from the list of subscribers to the first Hebrew prayer book to be published in England, in 1770. The list includes the leading figures in the Great Synagogue, the Hambro Synagogue, and the newly established Western Synagogue.[11] By this time Falk was no longer a struggling wonder-worker and certainly could afford to subscribe. When he prayed, he preferred to do so in his own home, where he maintained a small private synagogue, both in Prescot Street and in Wellclose Square, even though the Great and the Hambro were an easy walk from where he lived. This caused some controversy, for it contravened a regulation of the chief Ashkenazi synagogue in Duke's Place, which banned the establishment of rival houses of prayer so as to ensure its own financial stability. In spring 1749, on the festival of Shavuot, a decade before Falk fell under suspicion of being a secret follower of the long-deceased false messiah Sabbatai Zevi (1626–76), one of the wardens of the Great Synagogue, the diamond merchant Elias Levy (1701–50), 'sent a spy to see who was attending the Sage's synagogue' (in Zevi Hirsch's words). (When Levy died not long thereafter, Zevi Hirsch recorded that Falk had predicted his early demise because of his actions on Shavuot.) The otherwise unknown Moses Fishman was caught and forced to repent publicly at the Great Synagogue during the afternoon service on the following sabbath. But as the London community was voluntary and lacked any police authority, the wardens of the Great Synagogue were powerless to close Falk's synagogue or, indeed, to supervise his occult activities in any way. They were able to discipline Fishman, but then he was a humble trader in fish (it would appear, given his name), a man of low status with no connections, who, we can speculate, turned to the synagogue for occasional relief or depended on the custom of the well-to-do who managed its affairs. Years later, in 1767, when Falk donated 10 guineas to the Great Synagogue in memory of his recently deceased wife, one of the *parnasim* (wardens) wanted to make him a *ba'al bayit* (householder, that is, privileged member) of the congregation, but Falk refused the offer, although he expressed his gratitude.

Zevi Hirsch's diary and that of the Ba'al Shem, which Oron transcribes and annotates extensively, describe the latter's wonder-working, alchemical, and mystical activities. However, because these documents were not intended to be read by others, their accounts of the Ba'al Shem's rites are often cryptic and elusive. Thus it is often difficult to envision exactly what Falk was doing at a particular point in a rite or why he was doing it that way—that is, what mystical purpose it was intended to serve. Oron's learned notes make the task easier, as do her notes on the Hebrew and Aramaic texts he had recourse to in the performance of his rites. The latter are especially important because Jewish mysticism, whatever its experiential dimension, has always been text-heavy and text-centric. Her notes allow us to see how Falk's

[11] *Tephilloth, containing the Forms of Prayers which are Publicly Read in the Synagogue and Used in All Families*, trans. B. Meyers and A. Alexander (London, 5530 [1770]).

practices were rooted in earlier kabbalistic ideas and how he read biblical texts in a mystical way, a way that obviously departed from their conventional understanding.

More accessible are the passages in the diaries that describe Falk's healing activities. Perhaps the most fascinating is Zevi Hirsch's account of his effort to cure the mental illness of the son of Simhah Segal (or Levy) in 1750. Segal brought his son 'Isaac the madman' to Falk's house in Prescot Street, and Falk examined him to determine whether his insanity was due to natural causes or to possession by a demonic spirit (*kelipah*). Having determined that it was the latter, Falk kept him in his house for twenty-four hours and performed rites to cure him. At one point Falk threw a flask of oil from the window of his house onto the street and the flask, miraculously, remained unbroken after hitting the paving stones. Six months later 'the madness returned to the boy Isaac', Zevi Hirsch wrote, because Falk had cancelled (for reasons that Zevi Hirsch fails to mention) the adjurations that he had cast against the *kelipah* earlier. However, Falk also announced that while the boy would continue to be mad he would not be as seriously ill as before.

The Ba'al Shem performed his rites in at least four locations in or around London—in his home, in his chamber on London Bridge (before the demolition of the buildings on the bridge), at various sites in Epping Forest (an ancient woodland north-east of London, bordering Essex), and occasionally at other sites along the Thames, east of the City. Throughout his residence in London he also remained in close touch with his early patrons in The Hague, members of the Boas family, and travelled there to execute mystical tasks on several occasions. When the radical *maskil* Solomon Maimon (1754–1800) visited The Hague in 1783 or 1784,[12] he met Tobias Boas's sons Abraham and Simeon, and they told him of the miracles that they had seen the Ba'al Shem perform during his stays there. (The arch-rationalist Maimon replied that 'as a philosopher', while he did not 'question the truth of their statement', he thought that 'perhaps they had not duly investigated the matter themselves and had presented their preconceived opinions as facts'. They, in turn, denounced his view as heretical.[13]) Falk buried a gold chest containing ritual objects with mystical import somewhere in Holland in 1758 or 1759, later moving it to different sites, including the Boas estate. From time to time he also dispatched members of his household to northern Europe on missions related to his kabbalistic activities—for example sending his stepson Gedaliah to Flanders in 1747 and Zevi Hirsch to Holland in 1751.

I stress the geographical reach of Falk's activity for two reasons. First, as a kabbalist, the arena in which he operated was metaphysical and otherworldly, not local. The scope of his activity transcended the British Isles, let alone London. While he worked

---

[12] In his autobiography Maimon does not give the date of his visit to The Hague. I am grateful to Paul Reitter, who is preparing a new translation of the autobiography, for this information.

[13] Solomon Maimon, *An Autobiography*, trans. J. Clark Murray, ed. Moses Hadas (New York, 1967), 83–4.

small-time wonders for London's Jews, healing them and writing amulets for them, the focus of his occult activity was literally cosmic. In his eyes and the eyes of his devotees he was an unrivalled spiritual virtuoso, the possessor of arcane, ancient knowledge that allowed him to plumb the depths of creation, explore unseen worlds, and influence the invisible forces that flowed through and energized the material world. Thus, when he refused membership in the Great Synagogue in 1767, he told the *ḥazan* (cantor), Isaac Polack (d. 1802), 'Heaven forfend that my name should be mentioned in such a matter, for I am *ba'al bayit* for all the world.' So while London may have been the site of his residence and the most frequent venue of his wonder-working, the scope of his activity was broader. Second, Falk was known in theosophical and mystical circles outside Britain. His longstanding ties to the Boas family in The Hague, as well as his activities in Germany before his emigration to London, help explain why Christian travellers and adventurers from the Continent sought him out when they came to London. We know the identity of several of them and no doubt there were more, since the diaries of Zevi Hirsch and the Ba'al Shem do not cover the entire period of the latter's residence in London.

Two French noblewomen, the marquise de Thomé and the marquise de la Croix, visited the Ba'al Shem in October 1747, seeking mystical knowledge. (The marquis de Thomé, who shared his wife's interest in the occult, was an early follower of the theosophist Emanuel Swedenborg.) When the Jerusalem-born rabbi Hayim Joseph David Azulai (1724–1806), also known by the acronym Hida, visited Paris thirty years later, in the winter of 1777/8, on one of his fundraising missions for the Hebron yeshiva, he met the marquise de Thomé and the marquise de la Croix, and the latter talked of the kabbalistic secrets that Falk had taught her. Azulai, himself a kabbalist (which explains why the pair visited him), did not approve, noting that, 'in his conceit and wilfulness' Falk had 'revealed practical kabbalah and incantations to many nobles, both men and women, to aggrandize himself'. Azulai's testimony suggests that other well-born Europeans visited Falk and that the marquise probably visited him on more than the one occasion in 1747 that Zevi Hirsch recorded. It is also worth noting that when Azulai visited The Hague as part of the same journey, in June 1778, Tobias Boas's sons Simeon and Abraham recounted 'remarkable things' about the Ba'al Shem of London—for example, that he had a sword that could fly and that he had walked in a forest dating from the six days of Creation. Like Solomon Maimon several years later, Azulai was not impressed and referred to these things as 'nonsense'. But he *was* impressed by what they told him of the Ba'al Shem's wealth.[14]

The charlatan and adventurer Theodore Stephen de Stein (1694–1756), Baron von Neuhoff, one-time king of Corsica, met Falk frequently, sometimes daily, for several months in 1749—presumably to obtain, by alchemical means, the gold he needed to

[14] Hayim Joseph David Azulai, *Ma'agal tov hashalem*, ed. Aron Freimann (Jerusalem, 1934), 124, 154, 155.

retake the island kingdom he had briefly ruled. They met at Falk's house and at King Theodore's country house at Upton in Essex, close by Epping Forest, one of the sites of Falk's mystical activities. Their connection ended when Theodore's money ran out and he was imprisoned for debt in the King's Bench in December 1749.

Emanuel Swedenborg (1688–1772), who visited London frequently after the onset of his celestial visions in the mid-1740s, also apparently contacted Falk, although his name does not appear in either of the Hebrew manuscripts in this volume. On a visit in 1744, when he became seriously ill, he was moved to the home of Dr William Smith, a specialist in mental illness and epilepsy who knew Falk—Zevi Hirsch mentions his name—and allegedly drew on Jewish medical and kabbalistic traditions in treating these illnesses. Some have speculated that Smith introduced Swedenborg to Falk and that the Swedish church in nearby Prince's Square, where Swedenborg worshipped, and the Swedish-owned King's Arms tavern in Wellclose Square, where Swedenborg lodged in 1764, further linked the Swedish mystic and the Ba'al Shem. However, if they were acquaintances, what Swedenborg learned from Falk is, as Oron explains, a matter of dispute.

The adventurer and charlatan Count Cagliostro—alchemist, healer, and cultivator of esoteric strains of Freemasonry—was also said to have learned kabbalistic secrets from Falk, on his visits to London in 1771–2 and 1776–7. Falk does not mention Cagliostro in his commonplace book, but this does not preclude the possibility that they met, since this text is not an exhaustive record of everyone whom Falk encountered. More significant than whether the Sicilian learned anything from Falk is that the claim was given widespread credence. The reputation of Falk as the bearer of arcane knowledge was such that persons wishing to assert their authority in occult matters often hinted or suggested that their knowledge derived from an authentic source. In a popular biography of Cagliostro, the Australian historian Iain McCalman wrote that many of the artisans and intellectuals who frequented small, mystically minded Masonic lodges in Soho and elsewhere in central London in the 1770s claimed to have been inspired by teachings of Falk.[15] Again, this tells us more about his reputation and, more generally, the appeal of the secret lore that he embodied than about the extent of his ties to these Masonic seekers.

Oron's treatment of Falk's ties to Christians who were seeking esoteric knowledge is bracingly sober and effectively counters the fanciful and speculative accounts of Falk that have flooded the scholarly marketplace in the last two decades. The best known of these are the articles of Marsha Keith Schuchard, an independent scholar with a Ph.D. in British literature, who has written extensively on the esoteric traditions of European secret societies in the modern period and their impact on Irish and English literature. Her work sensationalizes the scope and character of Falk's

---

[15] Iain McCalman, *The Last Alchemist: Count Cagliostro, Master of Magic in the Age of Reason* (New York, 2003), 145–6.

activities. She claims, inter alia, that he was a crypto-Sabbatian who participated in a clandestine, kabbalah-fuelled plot to restore the Stuart claimant to the British throne; that he taught kabbalistic sexual theosophy to Swedenborg; that he supplied kabbalistic secrets to Masonic lodges; and that his influence spread to the far reaches of Russia, Algeria, and Italy.[16] Oron, drawing on her deep knowledge of the history of kabbalah and the two texts that she has edited, politely and firmly dismisses these extravagant claims. The historian of Frankism Paweł Maciejko is more emphatic in dismissing Schuchard's penchant for discovering conspiratorial activities. For him, her 'imaginative description of the eighteenth-century Jewish-Christian international Masonic network' is 'more like a positive fantasy of modern enthusiasts of multi-culturalism than a historical reconstruction'.[17]

The truth of the matter is that we have no unambiguous evidence of the nature of Falk's ties with Freemasonry. There is nothing in his own or in Zevi Hirsch's diary indicating that he taught kabbalah to prominent Freemasons, as Schuchard claims, or that he exerted any influence on the lodges in London—or elsewhere, for that matter. To be sure, his circle of patrons included active Masons, most prominently members of the Boas and Goldsmid families, but this proves little, for hundreds of Jews in London, drawn from all but the lowest social ranks, were Freemasons in the Georgian period.[18] They were attracted by Masonic traditions of sociability, self-government, and toleration, by the possibility of intimate companionship with respectable Christians, and by the exoticism of Masonic rituals, which offered a counterweight to the humdrum nature of daily life. In the last decades of the eighteenth century some lodges in London and abroad grafted magical, mystical, and alchemical elements onto their rituals, forging an ethos that was simultaneously rational and theosophical. Charlatans and adventurers like Cagliostro and Casanova, who wanted to infuse Freemasonry with occult elements, frequently imagined that Jewish mysticism was a source of untapped knowledge. Its antiquity, its esotericism, its inaccessibility, and its association with the mysterious, uncanny powers often attributed to Jews lent it cachet in their eyes and in the eyes of those whom they beguiled. Whether it was true or not, they *claimed* to have learned kabbalistic secrets from Falk and other learned Jews. In all likelihood, their knowledge was no greater than that of celebrity followers of kabbalah in the contemporary era. The significance of the association of Falk with

---

[16] See e.g. 'Yeats and the "Unknown Superiors": Swedenborg, Falk, and Cagliostro', in Marie Mulvey Roberts and Hugh Ormsby-Lennon (eds.), *Secret Texts: The Literature of Secret Societies* (New York, 1995), 114–68; 'Dr. Samuel Jacob Falk: A Sabbatian Adventurer in the Masonic Underground', in Matt Goldish and Richard H. Popkin (eds.), *Jewish Messianism in the Early Modern Period* (Dordrecht, 2001), 203–26; 'Lord George Gordon and Cabalistic Freemasonry: Beating Jacobite Swords into Jacobin Ploughshares', in Martin Mulsow and Richard H. Popkin (eds.), *Secret Conversions to Judaism in Early Modern Europe* (Leiden, 2004), 183–231.   [17] Maciejko, *The Mixed Multitude*, 229.

[18] John M. Shaftesley, 'Jews in Regular English Freemasonry, 1717–1860', *Transactions of the Jewish Historical Society of England*, 25 (1977), 153.

Freemasonry is less the reality than the myth, that is, what his contemporaries imagined and fantasized about him because they linked Jews with dark, unseen forces.

The fact that Falk figured sympathetically in the imagination of well-known charlatans does not mean that he was himself a charlatan in the eighteenth-century mould. It would be an error to associate him with that informal clan of exotic itinerants who moved from court to court and salon to salon, selling their services as alchemists, pimps, magicians, and purveyors of arcane knowledge to gullible and greedy princes and nobles, swindling and defrauding, staying one step ahead of the law, flourishing one moment and languishing the next.[19] While Falk exploited Christian fantasies about the mysterious powers of Jews, he was not, as far as we know, a swindler like Casanova and Cagliostro, for whom embezzlement and forgery were a way of life. Moreover, unlike them, he was neither an impostor, inventing an exotic or noble background for himself to smooth his way into aristocratic society, nor a libertine and serial seducer of aristocratic women. He never pretended to be other than who he really was: a *ba'al shem* and learned kabbalist from Poland, steadfast in his observance of Judaism. His world-view, which emerges clearly from the two texts, was uncompromisingly traditional—bearing in mind that kabbalah, while esoteric, loomed large in the Judaism of central and eastern Europe at the time. His library, which Oron reconstructs in Appendix E, included dozens of kabbalistic texts and commentaries on them, some of which accompanied him on his travels. Together with the entries in his diary, it testifies to his learned immersion in the Jewish mystical tradition. The most persuasive evidence that Falk was not a charlatan is his unbroken residence of four decades in London. While he never succeeded in transforming base into precious metals (as far as we know!), his activities and his conduct more generally failed to arouse the suspicion or hostility that might have forced him to move elsewhere. In his travel narrative Rantzow claimed that Parliament had Falk arrested and then freed him on condition that he no longer practise kabbalah, but this is too far-fetched to credit. The very notion that Parliament took any notice of him seems ludicrous.

The wealth that Falk accumulated is also evidence that he gained the trust of prosperous members of the Jewish community. It would appear that for four decades bankers and brokers rewarded him for his kabbalistic endeavours on their behalf. If we rule out the possibility that he succeeded in making gold or that he won the lottery consistently, there is no other way to account for his affluence, which was impressive. He lived in a large, well-decorated house in a more than respectable residential square and travelled by horse-drawn carriage. In August 1764 he listed in his diary the French bonds that he owned. Their value totalled 128,600 'pounds' (*livres tournois*)—the equivalent of approximately £5,500 sterling at the time or £550,000

---

[19] For this point I am indebted to Maciejko's original treatment of Jacob Frank and Wolf Eybeschuetz as typical eighteenth-century charlatans.

sterling at present.[20] Falk's will (see Appendix F) also reveals how wealthy he had become. He had no heirs—his wife was dead and they had not had children—so he left the bulk of his estate to synagogues, both Ashkenazi and Sephardi, and communal charities, mostly in London. The range and amount of the bequests are staggering. Moreover, most were intended to be annual gifts in perpetuity, drawn from the interest generated by the corpus of his estate. While the value of the entire estate is unknown, it would have had to be substantial to generate an annual income sufficient to satisfy these bequests.

Falk's ties to well-known banking and trading families underscore the complex and uneven character of the transformation of traditional Jewish society in the eighteenth century. Falk himself was the embodiment of the world of traditional early modern Judaism, with its faith in revelation, divine omniscience and omnipotence, the binding authority of the *mitsvot* (divine commandments), and the reality of the unseen. But his patrons were men of the world, well dressed and well fed, attuned to the quickening pace of financial and mercantile life and to the ways of Christian society; men of substance, whose dress, deportment, and style of life differed little from those of the Christian gentlemen with whom they traded and even socialized at times, for example in Masonic lodges. (Many in the next generation of Goldsmids and Pragers were so indifferent to Judaism that they left the community and became Christians to enhance their social status.) As a whole, moreover, English Jews, rich and poor alike, were more secular in their behaviour and outlook than central European Jews. Even though London Jewry was one of the largest Jewish communities in Europe in the eighteenth century, it was a religious backwater, lacking yeshivas and outstanding talmudists.

But as the story of the Ba'al Shem of London and his wealthy patrons demonstrates, the transformation of London Jewry, however advanced, was not comprehensive. Just as, at this time, mysticism and rationalism coexisted in Masonic and revolutionary circles, and esoteric and scientific discourse in learned and aristocratic ones, so too acculturation and secularization did not preclude a belief in a holistic, dynamic cosmos throbbing with unseen forces, and a fervour for harnessing their energy. Michal Oron's book reveals to an English-reading audience in compelling detail the persistence of the old in the new and the complexity of the passage from tradition to modernity.

[20] I am grateful to my colleague David Hancock, a historian of the early modern Atlantic, for providing me with the rate of conversion.

INTRODUCTION

I

A BRIEF HISTORY OF BA'ALEI SHEM

THE PRIMARY representatives of Jewish magic in the seventeenth and eighteenth centuries were known as *ba'alei shem* (literally, 'masters of the [divine] name'; singular: *ba'al shem*), wonder-workers who employed the names of God (or of his angels), through certain techniques, for various theurgic purposes.[1]

Despite biblical opposition to magic (and sorcery) and their practitioners,[2] the rabbinic literature teaches of the existence, and spread, of the phenomenon among the sages in the Land of Israel and Babylonia, and not only among the uneducated members of society.[3] Evidence to this effect appears in the mystical *heikhalot* literature:[4] not only do these works include patently magical texts, but their descriptions of the qualities and aptitudes of the mystical elect ('those who descend to the *merkavah* [divine chariot]') resemble what would later characterize the *ba'alei shem*.

Thus, the book *Heikhalot rabati* specifies:

1. One who 'descends to the *merkavah*' to attain mystical elevation ('observation of the *merkavah*') must recite certain hymns (that contain divine names).

2. Such an individual, by virtue of his being such a 'descender', is capable of foreseeing the future: 'Who shall be brought down, and who raised; who shall be weakened, and who strengthened; who shall be made destitute, and who rich; who shall be put to death, and who kept alive; who shall be deprived of inheritance, and who shall inherit Torah; who shall be given wisdom.'[5]

3. He knows people's characters and their hidden actions: 'all creatures are before

---

[1] For *ba'alei shem* in Judaism, see 'Ba'alei shem' (Heb.), in Eisenstein (ed.), *Otsar yisra'el*, iii. 137; Scholem, 'Ba'al Shem' (*EJ*); Nigal, *Magic, Mysticism, and Hasidism*; Hillel, *Ba'alei shem* (Heb.); Rosman, *Founder of Hasidism*, ch. 1; Etkes, 'The Role of Magic' (Heb.).

[2] See Exod. 22: 17; Lev. 20: 27; Deut. 18: 9–14.   [3] See Urbach, *The Sages* (Heb.), 97 ff.

[4] The *heikhalot* literature has been the subject of much research. See e.g. Scholem, *Major Trends*, 40–78; id., *Jewish Gnosticism*; Gruenwald, *Apocalyptic and Merkavah Mysticism*; Dan, 'Anfiel, Metatron, and the Creator' (Heb.); id., '*Ḥadrei merkavah*' (Heb.); id., *Ancient Jewish Mysticism* (Heb.). See also the individual articles in a volume devoted entirely to *heikhalot* literature: id. (ed.), *Early Jewish Mysticism* (Heb.).   [5] Schaefer, *Synopse zur Hekhalot Literatur*, para. 82 (p. 40).

him as silver before the silversmith, who knows which is genuine silver, which is adulterated, and which is pure'.[6]

In other words, these mystics possess special qualities: their knowledge of incantations and divine names enables them to undergo mystical experiences and be in contact with the supernal spheres. These texts therefore attest to magical knowledge or activity for mystical and spiritual purposes, together with magical knowledge of the nature and fate of human beings (that would later be known as 'wondrous sight').[7] Such magical faculties enable them to have profound insight into other human beings. The *heikhalot* literature also proffers further magical knowledge, for the attainment of material goals. Such knowledge may be found in various works of the genre, such as *Sefer harazim*,[8] *Ḥarba demoshe*,[9] and *Havdalah derabi akiva*.[10] These works assume that a person knowing the secret names (of God and the angels) is capable of exploiting that knowledge for theurgic purposes in this world. Thus we find magical incantations of hidden holy names, accompanied by practical instructions for the preparation of potions, and for various other activities. The purpose of such actions, as presented in these works, is to exert influence on other individuals, to prevent illness and pain, and to save people from robbers, evil spirits, demons, and sorcery.

During the geonic period, Rav Hai Gaon received a query from the community of Kairouan in North Africa, concerning a *ba'al shem* who, it was rumoured, had been witnessed simultaneously in several places.[11] That is, this man was acquainted with the technique of *kefitsat haderekh* (miraculous 'shortening of the way'),[12] and, according to those who directed the query to Hai Gaon, he would employ holy names to achieve his aims. Judging from Hai Gaon's response he disapproved of the very rumour, and he sounds a warning against the dangers inherent in such actions when conducted by the impure. This responsum contains the earliest known occurrence of the term *ba'al shem*.[13] In a later period, the Hasidei Ashkenaz (the pietists of the Franco-German community in the twelfth to thirteenth centuries) made repeated use of the terms *ba'alei shem* and *ha'osekim bashemot* (those engaged with, or manipulating, holy names). Joseph Dan has pointed out the demonological concepts in the writings of these pietists,[14] and has published several such texts with obvious demonological

---

[6] Schaefer, *Synopse zur Hekhalot Literatur*, para. 86 (p. 42).

[7] For the ability to perceive people's character and future, see Scholem, 'Physiognomy and Chiromancy' (Heb.), 461; Gruenwald, 'New Fragments from the *Heikhalot* Literature' (Heb.).

[8] See the edition by Mordecai Margalioth.   [9] Available in Gaster (ed.), *Studies and Texts*.

[10] See Scholem, '*Havdalah derabi akiva*: A Source for the Tradition of Jewish Magic during the Geonic Period' (Heb.).   [11] Ashkenazi, *Ta'am zekenim*, 54–8; Lewin, *Otsar hage'onim: ḥagigah*, 16.

[12] For *kefitsat haderekh* as a magical motif, see Nigal, *Magic, Mysticism, and Hasidism*, 33–49.

[13] According to Rosman (*Founder of Hasidism*, ch. 1, n. 9), the earliest known use of the term occurs in the ancient midrashic work *Sifrei zuta* (he cites Liberman, *Ohel raḥel*, 5).

[14] Dan, *The Esoteric Theology of Hasidei Ashkenaz* (Heb.), 184–202.

leanings.¹⁵ Dan focused both on the theology underlying these texts and on their folk-tale/literary nature. In his view, the demonological stories attest to the influence of the non-Jewish environment in which the Jews of this community were then living.¹⁶ These pietist writings contain proofs of magical activity, both for purely mystical purposes¹⁷ and for material gain in everyday life. An example of the first category may be found in *Sefer haḥayim* (The Book of Life), attributed to Rabbi Abraham ibn Ezra but written within Hasidei Ashkenaz circles:¹⁸

A vision is that a person is awake and meditates on the works of the Lord, or does not meditate *but pronounces the holy names or the names of the angels* in order to show Him his desire or to reveal a secret matter. The spirit of divine inspiration is revealed to him and his flesh, which is worms and maggots and is like a [mere] garment, trembles and recoils before the might of the spirit of divine inspiration, and cannot endure [this]; then that person stands as one in a faint, not knowing where he stands, neither seeing, hearing, nor sensing his body, but rather [sensing] what his soul sees and hears. This is what is called a vision, and this is what most prophecies entail.¹⁹

This writer asserts that the mere utterance of the names of God or of the angels causes a person to have a vision or to experience prophetic powers. The implication of this passage is that someone pronouncing the holy names experiences physical changes—his body trembles to the extent that he faints and loses his senses—but compensating for this physical weakness is the greater receptivity of his soul, which is thus prepared to experience the vision.²⁰

An example of theurgic activity is to be found in a collection of demonological tales attributed to Rabbi Judah Hehasid,²¹ which includes two tales about a person who writes amulets: 'A man would write amulets, and the demon came and slept with his wife before him; he did not see, but his wife would see.'²² Fantastic though this short story may be, it reflects the opposition that existed to the writers of charms, and indicates the danger they faced. The next story in the collection (which exhibits greater literary sophistication) also concerns a writer of amulets. This person is kidnapped by a demon, who first seeks to kill him, but is persuaded to spare him on condition that he marry the demon's daughter. The story succinctly describes this man's life in the world of demons with his succubus wife, and his subsequent return home after the death of his wife and his complete release. This is an early version of a folk

---

¹⁵ Id., 'Demonological Stories in the Writings of R. Judah Hehasid' (Heb.); id., 'Princes of the Cup' (Heb.).   ¹⁶ Id., *The Esoteric Theology of Hasidei Ashkenaz* (Heb.), 189.
¹⁷ Idel, *The Golem* (Heb.), 73–106.   ¹⁸ See Kirchheim, '*Ketav tamim*' (Heb.), 85.
¹⁹ Ibid., emphasis added. See also Dan, *The Esoteric Theology of Hasidei Ashkenaz* (Heb.), 143.
²⁰ Similar descriptions appear in accounts of the Ba'al Shem of London, both in the diary of his factotum Zevi Hirsch of Kalisz and in the letter of Sussman Shesnowzi to his son (see below, Appendix C).
²¹ See Dan, 'Demonological Stories in the Writings of R. Judah Hehasid' (Heb.).
²² Ibid., para. 18 (p. 19).

tale that was popular in Hebrew literature, beginning in the medieval period, entitled *Ma'aseh yerushalmi*,[23] which describes the marriage of a human and a she-demon. Though it has a happy ending, the opening of the tale illustrates the dangers awaiting people who engage in incantations and the writing of charms. The existence of such admonitions against magical activities, whether explicit (as in *Sefer ḥasidim*[24]) or implicit, by literary means, clearly reveals the presence of such activity.

Writings by thirteenth- and fourteenth-century kabbalists contain references to magical 'uses' of the holy names.[25] The Castilian kabbalist Rabbi Isaac Hakohen wrote: 'there is a further tradition known to the *ba'alei shem* at certain times: [the use of] the sphere of demons. In order to attain a part of the prophetic attributes, that is, [the use of] the sphere of the Holy One, blessed be He, and *kefitsat haderekh*, they make use of the perception that is called the sphere of the use of demons.'[26] He goes on to relate that he has heard from a great sage in Narbonne, and from many others, that Rabbi Eleazar the Great of Worms would ride the clouds by means of an

---

[23] See Dan, 'Demonological Stories in the Writings of R. Judah Hehasid' (Heb.), para. 19 (pp. 19–20); see also Dan, *The Esoteric Theology of Hasidei Ashkenaz* (Heb.), 198; Zfatman, *The Marriage of a Mortal Man and a She-Demon* (Heb.); T. Alexander, 'Design of the Demon Story Genre' (Heb.).

[24] *Sefer ḥasidim*, paras. 170, 469, 1114, 1172. The last section states explicitly that evil spirits harm only those who provoke them, such as a person whose ancestors (or who himself) wrote amulets, dabbled in sorcery and incantations, or interpreted dreams: 'a person should therefore beware of such activities'. It is clear from the wording that the involvement with magic was generally passed on from father to son as a family tradition.

[25] A few typical quotations will exemplify this. R. Abraham Abulafia wrote, in a letter to 'R. Abraham': 'After receiving the wisdom of the kabbalah, that brings one to [mystical] perception, I quickly realized that one is the matron and the other the servant-girl. And then I knew, moreover, the great error of those certain people who call themselves in some well-known lands . . . using a name renowned in the paths of kabbalah, *ba'alei shemot*. The error is that they think that they will perform wonders with the power of the [divine] names in incantations, when they pronounce them with their mouth, without any knowledge and understanding of their meaning. They claim to fly though the air on sticks, to slay their enemies with their words, to quench fire and calm the stormy sea with a [divine] name, and similar unfathomable madnesses and imaginings.' Jellinek, *Philosophie und Kabbala*, 22.

R. Moses de Leon: 'I saw those who explain the matter of *sha'atnez* [cloth made from linen and wool, a mixture forbidden by the Torah], who are *ba'alei shemot*, and they say that a demon [*satan*, here assumed to derive from the word *sha'atnez*] has power over one who wears *sha'atnez* and is capable of harming him.' 'The Secret of Forbidden Mingled Plantings and Forbidden Cloth Mixtures' (Heb.), *Sefer hanefesh haḥakhamah*, fo. 1N (13a).

Todros Abulafia: 'The tradition of the sages of divinity in the secrets of the Torah is one thing, that of those who know the [divine] names, another'; 'And do not imagine that he is referring to Metatron the Great Prince, who is frequently referred to by the *ba'alei shemot*.' *Otsar hakavod*, fos. 20a, 20b.

Joseph Gikatilla: 'And now, my son, hear my voice and hearken to my counsel. "My son, if sinners entice you, do not yield" [Prov. 1: 10]—let them not say, Go with us and we will give you [divine] names and formulas that you will be able to use; my son, do not walk with them, keep your foot from their path, for those [divine] names and uses are all manner of nets and snares to trap souls and take them to perdition.' *Sha'arei orah*, vol. i, 46.

[26] See Scholem, 'The Treatise on the Left Emanation' (Heb.), para. 10 (p. 92).

incantation.²⁷ Rabbi Isaac expresses no disapproval of this report; on the contrary, he cites it in support of his own account. In the work cited here, *Ma'amar al ha'atsilut hasemolit* (A Treatise on the Left Emanation), Rabbi Isaac presents various traditions known to him concerning the forces of evil and their source. This section of his treatise (para. 10) therefore introduces and substantiates a further tradition deriving from Rabbi Isaac, concerning 'three spheres [*avirim*, lit. 'airs']', the third of which is 'the sphere of the use of demons'. This tradition relates to the powers responsible for the various demons and fiends and their influence on the world, and ascribes dreadful diseases such as leprosy and rabies, and such catastrophes as earthquakes, to these supernal demons and their spawn. In fact, the progeny of these mighty demons are present in our world: some come to mislead and deceive human beings, while others strive 'to do good and drive away hardships from people, and tell the future to people, while they appear to them in human guise'.²⁸ The names of the 'supernal demons' in Rabbi Isaac's work would later reappear in a manual of adjurations and charms.²⁹

Magical activities that would be typical of the later *ba'alei shem* are cited as qualities and virtues of prominent figures in Jewish cultural history.³⁰ Such depictions are common in the hagiographical literature that developed from the sixteenth century onwards. Though these exemplary individuals are not yet referred to as *ba'alei shem*, the stories about them and their wondrous deeds justify their characterization as 'wonder-workers'.

Gedalyah Nigal has suggested that such tales were decisively influenced by the stories of the Hasidei Ashkenaz. The early motifs seem to have provided the external garb for the new figures, which in its later manifestations was embellished and expanded by the addition of new motifs.³¹ It is only natural to ask whether such stories have any core of historical truth. Even if we agree with the assumption³² that the stories were designed to show the reader, in narrative fashion, the hero's greatness and sanctity, they patently also fulfilled a social function. The hagiographical tales described these spiritual leaders—the heroes of the tales—as *magicians*, with implicit recognition of their abilities and their considerable proficiency in mystical and magical lore.

The seventeenth century saw the emergence of the popular kabbalistic literature, a genre that includes both hagiographical books and ethical *musar* works, including the subclass of the latter literature known as *hanhagot* (prescriptions for proper conduct). The influence wielded by books belonging to this genre aided the spread

---

²⁷ This is a vestige of a hagiographical tale of R. Eleazar of Worms and the secret of *kefitsat haderekh*; see also Nigal, *Magic, Mysticism, and Hasidism*, 37 ff.

²⁸ Scholem, 'The Treatise on the Left Emanation' (Heb.), 95.   ²⁹ Ibid. 94 nn. 1 and 2.

³⁰ For example, such tales are told of R. Simeon bar Yohai, R. Judah Hehasid, Nahmanides, R. Isaac Luria, and R. Hayim Vital. For the hagiographical literature, see Dan, 'On the History of the *Shevaḥim* Literature' (Heb.), 82–100.   ³¹ Nigal, *Magic, Mysticism, and Hasidism*, 10.

³² Dan, 'On the History of the *Shevaḥim* Literature' (Heb.), 83.

of kabbalistic teachings, and the once-esoteric lore intended for the elect became a popular way of life.

In a detailed study of this conduct literature, Zeev Gries has noted the spread of popular works of the genre towards the end of the seventeenth century.[33] These books, which were based on kabbalistic teachings, offered their readers new modes of worship. The procedures and mystical aims of the kabbalists were set before the public in a lucid, easily understood manner, so that even individuals who were not learned could follow them in their everyday life.

The conduct literature intensified the general feeling that the most profound secrets of the Torah were to be found in kabbalah.[34] The wider dissemination of kabbalistic teachings placed them at the centre of everyday life, and those adept in them were honoured and respected.[35] This spread of kabbalah and the esteem in which it was held apparently led to the emergence of the *ba'alei shem*. The term was possibly now applied to individuals well versed in the secrets of kabbalah, that is, mystics for whom knowledge and utterance of the holy names and letter combinations were an important component of their mystical practices; some of these practices, relating to everyday life, were now taught to the public at large. But it was also given to those who, possessing knowledge of the ancient popular traditions that linked folk medicine and the use of holy names, were able to apply their knowledge: the phenomenon of folk healers, which became quite common in the seventeenth and eighteenth centuries, is no doubt related to the cultural atmosphere, to the belief systems that obtained in these and earlier centuries in eastern and central Europe.[36] Misfortune, sickness, and natural catastrophe were blamed on demons or sorcery. Naturally, this nurtured belief in those individuals capable of countering such ills: those who possessed the power to nullify acts of sorcery and heal disease. It was the force of circumstances and popular beliefs that promoted the proliferation of *ba'alei shem*, who were able to use their prowess in these matters to earn their livelihood.

Alongside such mystics, whose occupation was an outcome of their faith, there were numerous impostors and charlatans lying in wait for gullible believers. In the eighteenth and nineteenth centuries the combined ignorance and cunning of these *ba'alei shem* aroused general criticism and derision, and a sense of revulsion.[37] Such criticism also influenced the writers of modern historiography, who describe the *ba'alei shem* as being of low and even inferior social standing.[38] This conception

---

[33] Gries, *Conduct Literature* (Heb.), introduction.

[34] Elbaum, *Openness and Insularity* (Heb.), 184, 219, 253. [35] Rosman, *Founder of Hasidism*, 20.

[36] There is a considerable literature on magic in Europe. A few representative works are Cavendish, *A History of Magic*; Flint, *The Rise of Magic*; Ruderman, *Kabbalah, Magic and Science*; Storms, *Anglo-Saxon Magic*; Thomas, *Religion and the Decline of Magic*; Walker, *Spiritual and Demonic Magic*; Yates, *The Occult Philosophy*. [37] See e.g. Werses, 'Phenomena of Magic and Demonology' (Heb.).

[38] See Dubnow, *The History of Hasidism* (Heb.), 30–1, 47; Weiss, 'Beginnings of Hasidism' (Heb.), 53–5; Dinur, 'The Origins of Hasidism' (Heb.). A similar attitude is discernible in Martin Buber's version

was first challenged by Mendel Piekarz, who cites two examples of *ba'alei shem*, contemporaries of the Ba'al Shem Tov (the founder of hasidism), who were also prominent Torah scholars who occupied highly respected rabbinical posts and were accepted as halakhic authorities.[39] Gedalyah Nigal, Moshe Rosman, and Immanuel Etkes have all stressed that those known as *ba'alei shem* were not only among the elite of the Jewish society but also gained prominence as spiritual leaders in their respective communities.[40]

Sources for Our Knowledge of the *Ba'alei Shem*

There are both direct and secondary testimonies, some sympathetic and others critical, that shed light on well-known *ba'alei shem* of the seventeenth and eighteenth centuries. These accounts were written by people who either knew the *ba'alei shem* personally or had heard of them from others who had first-hand knowledge of them.

Direct Evidence

One instance of the first category is a book by Rabbi Pinhas Katzenellenbogen entitled *Yesh manḥilin*.[41] This author served as the rabbi of several communities and was the scion of a highly respected family.[42] In the book, which was written as an ethical testament to his sons, he recounts the annals of his family and the story of his own life. His detailed account, including specific references to members of his family and other contemporaries, sheds light on the lifestyle and world of a typical Ashkenazi family in addition providing information regarding contemporary society. Among other things, Katzenellenbogen speaks of the activity of several *ba'alei shem* with whom he had become acquainted.[43]

Katzenellenbogen, who grew up in a distinguished rabbinical family and received a traditional education, was not a kabbalist, nor did his family belong to 'kabbalistic circles'. Nevertheless, his writing reveals something of the spiritual atmosphere that pervaded the family home. The list of books in his library, some of which he distributed to his sons while keeping others for himself, includes many kabbalistic tomes.[44]

of the Ba'al Shem Tov stories, which he alters and censors whenever they refer to the Ba'al Shem Tov's magical activities.

[39] Piekarz, *The Beginning of Hasidism* (Heb.), 136–7.

[40] Nigal, *Magic, Mysticism, and Hasidism*; Rosman, *Founder of Hasidism*; Etkes, 'The Role of Magic' (Heb.).

[41] Etkes, 'The Role of Magic' (Heb.), 77–86, discusses this book at length; Nigal, *Magic, Mysticism, and Hasidism*, and Rosman, *Founder of Hasidism*, also refer to it.

[42] The editor of the volume, in his introduction, describes the history of the author and his family, tracing their lineage back to R. Judah Minz (b. *c*.1408, d. Padua, 1506). Among Katzenellenbogen's ancestors was Saul Wahl, who according to legend was king of Poland for one day.

[43] *Yesh manḥilin*, 41–51.

[44] Among the books he possessed were the Zohar, *Zohar ḥadash*, *Sha'arei orah*, *Marot hatsove'ot* (by

Moreover, it is clear that he had indeed read them, as he quotes from them in his book.[45]

Katzenellenbogen's attitude to practical kabbalah was ambivalent. In keeping with a time-honoured tradition that emphasizes the dangers inherent in the 'use of names', he cites his grandfather, Rabbi Saul Katzenellenbogen, who had warned his sons against dabbling in the divine names;[46] he then adds some admonitions of his own, quoting from *Sefer ḥasidim*[47] and the book *Asis rimonim* by Menaḥem Azariah of Fano,[48] also declaring that he had personally known *ba'alei shem* who had suffered harm as a result of their vocation and had died prematurely.[49] While Rabbi Pinḥas, like his forebears, warns his own son against the use of divine names, it is clear from the rest of the book that his father (who had issued similar cautions) was nevertheless adept in their use. He had found several *segulot* (charms) recorded in his father's notebook, which he copied down for his sons' benefit.[50]

The ambivalence in Katzenellenbogen's attitude is even more obvious when, while declaring 'I myself have never engaged in practical kabbalah, nor performed any act using the holy names', he relates: 'except in one thing that I have from the kabbalist, our master and teacher, the rabbi, Rabbi Benjamin Beinish,[51] the author of the book *Amtaḥat binyamin*: a charm for a woman having difficulty in childbirth, that has been tested and proved several times, and, with God's help, has been of avail'.[52] Further on he describes a charm that he learned from the book *Toledot adam*:[53] 'And

R. David b. Judah Hehasid), *Sefer kavanot ha'ari*, *Sefer derushei ha'ari*, *Sefer hagilgulim*, *Sefer magen david*, *Magid meisharim*, *Pa'amon verimon*, *Sefer sha'arei tsiyon*, and *Sefer otserot ḥayim*.

[45] See e.g. *Yesh manḥilin*, paras. 16, 91, 245, 246.

[46] See ibid., para. 15 (p. 87). To bolster his warning, R. Pinḥas tells a story that he had heard from his uncle about the latter's father-in-law, a master of practical kabbalah. The story tells of a servant boy who had looked into a book of practical kabbalah, despite being cautioned not to do so, and who went mad as a result.   [47] See *Sefer ḥasidim*, para. 469.

[48] Menachem Azaria of Fano, *Asis rimonim*, sha'ar 27, fo. 65b.   [49] *Yesh manḥilin*, para. 16 (p. 89).

[50] Ibid., para. 20: 'See this, too, that I found in that same book and on the same page, written there beside it, and this too I do not desire to conceal from you, my beloved sons, may my Rock and my Redeemer protect them, and my descendants after me. And this it states: A wonderful remedy for a boy or a girl who has been struck with falling sickness [i.e. epilepsy], provided they have not had an attack three times. Make a ring of pure silver and write on its other [i.e. inner] side, before you bend it into a ring, in the script used for Torah scrolls, *tefilin*, and *mezuzot*, the names "Igla Agaf", "Aflaon Afiman", and then bend the ring, immerse the ring [in a ritual bath], and hang it on the child. This is tried and tested.'

[51] R. Benjamin Beinish was known as a *ba'al shem* and as the author of two books of charms: *Sefer shem tov katan* and *Amtaḥat binyamin*.   [52] *Yesh manḥilin*, para. 24 (pp. 97–8).

[53] *Toledot adam* was a well-known book of charms. The editor of *Yesh manḥilin* (Feld) comments (p. 98, n. 2) that it was written by R. Moses b. Elijah Gallena, and first published in Constantinople (1515), and later printed in Offenbach (1715); the same information is provided in Ben Jacob, *Otsar hasefarim*, 617, s.v. *Toledot adam*. Maters, 'A Book of Charms' (Heb.), lists several books by that name, and discusses a similarly named work by R. Joel Ba'al Shem, first published in Zolkiew in 1720. Judging from the dates, Katzenellenbogen is, indeed, most probably referring to Gallena's work.

these I tested and had practical experience with them, as I found and saw with my first wife.' Katzenellenbogen tells his children about several *ba'alei shem* whom he had met and entertained in his home, from whom he had heard wondrous tales and received charms. In times of trouble and sickness, he relates, he used these amulets to cure members of his family.[54]

Another notable element in *Yesh manḥilin* is the author's reports of various 'encounters' between members of his family and demons, and how they fought these malicious spirits. It is quite likely that these autobiographical stories (in which the narrator, Rabbi Pinhas, is sometimes a detached 'reporter' and at other times an 'eye-witness narrator') were known to his sons, who had undoubtedly heard them from him personally. Nevertheless, he saw fit to record them in his book, in recognition of the interest and perhaps even importance of such stories, in order to ensure that they would be preserved and passed on to future generations of his family, just as he himself had received such lore from his father's notebooks.

In sum, Rabbi Pinhas Katzenellenbogen's book provides living, reliable evidence of the mood of his contemporaries and his family. They all believed in the existence of demons and fiends; moreover, they were convinced of the power of charms to combat these entities, though well aware of the dangers incurred by employing such means.

Indirect Evidence

Indirect evidence is to be found in the works of Rabbi Jacob Emden.[55] This great foe of Sabbatianism fought an implacable war against his arch-enemy Jonathan Eybeschuetz, rabbi of the Three Communities (as the union of Hamburg, Altona, and Wandsbek was known). Accusing the latter of being a crypto-Sabbatian, Emden persecuted him and his followers and admirers, tenaciously probing their actions, statements, and writings in an attempt to prove by all possible means that they were secret adherents of Sabbatianism.

Yehuda Liebes, in an article entitled 'The Messianism of R. Jacob Emden and His Attitude to Sabbatianism',[56] clearly demonstrates Emden's multifaceted attitude: on the one hand he fiercely fought Sabbatianism, but on the other he himself embraced various elements that he found in Sabbatian literature.[57] His almost obsessive preoccupation with interpreting the amulets that Eybeschuetz distributed demonstrates his broad knowledge of practical kabbalah, including the lore of divine names and amulets.

Emden himself admitted to engaging in practical kabbalah. Once, for example, he gave a sick girl a gold ring on which holy names were engraved, and the girl 'was affected by it, her visage changed, and she rocked to and fro "like a hut" [see

---

[54] Katzenellenbogen invariably portrays these *ba'alei shem* as mystics well versed in the kabbalah, while remaining silent regarding their halakhic knowledge.
[55] See Section IV below.
[56] In Liebes, *On Sabbatianism and Its Belief* (Heb.), 198–211.
[57] See ibid. 199.

Isa. 1: 8]'.⁵⁸ Emden engaged in harsh polemical critiques of contemporary *ba'alei shem*, whom he suspected of being friends and allies of Eybeschuetz. Here lies the origin of his general hostility towards *ba'alei shem*, such as we find in his *Igeret purim*:

> the scoundrels among the *ba'alei shemot* that are in the land, the false magicians, and the users of mendacity, 'base silver laid over earthenware' [Prov. 26: 23], who hear and do not speak in praise of the world, the world of perfection, but rather [in praise] of the world of chaos. All of their thoughts are to return the world to a state of chaos. And they wish to lay hold of the [divine] name like the great ones, the men of renown and distinction ... to heal every wound, every sickness, every wretch, everyone defiled, and all who touched him. Empty-minded persons, without strength, come to him and purchase his potions for good money ... for they believe in him.⁵⁹

Emden mentions several wonder-workers, including Samuel Essingen, Moses Prager, Jonathan Eybeschuetz, Moses David of Podhajce, and Samuel Falk,⁶⁰ whom he accuses of fraud and deception. Despite Emden's polemics, his writings constitute an important source for our knowledge of several *ba'alei shem* of his time.

Books of Incantations

The reappearance and great popularity of Hebrew books of incantations and remedies are associated with two central processes in Jewish culture and in the world more generally. Renewed preoccupation with magic during the Renaissance,⁶¹ as well as intense interest in the ancient sciences, engendered a new concern for Jewish kabbalah and kabbalistic magic.⁶² Moshe Idel has noted the relationship between the emergence of magic in Jewish thought in Renaissance Italy and the burgeoning interest in magic among Christian intellectuals. Several manuals of magic, he observes, were translated into Hebrew, and Jews were in contact with Christian magicians.⁶³

The growth of magic in the Christian world also affected the spiritual and cultural world of the Jews in eastern and central Europe. Quite possibly, as Gries has suggested, the general appearance of newly published tracts of popular medicine prompted Jewish authors to follow suit. Some of these Jewish works combined practices and *tikunim* (corrective prayers or practical measures) based on Lurianic kabbalah with charms and medical prescripts.⁶⁴

---

⁵⁸ Emden, *Migdal oz*, fo. 244a.

⁵⁹ Bodleian, MS Mich. 618, fo. 7 (Neubauer's *Catalogue of Hebrew Manuscripts in the Bodleian Library* refers to it as MS 2190); also cited in Nigal, *Magic, Mysticism, and Hasidism*, 216 n. 6; see id., 225 n. 80; see also Rosman, *Founder of Hasidism*, 23–4.

⁶⁰ See 'Ba'alei shem' (Heb.), in Eisenstein (ed.), *Otsar yisra'el*, iii. 137, and entries in Nigal, *Magic, Mysticism, and Hasidism*, following the index.

⁶¹ See the studies cited in n. 36 above, all of which speak of the revival of magic in this period.

⁶² See Yates, *The Occult Philosophy*, 1, 3, 12, 18–19, 22, 24, 45, 186, 189–90.

⁶³ Idel, 'Magical and Neoplatonic Interpretations of the Kabbalah' (Heb.), 66.

⁶⁴ Gries, *Conduct Literature* (Heb.), 95–6.

Nevertheless, the composition and widespread distribution of books of charms (*segulot*) was closely bound up with the appearance of *ba'alei shem* and the belief in their powers. These books contain instructions and advice concerning physical and mental health, as well as protective measures for the home. The word *segulah* appears first in the Bible (Exod. 19: 5; Deut. 7: 6; Eccles. 2: 8), where it means 'treasure' or 'valued possession'. In medieval Jewish literature its meaning shifted to being a positive quality of an object[65] or a useful means to an end.[66] In the introduction to a book of charms entitled *Mifalot elohim* it is defined as a quality inherent in a material or a person, of its very essence: 'for *segulot* are not subject to change and they remain the same forever'.[67]

Charms derive first and foremost from God and his names, as expressed in letters, biblical verses, the angels he created (and their names), and astronomical bodies, as well as natural materials in general (animal, vegetable, or inanimate). An amulet can be effective when the person using it (possessing the necessary knowledge) combines charms formed of various materials with appropriate linguistic formulas. In other words, the very use of charms requires a familiarity with their nature.

The collections of charms put their authors' knowledge at the disposal of the public. In other words, they were primarily handbooks for home use, a kind of almanac or compendium of practical instructions. Some of these books arrestingly combine medical matters with prescriptions for ethical conduct that were garnered from other books.[68]

An examination of the books of charms reveals that, alongside 'prescriptions' of 'drugs' for the treatment of various illnesses, they contain practical advice relating to various everyday problems, such as how to increase a nursing mother's milk, how to cure bed-wetting, how to catch a thief, how to protect one's home against fire, how to succeed in love, how to improve one's memory and succeed in one's studies, and so on.

Sometimes one finds in these volumes different formulas, presented serially, for dealing with the same problem. Such cases clearly indicate that the author received different traditions,[69] and testify to his personal experience in the use of one formula or another, whether applied to himself or to someone else, as we can see from the endings of charms: 'tested', 'tested and tried', 'I have tested'. The prescriptions in this literature are generally recorded in alphabetical order by subject (names of diseases, limbs of the body, and so on), by chapter (each including different topics), or calendrically.[70]

---

[65] Judah Halevi, *The Kuzari* 5: 12.   [66] Maimonides, *Commentary on the Mishnah*, 'Shabat' 6: 10.
[67] Joel b. Uri Heilprin, *Sefer mifalot elohim*, introduction (also cited in a book of charms by R. Reuben b. Abraham (Jerusalem, 1865)).
[68] Examples of books of this description are the two works by R. Benjamin Beinish mentioned in n. 51 above. This feature of the genre has been pointed out in Gries, *Conduct Literature* (Heb.), 95–6, and Etkes, 'The Role of Magic' (Heb.), 91.   [69] Maters, 'A Book of Charms' (Heb.), 9–10.   [70] Ibid. 16.

Each general subject is divided into sections in which a particular problem or sickness is presented, followed by an appropriate charm or prescription (setting out the ingredients in detail); then come instructions for use (with a description of how the charm works to remove the sickness, the mode of contact with the material employed, how a link is forged between this matter and supernatural forces, and the like). While the presentation of the problem to be treated is generally brief and not very detailed, the following two sections are much longer. Here one finds a description of the ingredients (with their names sometimes given in other languages, such as Yiddish, German, or Arabic) and detailed instructions for the preparation of the remedy and when to apply it.[71] Zevi Hirsch of Kalisz, Samuel Falk's factotum, lists at the end of his diary a collection of charms which he probably wrote down for his own use after hearing them from his master.

Amulets

A central activity of the *ba'alei shem* was the writing of amulets, slips of parchment, paper, leather, or metal on which various letters were written or incised. A person with an amulet would be protected from various misfortunes, so it was believed, or cured of sickness.

Opinions differ as to the source of the strange word *kami'a*, the Hebrew term for such an artefact, though it is not of Hebrew origin.[72] One view ascribes to it the meaning 'to tie, attach', as the charm was often attached to some part of the body. Others understand this as coming from the Aramaic/Hebrew *kima(h)*, meaning 'a little bit', since the amulet generally contains only a few letters or divine names.[73]

Amulets were in common use by various peoples in antiquity.[74] Rabbinic literature contains references to the belief in and wearing of amulets,[75] as do sources from the geonic period.[76] The use of these charms was prevalent during the medieval period.[77] The ambivalent Jewish attitude to magic related primarily to the writing and

---

[71] See e.g. 'Whoever has an injury to his body, let him take the bark of the nut tree called *suakh untsa*, cook it together with henna and a raw egg, and then eat this on an empty stomach; this will expel any injury in the body, even a deadly poison' (Lipschutz, *Kitsur segulot yisra'el*).

[72] The word is mentioned a number of times in the rabbinic literature, e.g.: 'leather—enough to make an amulet' (Mishnah *Shab*. 8: 3); 'A physician is accounted reliable to state, "This amulet [was made by] an expert; I have cured with it"' (JT *Shab*. 8: 3), and more.

[73] According to Elijah Levita, *Sefer hatishbi*; see also 'Kami'a' (Heb.), in Eisenstein (ed.), *Otsar yisra'el*, ix. 193.

[74] See Naveh and Shaked, *Amulets and Magic Bowls*. [75] See BT *Shab*. 53*b*, 60*b*, 115*a*, 116*b*.

[76] See Harkavy, *Teshuvot hage'onim*, para. 373 (p. 189). A literary work of this period, *Alfa Beta of Ben Sira*, tells of an amulet written by Ben Sira for the son of King Nebuchadnezzar of Babylonia, on which he inscribed the names of the angels Sanvai, Sansanvai, and Semanglof, who supposedly protect infants from the she-demon Lilith. See Yassif, *The Medieval Stories of Ben Sira* (Heb.), 50–9.

[77] For a detailed discussion, with examples, see Trachtenberg, *Jewish Magic and Superstition*. See also the critique of Trachtenberg in Gruenwald, 'Magic and Myth' (Heb.), 23–4.

use of amulets. Nonetheless, the writing of amulets was a fully fledged profession practised by mystics and kabbalists, who considered their work a sacred art.[78] The writing of amulets required preparations similar to those of a scribe writing Torah scrolls, *tefilin*, or *mezuzot*: the writer was to immerse himself in a ritual bath, fast, and pray before approaching his task. It was the knowledge and writing of the holy names, as well as the fashioning of amulets, that gave rise to the designation *ba'al shem* or *ba'alei shemot* for those who engaged in this activity.

Amulets could assume different forms: circular, triangular, square, rectangular, pentagonal, and the like; some, known as a *ḥamsah*, were shaped like the palm of a hand, others were in the form of a fish or a Star of David.[79] The amulet inscription generally consisted of divine names, the names of angels, or a benedictory text written in initials (or in permutations of letters). Amulets written on parchment could include longer and more complicated formulas: besides divine names, they sometimes presented angelic names in numerological fashion, acronyms of biblical verses written as 'magic squares', and so on.[80] Pieces of jewellery set with various gems were also used as amulets, reflecting the popular belief that every type of precious stone possessed a unique quality.[81]

The momentous controversy between Jacob Emden and Jonathan Eybeschuetz[82] revolved around amulets written by the latter in which, so Emden claimed, he had incorporated the name of Sabbatai Zevi. Emden even devoted an entire book to the deciphering of Eybeschuetz's amulets.[83] There are two examples of amulets in the diary of Samuel Falk; we also possess a manuscript of his *Sefer hasegulot* (The Book of Charms), that he wrote in his own hand. The book and amulets, in addition to the stories about him and his actions, are proof of his occupation with such affairs, and justify the title given Falk: *ba'al shem* or, as he was commonly known, the Ba'al Shem of London.

---

[78] See Davis and Frenkel, *The Hebrew Amulet* (Heb.), 7. [79] See Budge, *Amulets and Talismans*.
[80] See Davis and Frenkel, *The Hebrew Amulet* (Heb.), 19–33.
[81] In an appendix, Trachtenberg, *Jewish Magic and Superstition*, quotes from a manuscript (unfortunately, without properly documenting the source) of an alternative version of R. Bahya b. Asher's commentary on Exod. 28: 17; both versions list various gems and their magical properties. Such traditions also influenced Christian magic.   [82] See Section IV below.   [83] Emden, *Sefat emet uleshon zehorit*.

II
A BIOGRAPHY OF SAMUEL FALK

D<small>R SAMUEL FALK</small>, the Ba'al Shem of London, was probably born in Podhajce (then in Poland, now in Ukraine), at the beginning of the eighteenth century, and named Samuel Jacob di Falk Tradiola Laniado.[1] His father, Rabbi Joshua Raphael Hasefaradi (i.e. 'the Spaniard'),[2] was apparently descended from a Spanish New Christian family which, having arrived in Poland in the sixteenth century, returned to Judaism; other than this, we know nothing of the other members of Falk's family. 'Falk' is also the name of a family of distinguished lineage that included Rabbi Joshua ben Alexander Falk, author of the halakhic work *Sefer mitsvot aseh*, and Rabbi Jacob Joshua ben Zevi Hirsch, author of *Penei yehoshua*, a compendium of new insights into the Talmud.

During his childhood and youth, when he lived with his family in Podhajce, Falk made the acquaintance of Moses David of Podhajce,[3] and they apparently became good friends; the two may have jointly studied, and engaged in, practical kabbalah. Both Falk and Moses David would later be known as *ba'alei shem*. The latter was also said to be a crypto-Sabbatian, and professed special teachings and views within this sect. Their cordial relationship proved durable, and the two met in London after an interval of many years.[4]

Falk's family moved from Podhajce to Fürth in Germany, which had become a major centre of Jewish life after the authorities permitted Jews to reside in the city in 1528.[5] Crypto-Sabbatians and hidden Frankists were known to live there, as in Podhajce,[6] and his stay in both places undoubtedly influenced Falk's personality and the

---

[1] This full name appears in his diary (fo. 21*b*) in the entry in which he explains the meaning of his signature: דימעפלי or פעמ״י ד״לי, which was composed of the first and second letters of his names.

[2] Falk mentions his father's name in his diary (fo. 32*b*) when he recounts a dream in which he saw the latter.

[3] See Wirszubski, 'The Kabbalist Moses David of Podhajce' (Heb.); Scholem, 'The Sabbatian Movement in Poland' (Heb.), 114; id., *Sabbatianism Studies* (Heb.), 330, 613; Liebes, *On Sabbatianism and Its Belief* (Heb.), 81, 223. [4] For this encounter, see Appendix C, n. 95.

[5] Fürth is in Bavaria. Our information concerning the family's move there comes from Emden, *Sefer hitabekut* (Altona edn., 1762–9), 129. Owing to the poor quality of this first edition, references are sometimes to the 1877 Lvov edition; this is noted below accordingly.

[6] See Scholem, *Studies and Texts* (Heb.), 61, 83, 98, 108. Fürth was a way-station for the followers of

course of his life. In Fürth he married a woman who was either a widow or a divorcee, and adopted her son Gedaliah.[7] Falk's connection with this city continued for many years. His mother was buried there, and his diary records the sums of money that he sent to Fürth's Jewish community and some of its officials for the erection of a tombstone over her grave, and for charity.[8] In his will he bequeathed £20 to be given to this community each year, in perpetuity.

In his youth Falk wandered throughout Germany, appearing in Westphalia as a *ba'al shem*, a healer of the sick, as the revealer of lost treasures, and as an alchemist capable of turning base metals into gold. These occupations led to his being charged with sorcery, a crime for which a court in Cologne sentenced him to be burned at the stake.[9] Falk managed to extricate himself from this sentence, and was expelled from the city. Information regarding his activities in the 1730s that comes to us from the memoirs of Count Rantzow is of great importance: the memoirs shed light on that hidden period in Falk's life before he settled in England, and directly quote his views on the standing of the Jews and their role in the world.[10] Falk's speech as reported in these memoirs offers the reader a glimpse of his character and personality, and possibly also explains how he came to charm so many people; his diaries and those of his factotum, which depict concrete actions and events, lack this perspective. Rantzow's memoirs, in which he candidly describes his impressions of Falk, supply an important document and give us the mark of the man:

I learned that my father frequently received the renowned prince and High Priest of the Jews, by the name of Hayim Samuel Falk. My father told me that this prince considers himself to be a scion of the line of King David. He further informed me that this Jew had spent a considerable amount of time in Geilberg, with Baron von Donop, the court-counsellor of the empire, who was an intellectual and a person of merit, one who cannot be deceived by external appearances. Indeed, my father asserted, this Jew was 'subject to a rabbinical ban [*ḥerem*] in many lands, but this was not because he did things that disappointed those whom he met. . . .

R. Judah Hehasid travelling to the Land of Israel in the early eighteenth century: see Tishby, 'The Letters of R. Meir Rofe to R. Abraham Rovigo' (Heb.), 279, 284, 331; Benayahu, 'The "Holy Brotherhood" of R. Judah Hasid' (Heb.), 133–82 and n. 151.

[7] According to Emden, *Sefer hitabekut* (Lvov edn.), fo. 71a.

[8] Emden maintains that Falk himself was childless. When I was in London in 1992, after a lecture that I delivered at University College London, I met a man who introduced himself as a member of the Falk family. He told me of a family tradition of Falk's daughter and her marriage to a member of the family of Zevi Hirsch of Kalisz. In his article on Falk, 'The King and the Cabbalist', Cecil Roth tells of his own wife's descent from the family of Falk's factotum. In 1995 Mrs Roth published an article in which she asserted that she was Falk's granddaughter. I do not understand this claimed lineage. Falk's will indicates that his only descendant was his stepson Gedaliah. See below, Appendix F, 'Falk's Will'.

[9] See Emden, *Sefer hitabekut* (Lvov edn.), fo. 71a.

[10] See Rantzow, *Mémoires*. I am grateful to Dr Marsha Schuchard for drawing my attention to this book and providing me with a photocopy of these memoirs. She maintains that the Jesuits pressured the governor to pardon Falk because they used Falk's ability to find treasures.

Consequently, in order to understand, you must see him with your own eyes. My father brought me to the one whom I presumed to be the prince of the Jews. Curiosity, which is aroused within us by some wondrous idea, and obedience to my father's command are what led me to the apartment of this celebrated kabbalist. When I arrived, this new priest told me that he knew what was in my soul. 'You, sir', he told me, 'are of a distrustful nature, a sentiment that characterized our ancient Jewish forefathers, of whom Jesus Christ said: This race will never believe in me unless it will see signs and wonders.'

'You speak', I responded, 'of the New Testament as if you were a Christian.' In reply, he said: 'Quite possibly I have read it at least as much as you have.' 'That is possible', I answered, 'but if it were the case, I am surprised that you remain in your [state of] error.'

'I am hardly in error', the Jew replied, 'and like it so little that I labour greatly to free all my brethren from it. They await someone to extricate them from the oppression and slavery in which they find themselves. The time for that is approaching, but I can tell you nothing more of this.' 'Your doctrine', the Jew continued, 'claims that we were cast out from being God's Chosen People. But then you shall have to prove to me that God, who is immutable, could change His commands. And it is clear that God did not change them in regard to our people. At present we are under the hand that strikes us on the head, like the hand of a father who punishes his children. The Christians enjoy the praise of the world, while the Jews are in a state of wretchedness; in a certain sense, the Jews are the only Christians, because of their suffering. Jesus Christ died to proclaim to us the period of our humiliation, after which we shall fill the world to the ends of the earth, with God's wonderful and tremendous trumpet blast, with the glory of the [Israelite] nation. This nation has experienced all possible vilification, but despite all the powers on earth, it has preserved God's Name and His unity. We rely only on the mercies of Heaven, that shall burst forth as lightning by the avenging angels. Do not tell us that we are blind, we always see the finger of God on our heads. Do you, my lord, cease your regard for your father because he punishes you? Is not punishment the finest sign of true fatherly love that can be given? Only when all the Jews shall be humble of heart shall their salvation come forth.' At that moment we were informed of the arrival of the Baron von Donop. I left the one presuming to be the liberator of the Jews with a shrug of my shoulders; this was my only response to what he said. After this I attacked the Baron von Donop for the trust he afforded this Jew. The baron replied that he knew this Jew, and he saw him at prayer in Cassel, where his reputation is not called into question. At that time he cured the daughter of the court Jew. The girl fell almost every day due to some hidden malady, and he, by means of kabbalistic amulets, protected her from this mishap, without giving her any medicine. But this is not all, the baron continued, when the court Jew was required to leave the city on various matters, he took with him the key to the wine cellar; the 'High Priest pretender' sat at the table, and when he saw that no wine was served, he raised the napkin by its ends, wrote a few letters, and loudly proclaimed: 'My host shall be surprised upon his return.' And indeed, when the Jew [i.e. the court Jew] returned home, he saw that all of his bottles of wine had moved from their place. When he came up from the cellar, he saw the 'High Priest pretender' laughing heartily, and he gave his host several signs and marks to tie on the necks of the bottles. The court Jew went back down into the cellar, did this, and, behold, all the bottles returned to their place.[11]

[11] Rantzow, *Mémoires*, 197–222. I wish to thank Professor Ron Barkai for helping me to understand

In his memoirs the count tells of several additional miraculous acts that Falk performed in the presence of the nobleman and the members of his household. These wondrous deeds included the moving of various objects and causing them to fly, and the miraculous appearance of a spirit or angel accompanied by earsplitting sounds that shook the castle and all in it. Rantzow records the speech that Falk delivered:

He delivered a very fine speech in German all of which, it seems, I recall, without omitting anything: 'God our Creator', thus he commenced, 'O our Master, whose works proclaim themselves from the lofty heavens to the lowest depths. Do we think of You as of a skilled worker, when we see Your works? When faced with the Universe, we are cognizant of the eternal; and the wonders of Heaven were done to show Your praise. Verily, O great God, there is no place on the face of the earth to which we raise our eyes that would not turn our hearts to revere You. Let us confess before God! We revere Him like slaves. O God, our Creator who has created all, who has presented Your praise on behalf of Your creation—man. O God, sustain our thoughts until we come to know You by Your simple will among people. Every person with a modest heart who reveres his Creator can be considered wiser than the marvellous philosophers, who after much research into the nature of the universe are forced to say what the heavens proclaim: the praise of the All-Powerful. But, O God, why have You not given us the ability to comprehend You, other than by Your deeds? Was this in order to make us unhappy? Will the one who does not fathom You be less unhappy?'

Rantzow continues with additional stories of Falk that Baron von Donop had told him, and of events to which he had been an eyewitness. He relates the baron's response to his doubts:

You are correct, the baron said, laughing. I myself laughed, and I was so sceptical that I wished to be assured of this with my own eyes ... and so I brought him to my home in Geilberg. Upon his arrival he caused a spirit to appear in my home that, so he claimed, was an angel. This spirit appeared within a light whose colour I cannot describe, since I know of no such colour that exists on earth. . . . The Jew conducted a conversation with the spirit in Hebrew. He adjured the spirit, and motioned to me to follow him. We entered my park, and towards its centre, under an oak tree, he suddenly stopped and said to me, all a-quiver, that he was incapable of standing on his feet. He then said the following: 'I want to make you richer'. He drew a circle and held in his hand a 30-foot-long parchment scroll filled with letters. He prayed in Hebrew,

---

the original text. Passages from the book cited below have been slightly adapted from the original French. Rantzow was apparently of Danish abstraction, but signed his work as 'a descendant of the Holy Roman Empire'. The German historian Johann von Archenholz writes, in *A Picture of England*, that Rantzow was a 'major general' in the French army, and a protégé of the duke of Braunschweig-Luneburg. He dedicated his memoirs to the dukes of this house (Karl, Anton Ulrich). In 1739 Rantzow's father permitted Falk to live on his estate, so that 'the prince and High Priest of the Jews would reveal and yield great treasures'. Baron von Donop, a court-counsellor in the service of the Hapsburg empire, and his son, an officer in the Swedish army, were also present on the estate. It is quite likely that it was the former who recommended Falk to Rantzow, since Falk had previously spent several years in the home of von Donop in Geilberg. See Archenholz, *A Picture of England*, 181–2.

and I immediately saw that a fire issued forth from the ground and rose to a height of 7 or 8 feet. The fire towered over the Jew's head and burned the ends of his hair, and at that moment the Jew fell to his knees and prayed. Afterwards, he told me that this sign was definitely auspicious. The next day he conducted the same ceremony at the same place, and then he showed me that the ground had opened. The roots of the oak were exposed, and next to them was a tremendous quantity of gold. I cried out to him that this sufficed for me, and that it was necessary to cut down the tree, in whose roots these riches were concealed. But the Jew replied that whoever gave the order to cut down the tree would die the moment he gave the command.

The next day he tied different letters on his knife with the marvellous blade. In my presence, he tied the knife to a certain document in the room. He went out with me, and asked me to close the door of his apartment with my seal. We mounted horses and rode on them as honoured personages do, together with three servants, riding to the forest close to my house. When we arrived, the Jew dismounted and prayed, with his face towards the ground. Suddenly he straightened up, looked at the sun, and proclaimed: 'Do you, my masters, see what we see? —this is the hunting knife that flies through the air, without a sheath.'

He stretched forth his hands and said to the knife: 'Come in peace', and the knife answered him as if it possessed a soul. Suddenly, my young son appeared before us, alarmed, and told us that a piece of glass from the Jew's window had fallen on his head, and when he looked up, he saw the knife floating in the air without anyone holding it.

When we returned to my home, we all went up to the Jew's room. The seal that I had affixed was as it had been when I had placed it. The door was opened, we entered, and we saw the sheath of the knife floating in the middle of the room. He called upon the knife and the sheath to cease their flying about, and the knife came into his hands, while the sheath continued to fly about, and it came to him only after he called to it the third time.... The Jew tried to convince me that there would be a worldwide war that would continue for thirty years, after which peace would reign in the world....

The greater my repugnance for this person, who is so renowned, the greater is my sense of trust in him. He told me to purchase a sheet of paper and mark it with my seal, to remove any doubts I might have about what he would show me. I left the palace and went to the city to purchase paper. I returned and gave the High Priest the sheet of paper on whose four corners I had placed my seal.

He held the piece of paper for the amount of time that he needed to write the Hebrew word *YHVH* [the Tetragrammaton]. He then returned the page to me and told me to pin the paper to the tapestry. He made a circle, and began to chant in Hebrew. About an hour later, I heard three knocks that were louder than a cannon shot, and the castle shook to its very foundations. We saw neither fire nor smoke, nor did we sense any smell—there was no similarity between this noise and that of a cannon. The next moment the paper was filled with signs of writing. I told the High Priest this, and he fell on his knees, with his eyes bathed in tears. He raised his head, and shortly afterwards instructed me to go out and take the paper, to see what was on it. I saw on it the image of God sitting in a chair, and two cherubim covering Him with their wings. Below this figure there seemed to me to be an inimitable depiction, and I saw in green letters everything remarkable that had happened to me since my birth. I also read there a prophecy that would later be fulfilled, word for word. The High Priest asked me if I had seen everything, and he advised me that this was still not all....

That evening the High Priest informed us that the following day he would engage in his kabbalistic activity. He ordered us to tell all who were able to come and observe what he would do, accompanied by a threat of death, for they would have to bathe. He also said that no one could come in to him either barefoot or wearing new shoes. He warned adulterers of a severe punishment, and declared that they could not enter his room for a period of twenty-four hours if they were guilty of this sin. In the most polite manner he asked the women to rid themselves of the *Napoli Post* so as not to endanger their lives, since the spirit that would come would not abide any impurity.

The following evening, as was his wont, he made a circle, and in the middle he placed a small square board that he had prepared during the day. He covered the board with a new white kerchief, and placed eight torches on it. He also positioned eight chandeliers in which candles were placed, for the lights accorded with his fantasy. He placed his hunting knife in the corner of the room, and put a burning candle stub on its point. He turned his face to the ground, and began to engage in prolonged breathing; afterwards he prayed for about a quarter of an hour, and then we heard a terrible noise. Following this sound he saw a terrifying vision: the hunting knife flew above the heads of those assembled and very forcefully entered the corner opposite where it had been standing previously. At that moment the Jew said: 'In the place where the knife stops, there is the treasure of Baron von Donop.' Each of us extended his hand to this knife, but no one succeeded in taking it from the hand of the High Priest.[12]

According to Rantzow, Falk left his parents' home after they had been ordered by the duke of Braunschweig to send him away. Notwithstanding this unfortunate turn of events, Rantzow continues, 'the well-known and renowned Hayim Samuel Falk, the supreme ruler of the Jews, the descendant of King David, went forth to England, where the Portuguese Jews received him as their prince and supreme ruler'.

We do not possess any information from other sources concerning Falk's life during this period (1730–48). On his way to England he probably went through Holland, where he forged social and economic ties with the worthies of the Portuguese Jewish community and the members of the Boas family,[13] continuing from there to England. Rantzow also mentions in his memoirs that when Falk arrived in England he was arrested by order of Parliament, and released with a warning to desist from kabbalistic activities. On the basis of Rantzow's portrayal, Marsha Schuchard presents Falk as the prince of the Portuguese Jews in London.[14] This characterization, however, is refuted by diverse documents that depict Falk as spending his first years in London in

---

[12] *Mémoires*, 202–12.

[13] We possess first-hand testimony—Falk's diary—regarding the members of the Boas family and their ties with Falk. Tobias Boas and his two sons, Abraham and Simeon, were wealthy bankers and were prominent in Holland and throughout Europe. The mighty and the distinguished, monarchs and noblemen, all beat a path to their door and employed their services, namely, extending loans and engaging in investments on their clients' behalf. For the history of this family, see below, Appendix A.

[14] See Schuchard, 'Yeats and the "Unknown Superiors"', 140.

abject poverty, surrounded by a small circle of followers, drawn from the fringes of the Jewish community, who believed in him and his wondrous powers. If Falk had in fact occupied a prestigious place in the Jewish society of London, he most likely would have lived in more prosperous and respectable conditions than those known to us.

In sharp contrast to this early period, Falk's life from the late 1740s to early 1750s is described in great detail in the diary of his factotum Zevi Hirsch of Kalisz.[15]

[15] For biographical details concerning Zevi Hirsch, see C. Roth, *The History of the Great Synagogue in London*, 165; id., 'The King and the Cabbalist'; Barnett, *The Western Synagogue through Two Centuries*, 152, 169, 170; see also the extensive discussion in Section VI below.

III

FALK'S ACTIVITIES ACCORDING TO THE DIARY OF ZEVI HIRSCH

ZEVI HIRSCH, the son of Isaac Eisik Segal of Kalisz, a *shtadlan* (intercessor with the non-Jewish authorities) and a native of Poland who emigrated to London, was Falk's factotum for about four years. The diary that he kept during this time, which records his daily life in Falk's household, is written in faulty Hebrew interspersed with Yiddish and English words, and occasionally with terms that seem to derive from French and German. Zevi Hirsch refers to Falk as *heḥakham*, meaning 'the Sage', and towards the end of the diary as 'Admo', an acronym meaning 'my master and teacher'. According to Zevi Hirsch, Falk's life in London from 1747 to 1751 was marked by poverty and deprivation: he repeatedly writes of his visits to the pawnbrokers Flanders and Nicholas to pawn various household effects and clothes so as to meet his master's most basic needs.[1] The parsimonious Falk paid him very little and left him hungry and penniless. He did not even give his own wife, to whom Zevi Hirsch refers as 'the rebbetsin' or 'the *rabanit*' (the rabbi's wife),[2] sufficient funds for household expenses. Zevi Hirsch himself was able to outwit his master from time to time and give her money without his knowledge. Indeed, Falk was on very bad terms with his wife, and Zevi Hirsch records their quarrels. He was also an eyewitness to the curses that Falk rained on his wife for her inferior cooking (ruining a special sabbath dish), and hints at Falk's habit of throwing dishes at his unfortunate spouse. Falk in fact sought to avoid his wife, who harassed him and interfered with his mystical pursuits. This poor marital relationship also finds expression in Falk's own diary (which documents a later period in his life): among the dreams that he records he tells of two separate occasions on which he dreamed that his wife had jumped to her death from a window.[3]

During his early years in London, Falk lived in Prescot Street in the East End[4] (Zevi Hirsch refers to this street as 'Peskit' or 'Pas', since English orthography was

---

[1] Zevi Hirsch's diary (ZHD), fos. 1*b*, 4*b*, 8*b*, 24*b*, 31*b*.
[2] See ZHD, entry for 13 Menahem Av 5511/1751, fo. 33*b*.
[3] Falk's diary (FD), fo. 2*b*; see also below, Appendix B.
[4] This street, like many others in this district, suffered damage during the Second World War. It was restored, and is now part of London's financial district.

not his strong point). In addition to this house, which Falk left some years later for another not far away, in Wellclose Square, he also maintained premises 'on the bridge', referring to London Bridge, which he used for his experiments in alchemy and for mystical rites.[5] He gathered around him a group of Jews who, according to Jacob Emden, belonged to the lower classes.[6] These Jews believed in Falk and in his powers, worshipped in the synagogue in his house, and on occasion gave him some money. Some of the members of this circle are mentioned by name in Zevi Hirsch's diary, while others appear in Falk's *Sefer hagoralot* (Book of Fortunes).[7] One of these individuals featured prominently in the diary is a Jew referred to as 'the Little One' who took care of Falk and visited him frequently, sometimes leaving him small sums of money. Another frequently mentioned name in Zevi Hirsch's diary is Cosman Lehmann,[8] who also appears in Falk's diary and in his *Sefer hagoralot*. Cosman was a familiar in Falk's home; his smooth talking was apparently of use to the latter in his international dealings. He undertook various missions for Falk, and played an important role in his relations with central figures among the Freemasons. Although Cosman had a reputation in France as a womanizer and debaucher, towards the end of his diary Zevi Hirsch refers to him as having mended his ways.[9]

Falk was regarded as a wonder-worker by the various people who visited his home in London during this period. From time to time Zevi Hirsch describes such visits in his diary.[10] In the autumn of 1747 Falk received two Frenchwomen, about whom Zevi Hirsch writes: '*Wednesday, 14 Heshvan* [7 October 1747] . . . That evening, the nobleman who had visited him last Monday night came, with two important noblewomen, and the rebbetsin spoke with them in French. Afterwards he spoke with them in the parlour for about two hours. Afterwards they went together in their coach.'[11] Zevi

---

[5] See Adler, 'The Baal Shem of London'; see also C. Roth, 'The King and the Cabbalist'.

[6] See Emden, *Sefer hitabekut* (edn. not specified), fo. 119b. Emden notes that Falk 'found helpers for himself from the ends of the camp who promoted him for their own benefit and good among the non-Jews, but not a single wealthy member of our people was seduced, only the poor, who thought to profit through him and who worked on his behalf'. Emden states clearly that Falk's followers came from the lower classes of Jewish society, in marked contrast to Schuchard's assertion that Falk's connections during that period were with its upper echelons. Basing her portrayal on Rantzow's memoirs, Schuchard depicts him as 'the prince of the Jews' in London, but this characterization is accurate only for Falk's later years (the 1770s).

[7] This manuscript, among the holdings in the archives of the Jewish community of London, is in Falk's own hand. I possess a photocopy thanks to the good offices of Charles Tucker, archivist of the London Beth Din. It is written in Spanish rabbinic script, and contains different biblical verses that are dedicated to members of his circle, that is, Falk specifies the verses connected with the fate of each of his followers. The names of his followers that appear in this book are: R. Jacob, R. Abraham, R. Mendel, R. Tobias, R. Meir, Cosman, R. Simeon, and Gedaliah. This 'book of fortunes' is no. 128 in the Neubauer catalogue (*Catalogue of Hebrew Manuscripts*, 37; the Institute of Microfilmed Hebrew Manuscripts, National Library of Israel, does not possess a copy of this manuscript).

[8] See C. Roth, 'The King and the Cabbalist', 142, and below, Appendix A. [9] See ZHD, fo. 35b.
[10] Ibid, fos. 3b–4a. [11] Ibid.

III. FALK'S ACTIVITIES ACCORDING TO ZEVI HIRSCH

Hirsch here describes a meeting that Falk conducted in his home with two noblewomen, who were brought there by a nobleman who in turn had been presented to Falk a few days earlier by his friend Dr Philippe de la Cour.[12] We have independent evidence of this meeting, in *Ma'agal tov*, the autobiographical book recounting the travels of R. Hayim Joseph David Azulai (generally known by the acronym formed from his Hebrew initials as 'Hida'). In the course of his accounts of his travels and meetings with various personalities, he mentions an encounter in Paris with the marquise de Thomé[13] and marquise de la Croix:

9 Tevet [1777]. Thursday night, the marquise de Thomé came with the marquise de la Croix. She sat with me and asked that I might pray for her. Then she said that she studied the Scriptures, and that she had visions of angels and demons who spoke to her; and when they were from the S[itra] A[hra] [the 'other side', i.e. evil in all its various manifestations], she would rebuff them. . . . She mentioned the Ba'al Shem of London, and said that the Jew had given her a book on kabbalah. She said some other remarkable things. I answered her accordingly. Then she told me that she was a very important lady, that she had saved several Jews from the Inquisition in Avignon, that she was the daughter of a marquis, and that her husband was a marquis. All this nonsense spoken by this gentile woman and several other gentiles was caused by this so-called '*ba'al shem*', who, in his conceit and wilfulness revealed practical kabbalah and incantations to many nobles, both men and women, to aggrandise himself. Many asked me about him, and I answered them. . . .

12 Sivan[.] S. David and I went with them to the village of —, on the seashore. They showed me great honour, and we spent some four hours there. They said remarkable things about the Ba'al Shem of London, Samuel Falk, son of the rabbi Joshua Falk: that he wears a coat of gold with letters inscribed, his handiwork; that he has a sword that can fly, and all his [mystical] activities [carried out] in seclusion in forests and by the seashore. He claimed that he engaged [in this activity] for the good of the world, and that he was descended from the tribe of Judah; that no one had engaged in such activity for four hundred years; that he was the king of the land of Tubal, who had followed the 'paths of the sea' [i.e. gone to faraway places]. Joseph Della Reina and R. Judah he-Hasid had also engaged in activities [such as] his, and similar nonsense, such as having walked in a forest that dates back to the six days of Creation. What is revealed [i.e. as opposed to his esoteric activities] is that he possesses much wealth.[14]

Falk, so she claimed, had taught her kabbalah, a claim that evoked a disapproving

---

[12] Dr Philippe de la Cour is Dr Abraham Gomez Argas, a well-to-do Jewish physician who taught medicine in Leiden before moving to London.

[13] Schuchard, 'The Secret Masonic History of Blake's Swedenborg Society', 41, asserts that the marquis de Thomé was one of the heads of the Masonic lodge in France, and mentions de Thomé's ties with Emanuel Swedenborg and Falk.

[14] *Ma'agal tov hashalem*, 124, fo. 73b, 155, fo. 106a–b. *Ma'agal tov hashalem* also appears in English translation: *The Diaries of Rabbi Ha'im Yosef David Azulai*, trans. B. Cymerman (Jerusalem, 1997), 196, 255; the translation is only partially reliable. A translation of the first passage of the quotation also appears in Adler, 'The Baal Shem of London' (*TJHSE*), 161.

response from Azulai: 'In his conceit and wilfulness he revealed practical kabbalah and incantations to many nobles, both men and women.'[15]

The French noblewoman's interest in kabbalah is understandable against a background of widespread interest in mysticism among her contemporaries. Alchemy flourished in the eighteenth century, and its ties with kabbalah were stressed. Kabbalistic works were translated into many languages, and various groups were studying the subject—mainly 'practical kabbalah', applied magic. In particular, leading Freemasons in a number of countries claimed familiarity with kabbalistic lore.[16] The marquise de la Croix was, in fact, reported to be an enthusiastic supporter of Freemasonry, and this may explain how Falk had come to her attention.

January 1749 marked a turning point in Falk's life. Zevi Hirsch reports in his diary that 'a nobleman' came to Falk's house at midnight. The visitor sat with Falk in his room for two hours, and upon his departure he left 2 guineas on the table.[17] David Kahana identified this distinguished personage as a German nobleman, Theodore Stephen de Stein, Baron von Neuhoff, the 'king of Corsica'.[18] The baron, a notorious international adventurer and swindler, induced the Corsicans to rebel against the Genoese government and enthrone him as their king. Crowned in 1736, he was soon deposed and expelled by the Genoese, who regained control of the island with the aid of the French. The baron wandered through Europe in the hope of securing assistance to regain his crown, and when he arrived in England he appealed for aid to friends and relatives, but they turned a deaf ear to the pleas of this would-be monarch. Among his attempts to obtain money he turned to Falk, hoping he could supply him with gold to finance his plans to reconquer Corsica and ascend the throne once again.[19] Zevi Hirsch reports the baron's frequent visits to his master (to whom he refers as 'the authority') and the large sums of money that he left on each occasion.[20]

Zevi Hirsch's diary reveals that at this time Falk was engaged in chemical experiments, occult rites, and the writing of amulets. He recounts the details of one experiment that he heard about from Falk's landlord, in which gunpowder that his master ignited exploded, causing a fire in which Falk and the members of his household suffered severe burns.[21] Zevi Hirsch also tells of Falk's riverside experiments in

---

[15] *Ma'agal tov hashalem*.

[16] For the great interest in kabbalah and magic in the eighteenth century, and the influence of the former on Christian circles, see Scholem, 'The Career of a Frankist' (Heb.), 141–209; id., 'Reports of Sabbatians' (Heb.) (see also the bibliographical appendix by Y. Liebes, p. 630); and Patai, *The Jewish Alchemists*.

[17] ZHD, fo. 20b.   [18] Kahana, 'Those in Error and Those Who Lead Astray' (Heb.), 55.

[19] For additional details concerning Baron von Neuhoff, see C. Roth, 'The King and the Cabbalist', 152–3.   [20] ZHD, fos. 20b–24a.

[21] See ZHD, fo. 25. Zevi Hirsch relates in his diary (fo. 25a) that Falk regarded himself as responsible for what happened, and believed that this mishap resulted from an error in his mystical practices. It was revealed in a dream to Falk that all this befell him because he had given 'the seal' to the wrong person, and only the return of the seal saved him from certain death. An account of a similar setback appears in ZHD, fo. 27a; this occurrence, too, miraculously came to its conclusion without casualties.

III. FALK'S ACTIVITIES ACCORDING TO ZEVI HIRSCH

the writing and drawing of amulets and seals.[22] Despite all these attempts, Falk was unable to help the baron, who was sent to debtor's prison, where he remained for six years; shortly after his release he died a pauper.[23] Zevi Hirsch's descriptions of Falk's experiments during this period, recorded from the viewpoint of an outsider making covert efforts to catch a glimpse of what was going on, seem to indicate that his master was conducting chemical experiments mainly with the object of converting base metals into noble ones; most probably he was actually engaged in electroplating common metals.[24]

Despite his mystical pursuits and his renown in England and abroad, Falk was the focus of controversy within the Jewish community in London: some saw his unusual personality and his celebrated status abroad as proof that he was a sorcerer and crypto-Sabbatian. Zevi Hirsch describes the private synagogue that his master established in his house for the members of his circle. Falk's opponents were apprehensive of his influence on the members of the Jewish community, and the establishment of a private synagogue enraged the community's leaders since it contravened the regulations that forbade the introduction of new synagogues within the city's bounds.[25] Evidence of this episode and of the community's attitude towards Falk is provided by Zevi Hirsch, who recounts (fo. 24*b*) an incident that took place on the sabbath in the so-called 'Bressler' synagogue, which followed the Ashkenazi rite: following the prayers, a public prohibition was issued against worshipping in the synagogue established by Falk (whom they called the *ba'al tsafon*[26]). The opposition to

---

[22] ZHD, fos. 21*b*–22*a*.

[23] See C. Roth, 'The King and the Cabbalist', 162. Roth also reproduces (p. 163) the text of the epitaph on Baron von Neuhoff's tombstone, in St Anne's churchyard in Soho:

Near this place is interred | Theodore King of Corsica | Who died in this parish December 11th 1756 | Immediately after leaving the King's Bench prison | By the benefit of the Act of Insolvency: | In consequence of which he registered | His Kingdom of Corsica | For the use of his creditors | The grave, great teacher, to a level brings | Heroes and beggars, galley-slaves and kings, | But Theodore his moral learned ere dead; Fate proved his lessons on his living head | Restored a Kingdom, and denied him bread.

The epitaph also appears on printed sheets in the church that are given out free of charge to visitors.

[24] ZHD, fos. 7*a*, 24*b*.   [25] See C. Roth, *The History of the Great Synagogue*, 151.

[26] *Tsafon* refers to the direction north, and not, as Roth surmises ('The King and the Cabbalist', 165), 'hidden master' (with the vocalization *tsafun*, hidden, concealed). For kabbalists the north symbolized evil and its forces; Schuchard ('Yeats and the "Unknown Superiors"', 143–4, 164 n. 217) interprets it as referring to Emanuel Swedenborg: 'the man who came from the north [*tsafon*]', relying on a partial and flawed translation of Zevi Hirsch's diary given her by Mrs Roth. Both of these interpretations are completely divorced from their context in the text. Those applying this term to Falk sought to thereby associate him with the forces of evil, the mystical Sitra Ahra, which is related to the north. Liebes, 'New Sabbatian Kabbalistic Writings' (Heb.), 400 n. 52, demonstrated that the numerical value of *ba'al tsafon* (322) is equivalent to that of *kelev ra* ('bad dog'); Emden applied this epithet to the Sabbatians in his book *Tsitsim uferaḥim* (s.v. 'Jeroboam'). According to Liebes, this numerical-value equation was taken from the book *Megaleh amukot* by the Polish kabbalist R. Nathan Spira.

Falk appears to have stemmed from suspicions prevalent among the public regarding his occult activities, mistrust that was based primarily on allegations made by Jacob Emden. Zevi Hirsch tells how, about a year after this, Elias Levy, one of the leaders of the community, sent a spy to see who attended Shavuot eve services at Falk's synagogue.[27] Those spotted by the spy were publicly warned, and one, Moses Fishman, was publicly humiliated during the sabbath afternoon service: as the Torah scroll was removed from the Ark, Fishman was compelled to confess and ask the congregation's forgiveness. Word of this incident reached Falk, who was so incensed that he put a curse on Levy. Nine months later, in January 1750, Zevi Hirsch noted in his diary that Levy had died, adding that his body had lain for three days without burial. He interpreted this disgraceful fact as punishment for Levy's treatment of Fishman.[28]

From the spring of 1749 entries in Zevi Hirsch's diary report the mystical meetings convened by Falk in a structure that he had erected ('on the bridge') in which his followers assembled, and which both Falk and his factotum refer to as a 'camp' (*maḥaneh*):[29]

Monday. At ten o'clock, I went with him to the forest, where he practised like yesterday. We went back to the house in Pas, and from there he sent me to the Bridge. He ordered that the door of the camp should be sealed with holy names that he had written in the house on Pas and given me, and so I did. When I came back I went with him to a house near Woolwich, where he practised for about one hour in the room overlooking the water, and from there we went to the house.

When we came to the house he ordered me to go with R. Tuvyah to the ritual bath and immerse. From there he ordered us to go to the Bridge, to the room near the room of the camp, and he ordered us to recite, first, Psalms [a list of forty-one psalms follows]; *tikun ḥatsot* until *tikun hanefesh*; then Psalms 139, 140, 145 in their entirety; afterwards, the first chapter of *Sefer yetsirah*; and then seven Utterances of Creation. Then he ordered me to remove the amulet that I had used after midnight and replace it with other holy names than those he had given me after midnight. He also forbade sleep until ten o'clock on Tuesday, and so we did. We began one hour after midnight. The instruction of the Sage was to seal the door with these second names, half an hour before dawn, and so we did. And after we sealed it, we recited the Song of Songs in its entirety, and so we were engaged in prayer and supplication until ten o'clock in the morning.[30]

One month later, Zevi Hirsch wrote in his diary:

The Sage went to his domain after midnight, when he summoned me, R. Tuvyah, R. Itzik, and the Little One, and he began with Psalm 119, 'Princes have persecuted me without reason', until the end of the psalm, and then the Sage cast lots in the book of Psalms; the lot fell on Psalm 68, and he meditated with great intensity. I remember also that he meditated on verse 16: 'O majestic mountain, Mount Bashan!', the final letters of which form the word *maran*, and

---

[27] ZHD, fo. 24b. [28] ZHD, fo. 26b.
[29] The term *maḥaneh* for this place of assembly is of biblical origin: see Gen. 32: 21, and elsewhere.
[30] ZHD, fos. 7b–8a.

also verse 18: 'God's chariots are myriad'—the holy name of 45, etc.; 'among them in Sinai' is *yam*; 'You went up to the heights' is *tam*; 'captives, having received tribute' is *yod-tav-tav*; 'of men', etc., and also verse 29: 'strength for you, the strength, O God' is *khaf-heh-mem*, 'which You displayed for us'; I could not remember more, because I had to write, and also it was indicated by the breaths of his mouth. And then he summoned the Little One.

And we began to chant Psalm 82, and he meditated on verse 2, and also verse 6, and he ordered me to write *alef alef alef alef*, which comes from 'I had taken you for divine beings', etc.; and then Psalm 83, and he meditated on verse 17: 'Cover their faces with shame', the letters *alef-mem-nun*, etc.; and then Psalm 97, and he meditated on verse 9: *me'od* is the holy name of 45 letters; and also verse 10: *ohavei* is the holy name of 18 letters; and also verse 12: *vehodu*—the alphabet that is 27 letters—*lezekher kodsho*, 'His holy name'. Then he completed the writing which he had done on Thursday with great embellishment, all in engraved letters, and he also wrote many holy names on it. That was the completion of everything as a prophecy. He left at the top of the crown four spaces in which to conceal holy names, and then hung it from the blade of the sword. Afterwards he took the small strap from the camp gate and put it on his table. He shut himself in with the new rope that he had made on Thursday, and he wrote some holy names on the strap while we chanted the aforementioned *alef alef alef alef*. Then he ordered R. Tuvyah to light two large wax candles, and he fastened the gate with the strap on which he had written holy names. He took the second strap, which was broader, put it on his table, and ordered us to leave. Then he summoned us, we chanted Psalm 79, and he indicated to me the letters that I was to write in the big book of *kavanot*, 32 letters from the Utterance 'In the beginning'. We went out, and he told us to come back in half an hour, and then chant those 32 letters, and afterwards to chant the four *alef*s upstairs, and so we did. When we returned, I saw that he had also written holy names on the second strap and tied it to the two pillars from the camp where we were. The Sage was prostrate on the ground, that is, upon the hide, with outstretched arms and legs, holding only the two ends of the new strap in his hands. The first book of *kavanot* was placed before him, and he wrote an amulet. He ordered R. Tuvyah to light all the candles, except the two around the sword at the camp gate, and R. Tuvyah did so. Thereupon the Sage stood up and lit the two large wax candles and two small wax candles, and he also lit two wax candles on the two posts, the candles that he had made himself on Thursday. Then he himself lit two wax candles on the camp gate, as well as a new candle on the tip of the sword. He lay down again with outstretched arms and legs, and he wrote holy names. He then called R. Itzik to come with the Little One, and the Sage gave R. Itzik names folded up, and he ordered him to meditate with the Little One on the three letters: *nun*, *ḥet*, *peh*, and then to give the holy names to R. Tuvyah, and so he did. Then he ordered R. Tuvyah that they should chant with him the names that he uttered, but that he should take care when mentioning the letter *tet*. Then R. Tuvyah was to go and place the names in the cavity opposite the gate, in the aforementioned crown, and the Sage chanted with great tears. And at the moment that he placed the holy names in the crown, the sword left the camp gate, and the crown with the candle on the sword blade remained in the air. We left, and afterwards he summoned us, and we saw that the crown was suspended in the air with the candle, and the candle was burning.[31]

[31] ZHD, fos. 16*b*–17*a*.

Similar ceremonies are described in several diary entries.[32] A similar account was given by a Jew named Eliezer Sussman Shesnowzi in a letter to his son describing what happened when he visited Falk in London.[33]

The description of the ceremony in Sussman's letter corroborates that appearing in Zevi Hirsch's diary. These accounts present typical elements of mystical rites that are found as early as the thirteenth century in the writings of Rabbi Abraham Abulafia:[34]

1. The participants in these rites are required to engage in various preparations (such as fasting, abstention, seclusion, purification, and immersion in a ritual bath).

2. The rites are performed at night.

3. Burning candles are central devices in the ceremony.

4. The utterance of holy names derived from different biblical verses is a central element of the rite.

5. Considerable importance is attached to *nigun*, that is, the utterance of holy names and biblical verses employing variant vocalizations.

6. During the course of the ceremony the sage or mystic (here, Falk) kneels, prostrates himself with outstretched limbs, and carves out the holy names with a knife.

7. The participants murmur the holy names and enter an ecstatic state, in which they experience a vision of moving candles, a crown, and a sword glittering before them, as if suspended in the air.

8. The rites are generally performed in the forest or in the quarters near the bridge, that is, near the river (= water) or in an isolated place.

The descriptions of the magical ceremonies conducted in Falk's home, as they appear in Zevi Hirsch's diary and in Sussman Shesnowzi's letter, are of great importance for the study of magic. Hirsch's graphic and authentic depictions of the different stages of the rite present us with a detailed portrayal of the magic techniques used by practitioners such as Falk.

---

[32] See ZHD, fos. 13*a*, 19*b*, 21*b*, 29*a*, 31*a*.

[33] This letter fell into the hands of R. Jacob Emden, who published it in *Sefer hitabekut* (Altona edn.), fos. 126–8). The letter is reproduced in its entirety in Appendix C with Emden's additions and comments. Emden distorts Falk's name, using instead various disparaging terms. For Emden and Falk, see Section IV below.

[34] See Idel, *The Mystical Experience in Abraham Abulafia* (Heb.); id., *Studies in Ecstatic Kabbalah*, 1–3, 103–70.

III. FALK'S ACTIVITIES ACCORDING TO ZEVI HIRSCH

From the early spring of 1750 entries in Zevi Hirsch's diary include descriptions of healing.[35] Sick (epileptic?) children were brought to Falk, who attempted to cure them. In 1751 he continued his alchemical experiments: Cosman supplied him with gold plates, which he used both to plate other objects and to produce mystical plaques in which holy names and diagrams were inscribed.

Zevi Hirsch's diary ends in the summer of 1751, with a list of medications and charms, apparently the result of the diarist's sojourn with Falk; perhaps he had copied them down secretly. A number of these 'prescriptions' are well-known folk remedies. Some were tried by Zevi Hirsch himself, who writes alongside the remedy—as was common in the medical books of the time— 'tested and proven', or, occasionally, the more personal 'I have tested'.[36]

[35] ZHD, fos. 27b, 28a. [36] ZHD, fos. 38b, 39a.

IV

SAMUEL FALK AS SEEN BY JACOB EMDEN

OUR KNOWLEDGE of Falk's life in the period 1751–82 is sporadic. In the 1760s he was besmirched, cursed, and persecuted by Jacob Emden, while at the same time he was frequently celebrated by various members of Christian society, who beat a path to his door in order to learn the secrets of kabbalah. The extant testimonies, therefore, portray a controversial figure: according to some he was a fraud, a swindler, and a complete ignoramus, while according to others he was an enlightened and charming man—a teacher, guide, and spiritual leader for several prominent Freemasons. His high standing among the latter, his amassing of riches, and his international connections were the most likely reasons for the status he eventually enjoyed within the Jewish community towards the end of his life. In order to arrive at the complete picture we must therefore gather together all its elements, one by one, and classify and arrange them, before presenting them in the proper order.

The 1760s were a tempestuous time. Jacob Emden's campaign against Jonathan Eybeschuetz and his son Wolf reached a climax during these years.[1] Emden devoted his life to a crusade against Sabbatianism, which he regarded as the source of all evil, a plague that had come to corrupt and destroy Judaism. He closely followed the writings of those he suspected of Sabbatian leanings and spent much time identifying and deciphering allusions in their works that, in his opinion, confirmed his suspicions. He called on his fellow rabbis to place a ban on anyone whom he suspected of favouring, supporting, or sympathizing with the members of what he termed the 'sect'. He waged a personal war against them and castigated their writings. On occasion he was assisted in this war by 'informants' in different parts of Europe who wrote and told him of goings-on within Jewish communities that seemed tainted by a Sabbatian bent.[2]

The controversy between Emden and Eybeschuetz and the members of his coterie made a deep impression on their own and on later generations, and it is highly

---

[1] There is an extensive literature on Jacob Emden. For biographical details, see Bick, *Rabbi Jacob Emden* (Heb.); see also Scholem, *Sabbatianism Studies* (Heb.), 758; Liebes, *On Sabbatianism and Its Belief* (Heb.).

[2] One of these 'informants' was R. Joseph Prager, the author of *Gaḥalei esh*. For Prager, see Oron, '*Sefer gaḥalei esh*' (Heb.).

likely that Falk would have faded entirely from our consciousness if it had not been for Emden's stubborn struggle against the Sabbatians in all their manifestations. Emden received a detailed letter from one of his supporters who had taken pains to copy a piece of correspondence that had come into his possession: a letter from Sussman Shesnowzi to his son.[3] Emden reproduced (and falsified) this letter in his *Sefer hitabekut*, and appended his response to it.[4] His attack on Falk yields many important biographical details regarding the latter that, if we disregard the slander and calumnies, are useful for our examination of Falk's life. Emden links Falk with Moses David of Podhajce and with Jonathan Eybeschuetz, and even states that the latter wrote an amulet containing Falk's given name (Samuel) next to that of Sabbatai Zevi. Emden's book is full of his hatred of Falk, whom he derisively calls a *ba'al shed* (possessing or possessed by a demon) instead of the term usually applied to him, *ba'al shem* (wonderworker).[5] Although this antagonism towards Falk notionally derived from Emden's religious zeal and his battles against Sabbatians of all types, whom he considered enemies of Judaism and out to destroy it, in fact it also had a personal basis.

In 1764 Rabbi Zevi Hirschel Levin (Hart Lyon), the de facto chief rabbi of the London Jewish community, left his post in London and moved to Halberstadt. The community was left without a successor, and it was decided to appoint a new chief rabbi. The post was offered to two candidates, Rabbi David Tevele Schiff and Rabbi Israel Meshullam Zalman (Solomon), Emden's son. Competition for the post was fierce, and not without slanderous accusations.[6] Emden tells of threatening letters that he received and incitements against him that were organized by a person named Lazi, who was 'a disciple of that man [i.e. Jesus]'. This Lazi, or Lazer, who is mentioned in Emden's diary, was one of Falk's circle (he appears in the diaries of both Zevi Hirsch and Falk). Emden does not expressly accuse Falk, but he definitely hints at the influence he wielded. The position fell to Rabbi Tevele Schiff, who was supported by Aaron Goldsmid,[7] one of the most wealthy and influential leaders of the community and Falk's close friend. Meshullam Zalman, the loser in this 'competition', would eventually be appointed rabbi of the Hambro Synagogue.

The 1760s were rife with rumours concerning the conversion to Christianity of many Jews. In his article on Moses David of Podhajce, Chaim Wirszubski notes that a syncretic orientation combining Sabbatianism with Christianity is discernible in Moses David's sermons and in an amulet that he wrote.[8] Yehuda Liebes tells us, on the basis of documents and letters that he unearthed, of the existence of a secret sect

---

[3] Reproduced in Appendix C below.

[4] Emden's response to his supporter, which is printed in his book after Sussman's letter, is reproduced in Appendix D.   [5] For a discussion of *ba'alei shem* see Section I above.

[6] For this episode, see Duschinsky, *The Rabbinate of the Great Synagogue, London*, 74–7; Emden's autobiography, *Megilat sefer*, 209; D. S. Katz, *The Jews in the History of England*, 276.

[7] See below, Appendix A.

[8] See Wirszubski, 'The Kabbalist Moses David of Podhajce' (Heb.), 77–8.

of baptized Jews whose members were crypto-Sabbatians who believed in Jonathan Eybeschuetz and his son Wolf.[9] These Jews had clandestinely converted while outwardly continuing to live as Jews, and secretly conducted bizarre ceremonies that integrated Christianity with Judaism; many would later return to Judaism. Liebes connects this sect with Moses David. Was it possible that Falk, who was friendly with the latter, also belonged to this circle? A seeming allusion to this appears in an issue of *The Gentleman* from 1762,[10] which published an anonymous letter to the editor telling of a kabbalist who was a 'christened Jew' (i.e. who had been baptized), whom the writer accuses of engaging in 'villainies', fraud, and deception. The description of this individual corresponds to Falk's appearance as he is described in other sources. Several of the scholars who discuss Falk mention this letter, but without discussing its content; furthermore, they completely overlook the fact that Falk the 'rogue' is defined by the letter-writer as a Christian Jew.[11] This conjecture concerning Falk's conversion is also raised by Schechter in his essay on the *ba'al shem*, and by Marsha Schuchard, who states both that Falk converted and that he founded a sect that combined Jewish and Christian elements.[12] The scholars who place Falk in such a 'sect'

---

[9] Liebes, 'On a Christian Jewish Sect' (Heb.), 212–37. Professor S. Z. Leiman criticized this article in a lecture that he delivered at a conference on 'The Sabbatian Movement and Its Aftermath: Messianism, Sabbatianism and Frankism'. This episode requires further study.

[10] *The Gentleman*, 32 (1762), 418–20.

[11] I found a reference to this letter in a note by Adler, 'The Baal Shem of London', which says that the letter clearly refers to Falk, although he is not mentioned by name. A similar reference is supplied by Roth in 'The King and the Cabbalist'. I wish to thank Ms Doris Nicholson of the Bodleian Library for helping me locate this manuscript. See also Schechter, 'The Baalshem—Dr Falk', 15; Schuchard, 'Yeats and the "Unknown Superiors"', 117.

[12] Schuchard, 'Yeats and the "Unknown Superiors"', 117, asserts that during the last five years of his life Falk established a new quasi-religion of Jews, Christians, and Freemasons. Basing her claim on Schechter, 'The Baalshem—Dr Falk', and on the letter published in *The Gentleman*, she writes of Swedenborg's conviction that Falk had indeed converted. Schechter himself, however, refrained from offering a definite opinion on this question. A close reading of the (real or fictional) letter raises a number of troubling questions, the first of which concerns its reliability. The editors of *The Gentleman* preface it with the observation that the writer was apparently a foreigner, which would explain its numerous grammatical mistakes. Why did the magazine publish the letter in its original faulty English: to preserve its credibility, or in order to create the impression that it was an authentic communication? A study of the letter reveals that it is full of the antisemitic stereotypes that had been circulated by Christians from time immemorial. On the one hand, the writer, who witnessed these events, stresses that the 'cabalist' converted, while on the other he relates that the kabbalist demanded that the writer should not enter a church for six months, as (one of a number of) preconditions of being made privy to the secrets of kabbalah, and the writer attests that for the past six months neither he nor any member of his family has crossed the threshold of a church. This demand in itself is inexplicable: how could it be voiced by someone who had recently entered the Christian faith? Did Falk really abandon Judaism? The letter reports a demand by the kabbalist to be given a pint of blood taken from a Protestant before he will reveal these magical secrets: this is clearly stereotypical. An additional requirement is for the writer to

and air the possibility of his secret conversion base their hypotheses on various proofs that can be contradicted or refuted. Falk's social ties with Moses David do not indicate that Falk followed him and accepted his messianic views. It is more likely that Falk hosted his long-time friend during the latter's visits to London after he had been persecuted and defamed in his native land, as a fellow victim of discrimination during the time of his wanderings and his early years in his new home in London. Additionally, their shared occupation as *ba'alei shem* probably brought them together after many years in which they had not seen one another. (It is unclear whether their relationship was one of teacher and pupil, or of two friends who were engaged in the same sphere of activity.) Schechter does not adduce any proof to support his surmise, and relies on an enigmatic sentence in Falk's diary that he understands as an allusion to the latter's unwilling conversion.

This reliance upon the letter in *The Gentleman* and the attempt to identify the anonymous rogue with Falk are puzzling in the light of the letter's antisemitic tone; it should therefore come as no surprise that the historian Nesta Webster accepted this identification, just as she presented Falk as a Sabbatian, a Frankist, a fraud, a swindler, and a despicable traitor, who devoted his efforts and money to destroying enlightened regimes, effecting revolutions, and overthrowing the existing order.

Significantly, not even the slimmest of hints to Falk's conversion is to be found in either of the diaries, nor any suggestion of his belonging to some 'sect' (his social ties are possibly more indicative of financial manipulations than of religious or national

---

bring him a Hebrew Bible, together with a Bible in English translation, both books having to be stolen from the house of a Protestant together with all that house's contents, all for magical ends. The writer portrays his meeting with the kabbalist, after he has presumably met all these demands. According to the letter, in the writer's courtyard, by moonlight, the kabbalist smeared a lengthy row of crucifixes with the blood that the writer had procured for him; he drew three circles on the ground, and wrote scriptural verses in them, in Hebrew and in English, with this same blood. All this was presumably done to banish Satan, but the inevitable impression gained from this account is that the one performing these acts was the Devil himself. We can therefore hardly avoid the conclusion that the editors of *The Gentleman* wanted to include an antisemitic tale in their magazine while doubly distancing themselves from the story: first, by attributing the letter to an anonymous writer, and second, by depicting him as a foreigner. Several interesting points emerge from this episode: why do scholars such as Adler, followed by Cecil Roth, mention this letter, which they regard as characteristic of Falk and an accurate picture of him? Both scholars take note of the fact that Falk is not mentioned by name in the letter, but they ignore both the representation of the kabbalist as having converted and, more significantly, the patently antisemitic essence of the letter. The antisemitic historian Nesta Webster, though she mentions the fantastic nature of the letter, emphasizes Adler's disregard of the depiction of Falk as an apostate, which she sees as supporting her own position. In my opinion the letter should not be seen as a credible account of the kabbalist; it should, rather, be seen as a deliberate attempt, by those in certain circles of English society who opposed Falk's activities and took a dim view of his connections, to create a distorted picture of him and earn him the contempt of the magazine's readers, some of whom were apparently among the kabbalist's clients or admirers. Consequently, I totally reject Schuchard's hypothesis. See also the discussion of the possibility of Falk converting in Appendix F, 'Falk's Will', below.

ideology). Jacob Emden's enmity, which had its origin in personal concerns, was later linked to his war with Jonathan Eybeschuetz and his followers. Moreover, Falk's will, which was written and signed shortly before his death, reveals that he was a devoted Jew all his days.

V

SAMUEL FALK AND THE FREEMASONS

THE HISTORIAN Nesta Webster, who lived in England around the turn of the nineteenth century, was the first to indicate the ties between Falk and the Freemasons.[1] Webster was a prominent antisemite who took an active part in the distribution of the *Protocols of the Elders of Zion* and published a long list of inflammatory articles in which she charged the Jews with responsibility for the Russian Revolution, as well as all the world's ills. This antisemitic orientation is also evident in her book on secret societies, in which she attempts to link the Jews with various cultic sects that, in her mind, were political in nature. She considered the leaders of these groups to be the descendants of Jewish families, or to have ties with Jews. An entire chapter in her book is devoted to Falk, whom she depicts as a 'high initiate' of the Freemasons ('the supreme oracle to which the secret societies applied for guidance'),[2] and as a Frankist, offering various details concerning him that she culled from a number of sources. This section can therefore serve as a bibliographical source for references to Falk in non-Jewish works. Webster takes note of the fact that Falk's name is mentioned many times in the encyclopedia of the Freemasons written by Mackenzie,[3] and she directs the reader to the article by Gordon Hills on Falk's high standing within the Masonic movement.[4] As proof of her claim of Falk's high standing in this society, Webster quotes from a letter that Savalette de Langes wrote to the marquis de Chefdebain:

This Doctor Falk is known to many Germans. He is a very extraordinary man from every point of view. Some people believe him to be the Chief of all the Jews and attribute to purely political schemes all that is marvellous and singular in his life and conduct. He is referred to in a very curious manner, and as a Rose-Croix in the *Memoirs of the Chevalier de Rampsow* [i.e. Rentzow]. He has had adventures with the Marechal de Richelieu, great seeker of the Philosophers' Stone.... He is at present in England. The Baron de Gleichen can give good information about him.[5]

Webster then speculates about Falk's connections with Cagliostro; she maintains that

---

[1] Webster, *Secret Societies*, 185–95. [2] Ibid. 189.
[3] Mackenzie, *The Royal Masonic Cyclopaedia*, 212–14, 262–7. This is correct, but it is not stated outright anywhere that Falk was a Freemason.
[4] Hills, 'Notes on the Rainsford Papers in the British Museum'. [5] Webster, *Secret Societies*, 189.

the latter received his knowledge from Falk, and that the mystery rituals that he conducted followed the instruction he received from him. As proof of Falk's role in the Freemasons, Webster cites Lessing's play *Ernst und Falk* (also called *Lessing's Masonic Dialogues*),[6] and links Falk with various French individuals who took part in the French Revolution and in the Paris riots. Contrary to the view held by many historians, she asserts that Lord Pitt was not the chief financier of the Paris disturbances but rather Falk the Jew, who gave the French gold from the many chests of precious metal that he possessed. According to Webster, Falk was therefore one of those subversive individuals and adherents of underground movements who aspire to destroy the existing order and establish a new regime.[7]

Falk's ties with the Freemasons were examined by Marsha Schuchard in connection with her study of the Swedish philosopher and mystic Emanuel Swedenborg (1688–1772), who was one of the 'enlightened' spiritual leaders of the Freemasons and whose teachings served as the basis for a new order, the 'New Jerusalem Church', that was organized by his pupils and followers.[8] Swedenborg first visited London in 1710–13. His activities after this period are veiled in mystery, apparently owing to the need for secrecy because of his participation in the French–Swedish–Jacobite conspiracy that sought to overthrow the English Hanoverian monarchy. On the numerous occasions on which Swedenborg returned to England during the years 1744–72 he apparently acted as an agent of the French king and the pro-French party in Sweden, the 'Hats'.

Louis XV most likely underwrote the anonymous publication in London of Swedenborg's theosophical writings, possibly in return for the latter's clandestine espionage activity. In 1744–5 Swedenborg sought to be accepted by the lodge of the Moravian Brethren, which counted among its ranks French, Prussian, and Swedish members. Despite their public protestations of loyalty to King George II, its members were suspect in the eyes of the authorities. Swedenborg was provisionally accepted by the group and participated in its ceremonies. From 1744 he stayed in the home of a member of the lodge, John Paul Brockmer, an engraver of gold watches who lived in Salisbury Court on Fleet Street. According to Brockmer's testimony, at the beginning of July 1744 Swedenborg suffered from a high fever and severe delusions. Worried, Brockmer asked for help from the Swedish ambassador; after the diplomat's refusal to extend any assistance, the ailing Swedenborg was moved to the home of one of his friends, Dr William Smith. In his researches and experiments, Smith made use of

[6] See pp. 54–5 below.

[7] I discuss Webster, who was an antisemite, only because her work contains references to additional sources not known to the historians who have studied Falk (Adler, Roth), and because she was the first historian, regardless of her motives, to connect Falk with the Freemasons.

[8] See Schuchard, 'Yeats and the "Unknown Superiors"'; ead., 'The Secret Masonic History of Blake's Swedenborg Society'. The following discussion is based on these works and on the sources (those that I checked) cited by Schuchard.

Jewish traditions and kabbalistic mystical meditations in the development of his theories concerning diseases of the nerves.[9] He was a frequent visitor to Falk's home, and Zevi Hirsch mentions him in his diary. Smith may very well have been the one who introduced Swedenborg to Falk.

The links between the Freemasons, on the one hand, and Judaism and kabbalah on the other had begun years earlier, as had the quest for the esoteric, the ceremonial, and the symbolic, and the incorporation of such elements into Masonic philosophy or, to be more precise, into the teachings of several orders within the ranks of this movement. Thus, for example, the teachings of the Order of the Asiatic Brothers incorporated Christian and (kabbalistic and Sabbatian) Jewish elements.[10]

Swedenborg, who had already taken an interest in subjects associated with Judaism and Christian mysticism, was naturally drawn to Falk, who had undoubtedly heard of the spiritualist from his friends in France and Holland. The location of the Swedish church close to Falk's home could also have been a connecting link between the two.[11]

---

[9] In his *Dissertation on the Nerves* (1768), Dr Smith presents his theory that man is an entity composed of two parts: one material, the other not material. These parts, according to his theory, are interdependent, with mutual ties, and exert a reciprocal influence: change in one causes change in the other. He also discusses the eternal nature of the soul that must be in the brain, which, he maintains, is a sort of shrine or sanctuary of this divine spark. The soul's limbs are the five senses that are located in the fibres of the mind. Smith believed in the existence of a universal ether that preserves the soul–body unity. When the balance between the cosmic ether and man's ether is disturbed, nerve disease results. In his view, by studying the reciprocal and analogous links between the internal and the external, the spiritual and the material, the physician can diagnose an illness and find its remedy. The attainment of the true balance is the eternal felicitous state that includes the elevation of all the senses. This theory could possibly explain Smith's paramount interest in different religious sects, including the Freemasons and kabbalists. He asserted that mystics who suffered from sexual repression channelled this sexual energy into religious ecstasy. In another book, *A Sure Guide in Sickness and Health* (1776), he relates that his theory concerning mental illnesses and recovery from them originated in his researches into Judaism (in the list of his sources, he mentions the Talmud, the writings of Maimonides, and the Zohar).

[10] See Scholem, 'The Career of a Frankist' (Heb.), 157–61; J. Katz, *Jews and Freemasons in Europe*, 35–53.

[11] Schuchard, 'The Secret Masonic History of Blake's Swedenborg Society', 133, links Swedenborg's interest in Jews with the ties that he forged in Holland with the pupils of R. Moses Hayim Luzzatto. Schuchard takes note of various individuals (who are known for their activity in Masonic lodges) and their ties with Jewish mystics. She also indicates the relationship between R. Jonathan Eybeschuetz and his son Wolf and the German seer Johan Daniel Müller, a musical director in Frankfurt. Despite his great professional success, Müller abandoned his work and immersed himself in the study of kabbalah. On his journeys through northern Europe, he met Eybeschuetz and his son Wolf in 1761. Müller found an affinity between Eybeschuetz's Sabbatian beliefs and his own ideas concerning the establishment of a movement for fraternity between Jews, Christians, and Muslims (see also Keller, 'Daniel Müller'). Idel, 'The World of Angels in Human Form' (Heb.), 64–6, stresses the influence on the writings of Emanuel Swedenborg of the kabbalistic notion of the world of anthropomorphic angels. The latter's writings ('Divine Love and Wisdom', para. 288; 'Heaven and Hell', paras. 59–67; *The True Christian Religion*, para. 80) portray heaven (that is a general appellation for all the angelic camps) arranged in the form of man.

Schuchard mentions that Swedenborg visited England for a third time in 1764. This time, he went directly to Falk's neighbourhood, and took lodgings at the King's Arms tavern in Wellclose Square. During this period Swedenborg was engaged in writing an essay on conjugal love that, as Schuchard relates, contains kabbalistic theories of sexuality, and that makes use of kabbalistic mystical symbols.[12] Falk's association with Swedenborg apparently influenced additional members of the Masonic lodge. The concern with kabbalah (mainly applied kabbalah) aroused great interest in Falk, and prompted prominent Freemasons to meet him with a view to absorbing some of his wisdom. Testimonies to this desire appear in the writings and correspondence of various individuals who documented these meetings. Captain Archenholz, a German officer in the service of the Prussian army, wrote a book in which he describes the people of England and their life and customs. The chapter on English Jewry focuses especially on Falk's singular character. Archenholz claimed that Falk, or 'Dr Falkon', had been 'renowned for some thirty years'. He visited Falk, and, after a description of his dwelling, he portrays Falk himself as a fine-looking elderly man with a white beard, wearing a white robe, who seemed to be about 70 years old (Falk was in his sixties at the time). During their conversation Archenholz was impressed by Falk's extensive knowledge of chemistry, which had led to the latter's experiments in alchemy.[13]

Giovanni Casanova,[14] a prominent figure in Europe who was even described as a 'free kabbalist',[15] was visiting London at the time. He forged ties with several leading Freemasons, and sought to arrange a meeting with Falk through the offices of Colonel Frederick Obcestva, a Polish Jew who claimed to be the son of Theodore Stephen de Stein, Baron von Neuhoff, and who was friendly with Falk. Casanova relates in his memoirs how he feigned an interest in lotteries and games of chance in order to be received by Falk;[16] he does not state whether this ruse was successful.

The 1770s brought Falk together with a colourful figure of international repute, Count Alessandro di Cagliostro. This relationship, which was first noted by Web-

---

Idel states that the kabbalah provides the key to understanding several vague statements by Swedenborg, and refers to Zimmer, *Philosophies of India*, 244–8, and Abelson, 'Swedenburg and the Zohar', 7–8. Idel further observes that Swedenborg might have heard lectures delivered by the apostate Jew Peter Loewe, about whom Yehuda Liebes wrote ('The Author of the Book *Tsadik yesod olam*' (Heb.), 331, 332). Swedenborg might have read passages from the Zohar with Falk, along with readings from other books in Falk's library, and these joint readings (Falk probably translated the texts for him) led Swedenborg to adopt those ideas that would later appear in his own tracts.

[12] There are many translations into English of this essay, such as that by Alfred Acton: *The Delights of Wisdom: Concerning Conjugal Love*.

[13] Archenholz, *A Picture of England*, 181–2.   [14] See Maynial, *Casanova and His Time*.

[15] For the application of the term 'kabbalist' to Casanova, see Scholem, 'The Career of a Frankist' (Heb.), 169 n. 87, which mentions the correspondence between Casanova and Frank regarding his 'kabbalah'.   [16] Casanova, *History of My Life*, iii. 58, x. 32.

ster,[17] is mentioned in many sources, especially since Cagliostro proclaimed that he was Falk's leading disciple. Born in Palermo, Italy, as Giuseppe Balsamo,[18] Cagliostro was generally regarded as a mediocre artist who specialized in copying ancient paintings and forging signatures. Like Casanova, who immediately viewed him as a rival and competitor, Cagliostro had studied kabbalah and dabbled in alchemy in Italy. In 1769 he went to Avignon with his family, where he probably learned the principles of Freemasonry. At that time ties were established between the Swedish lodge and the Jacobite lodge in Avignon, and Cagliostro became friendly with members of the former. He went to London in 1771 and took up residence near Wellclose Square on Leadenhall Street, next to the lodgings of Falk and Swedenborg. Schuchard is of the opinion that Cagliostro sought out Falk to learn from him the 'hieroglyphic secrets'— the 'mystical depictions' whose meaning, she maintains, Falk revealed to Swedenborg, from whom this esoteric knowledge then made its way to the other Masonic lodges.[19] She states that Cagliostro exchanged his theories for the kabbalistic system, which he called 'Egyptian Cabala'. His impressive demeanour, psychological acumen, and the various wondrous acts that he taught (which relied mainly on sleight of hand), explain his success in entering European high society. He was renowned as a healer of sicknesses, as one who possessed the secret of eternal youth, who could raise the spirits of the dead, and who could, and did, transform base materials into gold. It may be assumed that he gained knowledge in these realms from Falk, and was not necessarily privy to kabbalistic teachings, as Schuchard posits. In 1779–80 Cagliostro was in Russia, where he had gone to spread his new theories. His stay there is mentioned in a letter written by the Tsarina Catherine the Great to Baron Grimm,[20] in which she writes of 'a daring act' that Cagliostro performed in St Petersburg. She continues: 'M. Cagliostro, however, has come just at the right moment for himself, when several lodges of freemasons, which had taken up Swedenborg's principles, were anxious at all costs to see spirits; they therefore ran to Cagliostro, who declared he had all the secrets of Doctor Falk, an intimate friend of the Duc de Richelieu, and who formerly sacrificed to the black goat in the midst of Vienna.' Catherine also composed a satirical play about Falk and Cagliostro (*The Deceiver*, 1786), in which she joined the two names together as 'Cali Falkistron'. The play, which was translated into several languages, aroused the ire of the Swedenborgians in London, who regarded it as a personal attack on them.[21]

Another colourful figure who was connected with Falk during this period was

[17] Webster, *Secret Societies*, 191.

[18] See Mackay, *Extraordinary Popular Delusions*, 237–55. An extensive literature has been written on Cagliostro: see Phoiades, *Count Cagliostro*, 71–9.

[19] The meaning of the term 'mystical depictions' is unclear.

[20] This letter, of 9 July 1781, appears in Grot, *Lettres de Grimm à l'Impératrice Catherine II*, 212–13; Chettoui, *Cagliostro et Catherine II*, 59. The letter also appears in translation in Waliszewski, *The Story of a Throne*, 93–4.   [21] See Schuchard, 'Yeats and the "Unknown Superiors"', 147.

Simon von Geldern, a German Jewish adventurer who was known as Heinrich Heine's great-uncle.[22] Von Geldern was also known as *der Morgenlander* (the Easterner), reflecting his journeys and adventures in Palestine and Egypt. He was in London in the early 1770s, and asked to be accepted by Falk in order to learn from him. Moreover, he succeeded in convincing the princes of Hesse-Darmstadt that he was privy to Falk's kabbalistic esoterica. In 1771 the prince of Hesse-Darmstadt sent Geldern to London to make contact with Falk.[23] Heymann notes that not only did Geldern not meet Falk, but that he even spoke against the *ba'al shem* (apparently for political reasons). At any rate, when Geldern returned to Darmstadt he managed to convince the prince that he had indeed studied with Falk, and at the end of 1771 he was appointed 'court kabbalist' by the monarch.

The reports of Falk as teacher, guide, and clandestine leader of the Freemasons apparently spread throughout Europe, bringing him to the attention of the prominent philosopher Gotthold Ephraim Lessing,[24] the close friend of Moses Mendelssohn (whom he portrayed in his play *Nathan the Wise*).[25] Lessing's curiosity was aroused by the Freemasons, and he asked to be accepted by the Swedish Masonic lodge in Hamburg, called the Three Golden Roses. His attempt to gain acceptance in the higher degrees ('Strict Observance') of the order failed, but he continued to be a member with candidate status. His interest in the Freemasons also led him to read Masonic writings, expecting to find there an expression of his hopes and desires. Lessing's attempt to be accepted by the Freemasons embarrassed Mendelssohn, who urged the former to tell him everything about his Masonic experience. Lessing, however, apologetically explained that his pledge to secrecy prevented him from doing so.[26]

In 1778 Lessing published his *Masonic Dialogues (Ernst und Falk)*, giving vent to both his general impression of the Masons and his disappointment with Freemasonry. Certain allusions in the work indicate that he was only partially initiated into the Swedish secret rites, and his expectation that he would find in the Freemasons a worldwide movement that was open to all religions, a belief that would unite all, and a creed that was based solely on logic and nature was frustrated. The two characters in the book, Ernst and Falk, represent the questioning and enquiring aspects of the Masonic movement—Ernst (in the image of Lessing), and the Masonic leader and teacher Falk. Lessing's decision to use this name for the character representing the Masonic movement was clearly based on his knowledge of Falk's personality and

---

[22] See Heymann, *Der Chevalier, Von Geldern*, 304–7; Rosenthal, *Heinrich Heines Grossheim*, 44–62.

[23] See Heymann, *Der Chevalier, Von Geldern*, 334, 342, 347. [24] See Webster, *Secret Societies*, 191.

[25] See J. Katz, *Jews and Freemasons in Europe*, 23–5, 235 nn. 42–4. Katz mentions Lessing's play, but completely ignores the connection between the 'Falk' of the play and the real-life Dr Falk. Moreover, Falk's name does not appear in Katz's book, nor does Katz discuss the links between Swedenborg and the members of his circle among the Freemasons, on the one hand, and the Jews in England and in Holland on the other. Altmann, *Moses Mendelssohn*, similarly disregards this connection.

[26] Altmann, *Moses Mendelssohn*, 310–11; Rolleston, *Life of Gotthold Ephraim Lessing*, 152–3.

the latter's being considered the 'Unknown Superior' of the Freemasons (as Falk is referred to in various texts). Lessing paints a scene in which Ernst and Falk are sitting together in a forest, and Falk is explaining the goals of the Freemasons.[27] According to him, their aim is to change the world in such a manner that there will no longer be a need for philanthropy. He illustrates this by pointing to an anthill that is under a tree near where they are sitting.[28] He asks, 'Why is man incapable of existing without a government, as do the ants and the bees?' He then introduces his friend and pupil Ernst to the idea of a universal state built on political unity among the various countries in which men are not divided by national, social, or religious preconceptions, and in which equality reigns. At the end of the book's third dialogue, Lessing declares an intermission. During this time, the author states, Ernst becomes a Freemason. However, on his return in the fourth dialogue, Ernst tells Falk of his disappointment:[29] he claims that he has found 'many Masons' engaging in worthless pursuits such as alchemy or the raising of spirits.

Falk seeks to persuade Ernst that something extremely secret and ancient, with far-reaching aims, lies behind what is discernible. Ernst complains to Falk that the Jews are not permitted to join Masonic cells, to which Falk replies that he himself does not participate in them,[30] and that the great leaders who are privy to its secrets do not appear upon the public stage, but rather are hidden and not known to all.[31]

---

[27] This book was translated by Cohen as *Lessing's Masonic Dialogues (Ernst und Falk)*; see the translator's introduction (pp. 1–23).   [28] See the second dialogue, ibid. 40–50.
[29] See ibid. 69–81.   [30] Ibid. 77, and especially the fifth dialogue (pp. 96–108).
[31] Lessing sent Mendelssohn the manuscript of the *Masonic Dialogues*, to which Mendelssohn responded:

> I read your conversations about the Freemasons with great pleasure. But they did not satisfy my curiosity.... On the one hand, I rid myself of this evil spirit some time ago. I am certain that what people conceal from other people is rarely of value to research. On the other hand, I am well aware that your conversations were not intended to satisfy curiosity. At any rate, they led me to form ideas about an institution that, beforehand, had begun to appear to me to be worthy of contempt.

Lessing dedicated the dialogues to the duke of Braunschweig. The first three dialogues were published in 1778 in Göttingen. The author hoped that the work would be received favourably, despite the critique it levelled at the Swedish rite and its call for greater toleration and internationalism. The duke, however, thought that Lessing's revelations had gone too far, and he forbade the publication of the fourth and fifth dialogues. Lessing's Falk criticizes the projects of the Freemasons, such as the establishment of a hospital for orphans in Sweden, and regards them as insignificant in comparison with the Masons' true work, which he says is great and far-reaching, but which will only be properly appreciated in times to come. He argues that the goal of the Freemasons is to make everything that ordinary people call 'good deeds' unnecessary. Lessing apparently hoped to find the Freemasons advocating a new political theory that would advance religious tolerance. At the end of the third dialogue Falk succeeds in persuading Ernst to join the order. The publication of what Ernst finds there, however, was prohibited, and was plagiarized and published in 1780 without Lessing's permission. These dialogues reveal the disappointment felt by Ernst (Lessing) at the kind of rites that developed. He argues that Falk has deceived him, and that all that he has found there is a 'sterile wasteland'; he complains about the 'new members' or 'new brothers', who seek only to find gold or to awaken spirits. Lessing's Falk defends the 'brothers' who participate in

The presentation of Falk in Lessing's *Masonic Dialogues* as symbolizing the Freemasons once again raises several long-standing questions: why was Falk considered to be the teacher and spiritual guide of several prominent Freemasons? Why do the latter call him 'The Unknown Superior' (that is, the concealed leader) in their literature? Just what did Falk teach Swedenborg and the others who came to him? Schuchard argues that Falk offered Swedenborg (and possibly others as well) a kabbalistic interpretation of the Egyptian paintings (or hieroglyphs) possessed by Swedenborg, and notes that Falk taught them the principles of early Christian kabbalah. She also talks of the influence on the Freemasons of kabbalistic theories of sexuality, and links the sexual symbolism in the Zohar with Sabbatian and Frankist sexual teachings and with Falk (whom she depicts as a pupil of Barukhyah[32]). She further writes: 'Secretly associated with the radical Sabbatians of Poland and with French agents of the Stuart cause, Falk instructed Swedenborg in Cabalistic trance techniques and sexual magic.'[33]

the ceremonies (*Lessing's Masonic Dialogues*, 69–81). He maintains that all these dreams are merely way-stations on the true path (see Cohen's introduction to the dialogues; Altmann, *Moses Mendelssohn*; Schuchard's comments on this issue follow Cohen, but without specifying their source).

[32] Barukhyah Russo b. Judah (b. Salonika 1660, d. *c.*1720/5), also known as Baruch Kunio or Mustafa Jibili ('Senior Santo', i.e. 'the holy master' in Ladino), was considered to be the ideological successor of Sabbatai Zevi and Nathan of Gaza. Barukhyah founded an extreme new religion of a syncretic nature, whose followers were known as Konyoses. His teachings were based on the abandonment of the commandments and the abrogation of the Torah. The new believers were said to have engaged in acts of sexual licentiousness, for which a religious rationale was given: that these promiscuous acts were, in actuality, religious *tikunim* (measures aimed at restoring correct order to the world). The new religion preached God's descent to the world and his manifestation as the Redeemer, who was none other than Barukhyah (= God).

[33] Schuchard, 'The Secret Masonic History of Blake's Swedenborg Society', 40; her concepts of kabbalistic sexuality are taken in their entirety from secondary sources. There is no basis for her emphatic assertions that Falk was a guide for Egyptian kabbalah or for her theory of sexuality in the kabbalah. The reference that she gives ('Yeats and the "Unknown Superiors"', 152) that, presumably, Zevi Hirsch's diary speaks of Falk's ties with Sabbatians and Frankists in Hamburg and in Altona is a complete fiction. Her claim that Falk was a pupil of Barukhyah is also groundless (her reference to the article by Scholem is misleading—and incorrect; Scholem never mentions any relationship between Falk and Barukhyah, nor does he indicate any connection between Falk and Jacob Frank). Schuchard follows Webster in linking Falk and Frank; I did not find any indication of such ties, either in Falk's diary, or in Hillel Levine, *The Kronika* (Heb.), or in Jacob Frank's *Księga Słów Pańskich*. The existence of ties between the Freemasons and the members of Frank's sect still does not attest to the presence of such bonds between Falk and Frank.

By contrast, links between Falk and the Eybeschuetz family are more plausible, and Falk may very well have been in contact with Wolf Eybeschuetz and his followers. There is no evidence of such a relationship in Zevi Hirsch's diary, but allusions to it can be found in statements by Jacob Emden, and possibly also in veiled references to Wolf in Falk's diary, but this remains in the realm of conjecture (see the glosses on Falk's diary below).

Schuchard's use of the term 'Egyptian kabbalah' is also imprecise, and is used instead of the more commonly accepted terms 'hermetism' or 'hermetic teachings' which are primarily related to Hermes

Schuchard's assertions, no matter how vigorous, seem off track. The connection she draws between the sexual symbolism of the Zohar and Sabbatian teachings betrays her lack of knowledge in this area. Falk, like other kabbalists before him, did not engage in 'sexual magic', and certainly did not teach this 'subject' to Swedenborg and those of his circle. Rather, Falk could have taught Swedenborg the following:

1. Basic kabbalistic concepts, such as the system of divine *sefirot*,[34] and that of kabbalistic symbolism. (The term *madregot* ('levels') also appears in the Masonic writings, as do several kabbalistic symbols that connect the two *sefirot* representing the male and female powers in the world of the *sefirot*: Tiferet (Beauty) and Malkhut (Kingdom).)

Trismegistus, a name given to the Egyptian god Thoth ('Hermes the thrice-greatest'). According to early Egyptian belief, this god was the inventor of writing, the sciences, and magic; he is identified with the Greek god Hermes. Moshe Idel (*Kabbalah: New Perspectives*, 40–1) notes that ancient corpuses of hermetic writings of a clearly magical character were known in antiquity, and later in the medieval period. These works contained techniques such as incantation, the combination of letters, and exercises in concentration to enable the magician to make contact with higher entities and bring about their descent to the world (or their entry into the soul of the magician himself). These techniques also entered Judaism, and Idel (in various passages in his book—see the index) discusses their influence on kabbalah, especially ecstatic kabbalah. During the Renaissance, when magic, astrology, and alchemy flourished once again driven by the desire to control and change the forces of nature, we witness a return to those ancient texts, in the hope of finding in their teachings the means to realize this ambition. The character of Falk emerges, from both the diary of Falk himself and from that of Zevi Hirsch, as a practitioner of practical kabbalah. Despite the many books of theosophical kabbalah, including the Zohar, in Falk's library, their presence is not felt in the diaries, an omission that is even more striking in light of the frequent mention of, and reliance upon, prominent kabbalists and kabbalistic tracts by other *ba'alei shem* to give added authority to their own words. The question nonetheless arises: what led these prominent individuals to welcome Falk and seek to meet him in his house, and then mention this, either in writing or orally? The answer to this puzzle is to be found in the two diaries and other testimonies that we possess. Falk used techniques involving the numerical value of words and acrostics to foresee the future; these methods were likely to have been common among a number of *ba'alei shem*, as is attested by the *Sefer hagoralot* written in Falk's hand. Falk could tell people details about their character and fate, and served as their counsellor and guide. His knowledge of popular medicine, and of fields allied with chemistry (the plating of metals, the preparation of various compounds) also aroused interest (and perhaps was also of material and economic import). To these we should add his knowledge or skill in the areas of telekinesis and manual dexterity (and possibly also sleight of hand), and, above all, his meditative knowledge and activity, which he combined with his other paranormal knowledge in the ceremonies that he conducted in his house.

These characteristics and proficiencies attracted those among Falk's contemporaries who believed in his supernatural powers and who, accordingly, hoped to benefit from their acquaintance with him. On the other hand, the absence of his name from writings by kabbalists, rabbis, and Torah scholars, as well as a similar disregard for him by the *maskilim* (advocates of the Jewish Enlightenment) of his time speaks eloquently of their sceptical attitude towards Falk.

[34] One of the fundamental principles of kabbalah speaks of the concealed God, the Ein Sof, and of the godhead that is revealed in ten *sefirot*, a term that first appears in *Sefer yetsirah*. They are also known by other names, such as *ketarim*—literally, crowns; *madregot*—steps; *otserot*—treasures; *kelim*—

2. Numerology (*gematriyah*) and the transposition of letters (*temurah*). Falk employed these methods, which appear in his diary, both for interpretation of the Bible (understanding the biblical texts as having an alternative meaning either after considering the numerical value of the letters of a word or phrase or by rearranging the letters) and for magical ends.

3. Practical kabbalah. Falk may have taught his pupils the hidden meanings of texts of a mystical nature, instructed them in kabbalistic exercises and meditations, and possibly also trained them in various stratagems for moving objects and changing their shape.

There was also a political aspect to Falk's ties with the Masonic leaders. He was a prominent individual, and had international connections with well-known people who were active in the governments of their respective lands (France, Prussia, Russia, and Sweden), and with political figures who had revolutionary aims (such as the opponents of the royal house of Hanover in England). These individuals and their followers probably recruited Falk and the members of his circle to act as their contact in England (Falk's residence near London Bridge was an excellent observation point for spying on incoming ships). It is quite plausible that the missions on which Falk sent his followers (which are mentioned in both diaries) to various lands—France, Holland, and Prussia—were related to acts of espionage, but we have no proof of this. Moreover, Falk's knowledge of chemistry and his experiments in plating metals were well known, and led those political leaders and their agents to his door in the hope of thereby financing their activities. This is most evident in Falk's ties with the Polish Prince Czartoryski (referred to in Falk's diary as 'Duke'),[35] who was a Freemason and

---

implements; *orot*—lights; *gevanim*—shades/colours; *koḥot*—powers; and *havayot*—[modes of] existence (*shem hahavayah* is the Tetragrammaton). The system of these *sefirot*, which are the manifestations of God or his attributes, reflects only a portion of the divine existence that is immanent in the world that (only seemingly) is beyond Ein Sof. It is this system that implements divine providence, for there is no change within Ein Sof. Each *sefirah* expresses a different aspect of the manifestation of the godhead. The ten *sefirot* are Keter—Crown; Hokhmah—Wisdom; Binah—Intelligence; Hesed—Love; Gevurah—Power or Judgement; Tiferet—Beauty; Netsah—Lasting Endurance; Hod—Majesty; Yesod—Foundation; and Malkhut—Kingdom (also known as the Shekhinah, the Divine Presence) (the translation of these terms follows Scholem, *Major Trends*; see his ch. 6). The *sefirot* are divided into two groups: the first three 'superior' ones, and the other seven, also known as *yamim* (literally 'days'). Kabbalists draw an additional distinction in this system between the male and the female aspects (Binah and Malkhut respectively, the third and tenth *sefirot*), and they differentiate between the right side, that of Hesed, and the left, that of strict judgement; the median line between these two aspects expresses compassion.

As mystics, kabbalists employ symbolic language; thus they apply to the *sefirot* symbolic appellations that reflect their essence. They also employ this symbolic language in their reading of the Bible and other religious texts (i.e. the rabbinic literature); in other words, the sacred texts reflect the godhead in symbolic fashion.

[35] Prince Czartoryski (1739–1823) was known for his struggles on behalf of Polish unification, and in 1781–2 he was president of the tribunal of Lithuania. In 1765 he met Casanova, and quite possibly was the

maintained close ties both with Swedenborg and Cagliostro and with the Jewish Freemason Simeon Boas.[36] Falk writes in his diary of the recommendation that he received from his friend Simeon, who asked him to meet the prince; he also includes in his diary the text of the letter that he sent to Czartoryski.

The ramified relations described above are barely mentioned in Falk's diary, in which he recorded various things that happened to him, or which were done by him, from 1772 to 1782. This document clearly indicates that he lived a comfortable and wealthy life during this period, and that his standing in the Jewish community had been completely transformed. His numerous financial contributions to the community (which he recorded in his diary) apparently led to the request (also documented there) by Isaac Hazan, acting on behalf of the *parnas* (warden) of the synagogue Meir (referred to by Falk as 'R. Meyer'), to be a *ba'al bayit* in the community.[37] Falk records his shocked response to the proposal: 'Heaven forfend that my name should be mentioned in such a matter, for I am *ba'al bayit* for all the world.'[38] This declaration reveals his cosmopolitan outlook, which closely corresponded to the Masonic worldview and which was possibly also in harmony with the messianic pretensions of the man who was called 'the king of the Jews' or their 'prince'.

Shortly before his death Falk drew up his will,[39] in which he bequeathed the majority of his estate to the institutions of the London Jewish community. A few days after writing and signing this as required by law, he died, suddenly, on 17 April 1782.

Falk's personality and great influence were captured in books by Freemasons,[40] who regarded him as 'the Unknown Superior', but he has been ignored by scholars of Jewish studies, who refer to him—not necessarily by name, but as the 'Ba'al Shem of London'—only in passing. All that remains of him is a single portrait painted by one of the artists of the period,[41] in which we see a seated, white-haired figure, with

---

person who introduced the latter to the Sabbatian circles in Poland with whom the nobleman maintained good relations (his enemies said that he himself was a quasi-Sabbatian). Through Casanova, Czartoryski might have made contact with the Boas family in Holland. He first visited England in 1768, and went there a second time (as recorded in Falk's diary) in 1772. The prince probably sought Falk's help in financing his political plans and in forging ties with Masonic circles throughout Europe.

[36] For Prince Czartoryski's connections with the Freemasons, see Schuchard, 'The Secret Masonic History of Blake's Swedenborg Society', 127.   [37] *Ba'al bayit*, in the sense of communal leader.

[38] FD, fo. 32a. In the initial stages of my research, I thought that Falk's statement was pretentious, and possibly also hinted at his Sabbatian belief, but Yehuda Liebes drew my attention to a cosmopolitan tone in this diary entry. This entry may possibly allude to Falk's identification with the strand of thinking in Freemasonry that negates nationalist concepts that separate people from one another and views the world as a single unit composed of many individuals.

[39] The will is among the holdings of the National Archives at Kew in London; see Appendix F.

[40] e.g. Mackenzie, *The Royal Masonic Cyclopaedia*, 212–14, 626–7; Westcott, *History of the Rosicrucian Societies in Anglia*, 45; id., 'The Rosicrucians Past and Present', 43.

[41] For the history of the painting, see Adler, 'The Baal Shem of London', and C. Roth, 'The King and the Cabbalist'. The painting is attributed to the American painter John Singleton Copley, who visited

his right hand holding a compass (a Masonic symbol) and his left hand pointing to a Star of David.[42]

The name given to the painting, *Ba'al Shem*, led to its erroneous identification with another celebrated contemporary of Falk's, the Ba'al Shem Tov, Rabbi Israel ben Eliezer, the founder of hasidism. The painting appears in many history books with the mistaken caption underneath. The original painting travelled widely and went as far as Australia before finally being purchased by the family of Cecil Roth, in whose possession it remains at present.

Falk was buried in the Jewish cemetery in Mile End, where his tombstone bears the inscription:

An aged and honourable man, a great personage who came from the East, an accomplished sage, an adept in Cabbalah, the learned Rabbi Samuel, son of the learned Rabbi Raphael of blessed memory. His name was known to the ends of the earth and distant isles. During the forty years that he resided here he uplifted the banner of the Law and of Divine Worship. He studied and kept the Law, the Commandments, and Statutes. At the time of his decease he devoted all his possessions—a great substance—among many different charities. For the merit hereof may the Creator of the heavens and the Founder of the globe bind up his soul in the Garden of Eden with the other righteous men. And may He grant him the privilege of arising at the Resurrection with the other dead of Israel, whom He will hereafter raise up. He departed with a good name on Thursday, the fourth of the month of Splendour, *i.e.* Iyar (April

---

London in the late eighteenth century. Schuchard, 'The Secret Masonic History of Blake's Swedenborg Society', 164 n. 220, observes that the painting was examined by the art scholar Stephan Lloyd, who maintains that it was executed by Philippe Jacques de Loutherbourg, who was himself a Freemason and painted Swedenborg's portrait in 1771.

[42] In her description of the portrait, Schuchard states that Falk appears to be engaged in the composition of kabbalistic figures (namely, the Star of David that seems to be drawn on a sheet of paper lying on the table, and that Falk is touching); see 'The Secret Masonic History of Blake's Swedenborg Society', 164 n. 220. I would certainly not define the Star of David (*magen david*) as a kabbalistic drawing. Gershom Scholem clearly states in his article '*Magen david*: The History of a Symbol' (Heb.) that 'The *magen david* is not of Jewish lineage, nor does it possess any Jewish significance, neither overt nor concealed, at any rate [it does not have such significance] in the esoteric world of those within the fold of Judaism'. Scholem surveys the history of this symbol in Judaism, as in other religions, and notes the connection between it and practical kabbalah and Jewish magic. He describes how it became a Jewish symbol at a late period, incorporating different meanings (magical and messianic). Scholem stresses the use made of the *magen david* in Sabbatian circles, and relates this to its use on Falk's grave: 'At times the magical meaning is incorporated into the representative meaning that we have just discussed, as on the tombstone of that arch-magician Dr Falk, who was renowned in his time.... Such a use of the symbol on tombstones was still quite rare during that period' (ibid.). In the portrait of Falk by a Masonic artist (both Copley and de Loutherbourg were identified as Freemasons), Falk points to a Star of David, thereby possibly expressing the desire of the artist to indicate the magical practices of his subject, who was known to be a *ba'al shem*. Another very likely possibility, however, is that when Falk posed for the painting, he deliberately drew attention to this symbol, which several of his Sabbatian friends during this period had infused with magical-messianic significance.

17th), and was buried with honour and with mourning on the morrow, Friday, the twentieth day of the Omer [see Lev. 23: 15–16], 5542 A.M. (April 18, 1782).

May his soul be bound up in the bond of life!⁴³

The original inscription suffered the ravages of time, and nothing remains of it. However, the eulogy that appears in Adler's article on Falk was photographed, enlarged, and affixed to the tombstone. The large and impressive marble monument erected by the London Jewish community at the entrance to the cemetery in memory of the worthies interred there also mentions our hero, Hayim Samuel Jacob Falk, the Ba'al Shem of London, who won praise and glory in his old age and posthumously. The *ba'al shed* had finally became a *ba'al shem*—a wonder-worker and the 'possessor of a [good] name'.

⁴³ As translated by Adler in 'The Baal Shem of London' (*TJHSE*), 169.

VI
THE DIARIES AND THEIR RESEARCH

THE FIRST DESCRIPTION we have of Falk's diary is in an article by the scholar Adolf Neubauer, sublibrarian at the Bodleian Library in Oxford and reader in rabbinic Hebrew at the University of Oxford, which was published in the *Jewish Chronicle*; a second description followed in his catalogue of Hebrew manuscripts in the library of the United Synagogue.[1] In 1888 Solomon Schechter, then a tutor in rabbinics in London and soon to be appointed a tutor in rabbinics at the University of Cambridge, published an article, 'The Baalshem—Dr Falk'. Schechter apparently had difficulty understanding the contents of the diary, humorously observing: 'The language used is Hebrew, but the writer does not seem to have been on good terms with Dr. Syntax.' Schechter provided the details of Falk's will, and, for the convenience of his readers, also translated what Jacob Emden wrote concerning the *ba'al shem*. Schechter questioned Emden's charges regarding Falk's presumed crypto-Sabbatianism, and declared that he was leaving the examination of this issue for others.

In 1903 Rabbi Dr Herman Adler, chief rabbi of the British Empire, delivered a lecture on 'The Baal Shem of London' that was published in Berlin and in London,[2] in which he collected details and testimonies about Falk from various sources. Although Adler disregarded the kabbalistic material in the diary, his study opened a window onto Falk's world.

In 1953 and 1955 Professor Cecil Roth lectured about Falk on the radio and before the Jewish Historical Society of England; this lecture was eventually published in his *Essays and Portraits in Anglo-Jewish History*.[3] Roth based the essay primarily on the previous study by Adler, from which he copied many passages, but in addition he possessed the diary of Samuel Falk's factotum Zevi Hirsch of Kalisz, who was also the great-grandfather of Roth's wife, Irene.[4] Roth's essay examines a single, previously unknown, episode from Zevi Hirsch's diary, that of Falk's relationship with the

---

[1] See Neubauer, 'Literary Gleanings'; id., *Catalogue of the Hebrew Manuscripts in the Jews' College*, no. 127 (p. 37).

[2] Adler, 'The Baal Shem of London' (Berlin, 1903); an expanded version of this article was published in 1908 in *Transactions of the Jewish Historical Society of England*.

[3] Roth, 'The King and the Cabbalist', in *Essays*, 139–64.

[4] See ibid. 143.

'king of Corsica' Theodore Stephen de Stein, Baron von Neuhoff. Roth claimed exclusive rights to the identification of the king (whom Zevi Hirsch's diary calls *ba'al haserarah*—'the one holding power') with the baron, even though the connection between the two had been noted, and published, many years earlier by David Kahana,[5] and was also mentioned by Adler in his article. Roth hardly referred directly to Falk's diary, and his quotations from it come from a secondary source. Roth also wrote the entry on Falk in the *Encyclopaedia Judaica*.

Gershom Scholem mentioned Falk in the course of other discussions, mostly in very short references.[6] In general, Falk was forgotten and almost totally disregarded by scholarly research into eighteenth-century England.

In 1994 David Katz published his *Jews in the History of England 1485–1850*, which contains a chapter devoted to Falk,[7] and which is based mainly on earlier studies. For the first time, however, a contemporary scholar discussed the important place occupied by Falk and his circle in the history of the Jews in England, and the ties of the former with English society in the second half of the eighteenth century.[8]

Falk's diary was initially kept among the holdings of Jews' College in London (and is so marked in the Institute of Microfilmed Hebrew Manuscripts of the National Library of Israel in Jerusalem). Following a move by this institution within London the diary could not be found, and the efforts by several scholars to unearth it proved fruitless.[9] After many years of searching, the diary was rediscovered in the Jewish Museum in London, though it formally still belongs to the United Synagogue archive.[10]

Falk's diary has never appeared in print. Consisting of fifty-nine folio pages, some blank (the numbering of the pages is faulty), it is written in Hebrew, mainly in Spanish rabbinic script (although some pages are written in cursive Ashkenazi script). It opens in 1722, albeit with references to events that occurred earlier than this. Not a diary in the accepted literary sense of the term, it is, rather, a gathering of sundry recollections and notes written down by Falk so that he would not forget them. It contains inventory lists of different household articles that he stored in boxes in his house and elsewhere; notes regarding bottles of wine that he prepared; recipes for

---

[5] Kahana, 'Those in Error and Those Who Lead Astray' (Heb.), 55–6.

[6] See Scholem, *Studies and Texts* (Heb.), III, 168; id., *Kabbalah*, 282, 311; id., *The Messianic Idea in Judaism*, 279.

[7] *The Jews in the History of England*, ch. 7, para. iii.   [8] Ibid. 301 n. 51.   [9] Ibid. 300–3, 311–12.

[10] The diary was found with the assistance of Professor Ada Rapoport-Albert. Mr Edgar Samuel, then the director of the Jewish Museum in London, where the diary was found, permitted me to examine the manuscript and compare it with the version in the copies in my possession, for which I am grateful. The Chief Rabbi of the United Hebrew Congregations of Great Britain and the Commonwealth, Lord Sacks, and the director of the United Synagogue archive, Charles Tucker, graciously permitted me to publish the diary, for which I am also grateful. (The United Synagogue archive is in fact now part of the London Metropolitan Archive.)

cakes, biscuits, wine, and the plating of metals; lists of the duplicate copies of books in his library, and the lists of books that always accompanied him on his travels; the record of his meetings with various people, along with the accompanying correspondence; the monies that he paid and that he received, as loans or for items that he had pawned; the dreams that he had experienced; the measurements of different objects that he prepared for the room where his circle assembled; and amulets derived from biblical verses, using numerology, acronyms, and final letters to form incomprehensible words. In many places the text is difficult to decipher, since the Hebrew is frequently plagued by mistakes; additionally, Falk uses words from other languages (German, French, Yiddish, and Dutch) that he spells incorrectly.

The diary does not provide us with the picture of Falk the man that emerges from the other sources. His international relations, as set forth in the external sources, are barely mentioned there, nor does his outstanding personality shine through; his philosophical and cultural opinions are similarly not in evidence. Except for the list of duplicate books, the diary is silent on the influence exerted by these basic books of kabbalah and Jewish culture in general. The few entries in which Falk speaks of his private life refer mainly to his monetary dealings; only his dreams, which are portrayed in the diary, offer a glimpse of his personality.[11] Falk mentions the names of individuals who came to his home, some of them prominent figures, others now unknown. While Falk's diary is a fascinating document telling of the daily life of a unique Jew in eighteenth-century England, it cannot tell us about the man himself.

The diary of Falk's factotum Zevi Hirsch of Kalisz, which was discovered by members of his family,[12] is of a different nature. In the first half of the eighteenth century Zevi Hirsch left Poland for London, where he spent his first few years in the country before moving with his family to Bristol to serve as a cantor. Towards the end of his life he returned to London and became a member of the Great Synagogue.[13] His son founded the Collins family line, whose descendants include prominent architects, artists, and members of the theatrical profession.[14]

Zevi Hirsch wrote his diary over four years, during his period of service as Falk's factotum. This remarkable document chronicles Zevi Hirsch's daily life in the Falk household, which revolved entirely around the personality of the 'Ba'al Shem of London'. Reading between the lines, we become acquainted with Zevi Hirsch himself, as a simple and good-hearted Jew who faithfully serves his master but who is nonetheless aware of the injustice he suffers at his hands such as the withholding of his wages and other slights. Zevi Hirsch almost never complained about this in

---

[11] See below, Appendix B.

[12] For passages from the diary, see C. Roth, 'The King and the Cabbalist'.

[13] For details concerning Zevi Hirsch, see C. Roth, *The History of the Great Synagogue in London*, 164–5; Bet-Halevi, *History of the Jews of Kalisz* (Heb.), 372.

[14] See C. Roth, 'The King and the Cabbalist'.

VI. THE DIARIES AND THEIR RESEARCH

public, and gave free rein to his feelings only in his writing. He thus took refuge in his diary, where he could secretly record all that he did and everything that he experienced in Falk's house. Despite the criticism expressed in the diary of Falk's parsimony, and his indifference to Zevi Hirsch's suffering, Zevi Hirsch seemingly revered his master, referring to him mostly as 'the Sage' and later as 'Admo', an acronym for 'my master and teacher'. Zevi Hirsch records Falk's occult activities and the ceremonies at which he was present. In fact, the importance of the diary lies in the accuracy with which it documents the rites that Falk conducted. It also reveals the names of several members of Falk's coterie, along with those of other prominent visitors. Zevi Hirsch apparently accompanied Falk in his travels, and notes in his diary that he recorded their trip to Holland in another notebook (which has apparently been lost).

The original of Zevi Hirsch's diary, which is currently held by the Jewish Theological Seminary in New York,[15] is a small notebook (10 × 15.4 cm) comprising sixty-two pages, written in cursive Ashkenazi script. Some of the written pages were torn out and have been lost. The diary ends with folio 36a, which is followed by a list of debts (fo. 36b), then by blank numbered pages (fo. 37a–b), and then medicinal remedies (fos. 38a–39a).

The diary is written in poor Hebrew;[16] occasionally with Yiddish words or English words in Hebrew transliteration interspersed, and even more occasionally with words deriving from French and German, also in Hebrew transliteration. Numerous words are spelled incorrectly, hindering their decipherment. Many lines were erased by the author, and despite my efforts at reconstruction some passages remain illegible. At the end of the diary are two pages of 'medications' for various illnesses that Zevi Hirsch most probably learned from his master and committed to writing. The various details pertaining to everyday life in Falk's house shed light on his personality from a Jewish perspective, and enable us to construct a more complete picture of Falk's life and connections during the period covered by the diary (1747–51).

---

[15] I wish to thank Professor Schmeltzer and Dr Meir Rabinowitz, the directors of the manuscript collection of the Jewish Theological Seminary, for enabling me to photocopy and publish the diary (EN Adler 2441 Mic 3599).

[16] The very fact that an eighteenth-century diary was written in Hebrew, when it was not a spoken language and was reserved primarily for the writing of religious tracts, is itself praiseworthy. Zevi Hirsch's diary contains a wealth of information for the study of linguistics and its history; its publication provides scholars with much fresh material.

THE DIARIES

THE DIARY OF
ZEVI HIRSCH OF KALISZ

|fo. 1a| *London, Tuesday, 23 Elul 5507* [18 August 1747]. *He had intended to practise [his mystical devotions] but instead he went in the coach with *R. Mordecai Franzmann to *the house in Pas, *and he took books from there with him, that is, the best ones, also pictures, and also the staff that was with him, *for a pledge, that belongs to *the Sage. For this reason he cancelled his practices that night.

Wednesday. Today's practising was also cancelled, because he went to buy things for the new house he had bought at 35 Prescot Street.

Thursday. Also wasted because of the said things. *R. Zalman and R. Tuvyah came only in the evening, and he began to practise after midnight. First we recited Psalms

He the reference here is to Falk, in whose house ZH served as factotum. [ZH never refers to Falk by name, possibly for mystical reasons connected to warding off the evil eye, references to 'he' and 'him' throughout the diary are generally to Falk; likewise, references to 'she' and 'her' can generally be understood as references to Falk's wife.]

R. Mordecai Franzmann possibly Mordecai b. Getz Frank; see C. Roth, 'Membership', 178.

the house in Pas ZH refers to Falk's house in Prescot Street in east London as 'Pas', which he spells *peh-alef-samekh*. [The abbreviation apparently derives from his misspelling of the street name, which he renders as 'Pascot'.]

and he took the books ... with him [It is not clear whether 'he' here refers to Falk, as it normally does, or to Franzmann, meaning that the latter was taking the various objects as a security against a loan he had made to Falk.]

for a pledge [ZH's entry here is not clear, but it becomes evident from the diary that Falk is continuously leaving his possessions as a pledge with pawnbrokers to finance his day-to-day expenditures.]

the Sage an appellation that ZH sometimes uses in referring to Falk, though 'he' is more common. [In fact he writes the Hebrew word for 'sage' in an abbreviated form without the final letter, so even in using this term the reference is intentionally obfuscated, presumably to ward off the evil eye as explained above.]

R. Zalman and R. Tuvyah came only in the evening, and he began to practise after midnight ZH describes how he and other members of Falk's circle gathered in his house and prepared themselves the mystical ceremony subsequently performed by Falk, giving a precise listing of the verses recited. R. Tuvyah, mentioned a few times in the diary, apparently belonged to the circle of admirers who gathered around Falk and saw him as their rabbi, leader, and spiritual guide. He is also mentioned in Falk's *Sefer hagoralot* (for fortune-telling).

61, 32, and afterwards 27, and we recited the entire psalm *in the plural, and then Psalm 97, also *the Sixth Utterance, and then a verse from *Sefer yetsirah, chapter 1, from *'sealed north'. So we recited first a verse from Psalm 97, then a verse from the Sixth Utterance, and then a verse from Sefer yetsirah, until we finished the said psalm. *He then ordered us to leave, and he stayed in his room and practised for about four hours, also blowing the shofar, and he stopped.

Friday, 26 Elul. I went with him and he bought two mirrors for five guineas, a table, and also a small mirror for 30s. 0d., a pair of candlesticks and a coffee mill, and also a small bell for the house for 8s. 6d., a tray for *one guinea, also one chest to serve as a Torah ark for 10s. 0d., and also bedding for one [shilling?].

On Thursday, 25 Elul he redeemed his pledges from *the gentile Flanders: £1. 0s. 0d., also pewter for 14s. 0d., and also two *stot pens for 5s. 0d. *In total £10. 13s. 6d.

On Thursday, 25 Elul he redeemed his pledges from the gentile Flanders, that is, *a silver egg, a watch, and seven gold stars, and also his big lamp, for £37. 17s. 0d., and he also took from him thirty *arems, as well as three pairs of candlesticks. He said that he needed these things for his *rituals, for without them it was not possible to do anything.

in the plural i.e. changing the text of the psalm.

the Sixth Utterance see Mishnah *Avot* 5: 1: 'With ten utterances the world was created', which is interpreted as referring to the first verse of Genesis and nine subsequent occurrences of the words 'God said' in the biblical account of Creation. Kabbalistic doctrine considered these Ten Utterances to be parallel to the ten *sefirot*.

Sefer yetsirah the mystical Book of Creation.

'sealed north' *Sefer yetsirah* 1: 3: 'He sealed north. He turned left and sealed it with [the Hebrew letters] *vav heh yod*' (following the translation by I. Friedman (New York, 1977)). On the significance of 'north' in kabbalah, see also note to *ba'al tsafon* on fo. 7b (see p. 89).

He then ordered us to leave after the preparations for the ceremony, Falk ordered his followers to leave the room so he remained alone to engage in the occult rite.

one guinea [A guinea was worth £1. 1s. 0d.]

the gentile Flanders a pawnbroker with whom Falk left some of his belongings as pledges.

stot pens possibly meaning 'sauce pans', or perhaps deep and sturdy pans: 'stout pans'.

In total £10. 13s. 6d. [How ZH calculated this total, which he gives in words as well as in figures, is unclear.]

a silver egg, a watch, and seven gold stars [The items pawned suggest that Falk received expensive items in lieu of payment from the wealthy people who sought his services, but he did not have cash to cover his living expenses and so had to resort to pawnbrokers.]

arems to arm, i.e. to plate, possibly referring to pieces of metal that were to be plated; perhaps from the word 'armlet', since armlets could be of metal.

rituals [The term ZH uses for what Falk engages in is *avodah*, a term which in modern Hebrew means 'work' but which was used historically to refer to the rituals of the Temple. Given the mystical nature of Falk's endeavours, the use of 'ritual' and 'rituals' seems more appropriate than 'work'.]

|fo. 1b| Thursday, aforementioned: I brought his pledges that I had pawned for him, amounting to £3. 14s. 4d., and a further four guineas; and *R. Hirsch Hazan for his clothes, a total of *£7. 16s. 4d.

On Friday, 26 Elul, *We moved, may it be fortuitous, to the house in Prescot Street.

Sunday. He gave me half a guinea *to buy myself shoes and stockings, for he saw that I had no shoes on my feet. Even so, I had to beg him for the money.

Saturday night, 28 Elul, *the rebbetsin fell ill.

Eve of Rosh Hashanah, 5508. In tears, I begged him to give me 6s. 0d. to buy myself leggings.

For a reminder: my expenses for Rosh Hashanah 5508: a pair of shoes and a pair of stockings for 9s. 3d., leggings for 8s. 4d., a hat for 18d., a *camisole for 3s. 6d., *£1. 1s. 1d.

*For a reminder: he received from *the Little One eight days before Rosh

---

R. Hirsch Hazan possibly Samuel Hirsch of Schwersee, the assistant *hazan* (meaning, assistant cantor) of the Great Synagogue, also known as *hameshorer* ('the Poet'). See C. Roth, *The History of the Great Synagogue in London*, 81. [It was not uncommon to use a person's trade or calling as a surname.]

£7. 16s. 4d. [Actually, £7. 18s. 4d.] The fourpence is written as '4 b-sh', presumably an abbreviation for *beit-shin*, which appears to be ZH's term for a penny. [Perhaps connected with 'backsheesh' (from Persian), a relatively small amount of money given as a tip.]

We moved...to the house in Prescot Street Prescot Street was where Falk lived during his early years in London. Some years later he moved to a larger house not far away, in Wellclose Square, which belonged to the family of one Eli Levy [perhaps the 'Elias Levy' mentioned on fo. 24b (p. 126) and discussed in Appendix A]. After the latter's death his widow put the house on the market and Falk purchased it.

to buy myself shoes [This is the first of nine times that ZH mentions buying shoes. Marcin Wodziński suggests that the frequent need to do so was probably because shoes at the time were rather too flimsy for the state of the roads (personal communication).]

the rebbetsin ZH's appellation for Falk's wife, deriving from the Yiddish term for the wife of a rabbi. The next two lines were erased and cannot be reconstructed.

Eve of Rosh Hashanah...5508 [It is not clear what precisely ZH was referring to as the eve of Rosh Hashanah, but since he goes on to talk about needing money it was probably not the evening that Rosh Hashanah began (when the use of money would have been forbidden) but rather 29 Elul 5507, viz. the day at whose close the new year (1 Tishrei 5508) would begin. In the Julian calendar that would have been 24 August 1747 (4 September 1747 in the Gregorian calendar).]

camisole ZH transliterates the English word, which historically meant a waistcoat or undershirt.

£1. 1s. 1d. [Actually £1. 2s. 7d.]

For a reminder [ZH seems to be mentioning the relatively significant sum Falk had received from the Little One to highlight that his request for funds for his own needs was relatively modest.]

the Little One one of Falk's circle whom ZH

Hashanah 5508 more than £80 (in fact, the Little One paid out this sum on his behalf), and I know that he received from the Little One in cash more than £70.

At *Nicholas's near Aldgate, for £7, six gold stars, weighing 1 oz. and 18 dwt.

First day of September, that was a Tuesday, 8 Tishrei 5508. Nicholas had also had a gold watch that *Gedaliah pawned on 14 Tishrei 5507 for £4. 2s. 0d.—*lost.

|fo. 2a| For a reminder: on Friday, 26 Elul, when the Sage went from *the Bridge to his house, *he ordered me to stay in the room on the Bridge for at least fourteen hours and not to move from there. *And so I stayed until Sunday, 6 Tishrei, and on Sunday at twilight I went with him to the Bridge, and he did what he did, I know not what, and then he ordered me to behave as before, and so I did.

On Tuesday, 8 Tishrei 5508, *a Polack from the town of Lissa brought R. Hirsch Hazan a letter from my father, may he live long, written on Sunday, 2 Menahem Av 5507 [28 June 1747 in the Julian calendar], in Hamburg. But to me he did not send a letter, only adding three lines for me at the bottom of R. Hirsch's letter. And he wrote explicitly that he does not want to send me a letter by post because of the expense. *What can one say to that?

mentions here and elsewhere in his diary as giving Falk money from time to time. [His identity remains unknown.]

Nicholas's ZH records taking Falk's possessions to a pawnbroker and jeweller near Aldgate in the City of London. The legends woven around Falk include tales of 'wondrous events' that sometimes occurred when he pawned his belongings—perhaps that they mysteriously returned to his home. See Picciotto, *Sketches of Anglo-Jewish History*, 237.

Gedaliah [Falk's stepson.]

lost [Perhaps ZH meant that it could not be redeemed because so long had elapsed since it was originally pawned.]

the Bridge presumably, London Bridge; Falk appears to have had a room there as well.

he ordered me to stay ... for at least fourteen hours [No reason is given as to why ZH had to stay for this period of time. In the Hebrew edition Oron speculates that Falk might have told him to remain for fourteen hours in order to guard sacred objects there, but this seems unlikely given that had he left at the end of this period the objects would still have been there: since the 'fourteen hours' that Falk required him to stay would have ended during the sabbath, he could not have taken them with him. The need to remain in the room for fourteen hours recurs a few days later, on Yom Kippur.]

And so I stayed until Sunday, 6 Tishrei [ZH stayed a full nine days after Falk left. No explanation is offered as to why he stayed on after the sabbath, but it might have been because the intervening period until 6 Tishrei included the two days of Rosh Hashanah, the Fast of Gedaliah, and yet another sabbath.]

a Polack from the town of Lissa 'a Polack' is the Yiddish term for a man from Poland. 'Lissa' is the Yiddish name for the Polish town of Leszno. [We do not know how ZH's father knew the man, but Leszno was a small town and presumably everyone would have known about someone travelling to London.]

What can one say to that? ZH is evidently angry that his father sent a letter via an emissary to R. Hirsch Hazan while addressing only three lines at the end of the letter to him, his son. ZH's ire is twofold: he

On Monday, 7 Tishrei, I pawned at Milper's in New Street the king of England's coat of arms embroidered in silver and gold on suede. Most of what he had bought on Sunday, 6 Tishrei, for 14s. 0d., I pawned for 9s. 0d.

Eve of Yom Kippur. I redeemed the pledges that had been for three years at *the Minories, that is, two chandeliers, as well as a *curtain, a table cloth, a valance for the Torah ark curtain, and a mantle, for two guineas.

Yom Kippur. After I had finished reciting *musaf* I had to go to his room on the Bridge, so that fourteen hours should not pass, as he had ordered me on Friday, 26 Elul, as mentioned previously.

On Yom Kippur the Little One was also in the synagogue. He came at the beginning of *musaf* and stayed almost until the concluding service *ne'ilah*, and, moreover, he fasted all day long.

Sunday, 13 Tishrei. *He gave me a *genizah* and instructed me to go to the water, open it and render its contents unfit, that is, to erase a letter on each page. And there was a second one in addition, cut up to make pointed ends. As to that one, he ordered me to render a *beit* or *ḥet* or *mem* there unfit. I went to the Bridge, to our room, that is, down by the shops, and opened the window so that I could see the water, and I made them unfit as he had commanded, that is, I had a white cloth on the table when I made them unfit, and all this he commanded me to do |fo. 2b| so that he could use them as

is angry at the way comments intended for him are not kept private, and also at his father saying outright that he does not want to write to him separately because of the cost of postage.

the Minories an area near the Tower of London where evidently another pawnbroker was located.

a curtain ... and a mantle [Though seemingly disparate, these could all be items used for ritual purposes: a Torah ark curtain, a cloth to cover the desk from which the Torah is read, a valance for the Torah ark curtain, and a mantle to cover the Torah. The fact that they were being redeemed on the eve of Yom Kippur makes this all the more likely. Since such ceremonial textiles are needed in the synagogue on a regular basis, perhaps this was a special white set, symbolizing purity, reserved for use on Yom Kippur.]

He gave me a *genizah* and instructed me to ... render its contents unfit Falk orders ZH to render the pages that had been deposited in two *genizah* repositories unfit for ritual use so that he can use them to decorate his sukkah. [The date, 13 Tishrei, is important because the festival of Sukkot would begin the following evening, and the sukkah would have to be prepared in advance.] The actions Falk requires ZH to do are reminiscent of the *tashlikh* ceremony in which one's sins are symbolically cast into a body of water. [This ceremony is normally done on Rosh Hashanah but can be done later, some say as late as Hoshana Rabba (21 Tishrei).]

sukkah decorations, for if they were not made unfit I would not be able to use them elsewhere, only put them back in the *genizah* *or burn them.

Monday, 14 Tishrei. I pawned at Milper's a ring for 18*s*. 0*d*., and I gave 3*s*. 0*d*. to the rebbetsin without his knowledge.

I pawned her watch for 30*s*. 0*d*., and I gave her 2*s*. 0*d*. without his knowledge, that is, 2*s*. 0*d*., *a total of 5*s*. 0*d*. short.

Friday, 18 Tishrei 5508. I pawned a silver egg at Nicholas's for two guineas, its weight being 15½ oz. I gave her 2*s*. 0*d*., and the rest I gave him.

For a reminder: he had expenses on Simhat Torah, about two guineas, and all for nothing.

Thursday, 24 Tishrei. *I made a deal with R. Berele and gave him his writ of exchange for thirteen guineas for £6. 10*s*. 0*d*. and he also gave me a writ of exchange from the Little One that he had given to *R. Juda Polack for two guineas, and R. Berele returned the note to me.

Friday, 25 Tishrei. I pawned her *vaysn koymen* for 12*s*. 0*d*. at Milper's, and I gave her 3*s*. 0*d*. without his knowledge.

Expenses that I had for myself: I received from him only 16*s*. 6*d*. and I bought shoes, 6*s*. 0*d*.; stockings, 3*s*. 6*d*.; a hat, 18*s*. 0*d*; leggings, 8*s*. 6*d*.; a camisole, for 10*s*. 6*d*.; a small one, ditto, for 2*s*. 6*d*.; and a Pentateuch with Rashi's commentary and Targum Onkelos for 3*s*. 0*d*. [—].

Monday, 28 Tishrei. I pawned a gold star weighing 5 dwt. 3 gm. for 19*s*. 0*d*. with Nicholas the jeweller, of which I gave him only 16*s*. 0*d*.

|fo. 3a| I pawned two small lamps for 16*s*. 0*d*. with the widow at Houndsditch.

or burn them [The next two lines were erased.]

a total of 5*s*. 0*d*. short [ZH does not say from what, but we can surmise that he means that 5*s*. 0*d*. was missing from the total due to Falk on these two transactions because of the money given to the rebbetsin.]

I made a deal with R. Berele an account of negotiations that ZH conducted with an unidentified man called Berele concerning a monetary debt. ZH proudly relates how he eventually negotiated a compromise, and received, in return for Berele's promissory note (which ZH held), both money and the promissory note of the Little One, which had been transferred to one Juda Polack and from him to Berele before now being returned to ZH.

R. Juda Polack a member of Falk's family; see C. Roth, *The History of the Great Synagogue in London*, 82, 83. [One may speculate on the connection between 'Falk' and 'Polack' as names, viz. that 'Falk' can be understood as an Anglicization of 'Polack'.]

vaysn koymen possibly a white bowl; *Kumme* means 'bowl' in German.

For a reminder. *R. Laze Segal of Hamburg came to me in tears here in London and told me what straits he was in here, and what his condition was now, wanting for bread and with only one shirt to his body—all his possessions had been pawned. He asked me to help him with three guineas, but if that were not possible to at least give him 9s. 0d. as a loan to pay the landlord of the Amsterdam coffee house. I gave him half a guinea, and then he told me that he had not been at his lodgings these three nights because he owed the landlady 12s. 6d. He also told me other things, and then I took pity on him and gave him 13s. 0d. For this he promised me with solemn oaths that he would write this down in his diary, so that he would not forget what I had done for him, and he wanted to share a piece of bread with me. He promised me other things as well, because he had a relative here in London, named R. Selig of Hamburg, but despite that, he [R. Selig] had refused to lend him even one shilling, while I gave him three guineas to redeem his pawned property and to pay his debts.

Thursday, 1 Heshvan. I pawned a gold object weighing 15 dwt. with Nicholas the jeweller for £3. 5s. 0d., and I gave him only three guineas.

The Sage gave me 18s. 0d. for shoes.

An important reminder: *on Friday Meyer Bozbach came to me and asked me to lend him two guineas for six days just to maintain his standing with the stocking merchant, saying also that he wanted to give me 5s. 0d. as a gift. I gave him two guineas. I waited until Friday, 2 Heshvan, and he finally paid me, but only the principal, not giving me a penny as a gift. But I remained silent.

R. Laze Segal of Hamburg also known by the names of Laze Levi of Hamburg, Lazar Hamburger, and Lazarus Joseph. His descendants included the Franklin family of London. Laze Segal was a member of Falk's household, and was sent by him on various secret missions, to Germany and Holland. E. N. Adler (*London*, 144, 145) is of the opinion that Laze conducted negotiations with Sabbatian circles. His name also comes up in relation to the election campaign for the chief rabbi in London, as acting against the election of Jacob Emden's son; see Duschinsky, *The Rabbinate of the Great Synagogue*, 77; Adler, *London*, 144, 145; and Emden's autobiography *Megilat sefer*, 209. Laze was related to one of London's richest individuals, Selig Hamburger, but the latter ignored him and refused to help him in his distress. ZH relates in his diary, on various dates, how he helped Laze, whom he calls *ru'aḥ*, a term meaning 'wind' that can perhaps be interpreted by extension as 'hot air' and therefore implying one who talks a lot and is boastful, capricious, and highly strung.

on Friday, Meyer Bozbach came to me ZH describes a loan that he made in the hope of receiving some interest. Not only did Bozbach not return the money within six days as he had promised but only on Friday 2 Heshvan (presumably, a whole week after ZH had given him the money), but he also failed to return anything beyond the principal (though to do so would in any case have been forbidden by Jewish law).

Sunday, 4 Heshvan. A reminder: today I was staying with *Schwartz Leib and R. Joseph began to speak ill of the rebbetsin for gossiping about Schwartz Leib's wife, and about him as well. Then I fell into a rage, and R. Joseph and I had a great quarrel, but a word to the wise is sufficient. Then I vowed never to go to his house again while R. Joseph was staying there.

|fo. 3b| *Monday, 5 Heshvan.* I pawned his shirt for 3s. 0d. at Milper's.

Monday night, 6 Heshvan. I took a solemn oath *not to play cards, not even for a paltry sum, and I took this upon myself, as a vow and a solemn oath, for three weeks.

Tonight *Dr la Cour was with him in his house in Prescot Street with *a certain rich man and great nobleman, staying for about one hour. The youth Leib, son of Wolf Praeger, was also there that same night, as was R. Itzik of Zamość, but they did not see each other.

Schwartz Leib ['Schwartz Leib' has been capitalized as if it were a name, though since Hebrew does not use capital letters it is not known if that was ZH's intention. However, it would be an unusual name with strange associations because 'Schwartz', meaning 'black' would usually be a surname. 'Leib' could be a Yiddish form of the Hebrew name Aryeh, meaning 'lion' (from the German *Loewe*), but it could also mean 'heart'; in other words, *schwartz leib* could also mean 'a black heart'. Is ZH trying to tell us something by using this name? The phrase 'a word to the wise is sufficient' suggests that this is indeed the case. He is not very clear as to who 'Joseph' is, but since the whole account is about how Joseph slanders the rebbetsin, perhaps ZH feels that 'Schwartz Leib' is an apt moniker. Perhaps significantly, it is not preceded by the honorific 'R.' that ZH attaches to most names.]

Monday, 5 Heshvan ... Monday night, 6 Heshvan the apparent discrepancy in the dates is because the Jewish day starts at nightfall.

not to play cards ZH vows to stop gambling by playing cards; both diaries reveal that ZH and Falk were accustomed to engaging in games of chance such as dice and cards.

Dr la Cour Dr Abraham Gomez Argas, also known as Dr Philippe de la Cour, was a wealthy and fashionable Jewish doctor who had come to London from Holland. He was among the founders of the London Jewish Hospital, and practised medicine in Bath and in London. He married Abigail, the niece of Samson Gideon, a leader of the Portuguese community in London. Dr de la Cour maintained his ties with the Jewish community in Holland, where he returned towards the end of his life, and where he died in 1786. In London he became friendly with Falk, to whose home he frequently brought visitors (especially curious Christians) who wished to meet 'the Ba'al Shem of London'. See Hyamson, *The Sephardim of England*, 83, 84, 105, 213.

a certain rich man and great nobleman this might have been the marquis de Thomé, who was apparently a Freemason. The marquis paid an additional visit to Falk's home, this time bringing with him his wife and her friend (see below, diary entry for evening of 14 Heshvan, p. 77).

Tuesday, 6 Heshvan. I received a letter from my esteemed father, may he live long, that was written in Breslau on Friday of the intermediate days of Sukkot, 18 Tishrei. He sent the letter with *the brother of R. Jacob of Zamość, *blegart*, unsealed and *without the *ḥerem*. Although this was a confidential letter, concerning a match made for the daughter of R. Hirsch Hazan, he nevertheless sent the letter open (Do they have no sense in Poland?). He wrote no addresses, either for me or for R. Hirsch, and I had to pay a 1s. 0d. postal fee to R. Jacob of Zamość.

Thursday, 8 Heshvan. I pawned the ceremonial objects at Wyleport's for 10s. 0d.

Friday, 9 Heshvan. I sent a letter by post and paid here 1s. 0d., *franka* Green Barg, and from there to *Kalisz. R. Hirsch Hazan also sent two missives in my letter, one to my father, may he live long, and the second to his relative, to R. Samuel from his family.

Monday, 12 Heshvan. I received from R. Laze Segal two consignments. I loaned him four guineas. [Something pawned] for 6s. 0d. at Milper's.

Wednesday, 14 Heshvan [7 October 1747]. I pawned his *black garment for 8s. 0d. at Milper's.
 *That evening, the nobleman who had visited him last Monday night came, with two important noblewomen, and the rebbetsin spoke with them in French. Afterwards he spoke with them in the parlour for about two hours.

the brother of R. Jacob of Zamość [Possibly the brother was the aforementioned R. Itzik of Zamość.]

blegart possibly a distortion of the word *legat* (agent), meaning 'by an emissary'.
[Or perhaps a combination of Hebrew and English, using the Hebrew *be*, meaning 'with' or 'by', together with *legat*.]

without the *ḥerem* without noting [presumably, on the envelope or the letter itself] the ban imposed by Rabbenu Gershom (*c.*960–1028), one of the first great Ashkenazi talmudic scholars, against any unauthorized person reading a private letter addressed to someone else. ZH is angry at his father for sending an open letter, that is, one that could be read by anyone.

***franka* Green Barg** *franka* probably means 'collect', i.e. the addressee was liable for payment; Green Barg—the name of the postal company.

Kalisz ZH's home town, where his father was still living. A city in the Poznań district (in west-central Poland), it was the oldest Jewish community in Poland, dating from the late twelfth century.

black garment [Possibly the long black overgarment of silk or gabardine traditionally worn indoors by Jews of eastern Europe.]

That evening properly, 15 Heshvan.

the nobleman who had visited him the marquis de Thomé; see above, p. 76. ZH here recounts his return visit to Falk's home, this time with two French noblewomen, probably referring

|fo. 4a| Afterwards they went together in their coach. The Sage told me what they had requested, and he said that he was sure only of *the gentile nobleman, as the nobleman had said he wished to let him know two days in advance, through Dr la Cour, when he wished to visit him. Money remained, and they gave me 3s. 0d.

Thursday, 15 Heshvan. I visited *the esteemed R. Cosman in prison, and I spoke to him for about three hours. It caused me great pain to see him in that situation.

Sunday, 18 Heshvan. I brought R. Cosman fruits *from her.

Tuesday, 20 Heshvan. I brought R. Cosman a goose to eat.

Thursday, 22 Heshvan. I pawned her new [*word missing*] with two serviettes for 4s. 0d. at Milper's.

Friday, 23 Heshvan. I pawned his shirt for 4s. 0d at Milper's.

Tuesday, 27 Heshvan. 3 *kartinen, 4 [*unit missing*] wide, each three yards long, for 25s. 0d. at Houndsditch harbour, 28s. 9d.

to the visit by the marquise de Thomé that is mentioned in the diary of Hayim Joseph David Azulai, *Ma'agal tov*. According to Azulai, when the marquise visited Falk she told him how she had rescued Jews from the Inquisition; in response, Falk revealed several kabbalistic secrets to her, and gave her books and amulets. See the Introduction, Section III, above.

the gentile nobleman an apparent reference to the marquis de Thomé.

the esteemed R. Cosman Cosman Lehmann (see Appendix A) was a French Jew who had come to live in London and was a frequent visitor to Falk's house. Despite coming from a distinguished family (and hence the 'esteemed') he was known to be frivolous and had a bad reputation, perhaps because of his business affairs or perhaps because of his affairs with women. At this point he was apparently in prison for debt (he had become embroiled in business affairs), or perhaps in relation to his affairs with women. As part of Falk's circle he carried out various tasks for Falk and was in fact his contact with the outside world, that is, with the Christians who took an interest in Falk and his activities. He also supplied Falk with the gold tablets that he needed for his metal-plating activities. Cosman's ties with prominent members of society are documented in the letters of General Charles Rainsford (see Hills, 'Notes on the Rainsford Papers', 127–8).

from her most likely from the rebbetsin, Falk's wife.

kartinen ... 28s. 9d. a sort of fabric (perhaps from the Yiddish *kartin*, a thin and simple fabric). [£1. 8s. 9d. is presumably the total paid, though it is not clear what it relates to as the sums do not add up.]

Last night I pawned his silver quill and his pen for half a guinea, because the Little One was imprisoned by Bela Aaron. Finally, I and the Sage *persuaded him, for the Sage had promised to pay him within four weeks. The expenses relating to his imprisonment tonight were 22s. 9d., for that purpose he afterwards gave me those items to pawn, and *the rest came from the pockets of Houndsditch.

Friday, 1 Kislev. 10 *kamertin, belonging to *the aforementioned three, for 4s. 6d., *Houndsditch 3 harbour.

The Sage pawned, through R. Mordecai Franzmann, 25 lb. of copper from the large lamp for 27s. 10d.

Tuesday, 5 Kislev. 15 pieces of copper, weighing 24 lb. 12 oz., for 12s. 0d., *for the aforementioned.

|fo. 4b| On Tuesday, 6 Heshvan I pawned for 26s. 0d. copper from a menorah weighing 53 lb. 8 oz.

Friday, 8 Kislev. I pawned her *shtes, her apron of *ke'urit, and his small garment, for 8s. 0d. with Hervir.

Monday, 11 Kislev. I pawned her small knife and silver thimble for 6s. 0d.

The Sage bought a lottery ticket through Moses Nina for £10. 2s. 0d., number 20356. At this time there was really no bread in the house, and this is the proof: he pawned his clothes, as well as his hat, for 15s. 0d. and he had no shirt for his body except for one.

Wednesday, 13 Kislev. I pawned at Milper's two pairs of candlesticks, two big and two small, for [?] shillings.

Thursday, 14 Kislev. I visited R. Cosman, and as I came to the door of his room I could hear that they were seated by the table and eating together, he, the Little One, and a gentile whose name was Sherit, *ba'al muzi. I did not want to enter his room so

persuaded him [Presumably, persuaded Bela Aaron to release him.]

the rest came from the pockets of Houndsditch 'the rest' is presumably the difference between the half a guinea (10s. 6d.) obtained from the pawnbroker and the charge of £1. 2s. 0d. It is not clear what ZH meant by 'the pockets of Houndsditch'.]

kamertin a sort of fabric.

the aforementioned three [The reference is unclear.]

Houndsditch 3 harbour [The reference is unclear.]

for the aforementioned [Again, it is not clear to whom ZH is referring.]

shtes meaning unclear.

ke'urit apparently some kind of fabric.

ba'al muzi perhaps a musician (*muzi* could be an abbreviation for *muzikah*, music). [Or perhaps indicating that he had a moustache, which would have been unusual enough at this time to be worthy of comment because

as not to shame him *for eating improperly; I knocked on the door and R. Cosman came out to me, and he ordered me to wait for him for half an hour in the courtyard. I did so, and he came out to me and I spoke with him. Then I heard from the Little One that they had eaten the leg of a non-kosher animal, fried with butter and onion.

Friday, 15 Kislev. For a reminder, he did not give me even a paltry amount for the sabbath, and *there was neither bread, nor wick, nor candles in the house. I myself did what I could, and we observed the sabbath properly.

Tuesday, 19 Kislev. I pawned two large candlesticks used at Rosh Hashanah for 13*s*. 0*d*. at Milper's.

**Monday, 20 Kislev.* I brought R. Leib Praeger to his house. The efforts of R. Itzik of Zamość to achieve this over ten weeks had been to no avail, but I effected a reconciliation, and he spoke with me, and R. Leib promised to help him.

Monday, 20 Kislev. *Gedaliah returned from Flanders without any profit, and *I brought him to our house in Prescot Street.

|fo. 5a| *Monday, 25 Kislev.* A white cloth and a silver seal pawned with Hervir at Houndsditch for 3*s*. 0*d*.

facial hair was not well regarded; see <https://goodmenproject.com/featured-content/beards-moustaches-and-facial-hair-in-history-wcz/>.]

for eating improperly [It is not clear how at this point ZH knows that Cosman was 'eating improperly', since he had not yet entered Cosman's room nor heard from the Little One, as later recounted, that the food they had been eating was decidedly not kosher. Perhaps he suspected as much.]

there was neither bread, nor wick . . . in the house [These are items that would have been needed for the ritual celebration of the sabbath.]

Monday, 20 Kislev [If the day and date of the previous entry are correct, this entry is wrong; here and in the next entry it should have been either Tuesday 20 Kislev or Monday 25.] ZH tells of his success in mediating a reconciliation between Falk and Leib Praeger [though he does not say why a reconciliation would have been necessary]. Leib Praeger was of the family of Wolf Praeger, one of the pillars of the Ashkenazi community in London; Falk might have wanted to meet the latter and enlist his help. The efforts of R. Itzik of Zamość to being the two men together had evidently not borne fruit [ZH had recorded that Itzik and Leib had in fact met with Falk about six weeks earlier; see entry for 6 Heshvan], but ZH, acting on his own initiative, now succeeded in bringing about this meeting.

Gedaliah returned from Flanders Gedaliah had most probably been sent to Belgium by Falk on some mission, but according to ZH the mission was unsuccessful. [Though Flanders was also the name of a pawnbroker; see note on 'the gentile Flanders' on fo. 1*a*.]

I brought him to our house during the time that Gedaliah was absent, Falk and his household had moved to their new premises

Wednesday, 27 Kislev. A pair of tall candlesticks pawned with Wyleport at Houndsditch for 3s. 6d.

Night of 28 Kislev. A silver chain pawned for 1s. 6d. *at Milper's.

Friday, 29 Kislev. *Gedaliah pawned his watch for £3. 10s. 0d. I took from the money 2s. 0d., and he gave me only £2. 8s. 0d. Houndsditch. [—] also *Catherine's watch.

Thursday, 5 Tevet. Gedaliah pawned a crinoline with Wyleport for 3s. 0d.

Friday, 6 Tevet. I pawned three volumes of *Ein ya'akov* with R. Hirsch Hazan for half a guinea, and I already owed 1s. 6d., a total of 12s. 0d.—*15: 6.

Yesterday *the workman sent the chest that he had ordered a year and a half ago. The gentile had made it as commissioned, but I could not take it from him for lack of funds. Then the gentile sent to the home of the Little One and wanted to send him to prison for the money, as the Little One had been a guarantor, and I did not know how much had to be paid for the chest. Afterwards I saw the workman's bill, and it was £13. 0s. 0d.

in Prescot Street, which is presumably why ZH had to take him there.

at Milper's [One cannot but conjecture why ZH would have used three different pawn brokers on three different days. Perhaps they were all small firms that could not have extended many loans, but perhaps ZH wanted to conceal the extent of Falk's financial problems as indicated by the frequent recourse to pawnbrokers; or perhaps they each had different specializations.]

Gedaliah pawned his watch [Presumably, 'his' here means 'Falk's'. It would seem that Gedaliah gave ZH the £3. 10s. 0d. he received, and the latter took 2s. 0d. for himself before giving the balance to Falk. Falk then gave him £2. 8s. 0d., but ZH does not specify what this money was for.]

Catherine the maidservant, whose name crops up later in connection with some gossip (see diary entry for Tuesday night, 27 Adar I). [One is left wondering why a maidservant would have had such a valuable item as a watch.]

Ein ya'akov a collection of the aggadic (non-legal) material in the Talmud, compiled by Jacob b. Solomon ibn Habib (Amsterdam, 1725).

15: 6 [Half a guinea is 10s. 6d., so a further 1s. 6d. would indeed be 12s. 0d., so the reference to '15: 6', presumably 15s. 6d., viz. 3s. 6d. more, is unclear.]

the workman sent the chest according to ZH's account, Falk had ordered a special chest from a carpenter. The craftsman, who was not a Jew, had made the chest in accordance with this special order, sent the item, and demanded payment. Falk, however, refused to accept the chest since he did not have the money to pay for the transportation. The craftsman accordingly turned to the Little One, who was a guarantor for the payment. [ZH does not say whether the money was eventually found, but perhaps the flurry of visits to pawnbrokers mentioned in the preceding and following entries was somehow connected.]

On Wednesday, 4 Tevet, R. Meyer Posner had come with his son to our house in Prescot Street for the first time, and *I knew what he had said last year; and a word to the wise is sufficient.

Monday, 9 Tevet. *Gedaliah pawned a bed-covering for 4s. 0d., a white [*unclear*], and Catherine's watch at Houndsditch.

Wednesday, 11 Tevet. Gedaliah pawned on my behalf a pewter bowl for 1s. 0d. at Milper's.

Thursday, 12 Tevet. Gedaliah pawned a pair of *pistols with holsters for 9s. 0d. with Hervir [*unclear*] Houndsditch.

Friday, 14 Tevet. Gedaliah pawned his shirt for 3s. 0d. with Hervir, Houndsditch, 1.

|fo. 5b| *Monday, 16 Tevet.* I pawned five plates for 20d. with Hervir, Hounsditch. Gedaliah pawned four plates for 16d. with Hervir.

Wednesday, 18 Tevet. Gedaliah pawned three [?], two candlesticks, for 1½ pence, Milper's.

Thursday, 19 Tevet. Gedaliah pawned two mirrors for two guineas near Wall Park Alley, Houndsditch.

Friday, 20 Tevet. I pawned for the Little One a small, gold-plated deer's foot for 10s. 0d. with Nicholas the jeweller.

Wednesday, 25 Tevet. Gedaliah pawned one bowl and two candlesticks for 2s. 6d., Milper's.

Friday, 27 Tevet. Gedaliah pawned a *raklar* and two bed *garkhen* for 11s. 0d. with Hervir.

I knew what he had said last year ZH hints that Posner had apparently spoken ill of Falk the previous year, but he nevertheless visited the latter.

Gedaliah pawned ... Catherine's watch [ZH has recorded that Gedaliah had pawned the watch on Friday, 29 Kislev; maybe it had since been retrieved, or maybe ZH was confused as to the details.]

pistols with holsters ZH uses the terms *foistolen* and *halftert*. I am grateful to Shmuel Ram for helping me decipher these terms.

raklar presumably from the French *roquelaire*, meaning a man's knee-length cloak.

garkhen some sort of bedding.

Monday, 1 Shevat. Gedaliah pawned [?] for 4s. 0d. with Milper's.

Thursday, 4 Shevat. Two wall candlesticks from the synagogue for 2s. 6d. with Hervir. One candlestick for 8s. 0d.

Friday, 5 Shevat. *I used cunning and told the Little One that there was a letter in the house, and indeed, *he had written a letter with guile from R. Zalman, the brother of R. Moses Hart. And today was *Shmistmes. I did this until the Little One gave one guinea for the sabbath, but they did not know of all this. He started an argument with me, he quarrelled with me on the sabbath night because of *Collier, and he quarrelled with me on Sunday because of *the dog.

Friday, 12 Shevat. Gedaliah pawned two pairs of candlesticks from the synagogue for 6s. 0d. with Hervir.

For a reminder: *he had uttered strong curses against her *on the holy sabbath of 'Beshalaḥ' because of the food she had cooked. He said, by way of justification, that this was because she had made the *kugel* in a large vessel, and that was a disgrace for him before [unclear]; if he had not been ashamed because of Jacob the baby, he would have wanted to take the plate and throw it at her head; and a word to the wise is sufficient.

Tuesday, 16 Shevat. My little waistcoat was pawned for 2s. 0d., with Hervir, Houndsditch.

I used cunning ZH recounts how he craftily got money from the Little One. He gave this to Falk and his wife, and they gave him a few coins to repay their outstanding debts.

he had written a letter with guile ZH seems to suggest that Falk himself might have written a letter that purported to come from Zalman, the brother of Moses Hart. The latter was a warden of the Ashkenazi community, renowned for his wealth and for his activities on the community's behalf. Another brother, Aaron, was one of the founders of the Hambro Synagogue. See E. N. Adler, *London*, 116, 119, 140; Picciotto, *Sketches of Anglo-Jewish History*, 90, 126–7, 129, 139, 408, 460, 462; Wolf, *Essays in Jewish History*, 127, 140–2; C. Roth, *The History of the Great Synagogue*, 206, 211.

Shmistmes a derogatory term for Christmas. [Traditional Jews like ZH would avoid saying 'Christ.']

Collier Falk's landlord.

the dog the intention here is unclear. [Perhaps this another reference to Collier, given that a collie is a breed of dog.]

he had uttered strong curses against her ZH depicts a quarrel between Falk and his wife [referred to simply as 'she' and 'her'—as with references to Falk, her own name is never used] because of the way she had cooked the sabbath *kugel*. He quotes the angry Falk as having cursed his wife and wanting to throw the full plate at her.

on the holy sabbath of 'Beshalaḥ' [Meaning, the sabbath on which this portion of the Torah, viz. Exod. 13: 17–17: 15, is read in the synagogue.]

Friday, 19 Shevat. I sent a letter to my father, may he live long, by post, to *Leipzig. R. Tuvyah pawned six books for 30*s*. 0*d*. R. Hirsch Hazan loaned me 3*s*. 6*d*. to buy shoes.

Wednesday, 24 Shevat. I pawned my shirt for 18*d*. with the widow.

Friday, 27 Shevat. One bowl, two plates, two kettles from the synagogue, for 5*s*. 6*d*., with Hervir.

|fo. 6a| **Tuesday 4, 1st day of the new moon of Adar I.* The Little One gave the Sage two guineas to pay Bela Aaron, and the Little One told me that he had given him more than ten guineas, besides the debt of Bela Aaron, and he gave me only 18*d*. to redeem my shirt from pawn.

Thursday, 2 Adar I. The Sage asked Gedaliah to buy him six pewter plates.

Yesterday he gave those who were part of the circle frequenting the house on the Bridge two guineas, and also redeemed what had been pawned this week. All this is really a waste, because he does not know when he might have more.

Friday, 9 Adar I. I pawned for him, once more, a synagogue lamp, for what was needed for the sabbath.

Thursday, 16 Adar I. I pawned a sabbath lamp, as well as a cauldron and a pan, for half a guinea, with Hervir, Houndsditch, 10*s*. 6*d*.

On the holy sabbath, 18 Adar I, R. Laze of Hamburg was sent to prison by the manservant of the Venetian ambassador for the sum of £5. 0*s*. 0*d*., and he was in prison for two days.

Monday, 20 Adar I. One bowl, four plates, at Milper's, 2*s*. 6*d*.

Leipzig a city in south-central Germany, which had a Jewish community from the thirteenth century. The Jews were expelled from there in the sixteenth century, and returned to it only in 1710. [ZH does not say what his father, whom he had previously mentioned as being in Kalisz, was doing there.]

Tuesday 4, 1st day of the new moon of Adar I the '4' here is redundant. The dates of the following entries are confused, in that often the days of the week and the dates do not correspond. However, the name of the month is correctly recorded as 'Adar I' because in a leap year there is a second month of Adar immediately following the first. [The reference is presumably to Tuesday evening; the second day of the new moon would have started on Wednesday evening and continued on Thursday, as ZH has it.]

Tuesday, 20 Adar I. Two plates, two candlesticks *from *alef-heh*, and other kinds of copper, in a leather sack, for 2*s*. 0*d*., with the widow at Hounsditch.

Wednesday, 22 Adar I. The Little One received his money. He gave him forty guineas, and he began to spend it. He bought meat for 15*s*. 0*d*. to make dried meat and other fripperies.

Wednesday night, 23 Adar I. *The maidservant Catherine told me what had happened to her in our house (in the first year) on Hoshana Rabba and on other occasions too. The main thing was at the end of the month of Tevet, and I, too, saw a proof of this, and I told this story *in her presence (because she wanted to know the truth of the matter).

Tuesday night, 27 Adar I. The rebbetsin came and said to me that the maidservant had told her the affair of the *shaygets*, all in tears, and she tried to deny what I had told her, that this was all a lie. But I know for certain that it is true. She started to curse me, and I became enraged and showed my contempt for her, until she said that she would never do me any favours again, and she cursed me dreadfully. Her [the maidservant's] father took her hand and wanted to kill me.

|fo. 6b| *Saturday night, 2 Adar II.* The chest that the Sage had ordered a year and a half ago arrived—in my humble opinion, this, too, was a waste.

Friday, 8 Adar II. The Sage gave me 9*s*. 0*d*. to buy leather leggings.
    Wednesday, 6 Adar II. I bought a black garment and a cloth coat, for 15*s*. 0*d*.

---

from *alef-heh* an abbreviation possibly meaning 'from the *aron hakodesh*'—the Torah ark. [Though given the items mentioned this seems unlikely.]

The maidservant Catherine told me this passage and what follows it was erased but I have deciphered and reconstructed it. The reason it was erased may have been because it describes illicit relations between Catherine and someone who is called here 'the *shaygets*' (a derogatory term for a non-Jew). Deciphering the deleted text, it transpires that ZH, who heard the story from Catherine herself [and who indeed claims to have seen evidence of the truth of what she told him] related the story to the rebbetsin, who challenged the maidservant about it. Denying the story, Catherine became incensed and cursed ZH. We learn further that she was dismissed from her position, and that her father became angry and wanted to murder ZH. This narrative may possibly point to acts of sexual harassment of the maid by Falk [even though the maid seems to have told Falk's wife that the perpetrator was a *shaygets*] that ended with the maidservant's dismissal. [If that is true, it might also explain how Catherine, who was only a maidservant, owned a watch, and why Falk felt at liberty to pawn it.]

in her presence to the rebbetsin, Falk's wife.

Sunday, 10 Adar II. He commissioned the tailor to make for him a *roquelaire and a waistcoat. His expenses for these and other things were £6. 0s. 0d., for nothing.

Thursday, 14 Adar II. He gave me 6s. 0d. to buy shoes.

For a reminder: he had expenses on Purim of £8. 0s. 0d., and he invited R. Zalman with his wife for the festive meal, and also R. Itzik of Zamość. He also hired someone to cook, and it was all for no purpose.

Sabbath night, 16 Adar II. She fell ill, Heaven forfend, with the dropsy.

Monday, 18 Adar II. Gedaliah pawned *his clock for 50s. 0d.

Friday, 22 Adar II. Gedaliah pawned *a blue mantle.

For an important reminder about *what the Sage did for the boy Jacob for his barmitzvah: he dressed the boy from head to foot, and also held a festive meal for him *on the sabbath of 'Shemini'. He spent £2. 5s. 0d. on the clothing and £1. 0s. 0d. on the meal, in total £3. 5s. 0d. But for me he could not spare 3s. 0d. to pay the tailor on Friday, 22 Adar II, to repair my black garment; no more need be said.

Monday, 25 Adar II. Early in the morning Laze left London for the city of Portsmouth, just as I had interpreted [a dream] for him three months ago. I gave him a shilling for provisions, because he really had nothing at all, even for a single meal, and he had nothing but the clothing on his body. In the end *R. Jacob Sofer did him great

roquelaire a knee-length cloak.

his clock [Presumably, the Sage's clock.]

a blue mantle [In the Hebrew edition, 'mantle' was glossed as 'coat', on the assumption that ZH was using the German or Yiddish word for 'coat'. But the Yiddish term is also used for the ceremonial cloth covering, often of a richly coloured velvet, in which a Torah scroll is kept, and therefore more likely than Falk's coat to have been blue.]

what the Sage did for the boy Jacob ZH describes the barmitzvah celebration that Falk conducted for a boy named Jacob, who was raised in Falk's home. As we learn from the diary (see for example the entry for 14 Nisan, below), Falk engaged in the education and training of young boys and youths who had been brought to his home by their fathers, whether because they believed in his powers to effect cures or because they wanted him to educate them. [It could be that this was the Jacob referred to as 'the baby' in an entry for 12 Shevat, perhaps because he was 'the baby' at the table, but perhaps—given that Falk had other youngsters living in his home—it was another Jacob.]

on the sabbath of 'Shemini' the sabbath when the portion of the Torah read in the synagogue is Lev. 9–11. Very possibly the reference is to the following day.

R. Jacob Sofer this is a reference to Jacob ben Eliezer Eisenstadt (the grandson of the rabbinical authority Meir Eisenstadt), who had come to London from Poland. He was the author of a book [hence the moniker 'Sofer', a Hebrew term that means 'scribe' or

favours, and on Sunday night he sent him provisions for the journey, and made him a small contribution, and this was a great disgrace.

Wednesday, 27 Adar II. I employed all my cunning so that the Little One would give me a *firework that he had borrowed from his landlord, who has an inn, for 12*s*. 0*d*.

Friday, ten o'clock. There was still nothing in the house for the sabbath, until he asked Gedaliah to pawn something so he could prepare for the sabbath of *Shabat Haḥodesh and the new moon of Nisan.

|fo. 7a| *Wednesday, 5 Nisan.* I bought a shirt, a cotton hat, and a white cloth that had been pawned by Hayim, R. Laze's manservant, that belonged to the said R. Laze, *for 5*s*. 5*d*., £5. 5*s*. 6*d*.

**Friday, 7 Nisan.* He pawned the clothes that he had had made on Sunday, 10 Adar II, for 35*s*. 0*d*. *to buy raisins to make wine for Passover.

Wednesday, 12 Nisan. I received a letter from R. Laze through Joseph Franch.

Thursday 13 Nisan. I sent him an answer.
    For an important reminder of the trouble that it was to prepare Passover in our house: R. Itzik of Zamość had had to struggle to raise 9*s*. 0*d*., and the Sage pawned his hat for 6*s*. 0*d*., a total of 15*s*. 0*d*. to buy matzas for Passover.
    The Sage gave me a little gold to sell, and I sold it for 37*s*. 2*d*. to buy what was needed for Passover and also to redeem pawned goods for 25*s*. 0*d*.

Friday, 14 Nisan. I received a letter for R. Laze from his father-in-law in Italy. I paid the postal fee from my own pocket, and sent this letter on Monday, 17 Nisan, to R. Laze in the city of Portsmouth; in my humble opinion, this letter, too, is for no purpose.

'writer'] entitled *Toledot ya'akov*, published in London in 1770. See C. Roth, *The History of the Great Synagogue in London*, 148.

firework a tool used for working with fire, or a firearm.

Shabat Haḥodesh [The sabbath before the new moon of Nisan. The name derives from the special additional Torah reading for this sabbath, Exod. 12: 1–20, which says that *haḥodesh hazeh*, 'this month', the month of the Exodus from Egypt, is to mark the beginning of a new calendar for the Jewish people.]

for 5*s*. 5*d*., £5. 5*s*. 6*d*. [The arithmetic is unclear.]

Friday, 7 Nisan [ZH records the date erroneously as 2 Nisan.]

to buy raisins to make wine for Passover [Kosher wine was seemingly not available to buy so the Falk household would have had to make their own; this was commonly done in countries that did not produce wine.]

On the holy sabbath, the first day of Passover, *he took the child of *the honourable Joseph Teschen Spieler into his home to rear him, and the child was 6 years and 9 months old.

For a reminder: what penury there was on Passover! There were no candlesticks in the synagogue, just the lamp. There was *only a single Torah scroll, without any ceremonial appurtenances, and that is a great disgrace.

On Thursday, 13 Nisan. I pawned my leggings for 5s. 0d. with the widow, and for 3s. 6d. I bought stockings, and for 1s. 3d. a cap.

Tuesday 18 Nisan. *I received a letter from my father, may he live long, that was written from the city of Breslau on Tuesday, 4 Nisan. It reached me today in London.

Monday, 24 Nisan. The boy Jacob left the house and returned to his father, because his father wanted to teach him how to engage in business, so that he would have something practical in hand.

I bought a shirt from R. Hayim, which he said had been pawned for 4s. 6d. I gave him 4s. 5½d., but I found out that it had been pawned for only 3s. 0d., and indeed it was worth barely 3s. 0d. as it had no cuffs.

Wednesday, 26 Nisan. I bought from R. Hayim a prayer shawl, and also *the book *Eleh hamitsvot* and a book of Psalms for 5s. 0d. This was the property of Mordecai Schuster, and the prayer shawl was not worth 2s. 0d.

he took the child ZH tells of an additional child who was sent to Falk's home to be raised by him.

the honourable Joseph Teschen Spieler [This could perhaps be a reference to Joseph Froelich (1694–1757), described as 'Taschenspieler und Spassmacher am Hofe August des Starken', in Dresden; see Rainer Rückert, *Der Hofnaar Joseph Froelich*. *Taschenspieler* would normally mean 'pickpocket', but since ZH described him as 'honourable' and he appears to have been a court jester, perhaps the term can be understood as referring to a magician.]

only a single Torah scroll, without any ceremonial appurtenances [There are two different readings from the Torah on each day of Passover, which would normally be read from separate scrolls so as to avoid having to roll the scroll to a different place during the service, which can take some time. Reading from a single scroll is possible, but it reduces the majesty of the service also because the procession of Torah scrolls through the synagogue before and after the Torah reading would be far less impressive, especially in the absence of the silver appurtenances—bells, breastplate, and pointer—that would normally adorn a Torah scroll being carried ceremonially.]

I received a letter from my father ... from the city of Breslau [ZH's father seems to be peripatetic but we do not know why; on 8 Tishrei he wrote from Hamburg, on 6 Heshvan from Breslau, on 19 Shevat from Leipzig, and now again from Breslau.]

the book *Eleh hamitsvot* a book by Moses Hagiz (Amsterdam, 1713). The title translates

|fo. 7b| I pawned my shirt for 4s. 0d., Milper's.

On Tuesday, 25 Nisan, I pawned my shirt for 2s. 0d., Milper's.

Today, I pawned my black garment for 6s. 0d. near Wall Park.

On the eve of Passover Gedaliah had pawned the Sage's ordinary sword—which I thought was still in the place where it was supposed to be, that is, *in the forest—but he pawned it for half a guinea.

For a reminder, that on the sabbath of *'Aḥarei mot', on the eve of the new moon of Iyar, *they proclaimed in the Bressler synagogue that no man should attend the *minyan* in the home of the *ba'al tsafon*, on pain of excommunication, and anyone who did so would be punished to the extent of their ability.

Wednesday, 3 Iyar. R. Laze's brother came here to London from Hamburg. And on Thursday I sent a letter to R. Laze; in my humble opinion, his brother is *also a [kindred] spirit, and he has a big door; and his brother also wrote in my letter.

---

as 'These are the commandments', and it enumerates the 613 commandments in the Torah.

in the forest [Perhaps Epping Forest, as the nearest forested area to where Falk lived in east London.]

on the sabbath of 'Aḥarei mot' [That is, when the prescribed Torah reading is Lev. 16–18. This entry was obviously not written on Wednesday 26 Nisan as the event it describes took place on the following Saturday.]

they proclaimed in the Bressler synagogue ZH mentions an episode in which the worthies of the London Ashkenazi synagogue, formally known as the Great Synagogue but informally as the 'Bressler' [or more correctly as the 'Breslauer', since its rabbi from 1704 until his death in 1756 was Aaron Hart, who was born in Breslau] censured Falk (referred to in ZH's diary note as the *ba'al tsafon*; see below), based on a regulation of the board of the community that forbade the establishment of private synagogues. As the text indicates, a ban was placed on any member of the congregation who went to pray in Falk's synagogue (for the continuation of the episode, see fo. 24*b*, diary entry 'For a reminder, on the festival of Shavuot' below; see also C. Roth, *The History of the Great Synagogue in London*, 164, 165).

ba'al tsafon lit., 'master of the north'. In kabbalistic circles, north symbolized evil and its forces [based on Jer. 1: 14, 'From the north evil shall break forth'. It is likely that this term is ZH's rather that of the worthies of the Great Synagogue, as they would have had no problem naming names, whereas ZH, as we have seen, never referred to Falk by name. 'Master of the north' would of course have meant 'one who can control evil'.] The *gematriyah* of *ba'al tsafon* is equivalent to that of *kelev ra*, meaning 'evil dog', as pointed out by Jacob Emden in his book *Tsitsim uferaḥim* (Altona, 1768). For further details, see Introduction, Section III, n. 26.

also a [kindred] spirit, and he has a big door ZH might be trying to say that Laze's brother resembles him, and is also loquacious. ['Big door' could perhaps mean 'big mouth'; on fo. 29*a* ZH refers to Laze as a 'windbag', see p. 139.]

Monday, 8 Iyar. *I did nine *kabin*, and I went with *R. Gabriel into the parlour and wrote on four gopher-wood plaques with a quill pen, on each plaque *thirty-nine names of the angels of Gevurah, and also an incantation to summon them to us into the room. And after the writing we—I, R. Gabriel, and R. Tuvyah—recited Psalm 91 and Psalm 12, then we hung the four plaques in the four corners of the room, and then we made *warning after warning without an incantation. We did this for three consecutive nights, but to no effect.

    Today the Little One was imprisoned in the *sponging-house at Poultry Counter, but on Tuesday at midnight he was released because he had that day received some money by post.

Tuesday, 9 Iyar. The Little One gave the Sage a total of fifty and forty guineas in cash, and from this money he bought the things needed for his rituals. He also gave me 25*s*. 0*d*. to buy clothes for myself, and 5*s*. 0*d*. to redeem my leggings.

The holy sabbath, 13 Iyar. *I received a letter from my father, may he live long, that was written on the eve of the new moon of Adar II, by R. Michael, scribe of *the holy congregation of Krotoszyn; he also wrote to R. Hirsch Hazan.

Sunday, 14 Iyar. I was with the Sage in R. Cosman's home, and he gave him half a guinea, and 2*s*. 6*d*. to R. Aaron Pollack; *his expenses today were 19*s*. 0*d*.

I did nine *kabin* i.e. immersed in nine *kabin* (approximately 4.5 gallons) of water, the minimum volume needed for a man to purify himself when ritual immersion is required only by rabbinical law; for regular immersion, a ritual bath containing about 120 gallons of water from a natural source is required.

R. Gabriel probably R. Gabriel the *shoḥet* (ritual slaughterer); see C. Roth, *Records of the Western Synagogue*, 28. On R. Tuvyah see note on fo. 1*a*, p. 69.

thirty-nine names of the angels of Gevurah the names of the angels associated with the *sefirah* of Gevurah (the 'power' of God, as reflected in strict judgement), such as Gabriel, Nuriel, Casiriah, Dahariel, Gedudiel, Gadiel, and others.

warning after warning without an incantation apparently, the angels had to be warned of various forms of mystical activity.

sponging-house in Poultry Counter a 'sponging-house' was a debtors' prison. [Conditions there were better than in regular prisons because they were in fact places of temporary confinement; see <https://en.wikipedia.org/wiki/Sponging-house>. This one was in the counter, or prison, in the Poultry, the eastern continuation of a street called Cheapside.]

I received a letter from my father [The letter had taken some two and a half months to arrive.]

the holy congregation a translation of the traditional Hebrew term for a Jewish community. [Subsequent occurrences of this term in the two diaries are rendered simply as 'congregation'.]

his expenses today were 19*s*. 0*d*. [There were obviously other expenses too, since those listed here do not total 19*s*. 0*d*.]

In the evening I went with him to the forest; he practised in the forest for about half an hour, and we returned to our lodgings and stayed there that night.

Monday. At ten o'clock, I went with him to the forest, where he practised like yesterday. |fo. 8a| We went back to the house in Pas, and from there he sent me to the Bridge. He ordered that the door of *the camp should be sealed with holy names that he had written in the house in Pas and given me, and so I did. When I came back I went with him to a house near Woolwich, where he practised for about an hour in the room overlooking the water, and from there we went to the house.

*When we came to the house he ordered me to go with R. Tuvyah to the ritual bath and immerse. From there he ordered us to go to the Bridge, *to the room near the room of the camp, and he ordered us to recite, first, Psalms 11, 12, 15, 17, 18, 20, 43, 44, 64, 92, 93, 95, 96, 97, 98, 99, 102, 104, 105, 106, 107, 111, 112, 'Happy are those whose way is blameless' [Ps. 119], the 15 'Songs of Ascents' [Psalms 120–34], Psalms 136, 137, *tikun ḥatsot until *tikun hanefesh; then Psalms 139, 140, 145 in their entirety; afterwards, the first chapter of *Sefer yetsirah*; and then seven Utterances of Creation. Then he ordered me to remove *the amulet that I had used after midnight, and replace it with other holy names than those he had given me after midnight. He also forbade sleep until ten o'clock on Tuesday, and so we did. We began one hour after midnight. The instruction of the Sage was to seal the door with these second names, half an hour before dawn, and so we did. And after we sealed it, we recited the Song of Songs in its entirety, and so we were engaged in prayer and supplication until ten o'clock in the morning.

Monday night, 16 Iyar. The Sage went to the Bridge and stayed in the room where I and R. Tuvyah had engaged in supplicatory prayers, and he did not open the seal of the door to the room of the camp till three o'clock on Wednesday afternoon.

---

the camp Falk and ZH referred to the structure that Falk had erected on the bridge as the 'camp' (*maḥaneh*), using a biblical term (see e.g. Gen. 32: 21) for a place of assembly.

When we came to the house what follows is a rare and detailed portrayal of an occult rite that was performed by the water. Before it begins, Falk orders ZH and R. Tuvyah to immerse in the ritual bath to purify themselves—a common requirement in such ceremonies—and then to recite, as ZH records in detail, a series of psalms as well as passages from *Sefer yetsirah* as a preface to the rite itself. Only after these preparations does the ritual begin, with the sealing with holy names. The participants are required to stay awake the entire time. After this sealing, the ceremony concludes with the recitation of verses from the Song of Songs.

to the room near the room of the camp [The location is not explained very clearly.]

tikun ḥatsot a prayer recited at midnight in mourning for the destroyed Temple.

tikun hanefesh a kabbalistic prayer for the improvement of the soul.

the amulet that I had used to seal the door.

The same night I sent a letter to my esteemed father, may he live long, by *franka* Green Barg post, and *R. Hirsch also wrote in my letter a letter to my esteemed father, may he live long, and to his relatives.

Wednesday, 17 Iyar. The Sage went into his room at the camp at three o'clock in the afternoon. He stayed there for eight hours and returned before midnight, disappointed.

After midnight he returned and went to his room, where he stayed for an hour and a half. He fasted all day and all night, from Wednesday night (when he left his house), until Thursday at eleven o'clock.

Thursday night. At ten o'clock the rebbetsin came to him on the Bridge to kiss his hand, for the time had come, and at midnight she went. *He told R. Tuvyah and R. Itzik of Zamość that he had wanted to separate from her for at least a year and a half, or more.

On Thursday night at one o'clock in the morning. The Sage went by himself to his room and stayed there about two hours, and then he summoned R. Tuvyah, R. Itzik of Zamość, and me to his room. |fo. 8*b*| I saw that he was building a court, as before, and the small shofar of holy names was on the table, and a burning candle over it, as well as many other candles. He ordered R. Tuvyah to extinguish the big wax candle and place a small wax candle on the wick of the big one, and R. Itzik of Zamość did the same with the second candle. We went out, and he practised alone until seven o'clock in the morning.

Friday. The Sage recited the afternoon prayer in the *domain of the camp, then he summoned R. Tuvyah and myself to his room, and I saw what I had seen yesterday. I also saw on the table a small round lamp with seven small wax candles around it, and the scabbard of the holy sword was standing opposite it, and a wax candle over it, that

---

R. Hirsch R. Hirsch Hazan; see note to fo. 1*b* above, p. 71.

He told R. Tuvyah this passage more than hints at the state of the relationship between Falk and his wife. According to ZH, Falk told him, R. Tuvyah, and R. Itzik of Zamość that he had wanted for quite some time to separate from his wife. This and many other details in the two diaries attest to the tense relations between the couple. [At this point, though, they did not actually separate, and in fact she is mentioned again just a few days later in the context of something Falk wants from her.]

domain Heb. *gevul*, 'limit', 'boundary'; the word is used throughout ZH's diary, sometimes indeed referring to the boundary (or fence, wall) of Falk's camp, sometimes referring to the entire area in which he performed his rites (rendered as 'domain'). [In fact the relationship between 'the room' (sometimes 'house') on the Bridge, the 'camp' and the 'domain' is never clearly explained, though evidently it was clear to ZH.]

is, over the opening of the scabbard. And I saw a black hide lying on the floor, and the scabbard of the ordinary sword was lying on it, as well as two burning candles. And a large packet of his *drawings was also lying on it, while the ordinary sword was thrust before the gate of the camp. And then the Sage ordered R. Tuvyah to light a tallow candle on the table that could remain burning for seven hours. Then he lit two candles on the ground, that is, on the black hide. The Sage left the camp and sealed the room of the camp. He ordered R. Tuvyah to wait here on the Bridge till seven o'clock, which was the time of the sabbath. And the Sage went home with me safely in the coach to observe the sabbath.

Sunday, 21 Iyar. I went with the Sage to R. Cosman's home, where the Sage sat and talked with *Dr Lindy, and he stayed at R. Cosman's about two hours. From there I went with the Sage to his room on the Bridge.

On Sunday night R. Tuvyah was with us at the Bridge, and he stayed the whole night. The Sage himself practised the entire night, having begun at midnight and finished at seven o'clock. And then the Sage came to us and commanded me immediately to go home and tell the rebbetsin to buy linen to make him a *kitl*, for without it he could do nothing.

Monday 22 Iyar. I had to extend the railings as he needed to make his domain larger than before.

|fos. 9a–12b missing|

|fo. 13a| *and afterwards he wrote in *the book of *kavanot* the day of the week and of

drawings the reference is apparently to mystical drawings with symbolic meaning that served the mystic as he prepared for an occult vision or experience. See Idel, *The Mystical Experience in Abraham Abulafia* (Heb.), 110–11 and index.

Dr Lindy this is possibly Elias Lindo, a well-known *parnas* (warden) of the Spanish and Portuguese Jews' Congregation and a friend of the politician Lord George Gordon [1751–93, a colourful figure who converted to Judaism in 1787]; but possibly it was another member of this family, which included prominent bankers and communal figures. See D. S. Katz, *The Jews in the History of England*, 186, 187, 306; Ruderman, *Jewish Enlightenment in an English Key*, 158, 159; Wolf, *Essays in Jewish History*, 208.

kitl a white cotton robe, symbolizing purity, worn by the prayer-leader for the most important parts of the liturgy, such as for the annual prayers for rain and for dew and by all adult Jewish males on certain ritual occasions (in particular on Yom Kippur).

and afterwards he wrote [This phrase is preceded by an apparently meaningless string of 45 letters, but in fact the number of letters may have had kabbalistic significance, since the *gematriyah* of the letters comprising the divine name represented by the Tetragrammaton YHWH is 45. Because of the missing pages we do not know what preceded these letters.]

the book of *kavanot* *kavanot* are mystical meditations. Possibly this is a reference to the book of *kavanot* written in Falk's hand that is

the month, and holy names. He meditated on the letters *mem lamed*, and he took his big book of *kavanot*, that he allows absolutely no one to touch. He meditated on the letter *heh*, he instructed us to chant Psalm 15, and he meditated on that psalm in full, and then Psalm 43, etc. Afterwards he began to write additional holy names inside the aforementioned four plaques, and *we chanted *Ana bekho'ah* in full, with proper intent. Then he began to chant with us *alef, beit, gimel* in full, and then he once again began to chant from 'strengthen us, purify us' to the end. He left two plaques on the first table and two plaques on the second table, and he told us to go outside, while he remained alone in the room, wearing the *kitl*, until four o'clock on Thursday, and he stopped.

Thursday, 10 Sivan. Today I pawned with Nicholas the jeweller a gold watch of R. Cosman for nine guineas, and *I had to give him in exchange that if I do not redeem it after two months he is entitled to sell it, and then whatever is lacking from the principal I must make up to the principal that he gave me; and I gave R. Cosman only five guineas.

On Thursday night he practised alone for two hours before midnight. After midnight he went to his room, and afterwards he summoned us, R. Tuvyah, *R. Isaac, the Little One, and myself. *When we came into his domain, I saw that they had built a little camp, that is, only as much as the breadth of the camp gate, which was about three-quarters of a yard, and it reached lengthwise up to a place facing back towards the camp gate. In addition, there were two plaques on the two pillars of the camp, and on each a wax candle. There were also two shofars on two tables, and there was also

in the Jewish Museum in London (see Introduction, Section VI).

we chanted this refers to a mystical technique of chanting verses, in which the cantillation or vocalization marks function as musical notes. See Idel, *The Mystical Experience in Abraham Abulafia* (Heb.), 53–71.

Ana bekho'ah [A kabbalistic prayer traditionally ascribed to the mishnaic sage R. Nehunya b. Hakanah (see *Encyclopaedia Judaica*, vol. iii, cols. 25–6).]

alef, beit, gimel after the recitation of *Ana bekho'ah*, the initial words of which constitute the mystical 42-letter name of God, Falk repeats with the other participants in the ceremony the letters of this name (*ana bekho'ah gedulat*...), joining this with the phrase 'strengthen us, purify us' from this prayer. As fos. 9a–12b are missing, the description of the mystical rite is incomplete.

I had to give him in exchange ZH had to give the jeweller a written guarantee specifying the terms of the transaction.

R. Isaac [This is probably the same person referred to elsewhere as R. Itzik, the latter being the Yiddish diminutive of the Hebrew name Yitshak, rendered in English as 'Isaac'. Later instances are not highlighted.]

When we came into his domain ZH describes the place of assembly prepared for the rite, and the ceremony of the writing of the holy names and the casting of lots in the book of *kavanot*. He tells of the wondrous things that occur during the course of the rite: candles are extinguished by themselves, and the sword flies through the air and thrusts itself into the camp gate.

a *cellar opposite the camp gate. The Sage first cast lots in [the book of] Psalms, and the lot fell on Psalm 116, R. Tuvyah's lot fell on 52, R. Isaac's lot was 102, and my lot was 61. He began by first chanting Psalm 116 until verse 14, and he began to meditate on the verse 'I will pay my vows to the Lord'. He dictated in his big book of *kavanot* the day of the month, and also the day of the week; he also wrote some holy names with proper intent and continued until verse 18. He meditated on verse 18, 'I will pay my vows to the Lord'. He dictated a little more and completed the psalm, afterwards Psalm 52, afterwards Psalm 102, and afterwards Psalm 61, and he meditated on verse 5: 'O that I might dwell in Your tent for ever, take refuge under Your protecting wings. Selah', until the end. He meditated on the last verse, and he finished with the words *'day after day'. He then began the Second Utterance, first verse, and then verse 2 of Psalm |fo. 13*b*| 61, thus he finished verse after verse, the Utterance with the psalm. Afterwards he gave me the big book of *kavanot*, and ordered me to meditate with R. Tuvyah and R. Isaac on the holy names that he had written there. The Sage wrote other names, and he then gave over the holy names to the Little One, and he also told the Little One to light two wax candles that were standing on the two pillars of the camp, as mentioned above; then the Sage revealed to us the reason why he allowed the Little One to light the candles, and then he told us to go outside and he practised alone until nine o'clock Friday morning.

Monday night, 15 Sivan. He practised alone for two hours before midnight. After midnight he went alone to his room, and he practised for about one hour, all the while wearing his *kitl*. Afterwards, still wearing the *kitl*, he summoned R. Tuvyah, and also R. Isaac, the Little One, and myself, and there was one candle alight more than the number on the other table in the place where the Little One was sitting. We began by chanting the book of Genesis until *'And there was evening and there was morning, a third day [Gen. 1: 13]' and we repeated the verse. Then we recited Psalm 2, and also Psalm 5 and also Psalm 26 to the end. Then he resumed once again, and began from verse 7, 'raising my voice in thanksgiving', also to the end of the psalm, and he finished with 'And there was evening and there was morning, a third day'. He gave R. Tuvyah the *second book of *kavanot* to meditate on the holy names *of the cancellation of

cellar this seems to be ZH's term for the lower part of the vessel used to give light, viz. the part in which the candles actually burned.

'day after day' the concluding words of Ps. 61: 9 ('as I fulfil my vows day after day').

'And there was evening and there was morning, a third day' [Perhaps the emphasis on 'the third day', repeated a few lines later, links to the fact that according to the Jewish way of reckoning time, Monday night, which is when this ritual was taking place, is the beginning of the third day.]

second book of *kavanot* there were apparently two books of *kavanot*: one, the 'big' book, and this, the 'second' one.

of the cancellation of Wednesday night, 3 Sivan, as mentioned previously [We do not know what this refers to because the relevant pages are missing from the diary.]

Wednesday night, 3 Sivan, as mentioned previously. The Sage wrote holy names on the plaques that I had finished drawing on that day, and then he began to sanctify the letters that he had written on the above-mentioned two plaques—not an absolute sanctification, *because they were hollow letters, and these are the letters on the first plaque: *mem, resh, lamed, heh, resh, lamed, alef, beit, dalet, yod [—]. He began to chant and meditate on Psalm 79, from verse 10, and then on verse 11, meditating on the letters tav, lamed, alef, 'Let the groans of . . . reach You', until the end. He also meditated on verse 13: nun, lamed, lamed, lamed—'we shall glorify You for ever; for all time' etc. He said, 'He shall fell His enemies before Him', and he told R. Tuvyah that we should finish the holy names that he had given us first. While we did so he finished the above-mentioned second plaque, and then he began to sanctify them, as in the above-mentioned first plaque, and these are the letters: ayin, tet, zayin, zayin, tsadi, ayin, vav, yod, heh, samekh, mem; and he placed them on the hide that was on the floor, and we went outside. Afterwards he summoned us and commanded R. Tuvyah to sit in my place, and R. Isaac in the place of the Little One, and I and the Little One sat opposite the gate of the camp, just outside the domain. The Sage got down on his hands and feet on the hide, *and he wrote one charm in his big book of *kavanot*, and meditated on great things, all the while weeping. He then ordered me to write seven letters: mem, lamed, heh, resh, lamed, alef, beit. I then read these seven letters to the Little One, and he was to choose any two letters of these seven, whichever he wanted, and the Little One chose alef and resh. He then commanded that two tallow candles be lit for R. Tuvyah close to the camp gate, and the Sage lit the wax candle that was standing in the small shofar in the cellar opposite the camp gate; he meditated together with us on the aforementioned seven letters, and also on other holy names from the charm that he had begun to write in the big book of *kavanot*. And there was something totally new and wondrous from Heaven: the extinguishing of the wax candle |fo. 14a| in the cellar by itself, for the wick bent of its own accord, pointed downward, and extinguished itself. He commanded the Little One to light the wax candles that were standing *on the two pillars of the rope, but he was incapable, because of his fright; a word to the wise will suffice. Then with great speed and trembling the Sage caused the cellar to move from its place. The sword embedded itself in the camp gate, in the place where it had embedded itself when he first entered the camp before last

because they were hollow letters [Not clear; perhaps the meaning is that the letters were written in outline only and were thus not considered complete and worthy of sanctification.]

mem, resh . . . Zevi Hirsh notes that during the chanting of the verses Falk made use of the initial letters of the words in the verse (i.e. *notarikon*—acrostics); and similarly in the following sets of letters. 'Meditate' here means the recitation of the initial letters prior to chanting them.

and he wrote one charm sealing the fortune of each one.

on the two pillars of the rope [Perhaps meaning on the posts supporting the rope.]

Rosh Hashanah, that is, in the holy names that are in the camp gate. It was now more than three hours after midnight. And then the Sage stood up in a fury, with great trembling, and seized the blade of the sword and took it out to the edge of his domain, so that the hilt remained in the camp and the blade in his domain. And he stuck a wax candle onto the body of the sword, and thus the sword remained. He ordered R. Tuvyah to light the two large wax candles that he had made anew today, and also to hang above them the aforementioned two plaques. The Sage went outside with us, and we stayed outside for about five minutes, after which he commanded R. Tuvyah and R. Isaac to go to the edge of his domain, and see if either of the two wax candles had gone out; and they returned and said that no candle had gone out. Then he went with us to his domain, to his room, and he gave the Little One certain holy names folded up in a paper container, and the Little One had to write upon them ten letters. The Sage began to chant with us Psalm 64, and then Psalm 66, meditating on verse 12: 'You have let men ride over us, etc.', and he concluded the psalm: 'who has not turned away my prayer, or His faithful care from me'. Therefore, 'God will arise, His enemies shall be scattered, etc.', Psalm 68, and he meditated on great things, all the while with tears and a broken heart, particularly from verse 14, 'even for those of you who lie among the sheepfolds, etc.', up to verse 20, thus he engaged in great meditations. During the recitation of these verses, one wax candle of the above-mentioned two large candles, over which the plaques were hung, went out. The Sage finished the psalm with us; he ordered us to go outside, and we returned. He commanded the Little One to make a closed letter *mem* beneath the line that he had written over the holy names, that is, a large *mem*, as if along the length and breadth of the folded paper with the holy names, and thus he did. Afterwards the Sage wrote an open *mem* within the closed *mem*, and then I, too, wrote an open *mem* within it; and then he commanded the Little One too to write a *mem*. Then he commanded him to watch the sword, and especially the candle stuck on the point of the blade, and to meditate on the *mem*, and thus he did. He commanded me to write another open *mem*, and before the Little One had finished writing the second *mem*, the wax candle on the point of the blade went out, and this happened in the blink of an eye. He ordered us to leave, and thus we did, while he remained alone for about two hours and engaged that night in great things; *I could not believe your power is so great, to do such things in a small camp and in a small domain. He stopped at eight o'clock on Tuesday, and then he revealed to me that it was a great effort for him to send the sword away from his domain.

I could not believe your power is so great
  [Presumably, meaning 'his power', i.e. Falk's power.]

Tuesday night. He was practising in the camp in his domain, and he practised alone until after eleven o'clock, when he returned and waited until after midnight, and then he went, again alone, remaining for about one hour. |fo. 14b| Afterwards he summoned me, R. Tuvyah, and R. Isaac. There was no candle burning there, except for two candles burning on his writing table. He ordered me to light two candles, that is, one candle on each table, and he put them on the hide. He began to chant with us Psalm 2, meditating on verse 2, 'conspire together', great things, and he also wrote great things in his big book of *kavanot*. He also meditated on *alef, beit, gimel, dalet, heh, vav*, to *tav*, meditating on verse 4, 'He who is enthroned in heaven', and on the last verse, 'in the mere flash of His anger, happy are all who take refuge in Him'. Then he repeated Psalm 2 and then Psalm 7, meditating on verse 2, 'I seek refuge, deliver me from all my pursuers and save me', as well as verse 4, 'O Lord, my God, if I have done such things, if my hands bear the guilt of wrongdoing', and he said, *'A line with the hand, not with wrongdoing and not with a yoke.' The Sage then revealed his meaning to me, that he was drawing the line with his hands, that *there is a line of Gevurah and also a line of Hesed; the line of Gevurah is called 'wrongdoing', and the line of Hesed is called 'love'. *And this is something absolutely new: the numerical value of *kav* [line] is the same as *ayin-vav-lamed* [wrongdoing/yoke], but he draws the line, neither with wrongdoing, nor with a yoke. And he revealed more great things that we may not commit to paper. He completed the psalm, to *'the name of the Lord Most High', and then began *'From the mouths of babes and sucklings' in Psalm 8, and intensely meditated on this verse and he finished. He also meditated on verse 7, 'You have made him master over Your handiwork, laying the world at his feet', and completed the psalm. And again he began Psalm 8, and then he began to chant the Fourth Utterance to the fifth day, verse by verse. We began again Psalm 8, and he meditated on great new things, and then *Sefer yetsirah*, chapter 1, only of the charms, and no

alef . . . tav i.e. all the letters of the Hebrew alphabet.

'A line with the hand, not with wrongdoing and not with a yoke' Falk seems to be demonstrating here some occult interpretation of the Hebrew text; the word for 'line' (*kav*) sounds very similar to that used in the psalm for 'hand' (*kaf*), and the Hebrew words for 'wrongdoing' (*avel*) and 'yoke' (*ol*) are homonyms spelled with the same three letters *ayin, vav, lamed*.

there is a line of Gevurah and also a line of Hesed respectively, divine power and love, two of the ten attributes of the divine that comprise the kabbalistic *sefirot*.

And this is something absolutely new [ZH relates with excitement that Falk explains to him the numerical value of *kav* ('line') is the same as that of *ayin-vav-lamed* (meaning either 'wrongdoing' or 'yoke'). However, Falk does not explain how he calculates that; the basic numerological technique of adding the numerical equivalents of each letter does not give the desired result so it would seem that he is applying a more sophisticated method of calculation.]

'the name of the Lord Most High' Ps. 7: 8.

'From the mouths of babes and sucklings' Ps. 8: 2.

more. He meditated and wrote great things—the power of the Lord to see and hear from him psalms—and afterwards Psalm 20, Psalm 24 verse 6, 'Such is the generation of those who turn to Him, Jacob, who seek Your presence. Selah', and then he completed the psalm. And then Psalm 47, meditating on verse 5, 'He chose our heritage for us, the pride of Jacob whom He loved'—*the initials *alef-nun-alef* from *alef-beit-gimel*, which is a divine name in itself. He also meditated on verse 6, 'God ascends amidst acclamation, the Lord to the blasts of the horn, etc.', and he also meditated on the last verse, 'The great of the peoples are gathered together, the retinue of Abraham's God; for the guardians of the earth belong to God; He is greatly exalted.' And during the time we were with him in his domain, he wrote things and great meditations in the big book of *kavanot*. He ordered us to go outside, and then he came to us and ordered us to chant Psalm 47, and meditate on the initial letters of 'You are our heritage', and also in the last verse, the initials of 'the great of the peoples', *nun ayin*, are gathered together, the retinue of *nun ayin* the God of Abraham, whom he loved, for the guardians of all of them, of the earth, belong to God; He is greatly exalted, Amen'. Also, the final letters of 'The great of the peoples are gathered together, the retinue of Abraham's God; for the guardians of the earth belong to God; He is greatly exalted', that constitute 'sea', 'and water', 'sea'. He told us that we could recite the morning service, and also to recite Psalms, **Sha'arei tsiyon*, or other supplications, except that every ten minutes we should recite the psalm with the meditations that he gave us, and Heaven forfend that we should sleep. *And I was obliged to take the child Abraham from his bed, because of the danger.

|fo. 15a| And the Sage went to his domain, closed the door, and took the key of our room, and he also sealed the door. We remained like that, shut up tight, for four hours, and we did his bidding. At eight o'clock on Wednesday the Sage came back to us and stayed. The Sage remained without sleep, from Monday night to Thursday he slept two hours, and he said that he was not permitted to sleep within the domain, that is, in this house, and he stayed.

On Thursday evening the Sage went alone to his domain, stayed for about two hours, and began after midnight. Then he summoned R. Gabriel—and that was the

the initials *alef-nun-alef* from *alef-beit-gimel* *alef-nun-alef* is a reference to the initial letters of a phrase from Ps. 47: 5 which translates as 'He chose our heritage for us'. *Alef-beit-gimel* alludes to the 42-letter name of God that is formed from the initial letters of the *Ana bekho'ah* prayer, the first three words of which are in alphabetical order, i.e. starting in turn with *alef*, *beit*, and *gimel*.

Sha'arei tsiyon a collection by Nathan Nata Hannover (d. 1683) of *tikunim* (corrective prayers), other prayers, and *piyutim* (liturgical poems) based on Lurianic kabbalah and the writings of R. Hayim Vital.

And I was obliged to take the child Abraham from his bed because there was a sense of danger connected to the rite described by ZH, he felt compelled to remove the child Abraham (apparently one of Falk's charges).

first time he had brought him to his room—and he stayed with him for about five minutes and he came back. Afterwards he summoned R. Tuvyah and R. Itzik of Zamość and he chanted with them what he chanted—I do not know. They returned, and we recited the morning service. Then the Sage went home to sleep a little, because he was really ill after he had not permitted himself to sleep in his domain. He stayed home until two o'clock in the afternoon and came back. He found something new in his domain, but he did not reveal it to us, only he summoned *R. Jacob Cohen Barbariski to make something from gold and with silver, but R. Jacob was unable to do so. Then R. Tuvyah told me what psalms he had used with them last night. First, he began with them by chanting the Fourth Utterance and the Fifth Utterance, 'And there was evening and there was morning', also *'In the evening, I am weary, and in the morning with my groaning' in Psalm 6. And then he began again the Fourth Utterance, the first verse, also *verse 5, 'O Lord, do not punish me in anger, etc.' in Psalm 6. In this way he completed verse by verse, and ended 'and there was evening and there was morning' with the evening [mentioned in] verse 7, 'I am weary with groaning, etc.'. He began the Fifth Utterance, first verse, and then verse 8 from Psalm 6, and ended 'and there was evening and there was morning' with the morning, for in the morning, *'[all my enemies] will be frustrated and stricken with terror, etc.'. He also mentioned *'and in the seal, six'—'they will be frustrated and stricken with terror'. Then we recited with great conviction Psalm 16, and he meditated on the words *'I say to the Lord'. Initial letters: 'I have no good but [*bal*] in you', the initial letters of which are *tet beit ayin*, and with the word *bal* he meditated on *lamed beit* paths; and also *'As to the holy ones that are in the land', the initial letters of which, taken backwards, are *beit alef lamed*, *'they are the mighty ones', the end letters and the initial letters of which are *yod-heh-vav-heh*, 'my whole desire', the initial letters of

R. Jacob Cohen Barbariski I have been unable to identify this person.

'In the evening, I am weary and in the morning with my groaning' this combines Ps. 6: 7: 'I am weary with groaning' with the verse from Genesis just cited.

verse 5, 'O Lord, do not punish me in anger' in fact, verse 2.

'[all my enemies] will be frustrated and stricken with terror' Ps. 6: 11.

'and in the seal, six' a reference to *Sefer yetsirah*.

'I say...I have no good' Ps. 16: 2.

tet beit ayin perhaps because these letters spell out *teva*, the Hebrew word for 'nature'. [The significance of this is not explained.]

lamed beit the inversion of the letters comprising the word *bal*, with the numerical value of 32, i.e. 32 paths. [Presumably these are the 32 paths of wisdom mentioned at the beginning of *Sefer yetsirah*, associated with the fact that the word 'Elohim' ('God') appears 32 times in the story of the Creation in the first chapter of Genesis.]

'As to the holy ones' Ps. 16: 3.

'they are the mighty ones' the continuation of verse 3, as are the following two quotations.

yod-heh-vav-heh the Tetragrammaton.

which are *kaf ḥet*, *'in whom is', which is the holy name of 42; and he completed the psalm with great mystical significance, except for the holy names that he had mentioned in this psalm with *the breaths of his mouth. He then practised with R. Tuvyah and R. Itzik for about two hours, and he remained in his domain until five o'clock on Thursday, and he stopped.

On Thursday night the Sage practised alone until midnight, and after midnight he summoned me, R. Tuvyah, and R. Itzik, and we began the Fifth Utterance and the Sixth Utterance, until 'and there was evening and there was morning, the sixth day', and then Psalm 5, that also contains thirteen verses, corresponding to the aforementioned two utterances. Then he began reciting Psalm 30 from verse 2 *'We extol you, O Lord, for you have lifted me up', and also Psalm 5 from the last verse, 'For You surely bless the righteous man, etc.', and thus he finished the two psalms, that is, Psalm 30 forwards and Psalm 5 backwards, and then Psalm 36. |fo. 15b| He meditated on verse 2, 'Transgression says, etc.', and he also wrote something in the big book of *kavanot*, and then Psalm 83—he first began verse 5, and then verse 2, meditating on 'do not be silent' etc., until verse 13, and then he meditated on verse 13, as well, and also wrote something in the big book of *kavanot*. He finished up to verse 16, where he meditated on 'terrify them with Your storm', as well as on verse 17, 'Cover their faces with shame', to the end; and then Psalm 88. He ordered us to go outside, and then he ordered us to chant Psalm 88, and then he ordered us to chant the second letter of each word in the psalm, that is, beginning from verse 2, thus *producing the following names: ה'ל'ש'ו'ע'ל'ג'; ב'פ'פ'ט'ז'ר'; י'ב'ר'פ'ח'ש'ג'; ח'מ'ו'ו'י'ג'י'י'; מ'מ'פ'מ'ל'כ'ב'ש'א'כ'ו'ה'י'ג'; ת'ב'ח'מ'מ'; ל'מ'מ'כ'ש'נ'ל'; ר'י'מ'ת'ו'מ'ל'ל'צ'; י'א'נ'נ'ר'ה'כ'ו'ט'ל'פ'; ל'ע'ל'מ'פ'ק'ו'ל'; י'ק'ס'מ'א'; י'ח'ל'צ'א'ש'; א'ל'ה'ו'ב'פ'ק'; מ'ה'ז'פ'ס'נ'מ'; נ'נ'ג'נ'ש'מ'פ'; ל'ב'ר'ע'מ'; ב'מ'ל'י'ק'ל'ח'; ר'מ'ה'ר'י'ח'.

kaf ḥet [Letters which could be read as *ko'aḥ*, meaning 'power'.]

'in whom is', which is the holy name of 42 Falk is saying that the Hebrew word for this phrase, *bam*, whose two letters, *mem* and *beit*, have a combined numerical value of 42, is an esoteric reference to the divine name of 42 letters.

the breaths [*havlaḥot*] of his mouth ZH describes the manner in which the holy names were uttered. *Havlaḥot* means breathing or exhalation. This terminology therefore presents one of the mystical techniques related to the enunciation of the letters: the mystic is to inhale and exhale air while reciting the various vocalized letters. See Idel, *The Mystical Experience in Abraham Abulafia* (Heb.), 24–30. Below (fo. 21b, entry for 24 Shevat, first line), ZH writes that Falk 'chanted with the breaths of his mouth'; for this chanting, see ibid. 53–71.

'We extol you' the psalm actually reads 'I extol You'.

producing the following names Falk orders the participants in the rite to meditate on the second letters of the words in Ps. 88, beginning with the second verse, and thereby produce new holy names. The second verse, ה' אלהי ישועתי יום צעקתי בלילה נגדך, yields the name composed of the letters ה'ל'ש'ו'ע'ל'ג'; the third verse, תבוא לפניך תפילתי הטה אזנך לרנתי, produces the name ב'פ'פ'ט'ז'ר'; and thus for all the last eighteen verses in the psalm. Those gathered then return to verse 13:

And then three Hebrew words meaning 'Are Your wonders made known in the darkness?', thus he ordered us to recite, first, eight times, the aforementioned names from the psalm, and then the whole psalm; and then ten times; and then thirty times, as the numerical value of *yaḥel*. The Sage went to his domain to complete the amulets, and he completed eight. He also made a small rope, hung amulets on the rope that he had hung between the two posts of the camp [gate], hung two on the posts, and he completed the amulets before we finished chanting what he had given us. Then he signalled us to stop—even though we had recited the aforementioned psalm only forty-one times with the aforementioned names—and to recite the morning service. It was six o'clock on Friday morning, and the Sage stayed in his domain until an hour after midday. During that time R. Gabriel also came, for the Sage had sent for him to be brought.

And two hours after midday he summoned me, R. Tuvyah, R. Itzik, and R. Gabriel to his domain, and he began once again to chant *"gracious" is interpreted as meaning God', and then Psalm 111; it was a wondrous and marvellous thing, how he drew such mystical meanings from these two psalms, 111 and 112, and combined them with *Sefer yetsirah*; it was a miraculous discovery that he was granted from Heaven concerning their association, also the holy names, the vigil, and the ten *sefirot* and charms from *Sefer yetsirah*, all associated with the aforementioned two psalms. He continued to recite the two psalms for two whole hours, and then he began again. He ordered me that whenever he gave me a sign I should write one letter in square script in the big book of *kavanot*, beside the names that he was using on 17 Sivan 5502 [1742]. It was a great discovery, that the day of the month caused that it also should be on 17 Sivan 5508. *I wrote these names: א׳י׳ב׳; ב׳י׳י׳; ג׳מ׳י׳; ד׳ל׳ח׳, and in this way I finished these two psalms.

|fo. 16a| Afterwards he chanted Psalm 5 to verse 9; then he returned to his seat, which is where I had been sitting while I was writing, and finished Psalm 5. He then *began to chant from *Sha'arei tsiyon* from 'And You are He whose years' to 'Hearken

היודע בחושך פלאך׳, whose second letters yield ח, ל, י׳. In the next stage, the participants are to repeat these names a total of 48 times (the numerical value of the word יחל׳, as follows: in the first set they recite the names 8 times, and conclude with the recitation of the psalm in its entirety; in the second set, 10 times; and in the third set, 30 times. ZH relates that although they were supposed to repeat the name 48 times they only had time to do so 41 times.

"gracious" is interpreted as meaning God [The reference here is unclear.]

I wrote these names the names that ZH writes are the acronyms formed from the initial letters of the words in the first two verses of Ps. 111: אודה ה׳ בכל לבב בסוד ישרים ועדה׳ גדלים מעשי ה׳ דרושים לכל חפציהם׳ [excluding the preliminary salutation 'Hallelujah'].

began to chant from *Sha'arei tsiyon* the passage quoted includes an acrostic with the 72-letter divine name that is derived from the three verses of Exod. 14: 19–21. It appears in the chapter entitled *Sha'ar tikunei tefilot* ('the chapter of corrective prayers').

to my voice from the depths'. Then he took two candles with the shofars from the tables, and stood them on his table. He also ordered that two tallow candles be lit by the camp gate, and he also ordered R. Tuvyah to light two large wax candles, one on each table, and also two candles of those standing in the holy candlesticks *and covered with the shofars on his table. Then he ordered him to break the seal of the two curtains of the camp gate. The Sage went himself and opened the curtains, and the sword embedded in the camp gates in the holy names was seen as it had been when he first came, before last Rosh Hashanah. The Sage lit two wax candles on the place where the holy names were written and where the sword was embedded. Then the Sage took down the four amulets with the rope that he had made on his table. He commanded R. Tuvyah to chant the names that were written in the big book of *kavanot* on 17 Sivan 5502, as well as the names that I had written beside them this sabbath eve, Friday, 18 Sivan 5508, and he wrote on each seal. There was a circle on the seals, and within the circle he wrote three letters very beautifully. While he was writing, the large wax candle on the right-hand table suddenly went out, and he expressed regret that he had not been more careful; and while he was writing on the second seal, the large wax candle on the other table began to go out. The Sage announced that he did not give it permission to be extinguished. The candle spattered wax on the whole table but the Sage did not let it go out, and it had to remain alight. The great wonder, however, was what suffering the candle had, that he prevented the wick from going out, rather, it was forced to stand by itself and remain alight, thus the candle flickered for a quarter of an hour. Afterwards the Sage went and lit a new candle on the tip of the sword; I also saw that there was a small amulet hanging on the sword blade, and he ordered us to leave. Meanwhile he summoned R. Tuvyah and R. Itzik, and the small wax candle on the sword blade went out, and the Sage said that had to stop, since it was only an hour and a half until the sabbath. The Sage recited the afternoon prayer with R. Tuvyah and R. Itzik; it was a great wonder that he still had strength after he had practised continuously for eighteen hours, and all the while fasting.

|fo. 16b| *Sunday evening, 20 Sivan.* I was sick, Heaven forfend, and I could not go to the Bridge. The Sage went himself with Gedaliah at eleven o'clock on Sunday night, and I came to him on Monday before midday.

Monday night. He practised alone before midnight, and after midnight he summoned me, R. Tuvyah, and R. Itzik to his domain, and only four candles were burning. We began to chant *the First Utterance, the Second Utterance, and the Third

and covered with the shofars on his table [It is not clear what this might mean.]

the First Utterance from Gen. 1, which describes the first day of Creation. [In the Jewish tradition the world was created by ten acts of speech, here called 'Utterances'.]

Utterance, up to 'and there was evening and there was morning, a third day', and then Psalm 1 in its entirety. He repeated Psalm 1, first verse, and then the first verse of the First Utterance, and he completed the First Utterance with the first psalm, verse by verse, because there are six verses in the First Utterance, and also six verses in Psalm 1. Then he ordered me to write on blank paper the letters that he indicated to me. Again he began Psalm 1, and he compiled from the first three verses letters that are the initials, in order, of the first two verses from 'In the beginning' to 'the water', missing only 'and darkness', and for that reason he said instead 'and not darkness'. He ordered us to leave, and then he summoned us to his domain. He ordered us to recite and chant Psalm 137, and then he indicated more letters from Psalm 137 that I should write. First we recited the psalm in its entirety, then he repeated Psalm 137 and connected it with the Second Utterance, verse by verse, this to the end of the psalm and the Utterance. He again repeated the psalm, indicating the letters to me, and I wrote. There were, again, initial letters in order, from 'And God saw' to 'water from water', but the word 'good' [*tov*] was missing, and for that reason *he omitted the letter *tet*. He then said, *'Jerusalem has greatly sinned', and ordered us to leave. These are the names that he compiled from Psalm 1, that is, from the first three verses of the psalm: בבאאהו; הוהתועפ; תואמעכפה*. And these are from Psalm 137: ואאהכ*, lacking the letter *tet*, ואבהוהאליוקלואירבהום במל*. And he ordered us to leave, and he practised until seven o'clock on Tuesday.

Tuesday night. He practised alone before midnight, and after midnight he began his rituals alone in his domain. I, R. Tuvyah, and the Little One stayed in our room, and he practised continuously for nine hours.

Wednesday. I had to bring that small table from the house. The Sage made himself two new wax candles.

he omitted the letter *tet* [Perhaps because it is the initial letter of *tov*.]

'Jerusalem has greatly sinned' Lam. 1: 8.

בבאאהו; הוהתועפ; תואמעכפה i.e. the initial letters of the words in the first verses of Gen. 1.

ואאהכ the initial letters of the Hebrew for 'And God saw that the light was'; Falk omitted the letter *tet*, representing the Hebrew word *tov* ('good'). [No explanation is offered for why Falk omitted *tov*, but perhaps it relates to the statement that 'Jerusalem has greatly sinned', which is also not explained.]

ואבהוהאליוקלואירבהום במל these are the initial letters of Hebrew words from Gen. 1: 4–6 'and God separated the light from the darkness. God called the light Day, and he called the darkness Night. . . . And God said, "Let there be an expanse in the middle of the water, that it may separate water from water".' [In fact the letter *vav*, which is the first letter of *vayikra*, the word for 'and he called', is missing; no explanation is offered.] The connection with Ps. 137 is unclear.

On Wednesday night the Sage went to his domain by himself after midnight, and he practised all night, and also all day Thursday.

Thursday night. The Sage went to his domain after midnight, when he summoned me, R. Tuvyah, R. Itzik, and the Little One, and he began with Psalm 119, *"Princes have persecuted me without reason', until the end of the psalm, and then the Sage cast lots in the book of Psalms; the lot fell on Psalm 68, and he meditated with great intensity. I remember also that he meditated on verse 16: 'O majestic mountain, Mount Bashan!', *the final letters of which form the word *maran*, and also verse 18: *"God's chariots are myriad'—the holy name of 45, etc.; *"among them in Sinai' is *yam*; *"You went up to the heights' is *tam*; 'captives, having received tribute' is *yod-tav-tav*; 'of men', etc., and also verse 29: 'strength for you, the strength, O God' is *khaf-heh-mem*, 'which You displayed for us'; I could not remember more, because I had to write, *and also it was indicated by the breaths of his mouth. And then he summoned the Little One.

'Princes have persecuted me without reason' Ps. 119: 161.

the final letters of which form the word *maran* meaning 'our master'.

'God's chariots are myriad' Ps. 68: 18; ZH writes four letters in this verse ((*khaf*, *heh*, *yod*, *yod*) with horizontal lines above them, indicating that their combined numerical value is of mystical significance. In this case the value is 45 (*khaf* = 20 + *heh* = 5 + *yod* = 10 + *yod* = 10), an allusion to the idea that in reciting the verse one should meditate on the divine name of 45 letters.

'among them in Sinai' the final Hebrew letters of this phrase (also from Ps. 68: 18), comprise the word *yam*, sea.

'You went up to the heights' from Ps. 68: 19 (as are the following two quotes); the final Hebrew letters spell out the word *tam*, meaning: innocent, perfect. This phrase begins with the words *shavita shevi* ('having taken captives'); *shavita*, with its letters rearranged, is, as Professor Yehuda Liebes pointed out to me, 'Shabetai'. Indeed, the Sabbatians frequently made use of this verse, claiming that it alluded to Sabbatai (Heb. *shabetai*) Zevi. This may be an instance of the technique of forming new words from word endings and their attachment to words in the chapter. Using this technique, Falk could possibly have alluded to matters of a messianic/Sabbatian nature. This possibility, however, remains within the realm of conjecture, as it is supported solely by numerical-value calculations and acrostics. (I am sceptical concerning the acceptability of such allusions, but they should nevertheless be presented as an interpretative possibility.) The acrostics allude to the following messages: *yam* = *yavo menahem* (the consoler shall come), *yeshu'at meshiho* (the salvation of his messiah); *tam* = *torat mosheh* (the Torah of Moses); *yod-tav-tav* = *yafeh talmud torah* (It is good to study Torah—Mishnah *Avot* 2: 2); *kaf-heh-mem* is *kohen mashi'ah* (priest-messiah), *kevod hashem mimekomo* ('the glory of the Lord from his place'—Ezek. 3: 12; recited in the Kedushah prayer), *kol hamitsvot* (all the commandments), *ken hayah minhago* (thus was his practice). Falk might have had concealed intentions in these letter combinations, but ZH was unaware of them, especially since he states that his recollection was not precise.

and also it was indicated by the breaths of his mouth [Presumably, 'it' here refers to the mystical intensity.]

|fo. 17a| And we began to chant Psalm 82, and he meditated on verse 2, and also verse 6, and he ordered me to write *alef alef alef alef*, which comes from 'I had taken you for divine beings', etc.; and then Psalm 83, and he meditated on verse 17: 'Cover their faces with shame', *the letters *alef-mem-nun*, etc.; and then Psalm 97, and he meditated on verse 9: *me'od* is the holy name of 45 letters; and also verse 10: *ohavei* is the holy name of 18 letters; and also verse 12: *vehodu*—the alphabet that is 27 letters—*lezekher kodsho*, 'His holy name'. Then he completed the writing which he had done on Thursday with great embellishment, all in engraved letters, and he also wrote many holy names on it. That was the completion of everything as a prophecy. He left *at the top of the crown four spaces in which to conceal holy names, and then *hung it from the blade of the sword. Afterwards he took the small strap from the camp gate and put it on his table. He shut himself in with the new rope that he had made on Thursday, and he wrote some holy names on the strap while we chanted the aforementioned *alef alef alef alef*. Then he ordered R. Tuvyah to light two large wax candles, and he fastened the gate with the strap on which he had written holy names. He took the second strap, which was broader, put it on his table, and ordered us to leave. Then he summoned us, we chanted Psalm 79, and he indicated to me the letters that I was to write in the big book of *kavanot*, 32 letters from the Utterance 'In the beginning'. We went out, and he told us to come back in half an hour, and then chant those 32 letters, and afterwards to chant the four *alef*s upstairs, and so we did. When we returned, I saw that he had also written holy names on the second strap and tied it to the two posts from the camp where we were. The Sage was postrate on the ground, that is, upon the hide, with outstretched arms and legs, holding only the two ends of the new strap in his hands. The first book of *kavanot* was placed before him, and he wrote an amulet. He ordered R. Tuvyah to light all the candles, except the two around the sword at the camp gate, and R. Tuvyah did so. Thereupon the Sage stood up and lit the two large wax candles and two small wax candles, and he also lit two wax

alef alef alef alef the first letters of the words from this verse (Ps. 82: 6).

the letters *alef-mem-nun* the last letters of the words in this verse, spelling out the word 'amen'.

***me'od* is the holy name of 45 letters** the word *me'od* from Ps. 97: 9, 'You are exalted *me'od* ('high'; lit., greatly) above all divine beings', has the numerical value of 45, corresponding to the number of letters in one of the divine names of God.

***ohavei* is the holy name of 18 letters** the word *ohavei* from Ps. 97, 'O you who love [*ohavei*] the Lord', has the numerical value of 18.

vehodu*—the alphabet that is 27 letters—*lezekher kodsho the word *vehodu*, meaning 'and give thanks', from Ps. 97: 12, 'and give thanks to His holy name', has the numerical value of 27, the number of letters in the Hebrew alphabet (that is, including the final forms of the five letters that are written differently when at the end of a word).

at the top of the crown [The Hebrew term for scribal embellishments of Hebrew letters.]

hung it from the blade of the sword ['It' here presumably refers to what Falk has been writing on.]

candles on the two posts, the candles that he had made himself on Thursday. Then he himself lit two wax candles on the camp gate, as well as a new candle on the tip of the sword. He lay down again with outstretched arms and legs, and he wrote holy names. He then called R. Itzik to come with the Little One, and the Sage gave R. Itzik names folded up, and he ordered him to meditate with the Little One on the three letters: *nun, ḥet, peh*, and then to give the holy names to R. Tuvyah, and so he did. Then he ordered R. Tuvyah that they should chant with him the names that he uttered, but that he should take care when mentioning the letter *tet*. Then R. Tuvyah was to go and place the names in the cavity opposite the gate, in the aforementioned crown, and the Sage chanted with great tears. And at the moment that he placed the holy names in the crown, the sword left the camp gate, and the crown with the candle on the sword blade remained in the air. We left, and afterwards he summoned us, and we saw that the crown was suspended in the air with the candle, and the candle was burning.

|fo. 17b| The Sage sealed the impression of the sword in the camp gate with a seal that had been lying on the table, and we began to chant, with much weeping, Psalms 102, 63, and 38, and the Sage meditated on them with great concentration. When he recited *'The voice of the Lord kindles flames of fire'*, he pointed with his finger at the right-hand candle in the camp gate, and it was extinguished at the very moment that he spoke. We went out, and the wax candle on the crown burned until it reached the paper and then it too extinguished itself but nevertheless remained suspended in the air, and we went out. I forgot to write first that there were six amulets suspended on the rope of the camp, that is, three on each side; and four on the posts, two on each side; and also two below, on the posts near the table, one on each side; two on the candles on the camp gate, one on each side; and two on the tables, one on each side; for a total of sixteen amulets; and they were all suspended in paper bags, very finely embellished. And when we were outside, the Sage came to us and revealed to us only a minute part of the sacred rituals in which he had been engaged this night. He said that the aforementioned crown was like a prison with four cells.

Four cells for four names: and if one name placed in a cell does not banish the sword, then a second will be put in place, until all four have been so placed. And if all four do not banish the sword, then the crown with the four holy names in it must be burned. But the Holy One, blessed be He, who hearkens to Israel's prayers, gave the Sage success, so that the sword departed immediately with the first holy name. He also revealed to me that he had made this aforementioned new rope with the intention of banishing the sword, so that the sword would not have permission to return anywhere; for if the aforementioned new rope with all the aforementioned amulets is in any place where the Sage should build a small camp with the new rope, then it

---

'The voice of the Lord kindles flames of fire'
   Ps. 29: 7.

must come; but otherwise it does not have permission to come. He practised this night only six hours, and in those six hours there were more new things than in the six weeks that he had been practising; and a word to the wise is sufficient.

Friday, 25 Sivan. I pawned two small candlesticks for 2*s*. 6*d*. with the widow.

The Sage went home and stayed there until Tuesday night, the first day of the new moon of Tamuz.

Wednesday, 1 Tamuz. Gedaliah pawned a gold star, 10*s*. 0*d*., and a holy name, for £2. 10*s*. 0*d*., and their weight was 1 oz. 5 dwt.

At night the Sage came to the Bridge, went to his domain, and quickly returned. He stayed at the Bridge for about two hours.

|fo. 18*a*| The Sage pawned the gold star and the other gold seals for £4. 10*s*. 0*d*., to buy for the rebbetsin what she needs so that she can go to the wife of the ambassador of Cologne, whose name is Shampan. And so she went to her this day, and it was a waste of about two and a half guineas.

Sunday, 4 Tamuz. R. Hirsch Hazan's daughter died, her name was Bluma, may she rest in peace.

Monday, 5 Tamuz. I pawned my small camisole for 2*s*. 0*d*. with the widow.

Tuesday, 6 Tamuz. The Sage returned to the Bridge, to his room, and today he gave me a little wax to melt in a vessel. And afterwards, when it had melted, I found that the vessel contained a large wick made of *shemot, and he was greatly grieved by this; *then the Sage revealed to me the nature of the aforementioned wick.

He also revealed to me this day that the holy names that the Little One had held for a long time in his bosom secured with a seal, and also the holy names in another receptacle that was also sealed—all these holy names had disappeared, leaving only the sealed containers. The disappearance of these holy names took place at the same time as the disappearance of the sword, on Thursday night, the night of 25 Sivan, as mentioned above. The Little One knew nothing until Tuesday, the eve of the new moon of Tamuz, when the Sage summoned him to his house so he could take the holy names from him, and the Little One remained afraid and amazed at this.

On Tuesday night the Sage practised alone, about five hours, in his domain.

---

shemot literally, 'names', but the term is commonly used for any piece of paper on which the name of God appears, and which therefore cannot be used for secular purposes and must be disposed of respectfully (by archiving in a *genizah* or by burial).

then the Sage revealed to me the nature of the aforementioned wick [This presumably

Wednesday night, 8 Tamuz. The Sage made himself *thirteen wax candles, each weighing 2 oz., and he also made something like a beam, to put it in when he opens the camp.

One hour after midnight on the said night, the Sage went to his domain, and then he summoned me and R. Tuvyah. I saw a small copper lamp hanging there, also a cut piece referred to as 'the mirror' above the camp gate. We began first to chant Psalm 138, and then 139, 140, 141, 142, 143, and then he again repeated Psalm 138, first verse, and also the first verse of Genesis. He put these together, in the same way as 'and there was evening and there was morning, a first day [Gen. 1: 5]'. Then he ordered me to write the following names in the big book of *kavanot*: וביכגכי*, and they are the initial letters of verse 5 in Psalm 138. He also commanded me to write first, near that name, these names: ועוביא*, and they too are initial letters, of verse 5 in Genesis. He completed Genesis through the second day, altogether eight verses, together with the psalm, also eight verses, verse by verse. Then he ordered me |fo. 18*b*| to write these names as well: ועוביש*, and also ייביחלמיאת*. And then Psalm 139 with the Third Utterance in the same order as before, and I wrote ועוביש, verse 13 in Genesis, and also אוצועכ*, verse 5 in Psalm 139. In this way he completed the six psalms, and I had to write down the letters he had indicated to me in the psalms for it was not possible for me to keep so much in my head. And it was something new and marvellous, the knowledge that he had from Heaven. And afterwards we recited the morning prayers. Then the Sage ordered us to chant those holy names that I had written, and he wrote an amulet while we were chanting. Then he took the amulet that he had written, and he placed it between the two wax candles that were standing in the camp gate. He stopped, and it was nine o'clock.

---

relates to what is revealed in the text that follows, but this is not stated explicitly.]

thirteen wax candles, each weighing 2 oz. [Given the precise detail here one can but wonder whether there was significance in the fact that the total amount of wax needed for 13 candles of 2 oz. each was 26 oz., when 26 is the numerical value of the letters of the Tetragrammaton.]

וביכגכי the initial letters of the Hebrew words of Ps. 138: 5: 'They shall sing of the ways of the Lord, "Great is the majesty of the Lord!"'

ועוביא the initial letters of the Hebrew of Gen. 1: 5: 'And there was evening and there was morning, a first day.'

ועוביש the initial letters of 'And there was evening and there was morning, a third day' (Gen. 1: 13).

ייביחלמיאת the name composed of the initial letters of 'The Lord will settle accounts for me. O Lord, Your steadfast love is eternal; do not forsake the work of Your hands' (Ps. 138: 8).

אוצועכ the name composed of the initial letters of 'You hedge me before and behind; You lay Your hand upon me' (Ps. 139: 5).

Thursday night. The Sage went to his domain one hour after midnight, and then he summoned me and R. Tuvyah. *The Sage cast lots in the book of Psalms, and the lot fell on Psalm 62. He chanted the psalm with us, then we recited the Fifth Utterance and the Sixth Utterance, and then he cast lots once again. The lot fell on Psalm 76, and afterwards he chanted the same two Utterances. He cast lots a third time, and it was Psalm 46; a fourth time and it was Psalm 57; a fifth time and it was Psalm 58. And then he repeated the procedure, and again began with Psalm 62 with the same two Utterances, and the psalm had only verses as the number of the two aforementioned Utterances, and afterwards he chanted a psalm. It was a wondrous thing, the rituals, the knowledge, and the deeds that he did, about six hours consecutively, and he stopped.

Monday, 12 Tamuz. The Sage returned from the house on the Bridge. He stayed here the entire week, and he practised each night in his domain with new things, with the casting of lots in the book of Psalms, with the Utterances, and with *Sefer yetsirah*, wondrous, amazing things, and I had no time to write down what happened.

Thursday night, 16 Tamuz. I again had no time to record things while they happened. *Only this I remembered: that he made a new rope, because of what happened last night, that it broke by itself. He also made wax candles by himself, and he practised alone in his room from midnight to five o'clock in the morning. Then he summoned me, R. Tuvyah, and R. Itzik, also the Little One, and we began to chant Psalm 78; and he added what he added. Then he knelt in front the camp gate, and we began once again to chant Psalm 78, up to *verse 55: 'He brought them to His holy realm', as before. This utterance was a new thing, and I do not remember what he meditated on this psalm, and he wrote what he wrote, also great things. Afterwards he stood up, took the holy names that he had written, and wanted to place them in front of the camp gate. |fo. 19a| As he did so the camp gate, which had been sealed for eleven months, opened by itself. Then the Sage was angry with us, and said we had not meditated ceaselessly with him as we should have. Then he ordered that all the tallow

The Sage cast lots in the book of Psalms, and the lot fell on Psalm 62 the psalms on which the lots fell all contain twelve verses (excluding in each case the introductory verse).

Only this I remembered here too ZH mentions that he is recording events on the basis of what he can remember, rather than immediately after they occurred. In other words, the descriptions of the ceremonies in the two entries dated 'Thursday night, 16 Tamuz' and 'Friday, two o'clock in the afternoon' were written some time after they happened, when ZH had time to sit and record them.

verse 55 should read 'verse 54'. The word for 'realm' in this verse, *gevul*, is the term used by Falk to describe his 'domain'. [Perhaps implying that he considered his domain similarly holy.]

candles be extinguished, and that every time he uttered a letter R. Tuvyah was to light one of the wax candles that the Sage had made that day, whichever candle he wanted. He also ordered R. Itzik of Zamość to light on the second table the counterpart of the candle that R. Tuvyah had lit, and so he did. He also ordered R. Tuvyah and R. Itzik to light the wax candle that was in the crown each time that he uttered a letter; then he told R. Tuvyah to take the key from the camp gate, and so he did. Afterwards the Sage stood in front of the camp gate and meditated what he meditated, and the gate opened by itself. Then the Sage again shut the gate and returned to his place, and he began to chant with us with great concentration on what he meditated; and then the wax candle, which was standing on the large candle, went out by itself, effortlessly, really in the twinkling of an eye. He ordered us to turn our faces away, and thus the candle, its counterpart on the right-hand table, went out, and then the wax candle that was in the crown before the camp gate went out by itself; and then he ordered that the two candles standing in the little candlesticks be extinguished. He lit two other candles, and they went out by themselves, and this thing—the extinguishing of the candles this night—was a wondrous thing. Afterwards we went outside to pray, and he practised this night until 8 o'clock in the morning, and then he stopped.

Friday, 16 Tamuz, two o'clock in the afternoon. The Sage made a small seal within which was a letter *yod* of gold, and also another gold letter, and on the outside the Sage wrote certain names very beautifully. And he ordered the Little One to write the letter *tet*, near the hole through which the gold was visible from the outside, on the right side, and on the left a letter *kaf*. Then he ordered that the hole be filled up with ink, that is, that the Little One himself should do that. He then filled it with hot copper and the Little One put his seal to it. Then the Sage made a cover for it of paper and ordered the Little One to sign his name *in square letters, and then I signed my name on the other side. Then the Sage wrote under my signature *three letters with two *pataḥ*s, very beautifully, and then he made a cover for it resembling a *closed *mem* from a piece of iron wire, and then he made another cover of paper and he tied it to a stone. He ordered me and the Little One to go out on the river in a small boat and throw the names with the gold into |fo. 19b| the water, and so we did. The Sage

in square letters [Hebrew has two principal written forms: square letters, as used by scribes in writing the Torah and religious texts; and a cursive script used for other purposes.]

three letters with two *pataḥ*s a *pataḥ* is a Hebrew vowel indicated by a single line beneath the letter that it is vocalizing.

[The name of the vowel derives from a root expressing 'openness', and kabbalists take it as a symbol of the acquisition of knowledge about other worlds; see <http://www.biblical-hebrew-study.com/soul-of-the-letters-the-vowels-of-the-hebrew-alphabet/>.]

closed *mem* the shape of the letter *mem* when at the end of a word.

practised in his domain almost until the start of the sabbath. Then he extinguished all the candles in his domain, lit one wax candle opposite the camp gate, and sealed up the great gate, and went home. By now the sabbath had already started; we went home, and the Sage stayed at home until Tuesday.

Today Hirsch Hazan's son, the boy Mordecai, died, may he rest in peace.

Tuesday night, 21 Tamuz. An important reminder that today *the wife of R. Aaron Frank died; two months previously she had given birth to twin sons, and both died within two weeks, one after the other.

Wednesday night, 22 Tamuz. I borrowed from the landlord Collier one and a half guineas to pay the rent for the house in Prescot Street. I took this loan for only three weeks, and three guineas from R. Isaac Doctor.

After midnight, he summoned me and R. Tuyah to his domain, and we began to chant Psalm 16 in its entirety. He extracted many holy names from it and wrote them in the big book of *kavanot*. We then chanted Psalm 32 in its entirety, and he again extracted many holy names; and then Psalm 29, just like the first, *and he extracted *merkavah* from it; and then Psalm 150, like the first, as well, extracting the letter *heh* and writing a large *patah*. We then repeated Psalm 29 forwards, and also Psalm 1, and he stopped.

*Wednesday night. He cancelled, only he alone practised, and the delay was because *he had not finished the shofar.

---

the wife of R. Aaron Frank Aaron Frank was a trader in gems and jewellery in Hanover. In 1729 he settled in England and became one of the leaders of the Ashkenazi community in London. See C. Roth, *The History of the Great Synagogue in London*, 64, 88, 94, 131; id., *The History of the Great Synagogue*, 211; E. N. Adler, *London*, 135. Aaron Frank was the son-in-law of R. Moses Hart, another prominent member of the London Jewish community.

and he extracted *merkavah* from it . . . extracting the *heh* and writing a large *patah* . . . We then repeated Psalm 29 forwards [The word *merkavah* is the term used by the prophet Ezekiel to describe God's mystical chariot-throne, so it has mystical associations for the kabbalist. The letter *heh* is used to represent one of the divine names. On the mystical associations of the vowel *patah*, see comment above on the phrase 'three letters with two *patah*s' on fo. 19a. Note also that a *heh* is the first consonant in *merkavah* when the word is read backwards [albeit it is not vocalized with a *patah*; since ZH then goes on to say that they continued reading forwards, it suggests that until then they had been reading with the words in the reverse order, though the point is not made specifically.]

Wednesday night [The text that follows seems to contradict that immediately preceding it.]

he had not finished the shofar [ZH goes on to say that Falk was in the process of drawing a shofar, so that is presumably what he was referring to.]

Thursday night. He went to his domain after midnight, and then he summoned me and R. Tuvyah, and he began to sanctify the holy names on the new shofar that he had drawn, and I finished by day. When he finished, he hung them opposite the camp gate. He extinguished the tallow candles, he himself lit two wax candles, and he measured them with the compass. He also made a sign with his fingernail in both candles, and then he placed the holy names in what he had used to drive out the sword, and this he placed in the crown that he had hung in front of the camp gate. Then we left, and he stayed until seven o'clock.

Friday. At the time of the afternoon prayer he practised what he practised, and then he ordered me to light a single wax candle, as I had done last Friday. We then went out to the house, where he stayed until Tuesday night.

Tuesday night, 28 Tamuz. The Sage went to his domain, where he wrote *holy names relating to the shofar, to be inside, and he practised until four o'clock, when he went home and remained there until Thursday night.

Thursday night, 1 Av. The Sage went to his domain after midnight, and he summoned me and R. Tuvyah. We first recited the Torah portion of 'Ha'azinu' till the end [Deut. 32: 1–43], responsively and with devotion, and then he recited 'And there was evening and there was morning, the sixth day' [Gen. 1: 31]. Then we recited the Song of Songs, and this, too, was recited with great devotion, and afterwards |fo. 20a| we recited the Sixth Utterance, and also the Third Utterance, followed by Psalm 108, and he stopped.

That evening, the eve of the new moon of *Menahem Av, R. Cosman left prison and went to Guildford, *making himself a free man.

holy names relating to the shofar [In the mystical tradition, the various sounds emitted by the shofar are conveyed to the divine thrones by different named angels; it could be that ZH is referring here to their names.]

Menahem Av [The month of Av is the month in which both temples were destroyed. The first nine days of the month are marked as a period of semi-mourning that culminates in the fast-day of the Ninth of Av, the anniversary of the destruction; the remainder of the month is considered a period of consolation. Because of this the month is often known as 'Menahem Av' ('Av of Consolation'), also because following the destruction God consoles (*menaḥem*) his people as a father (*av*).]

making himself a free man [The phrase ZH uses for 'free man', *ben ḥorin*, is that which occurs in the Passover Haggadah to signify that the Children of Israel are no longer slaves. It is not clear why he would have gone to Guildford, a small town south-west of London, and come to the Sage only a few days later (see entry for 6 Av).]

Sabbath eve, at eight o'clock at night. The Little One was imprisoned by his landlord for the sum of £2. 14s. 0d., and on the sabbath a creditor presented him with a promissory note for fifty guineas and had him put in prison.

Tuesday night, 6 Av. The Sage came to the Bridge, to his domain, and he was in his domain for a short time after midnight.

And he stayed here Wednesday and Thursday, till we finished the holy names associated with the shofar, until midday on Friday, 8 Av.

Wednesday, 6 Av. The Little One left prison and gave his creditor new promissory notes.

R. Cosman, who had been released from prison, came to the Sage on the Bridge for the first time.

Tuesday, 19 Menahem Av. The Little One was imprisoned for £58. 0s. 0d., the rent for his house, and he was in prison until Thursday, 21 Menahem Av. I received a letter from my esteemed father, may he live long, *written in Piotrków on 27 Sivan and *brought by Jews from Zamość.

Thursday night, 22 Menahem Av. The Sage sent R. Tuvyah with me to the Bridge, to his domain, and he gave R. Tuvyah something like a piece of paper, and he ordered him to throw it into a crack of the door, between the lintel and the room of his domain, and so he did, and R. Tuvyah left.

---

14 Elul. For an important reminder, that today, the sabbath of the Torah portion of 'Ki Tetse', there were no candlesticks in the synagogue, nor did we have any fish or meat, nor any pewter or copper vessel *in the summer; and the child fell ill with the measles. This distress began on the holy festival of Shavuot, and it was so until—

Sabbath eve, at eight o'clock at night [In London in July/August, when the month of Av would normally begin, eight o'clock on a Friday night might well be still before the 'start of the sabbath', i.e. 'sabbath eve'.]

written in Piotrków on 27 Sivan [That is, some seven weeks previously.]

brought by Jews from Zamość [Zamość is some 200 miles south-east of Piotrków; it is not clear what Jews from Zamość were doing in Piotrków but perhaps it was just a convenient place to stop on the way to London.]

in the summer; and the child fell ill ... This distress began on ... Shavuot [The relevance of the summer is unclear. ZH does not say which child he is talking about (he has previously said that there were several staying with Falk), or what state of distress he is talking about; Shavuot was some three months previously. However, from the entry for 22 Elul, it seems that the distress was financial.]

Sunday, 22 Elul. *I sent a letter to my esteemed father, may he live long, with the Jews who had come from Zamość.

For a reminder, what distress there was on Rosh Hashanah 5509, until I helped with £2. 0s. 0d., and R. Gabriel, as well, with £1. 10s. 0d.

Thursday, 26 Elul. The Sage went to the Bridge and took the shofar from his domain, as well as the linen, that is, the curtains of the domain, and he went home.

|fo. 20b|

5509 [1748/9], here in London, may it be propitious

Saturday night, 21 Tishrei. I pawned my shirt for 2s. 0d. at Milper's.

*Monday, 28 Tishrei. I pawned my black garment for 6s. 0d. near *Wolpeck.

Monday, 13 Heshvan. For a reminder: on the holy sabbath of the Torah portion of 'Lekh lekha', 11 Heshvan, we had *only half a head, yet we celebrated the sabbath. R. Cosman, too, dined with us, but we did not even have candlesticks for a sabbath candle, and we had to borrow two candlesticks from R. Noah's wife for candles, and a word to the wise will suffice.

I received a letter for the Little One with a written note for £92. 3s. 7d. On Tuesday I cashed it, and I gave the Sage seventy-eight guineas [£81. 18s. 0d.], and the rest I brought to the Little One. Early on Wednesday morning I was with him at the Little One's, and then I brought the Little One £61. 0s. 0d. and the Sage kept twenty guineas [£21. 0s. 0d.], but I had nothing from that money, not even a penny, from either party.

Wednesday, 15 Heshvan. He gave the landlord Collier £6. 0s. 0d. for rent of the house for two quarters, so he would owe him nothing until *Shmistmes, only £3. 0s. 0d. per quarter.

I sent a letter ... with the Jews who had come from Zamość [We do not know what the Jews from Zamość were doing in London but they appear to have stayed for at least one month, given when they had delivered the letter to ZH.]

Monday, 28 Tishrei the day and date are inconsistent with those of the preceding entry; 28 Tishrei fell on a Saturday night/Sunday.

Wolpeck [Perhaps a reference to Wall Park or Wall Park Alley, mentioned elsewhere.]

only half a head presumably of fish.

Shmistmes Christmas (derogatory; as at fo. 5b, p. 83 above).

Monday, 11 Kislev. I received a written note from France addressed to the Little One, in the amount of £22. 0s. 0d., and I brought six and a half guineas [£6. 16s. 6d.] to our home; the Little One kept the rest.

Wednesday night, 11 Shevat. Tonight *a great nobleman came from a vast distance, just like a messenger from Heaven, to communicate with the Sage and conclude dealings with him. The Sage was with him in the room about two hours, and the nobleman departed and left two guineas on the table.

Friday, 12 Shevat. The nobleman sent ten guineas with R. Cosman.

Monday, 15 Shevat. The Sage went to the forest with Gedaliah.
The great nobleman came to our house and talked *to her for about two hours. Meanwhile the Sage returned from the forest and spoke to him. This evening the nobleman wrote his signature |fo. 21a| in his book of *kavanot*, and he departed.

Friday, 19 Shevat. The great nobleman sent four guineas with R. Cosman.

Sunday, 21 Shevat. On Friday night, 20 Shevat, the great nobleman came unannounced, spoke with the Sage, and went away, and he gave the Sage ten guineas.
Today I went with the Sage to the Bridge. The Sage took the chest and also the holy names that he wanted to take from there. He gave the landlord Collier four guineas and he went home.

Monday, 22 Shevat. He built a little table above the long table containing the holy names, and he also placed the two chests of the shofars near the table, one on each side. He also hung the holy names—that is, the *genizah* that he had taken yesterday from the room on the Bridge—above the table. *He made a curtain in front of it, like a small camp, but without a rope.

Tuesday, 23 Shevat. I went to the forest with the Sage, and I stayed with him in the inn near the forest. The Sage went up to the room, where he began to draw an amulet in his book of *kavanot*. He remained there about three hours, and then he rode a

a great nobleman came...just like a messenger from Heaven thus begins ZH's account of the relationship between Theodore Stephen de Stein, Baron von Neuhoff (the deposed 'king of Corsica') and Falk; see Introduction, Section III. Beginning with this entry, ZH lists the sums of money that von Neuhoff either brought with him or sent from time to time [which may explain the phrase 'just like a messenger from Heaven'].

to her i.e. to Falk's wife, the rebbetsin.

He made a curtain in front of it [The construction here is difficult to visualize.]

horse into the forest, alone. It was time for the afternoon prayer and he stayed there about half an hour and came back. I went with him into the inn that stands on the road by the water, where he went to the room and drew in the book of *kavanot*, staying for about an hour. Afterwards we went home; it was nine o'clock at night. The great nobleman was in our house with R. Cosman, but they did not know that the Sage was coming, and they left the house. Afterwards the Sage went to our house.

Wednesday, 24 Shevat. The Sage fasted and went into the parlour, into the place that he had built on Monday. He wanted to finish the amulet, but I do not know whether he finished or not. And at night, when I went to sleep at the Bridge, the landlord Collier told me that there had been great commotions in the camp at three o'clock in the afternoon. I immediately rushed to tell the Sage, and he went with me to the Bridge straight away. The Sage entered the room of his camp and lit candles, as he knows how.

|fo. 21*b*| He chanted with the breaths of his mouth, stayed about half an hour, and came back, remaining all night on the Bridge in the other room. The Sage told me that if he had possessed good horses, he would have ridden into his forest during the night.

Thursday, 25 Shevat. I went with the Sage to the house at eleven o'clock in the morning. Almost half an hour later, there was a great commotion in his camp, and the landlord Collier sent his servant with this information. Then the Sage told me to go immediately to the Bridge, and he ordered me to wait there, in the domain in the house, until six o'clock in the afternoon, which I did. *He also ordered me to look outside the gate, whether there was a big light or a small one, but I could see nothing because it was shut up tight. After six o'clock I went home.

The great nobleman came with R. Cosman to our house at twilight, unannounced, and he gave the rebbetsin six guineas. *He had a reason, that his wagon had broken on the way too.

This night, too, the Sage had some reason: I brought the great nobleman into the parlour, and there on the table was the book of *kavanot* with the amulet in it. I was coming and going from the parlour, and while I was out of the room the nobleman opened the book of *kavanot*; but because he had set eyes on it and touched it *the amulet was rendered invalid, and a new one was needed.

He also ordered me to look... whether there was a big light or a small one Falk apparently feared a fire which is why he ordered ZH to return to the bridge to investigate, but ZH could see nothing since the camp was locked.

He had a reason ZH relates that Falk stayed at home for some reason that prevented him from going to the 'camp'.

the amulet was rendered invalid [An interesting parallel is the esoteric belief that if

Sunday night, 29 Shevat. The great nobleman sent ten guineas with R. Cosman.

Tuesday, first day of the new moon of Adar. The great nobleman came unannounced with *Dr Smith, but he did not see the Sage.

Wednesday, second day of the new moon of Adar. I went with the Sage to the forest, where he drew a new amulet, and then he rode by himself from the inn to the forest, where he stayed about half an hour. He came back to the inn, and I went with him from there to the inn by the river. There he drew what he needed, and we came home, because he thought the nobleman was in our house. But when we came home the nobleman was not there because he was ill.

On Tuesday, first day of the new moon of Adar, I went to the ritual bath to immerse myself, as well as the gold letters that the Sage had given me to immerse, *for they had to be in my hands while I immersed myself.

Monday, 6 Adar. I went with the Sage to the forest, *to the water that is called Tevils House, and there he drew something in the new seal that he had made on the aforementioned Thursday. He stayed about half an hour, and we went back to the Pas house. From there we went home and we found the nobleman |fo. 22a| in our house. The Sage went to the parlour, practised with the amulet that he had made at the water, and then summoned the nobleman. It is my humble opinion that he showed the aforementioned nobleman some new supernatural thing; I also heard from the Sage that the place by the water was auspicious for him. He practised with him for about three hours.

That night the nobleman gave the rebbetsin four guineas, and three guineas to the Sage.

---

a gentile touches or even sets eyes on kosher wine, that is sufficient to render it not kosher; some hasidim wrap the bottle from which they are serving wine if a non-Jew is at the table.]

Dr Smith Dr William Smith was a well-known English physician and a friend of the spiritualist and mystic Emanuel Swedenborg. As well as treating bodily diseases he applied kabbalistic methods to treat psychological disturbances. Smith was interested in Falk and in his methods for treating epilepsy and mental illness, and he visited him in his home a number of times. He was probably Swedenborg's physician, and he introduced him to Falk. See Schuchard, 'Yeats and the "Unknown Superiors"', 143; see also above, Introduction, Section V.

for they had to be in my hands while I immersed myself [This is contrary to the normal practice during ritual immersion; nothing at all must be held, so that the water can flow freely over all parts of the body.]

to the water that is called Tevils House perhaps meaning *tevilah* house, i.e. the house of ritual immersion.

Wednesday, 8 Adar. The nobleman sent five guineas with R. Cosman.

Tuesday, 14 Adar [Purim]. The nobleman sent nine guineas with R. Cosman.
   For a reminder, that the Sage conducted a Purim feast on Purim as if he were a rich man, *from ten thousand. His expenditure for Purim was surely more than fifteen guineas, together with other expenses until after the sabbath of 18 Adar.

Sunday, 26 Adar. The rebbetsin visited the nobleman, and he gave her four guineas.

Thursday, 1 Nisan. The nobleman visited the Sage and spoke with him in the parlour.

Saturday night, 4 Nisan. The nobleman sent seventeen guineas with R. Cosman and Gedaliah.

Monday, 5 Nisan. The Sage gave me a guinea to buy a *kepkart* and shoes for myself.
   On Tuesday, 28 Adar, the nobleman had sent five guineas with R. Cosman—I forgot to record this above.
   On Wednesday, before noon, I visited the nobleman, and I brought him *holy names that had been invalidated. I then went back to the Sage at Pas in Bethnal Green. From there I went with the Sage to the river near Woolwich, where he practised something at the time of the afternoon prayer and then we returned home safely.
   Today, Monday, 5 Nisan, a note came from the Little One, from the city of Paris, for the sum of £95. 9s. 8d. I kept it until Tuesday, 13 Nisan, when I cashed it and gave the money to the Sage.

Monday, 12 Nisan I received a written note from the Little One, from Paris, for the sum of £65. 2s. 0d. I handed it over to the Sage, and he kept £59. 0s. 0d.

Tuesday, 13 Nisan. I received from the Sage four and a half guineas for the debt for *what he had spent a year ago.
   |fo. 22b| *For the holy festival of Passover 5509 [1749], he spent £2. 0s. 0d. on me, just for linen for a shirt.

---

from ten thousand i.e. as if he had ten thousand guineas or pounds sterling—in other words, as if he were a millionaire.

kepkart a sleeveless cloak [perhaps related to the English term 'cape'].

holy names that had been invalidated [Perhaps Falk needed to render them powerless before giving them to a gentile.]

what he had spent possibly meaning 'what he had owed'.

For the holy festival of Passover [Due to begin the next day.]

The eve of the festival of Passover, the Sage gave me 12s. 0d. to buy leggings and a waistcoat.

The nobleman sent ten guineas with R. Cosman for Passover expenses.

Monday, intermediate days of Passover. The nobleman sent four guineas with R. Cosman; also *a watch of pinchbeck, a gift for the Sage, worth four guineas.

Monday night, 26 Nisan. I went with the Sage to visit the nobleman, and he stayed about three hours. The Sage took from him the holy names that I had given him on Wednesday, 7 Nisan. He also took from him three guineas; the nobleman prevailed on him to take this to pay for the coach.

Friday, first day of the new moon of Iyar. At eight o'clock the nobleman sent his manservant to the Sage to invite him to his country house, and the Sage gave the manservant a gift of a guinea. Afterwards I went with the Sage to the *country, to the nobleman, that is, in a chaise and horse, and he gave the Sage two guineas to pay for the chaise.

Friday, 8 Iyar. I was with the Sage, visiting the nobleman in his country house, where he *gave him some holy names in a sugar container. He stayed there about two hours, and the nobleman then went somewhere else and so did we.

Monday, 10 Iyar. I went with the Sage to the nobleman's country house at seven o'clock in the morning, and he practised in the garden what he had begun the afore-

---

a watch of pinchbeck [Because ZH writes 'pinchbeck' in Hebrew letters, which has no capitals, his meaning is ambiguous; it could mean 'a watch made by Pinchbeck'—meaning, by the watchmaker Christopher Pinchbeck (1710–83)—or 'a watch made of pinchbeck', an alloy of copper and zinc that was invented by Pinchbeck's father, who was also called Christopher (1670–1732) and was also a clockmaker, which was used to imitate gold in jewellery; by extension, 'pinchbeck' meant 'counterfeit, cheap'. Since ZH gives the price of the watch at four guineas, perhaps the former is more likely since the younger Pinchbeck became the king's watchmaker by appointment to George III; <https://en.wikipedia.org/wiki/Christopher_Pinchbeck>.]

country the reference is to Baron von Neuhoff's country estate; ZH mistakenly renders 'country', meaning 'rural', with the Hebrew *medinah*, meaning country in the sense of 'political state'.

gave him some holy names in a sugar container [Since sugar was a valuable commodity in the eighteenth century it was often kept in fine containers, even of silver; a sugar container would therefore have been a high-prestige item that would have been deemed appropriate for the safe keeping of amulets such as holy names.]

mentioned Friday. He stayed about an hour, but the nobleman was there. I went with him from there to the forest. At twelve o'clock Gedaliah came to us, to the inn near the forest, and he said that the nobleman had passed by our house and asked for the Sage to come to him. The Sage went with us to the new place in the forest, not to his regular place, and from there we went together to the water. When we had come half-way, Gedaliah told me to ride quickly, and I replied that I could not, and then *he began to pursue. And when he had gone just 20 yards away from me, the horse fell with him. There was a large wound on the horse's forehead, and the horse was just as if dead, *killed on the road. Then we had great trouble. We brought it, with great difficulty, to the house of the surgeon in Stratford. From there I went with the Sage to *Upton, to the nobleman's country house, and he entered the garden once again. But before we went to the country house, I went with the Sage to the water, from there to Upton, and from Upton safely to our house.

|fo. 23a| *Wednesday, 12 Iyar.* The nobleman came to the Sage's house, and the Sage did something, and gave him holy names in seals in the sugar container. The nobleman stayed about two hours and then left.

Thursday, 13 Iyar. Thursday, the nobleman was in the Sage's house, and I was not there. He gave the Sage ten guineas, and in the afternoon *Madam Flemick was in our house, together with her sister and *Dr Smith.

Gedaliah returned from the house of the physician in Stratford, and the nobleman paid the physician three guineas for him.

Monday, 17 Iyar. Early in the morning, at four o'clock, I went with the Sage to the country, to the nobleman's house. He went straight into the garden and practised what he practised. We went from there to the forest; the Sage took my horse and rode into the forest, where he stayed about half an hour before returning. From there we went to the river near *East Ham, where he practised for about an hour.

he began to pursue perhaps with the meaning of ride quickly, gallop.

killed on the road [The translator points out that the phrase is reminiscent of the biblical case of the victim of an unsolved murder that imposes a heavy responsibility on the elders of the town nearest to the corpse, who must then engage in a special ritual, an association that obviously is inappropriate for a simple accident involving an animal. The use of the phrase suggests that ZH did not understand the original concept properly. See Translator's Note, p. xiv]

Upton [A town to the east of London, now part of the London Borough of Newham.]

Madam Flemick should be 'Fleming'. [Perhaps a reference to the wife of the nobleman's landlord.]

Dr Smith [See note on fo. 21b, p. 118.]

East Ham [A town to the east of London, now incorporated in the London Borough of Newham.]

He then returned to the nobleman's house; the nobleman gave him a gold watch worth £40. 0s. 0d. to pawn, and from there we went safely home.

Wednesday, 19 Iyar. Early in the morning, at four o'clock, I went with the Sage to the country, to the nobleman's house. He immediately entered the garden and practised what he practised, for about two hours. Afterwards, at eight o'clock, the Sage sent me to the river near East Ham. He gave me holy names and commanded me to open only the first container, and then he ordered me to seal with a seal that he had given me and come back to him, and so I did. When I came back, I went home with him.

Thursday, 20 Iyar. There were fireworks in the courtyard of the palace, and I went to watch them with the Sage and the rebbetsin. My expenses this day were about six guineas, and it was all a waste.

I received a letter from my father, also from my mother, and also from my sister, may they all live long, through R. Joseph of Zamość, that was written in Piotrków on *4 Adar 5509.

Monday, 24 Iyar. I went with the Sage with a good horse to the country, to the nobleman's house. When he was there *the Sage did not know what to do with the holy names that he had given the nobleman: he could not take them from him, nor could he leave them with him. The Sage gave orders to clear the room. He placed a table in the room, with two wax candles on it. He spread paper on the table, lit the candles, placed the holy names on the table, closed the room, and took the key with him. From there I went with him to the river near East Ham, and he did there what he did. Then he summoned me and said 'What a bad deed I did in taking the key into my possession. You must return the key to the nobleman'; in the room by the river something was revealed to him which he did not reveal to me. He said he had to go to the forest, and I went with him from there. When we came on to the road, the Sage went with the chaise along the circuitous path. When I asked him why he did not take the straight route, which is nearer to the forest, he answered me, 'Do not ask me, it is better that I go two *parasangs further, |fo. 23b| and not take the short route, which

---

4 Adar 5509 [Nearly three months previously.]

the Sage did not know what to do ZH tells of Falk's indecision as to whether to give Baron von Neuhoff the holy names. His prescience ('knowing in advance') that the act of taking the key from the nobleman entailed something adverse induced Falk to go to the forest (the location of some of his occult rites). In contrast to his usual practice, however, this time he chose to go there in his carriage, by a different route ('the circuitous path'), that is, not by the shortest and most direct route. As ZH relates, shortly before their arrival at Stratford their carriage collided with another; the carriage was destroyed, but they emerged unscathed.

parasangs a parasang is a talmudic unit of length, roughly equivalent to four miles.

is an evil way. I fear that something evil shall befall me today.' When I heard that, I fell silent and I followed him. As we approached Stratford another chaise with a man and woman in it came right up to ours. Our chaise overturned with the Sage inside, and then the horse began to gallop and the chaise was smashed into little pieces; thank God, the Sage was unharmed. No doubt another man would surely have been killed. We went to a nearby inn, and then the Sage sent me with the key that he had given me by the river. He ordered me to bring it to the nobleman, and this was a marvel, that he had known in advance that something bad would happen to him. I went to the nobleman and delivered the key to him. I went back to the Sage, and we returned home safely. The damage to the chaise was only four guineas, and there were also other expenses, two guineas.

The nobleman gave the Sage a gold toothpick case worth three guineas, and I pawned it with Nicholas the jeweller for £1. 5s. 0d.; it weighed 7 dwt.

Thursday, 27 Iyar. I went with R. Cosman to the nobleman in the country, and I took the key from the nobleman, from the upstairs room.

Monday, 2 Sivan. I went with the Sage early in the morning, at four o'clock, to the nobleman's country house. The Sage went up to the room and took the holy names from there. Then I went with him to the river near East Ham, where he engaged in his practices for about an hour. From there I went with him to our house, we stayed in the house about four hours, and then I went with him to the forest. He took the horse and rode alone into the forest, and he engaged in his practices for about half an hour. From there I went with him to the nobleman's country house, where we stayed about half an hour, and from there we went home safely.

Tuesday night. At nine o'clock, I went with him to the nobleman's country house. He stayed there in his room for four hours, and he did something in his room. And then, early in the morning, at four o'clock, I went with him to the forest by the river at East Ham, and he remained there. He practised alone in the forest for about half an hour, and then we went to the house. He stayed in the house until four o'clock in the afternoon, and then I went with him to the river near East Ham, where he practised alone about an hour. Then he returned to the nobleman's country house, where he stayed for about an hour, and then we returned home safely.

The nobleman sent the rebbetsin *nineteen guineas and one shilling, 20, with Dr Smith.

---

nineteen guineas and one shilling, 20
  ['nineteen guineas' is £19. 19s. 0d., so an additional shilling would make £20 in total.]

The eve of the festival of Shavuot. He clothed *R. Isaac the son of the late R. Ezekiel for about one guinea, and he also |fo. 24a| honoured him by having him eat with him at his table on the festival, together with R. Itzik Zamość, and he stayed thus until [*text indecipherable*]

Sunday, 8 Sivan. I went with him to the nobleman's country house at eleven o'clock, and he stayed there about four hours. From there we went to the river near East Ham. He practised there for about two hours, and from there we went home safely.

Monday. At three o'clock in the afternoon, I went with the Sage to the forest, where he practised alone for about half an hour and then came back. Afterwards we went home, and on the way he said that he wanted to drive a little in the country. He came to the country house belonging to the nobleman *Sir Fisher Tench, and he went into the garden, and into the house, as well; it was truly a very beautiful building. He gave gifts to the servants there, and he had expenses of 9s. 0d. We went from there, and he tarried on the way, until after ten o'clock. We came to *the nobleman's country house, and the Sage sent me to the nobleman, to ask him for what he had sent him. The Sage waited near the house, wanting the nobleman himself to come and invite him to come in. The nobleman, however, paid no attention, and he gave me the holy names. I went with him to the inn on *Rampart Street, to spend the night there. Early Tuesday morning, at six o'clock, I went with him to the nobleman's country house, where he stayed for about four hours. From there we went home safely.

On Wednesday, 4 Sivan, I had sent a letter to my father, also to my mother, and also to my sister Leah, may they live long, with *R. Moses Zamość.

Tuesday, 10 Sivan. For a reminder: today, the aforementioned R. Laze of Hamburg left here, London, completely destitute. He came to me and asked me to intercede

R. Isaac the son of the late R. Ezekiel possibly a reference to the son of R. Ezekiel b. Shalom of Zamość, a leading Sabbatian (see Scholem, 'The Sabbatian Movement in Poland' (Heb.), 137). This conjecture is supported by Falk's conducting a banquet in his honour, to which R. Itzik Zamość (who, as already noted, probably hailed from R. Isaac's home town) was also invited.

Sir Fisher Tench [Tench was a City of London financier who was a member of parliament and a director of several companies. The house ZH is talking about could be the Great House at Leyton, which Tench inherited from his father. See <https://en.m.wikipedia.org/wiki/Sir_Fisher_Tench,_1st_Baronet>.]

the nobleman's country house [Presumably he is referring here to Baron von Neuhoff's country house.]

Rampart Street [A street in the Whitechapel district of the East End of London.]

R. Moses Zamość one of Falk's visitors. His name suggests that he came from Zamość, a town in south-eastern Poland that was home to many Sabbatians.

with the Sage to give him **tefilin* for the journey. I asked the Sage, and he gave him *tefilin*, and also 5s. 0d., *provisions for the journey, because he felt greatly responsible, *to go to his room to take his belongings; a word to the wise is sufficient.

Today, too, R. Tuvyah left together with Leib Schneider with his merchandise for the fair at Frankfurt am Oder. The Sage undertook to pay Moses Fishman for him the sum of six guineas.

Wednesday. At three o'clock in the afternoon, the Sage sent Gedaliah with a note to the nobleman, and I and the Sage stayed at the inn *in the village of Stratford until he returned. Then I went with the Sage to the forest because he thought that the nobleman had gone there. From there we returned to the nobleman's country house and we stayed there all night. That night the nobleman went up to his room, and when he came back the nobleman fell down the stairs, causing himself great pain on his right side, but there was no danger, thank God, and we stayed there until Thursday morning. At ten o'clock we went home safely from there. The nobleman gave him a gold **toz* weighing 4½ oz., to help him out with money.

Thursday. At five o'clock in the afternoon, I went with the Sage to the nobleman's country house, I asked only if the nobleman was in good health, and we came back home.

|fo. 24b| *Friday, 13 Sivan.* I pawned the *toz* with the jeweller Nicholas for sixteen guineas.

I went with the Sage at one o'clock in the afternoon to the river near East Ham, and he stayed there about two hours. From there we went to the aforementioned nobleman at *Upton, we stayed there about an hour, and from there we went home safely. This week's expenses were five guineas, for nothing.

---

tefilin for the journey [Jewish men are required to wear *tefilin* (phylacteries) for morning prayer on weekdays; R. Laze may have pawned or sold his and been using someone else's while in London, but would need his own set while travelling.]

provisions for the journey see Gen. 42: 25. [ZH uses a biblical expression that recalls the provisions that Joseph gave his brothers when they left Egypt to bring him his brother Benjamin.]

to go to his room to take his belongings; a word to the wise is sufficient [Presumably, Falk instructs ZH to go to Laze's room and take his things so as to avoid any unpleasantness with his landlord for non-payment of debts; hence 'a word to the wise is sufficient'.]

in the village of Stratford [Stratford, today a district that is part of Greater London, is about six miles from the centre of London.]

toz possibly an abbreviation for the toothpick case that Falk had received from the nobleman, and that he was now compelled to pawn (see above, fo. 23*b*, entry for Monday, 24 Iyar). C. Roth, 'The King and the Cabbalist', 158, understands *toz* as a snuffbox.

Upton [Now part of the London Borough of Newham.]

For a reminder: on the festival of Shavuot, *Elias Levy, cursed be his name, sent a spy to see who was attending the Sage's synagogue. On Thursday, *the worthies of the congregation, cursed be their name, convened and summoned those persons, warning them that no man should do wrong again by going there. On the sabbath of 14 Sivan, they compelled a certain man, *Moses Fishman by name, to stand when the Torah scroll was being taken out from the ark for the afternoon service. The beadle read out to him, and he had to respond after him, saying, 'I have sinned and transgressed by going to worship in the synagogue of the *ba'al tsafon, and I beg the congregation's forgiveness.' And a word to the wise is sufficient.

Wednesday, 18 Sivan. I was at the nobleman's country house and I took the holy names from him.

Wednesday, 25 Sivan. I was with the Sage at the nobleman's country house, and the nobleman gave him two *moidores worth £1. 7s. 0d. From there I went with him to the river, and from there we went home safely. We had expenses of £1. 5s. 0d.

On the sabbath of 21 Sivan, young R. Zevi Hirsch Segal, the son of *R. Moses Chentchin, grandson of R. Samson Hazan of Chentchin (his father lives at present in the community of Chmielnik, and his uncle on his mother's side was the distinguished R. Dov Baer in the community of Chmielnik) came to me. He told me that he had met my father, may he live long, some seven weeks ago, in *Hotzenplotz in Moravia. He also told me other things, and that he was a member of our family. I did for him what I could, and I gave him first 7s. 6d., later 3s. 0d., and later a Pentateuch with the commentary of Rashi, for 3s. 6d., so he might be accepted as a manservant by R. Jonah of *Halberstadt.

Elias Levy in this entry ZH describes an episode that had taken place in the Great Synagogue on the eve of Shavuot: see above, Introduction, Section III (p. 40). For Elias's biography, see Appendix A.

the worthies of the congregation the congregation referred to is that of the Great Synagogue. [ZH referred to it earlier as the 'Bressler Synagogue'; see the note to fo. 7b above, p. 89.]

Moses Fishman [The fact that Fishman was publicly humiliated in this way may relate to the connection between him and Falk mentioned on fo. 23a, just above, entry for Tuesday 10 Sivan.]

ba'al tsafon see the note to fo. 7b above, p. 89.

moidores Portuguese gold coins.

R. Moses Chentchin ['Chentchin' is the Yiddish name for Checiny, Poland, which is presumably where this R. Moses came from.]

Hotzenplotz [The German name for the village of Osoblaha, at this period a Moravian enclave in Silesia; Jews took refuge there in the sixteenth to eighteenth centuries when they were not permitted to live in Silesia. In 1788 there were 586 Jews in thirty houses, so quite a substantial Jewish community. See <https://www.jewishvirtuallibrary.org>.]

Halberstadt [In the seventeenth and eighteenth centuries Halberstadt was

Sunday, eve of the new moon of Tamuz. He had a quarrel with me, that I should hire for him the chaise and the horses for the entire week, and so I did. I hired a chaise for two guineas, and then I heard that the nobleman was in town and all these expenses were for naught, so that about four guineas had been wasted.

Friday, 25 Tamuz, Today *the captain was released from the prison called *King's Bench. He sent the Sage one and a half guineas.

For a reminder: today I took from the money that I had collected for the Little One before he left prison, *a sum of 86, from which I took 20, and I immediately sent seventeen guineas with the esteemed R. Leib Nordom to my master, my father, may he live long, to the city of Piotrków. I also sent a short letter with him.

|fo. 25a| *Tuesday, eve of the new moon of Av.* I sent a letter from London to my master, my father, may he live long, *to the Jewish community of Piotrków, by the post *franka* Green Barg.

Wednesday, new moon of Av. I sent with Ber Pollack one *tubovni toz* for 12s. 0d. to R. Laze Segal in The Hague, for the *batelkhis* that I received through Meir son of Zelikle in *Gunheim, a total of 4 *batelkhis* of rice.

On Wednesday, 23 Tamuz, the Sage had told me to do what I could to persuade the Little One *to just £30. 0s. 0d., and he wants to abandon the camp at the Bridge. But for me this was like a sharp sword on my neck, for I know what troubles we may

considered a world-renowned centre of Torah study and philanthropy. It also served as a centre for the nearby smaller communities of Prussia such as Halle and Magdeburg. See <http://www.jewishvirtuallibrary.org>. Presumably R. Jonah was now living in London.]

the captain the reference is unclear [though perhaps it is the person referred to as the Little One who is mentioned in a second entry for the same day as having been released from prison].

King's Bench generally, a division of the English High Court; here, the King's Bench debtors' prison.

a sum of 86, from which I took 20 [The unit is not stated. Perhaps guineas, since ZH goes on to say that he sent seventeen guineas to his father.]

to the Jewish community of Piotrków [ZH's mention of the Jewish community in this context seems strange, but perhaps he did indeed send the letter care of the Jewish community. Marcin Wodziński explains that this was a common practice in Poland in this period (personal communication)]

tubovni toz possibly a small amount (a 'tuppenny', or two pennyweight) [of *toz* in a snuffbox (note to fo. 24a, p. 125 above)].

batelkhis bushels; or, perhaps, a package or chest ('bottlecase').

Gunheim [Possibly Gundheim, in the Alzey-Worms district in the Rhine Palatinate of Germany.]

to just £30.0s.0d, and he wants to abandon the camp at the Bridge [It seems that Falk is asking ZH to obtain £30 from the Little One, but seeing that just a few days earlier

yet have because he abandoned the camp in another house, and *for that I did what I did on 25 Tamuz.

Friday, 23 Menahem Av. There was a fire in the house of the painter by the Bridge, near the house in which the camp was situated, but it was extinguished and there was no serious damage.

Sunday night, 26 Menahem Av. *The Sage made fire with a pistol that he used to make fire to kindle a lamp in the house. Then they did a foolish thing with the powder-holder: the Sage wanted to put a little powder in that pistol, he lit the powder, and the powder-holder exploded. The Sage's face was burned, along with his hands, and the boy's face and hands were burned as well; some damage was also done to the rebbetsin's eyebrows. The Sage was in such great pain that he was beside himself, and he sent for the physician to heal him and the boy. On Monday, 27 Menahem Av, the Sage slept a bit, because he had not slept the whole of the previous night, and he had such a dream: 'Wicked one, what have you done, giving the seal to the Little One?' (the aforementioned seal of Monday, 24 Iyar). The Little One returned the seal to him on Friday, 24 Menahem Av, and said to him in the dream: 'If the seal had not been in your house, you would surely have been marked for death, Heaven forfend.' The Sage immediately awoke from his dream and told the whole story to the rebbetsin. His medical expenses were three guineas.

|fo. 25b| For a reminder that on Wednesday, 25 Sivan, *the nobleman had fled from

(25 Tamuz) ZH had had to collect money for the latter, the storyline here is unclear. It is also not clear who wanted to 'abandon' the camp (the verb ZH uses is 'cancel'), nor what that might mean.]

for that I did what I did on 25 Tamuz [The diary entry for that day is not clear on the specifics; note also that the reference here is being made in an entry dated 23 Tamuz but obviously made later.]

The Sage made fire with a pistol ... His medical expenses were three guineas. ZH describes Falk's alchemical experiments in his house in connection with his efforts to help Baron von Neuhoff by devising a technique to convert base metals into gold. This entry portrays how Falk was miraculously saved from death in an explosion in his house that was caused by one of these experiments. Falk, his wife, and a child who was in the house at the time were injured in the resulting fire. ZH repeats Falk's explanation for the mishap that 'the Sage' had received in a dream in which he was told that it was caused by a seal apparently containing holy names (a sort of amulet) that Falk had given to the Little One. The latter returned the seal, thus saving Falk from death, but the explosion occurred as punishment for the kabbalist having entrusted the charm to one unworthy of holding it—or so Falk explained the sorry events to his wife. ZH might have heard this theory from the rebbetsin, or possibly while eavesdropping on Falk from outside the door.

the nobleman had fled Baron Theodore von Neuhoff was forced to flee his country estate because of his debt to the jeweller, but the latter located him in the city. The baron's landlord, Mr Fleming, acted as guarantor for his debt, thus keeping the nobleman out of

the country to the city because of his creditor, that is, the jeweller, but then he was caught in the city by the jeweller, for a sum of £150. 0s. 0d. His landlord Mr Fleming was his guarantor, and he stayed at his home until Sunday 9 Tishrei; then he fled from there to his brother-in-law, Milord Kilmachnick, but he had no help from him from that day until [*text indecipherable*]

Monday night, 26 Elul. R. Cosman gave twenty-three guineas to redeem the nobleman's gold watch, *but it was only ten guineas. All that was the expense for the festival, he only redeemed some pledges for the kitchen.

5510 [1749/50], here in London, may it be propitious

The first day of Rosh Hashanah, I led the morning service, also the additional service, and I had a little pain in my throat. On the second day of Rosh Hashanah I blew the shofar, reciting the blessings, and also blowing *thirty blasts. But at night I fell ill, Heaven forfend, and I was sick for six weeks. The physician said that I was in danger, but 'the Lord punished me severely, but did not hand me over to death' [Ps. 118: 18]. Blessed be the Omnipresent, who sent me a cure from Heaven. My expenses, from my own pocket, were £4. 0s. 0d.

Tuesday night, 12 Tishrei. R. Cosman gave three guineas to make a *sukkah, and also for the other expenses of the festival.

The first night of Sukkot. R. Cosman gave one guinea for the Sage's clothing.

Monday, 17 Tishrei. I received a letter from my master, my father, may he live long, by the young man R. Judah, that was written in Breslau on Tuesday, 4 Tishrei—I was happy. On Tuesday, 18 Tishrei, I sent an answer to the city of Kalisz, by the post *franka* Green Barg.

prison. Von Neuhoff, however, did not succeed in obtaining the funds needed to repay his debt, and accordingly was forced to flee to his brother-in-law, Lord Kilmallock (to whom ZH refers as 'Milord Kilmachnick'). Von Neuhoff had married Lady Sarsfield, the daughter of an Irish Jacobite expatriate by the name of Viscount Kilmallock; see C. Roth, 'The King and the Cabbalist', 159.

but it was only ten guineas presumably, only worth ten guineas, i.e. he only received ten guineas for it.

thirty blasts of the shofar, i.e. the standard practice on Rosh Hashanah; the first day of Rosh Hashanah in that year fell on a sabbath, when the shofar is not blown.

sukkah the booth that must become a Jew's home for the week of the Sukkot festival.

Wednesday, 9 Heshvan. R. Cosman sent one guinea with Gedaliah for household expenses.

Wednesday, 17 Heshvan. R. Cosman gave one guinea, for household expenses.

Before Rosh Hashanah, R. Tuvyah had returned from Frankfurt an der Oder, and he remained in London until after *the festivals. On Tuesday, 25 Tishrei 5510, R. Tuvyah left London for Poland because he had been compelled to swear, and also give his word of honour, before the rabbinical court in Frankfurt, that he would go only once to London, and would return forthwith to Poland, for his wife. They held a pledge of his for twenty-three ducats.

Tuesday, 23 Heshvan. R. Cosman gave me *the donation that he had vowed on the festival, the sum of half a guinea; and on Friday, 19 Heshvan, in his house, he also gave me 4s. 0d.—a total of 14s. 6d.

|fo. 26a| R. Cosman gave her one guinea for household expenses.

Wednesday, 24 Heshvan. R. Cosman sent *one *cyderin* to our house, for £1. 12s. 0d.

Tuesday, the new moon of Kislev. I received an answer from my father, may he live long, that he had received the money that I had sent with *R. Leib Norde on 25 Tamuz 5509. He wrote me that he had married off my sister Leah *on 8 Heshvan, and I was very pleased. He also *replied to my letter of 18 Tishrei mentioned above.

For a reminder: there was such poverty in the house that we actually had no bread in the house on Tuesday, the new moon of Kislev, and also on Wednesday. He and she

---

Wednesday, 9 Heshvan the notation is incorrect; 9 Heshvan fell on Monday night/Tuesday. [Possibly the gift is mentioned in error and it was made only once rather than on two occasions.]

the festivals [ZH means the whole sequence of festivals that fall during the month of Tishrei: Rosh Hashanah, Yom Kippur, Sukkot, Shemini Atseret, and Simhat Torah.]

the donation that he had vowed Cosman had presumably received some liturgical honour (e.g. being called to the reading of the Torah) on one of the festivals and, as was customary, promised to make a donation to the congregation.

one *cyderin* ... £1. 12s. 1d. possibly apple cider. [The quantity is not stated but it must have been quite a lot for thirty-two shillings—half as much again as he had just given for household expenses.]

R. Leib Norde [Presumably the man referred to on fo. 24b as R. Leib Nordom.]

on 8 Heshvan [viz., about three weeks previously.]

replied to my letter of 18 Tishrei the letter from his father was in response to two letters sent by ZH, one in the month of Tamuz and the other on 18 Tishrei.

fasted all day until the night, when I gave them sixpence to buy something to eat; there was nothing in the house worth anything.

Thursday, 3 Kislev. R. Cosman gave one guinea, for household needs.

Monday, 7 Kislev. R. Cosman sent one guinea with Gedaliah, for household needs.

Tuesday night, 16 Kislev. R. Cosman sent one guinea in a letter, for household needs.

Friday, 25 Kislev. I went to R. Cosman, and he sent one guinea with me, for household needs.

28 Kislev. R. Cosman gave me one guinea, for household needs, as well as 11s. 0d. for fish.

Wednesday, 8 Tevet. R. Cosman gave me one guinea, for household needs.

On Tuesday, 7 Tevet, the Little One had given a guinea and a half; moreover, some weeks before, he had sent two guineas by *penny post, that the aforementioned great nobleman had sent to our house.

Sunday, 12 Tevet. *The aforementioned nobleman was seized from his brother-in-law's house, and he was brought to the *sponging-house, to the King's Bench prison guard. The nobleman took Mordecai Franzmann as an emissary, to send him to noblemen to intercede for him in writing, and he remained there in that prison until [*text indecipherable*]

Tuesday night, 22 Tevet. R. Cosman had *yahrzeit*, and he gave one guinea for household needs, and half a guinea for fish for the sabbath.

penny post the penny post was a system in which standard letters could be sent with postage of a single penny. [At this point it was well established in England, having been introduced in 1680 and taken over by the government in 1682. See <https://en.wikipedia.org/wiki/Penny_Post>.]

The aforementioned nobleman was seized from his brother-in-law's house [There is more than one 'aforementioned nobleman', but the reference to the brother-in-law suggests that this was Baron Theodore von Neuhoff.]

sponging-house a debtors' prison (see note on p. 90 above on fo. 7*b* re the diary entry for 8 Iyar 5508). Baron Theodore von Neuhoff was imprisoned for six years. He died shortly after his release from prison, in abject poverty, and was buried in the churchyard of St Anne's in Soho (see also Introduction, Section III, n. 23 above).

yahrzeit the anniversary of the death of a close

|fo. 26b| *Tuesday, 28 Tevet.* R. Cosman sent one guinea with me for household expenses.

For a reminder: on Monday, 27 Tevet, *the newspaper wrote that there had been a fire *in Kalisz, that is, in a particular *cloister, and that many people had been injured, both men and women.

Wednesday, 7 Shevat. R. Cosman sent one guinea with me for household expenses.

On Sunday, 4 Shevat, the Little One had lost the holy names that the Sage had given him in a little box that contained a gold final *mem*. That is, it was not lost, but *the harlot in his house had forcibly taken it from him and did not want to return it, and it stayed that way.

Tuesday, 13 Shevat. R. Cosman sent one guinea with Gedaliah for household expenses.

Tuesday night, 14 Shevat. *The landlord Collier died at the Bridge, nine days after the death of his child, so there were two corpses within nine days.

Sunday, 18 Shevat. May it be remembered that today *the esteemed Eli Levy, may the name of the wicked rot, died here, and he lay until Tuesday, 20 Shevat, before he was buried. This was appropriate for his reputation, cursed be his name. And thus did the Sage predict for him, that he would not live out the year, because of *what he had done on the last festival of Shavuot.

---

relative for whom one is required by Jewish law to mourn. [It is a custom on the *yahrzeit* to give charity in the name of the deceased so that the soul may enjoy repose, so this may explain R. Cosman's generosity.]

the newspaper ZH uses the Polish term *gazeta*. [Presumably someone from Kalisz had brought it to London, because an English newspaper would not have printed such local Polish news. This entry also suggests that ZH could read Polish at least well enough to understand a newspaper article.]

in Kalisz i.e. ZH's home town.

cloister ZH writes 'cloister' in transliteration [perhaps meaning *klasztor*, the Polish term for monastery].

the harlot [Presumably a derogatory term rather than a factual description.]

The landlord Collier from whom the house on the bridge was rented; the landlord died shortly after the death of his young son.

the esteemed Eli Levy ZH writes of the death of Eli(as) Levy, the prominent community leader mentioned above (fo. 24b, p. 126; see also Appendix A). Even after Levy's death ZH continues to curse him and, additionally, tells of the disgrace he suffered posthumously in that his corpse lay unburied for two days. ZH also adds Falk's explanation for Levy's sudden demise.

what he had done [See p. 126 above.]

Tuesday, 20 Shevat. R. Cosman sent one guinea with me for household expenses.

Monday, 26 Shevat. R. Cosman sent half a guinea with Gedaliah for household expenses.

---

28 Shevat. A robber attacked R. Cosman on the porch and robbed him of twenty-five guineas, and also of the *gold watch.

Tuesday, 4 Adar I. R. Cosman sent one guinea with Gedaliah for household expenses.

Sunday, 9 Adar I. R. Cosman sent one guinea with Gedaliah for household expenses.

Thursday, 13 Adar I. Between noon and one o'clock there was an *earthquake in London, and for just about a single moment the walls were trembling.

Tuesday, 18 Adar I. R. Cosman sent one guinea with Gedaliah for household expenses, as well as 10*s.* 0*d.* for fish.

Wednesday, 26 Adar I. R. Cosman sent one guinea with Gedaliah for household expenses.

Friday, 28 Adar I. R. Cosman sent ten guineas with Gedaliah, because *the rebbetsin had written a letter to him, in the name of the Sage, saying that there would be *great poverty on *Shabat Shekalim and she was sickly.

---

gold watch see p. 129 (fo. 25*b*) above, where ZH relates how Cosman gave money to redeem the 'nobleman's' gold watch.

earthquake ZH uses the Yiddish *Erdtsiternish*, breaking it into two words: *erd tsiternish*. [The earthquake occurred on 8 February 1750 and apparently toppled several chimneys and demolished some decrepit buildings; see <https://en.wikipedia.org/wiki/List_of_earthquakes_in_the_British_Isles>.]

the rebbetsin had written ZH writes of the intervention by Falk's wife, who wrote a letter to Cosman requesting financial aid; ZH also mentions the rebbetsin's illness.

great poverty i.e. they did not have any money for this sabbath (i.e. the following day).

Shabat Shekalim [The sabbath preceding the new moon of Adar (or on the new moon itself, if it falls on a sabbath), on which Exod. 30: 11–16 (the section on the half-shekel) is read; one of the four sabbaths in this period of the year with special Torah readings. The reference here is to 29 Adar I (24 February 1750).]

|fo. 27a| *Monday, 1 Adar II.* He received £60. 0s. 0d. from the Little One, and on Tuesday he paid *the landlord, the widow Collier, for a quarter-year before the coming Passover festival; he also paid *R. Hertz Posner five guineas for R. Gabriel.

For a reminder, *that of all the money he received, he gave me only £1. 10s. 0d. for shoes and other things—the same £1. 10s. 0d. that I received on Thursday, 4 Adar II.

Tuesday, 9 Adar II. The Sage received more money from the Little One, bringing the total of what he received from the Little One to £132. 0s. 0d., so the Sage admitted to me himself.

The Sage gave me two and a half guineas to repay me for what I had spent. The total I received from that money was £4. 2s. 6d, and I spent of this money more than £4. 0s. 0d.

Wednesday, 10 Adar II. For a reminder: the Sage brought from his room to ours pieces of paper on which he had written certain holy names, and he threw them into the fire to burn. While they were burning, *the 9-year-old Abraham came to the fire and stared at it; he may have poked it too. He immediately had a great pain in his eyes, becoming really blind and unable to see anything. A great fear immediately seized the Sage, and he asked if Abraham had been close to the fire, and we were all distressed. The Sage ordered everyone to leave the room, and he remained alone with the child and myself. The Sage tied a kerchief over the child's eyes, placed a pen in the child's hand, and he wrote a holy name with a *mem* open on both sides. He ordered the child to throw the holy name into the fire, but the child refused, lest it kill him. Finally, I forcibly took him and brought him near to the fire. He threw the holy name, and then the child was seized by an epileptic fit, Heaven forfend. I immediately brought a physician, who instructed us to draw blood from the child. The child lay as dead, and thus he lay for four hours, Heaven forfend. In the meantime, the Sage commanded me to write the aforementioned holy name, and so I did. I did not know

---

the landlord, the widow Collier following the death of Collier the landlord (i.e. the owner of the rented house on London Bridge), ownership of the house passed to his widow.

R. Hertz Posner [Perhaps the son of R. Meyer Posner, mentioned on fo. 5a, p. 82.]

that of all the money he received ZH complains that he received only a paltry amount of money (30s. 0d., or £1. 10s. 0d.) from the large sum that Falk had received (£60. 0s. 0d.); he is clearly disappointed by Falk's behaviour towards him.

the 9-year-old Abraham one of the children being raised by Falk. Falk had been writing holy names and had thrown the paper on which he had written the names into the fire. The child was near the fire and may have been poking it, causing sparks to fly into his eyes. There was a great commotion; Falk kept his head and ordered the room to be cleared save for ZH and the boy. ZH goes on to describe how Falk 'cured' the child.

what he did with it, I just heard some kind of spell recited by the fire, and by nighttime the child was as healthy as before. The Sage told me that if he had not done that, the child would have been blind, but *they did not have the power to kill the child.

|fo. 27b| *Thursday, 11 Adar II.* For a reminder: this was the *Fast of Esther. Early in the morning, between five and six o'clock, *there was a great earthquake, what we call in German *Erd zitternis*, that we thought the world would be destroyed in an instant, here in London, 5510.

Purim night. For a reminder: R. Cosman gave me *Purim money, in the amount of half a guinea, on Purim night.

Tuesday night, 24 Adar II. R. Simhah Segal brought his son, Isaac the madman, into the Sage's house, and the Sage examined him to determine whether he was insane from natural causes or *because of a *kelipah*. He found that it was caused by a *kelipah*. The youth was in our house for close to twenty-four hours, and *a wondrous thing occurred with the flask of oil that the Sage threw from the window into the street, about ten cubits onto the stones, and yet the flask was completely unbroken.

Friday, 27 Adar II. He began to pawn things again, and the first was his red garment, pawned by Rebecca.

Sunday, 28 Adar II. *I immersed myself, and the Sage did too.

they did not have the power to kill the child i.e. the forces of evil, demons.

Fast of Esther the fast-day preceding Purim, in commemoration of the fast observed by Queen Esther and the Jews in Shushan (see Esther 4: 16). [The fast was observed a couple of days early; it should have taken place on 13 Adar but that would have been a sabbath, when fasting is not permitted except on Yom Kippur.]

there was a great earthquake [This was the last earthquake to have its epicentre in London. The civil date was 8 March 1750; see <https://en.wikipedia.org/wiki/List_of_earthquakes_in_the_British_Isles>.]

Purim money two of the commandments associated with Purim are for Jews to send portions of food to one another and to give to charity. If Falk gave him the money in fulfilment of one of these obligations, ZH does not use the normal form of words; or possibly this was given as people give gifts for each Jewish festival.

because of a *kelipah* a *kelipah* is a kabbalistic term for a demon, or for the forces of evil in general.

a wondrous thing occurred ZH obviously considers it a miracle that the flask of oil Falk threw into the street did not shatter [but he does not say whether the youth was cured].

I immersed myself, and the Sage did too they immersed themselves in a ritual bath. [The date is no coincidence: it was the day before the new moon, regarded by some as a minor Yom Kippur and an opportunity for repentance.]

Monday, eve of the new moon of Nisan. Today I went with the Sage to the Bridge, and I thoroughly cleaned the room of the camp. At night, after midnight, he practised alone what he practised.

Tuesday, new moon of Nisan. He practised alone again, and on this day R. Cosman sent the key of the new house on the Bridge that he had bought. He forbade going there until he himself could come.

Wednesday. He practised alone once again, and R. Cosman came at noon. This day Cosman began giving him money for the completion of his work on the Bridge. Afterwards the Sage sent me to summon R. Mann and R. Itzik of Zamość to be with him this night. They came at night, and the Sage began to do his rituals after midnight. He went to his room, and we remained in our room. He ordered us to engage in Torah study, and we engaged in study until seven o'clock in the morning, when R. Mann and R. Itzik went to the synagogue. The Sage remained in his room until four o'clock in the afternoon, when he returned in a good mood and with a cheerful heart, and then said, 'Blessed be the Lord, that I have done a great thing', that *he had cancelled his camp, but he had permission to build *another camp on the Bridge; in so doing he had effected a great thing, that he had *permission to go to the water, that had been forbidden him for *fourteen years. Afterwards the Sage revealed to me what it had taken to cure this madman, the son of that Simhah; he did so only in order to have an excuse |fo. 28a| to enter his camp and cancel it, and indeed he succeeded in the endeavour. This is the proof, that the Sage told me that if he had been able he would have [?] this madman. And then, at six o'clock in the afternoon, we went home safely. That was Thursday, 3 Nisan 5510.

Sunday, 6 Nisan. *I went with the Sage in a chaise and horses to the madman in Bethnal Green, and the madman's father was there. When we came he did not want

he had cancelled his camp [The meaning is unclear; perhaps 'profaned it', meaning that its sanctity was cancelled?]

another camp Falk had apparently purchased another property on the bridge (in addition to the one he rented). ZH describes the preparations for the move to the new premises (the 'camp').

permission to go to the water in purchasing new premises Falk might also have acquired the right to use anchorage near the bridge.

fourteen years possibly an allusion to the fact that in the fourteen years since Falk's arrival in London, he had not been permitted to build on London Bridge, but now permission had been granted (this might also indicate the date of Falk's arrival in the city, which, according to this calculation, would have been in 1736).

I went with the Sage . . . and the madman's father was there ZH describes another attempt by Falk to cure insanity. The nature of the account indicates that this was the exorcism of a dybbuk (called by ZH a *kelipah*). Falk told his followers how they should conduct themselves with the madman,

to say anything, for fear of the Sage, until the latter drew him out with pleasant words, when the madman began to talk, saying to the Sage that he should walk alone with him. The Sage walked with him, and I behind them. He spoke with the Sage and disclosed that at times he felt in his bed something like a human head. The Sage had previously told me this, that he had an inner demon. He could exorcise it, but he did not want to do anything himself, he would rather entrust the task to scholarly and God-fearing people. He told them how to behave with the madman and he gave them instructions, how to write an amulet for him; if they were God-fearing, then it would be a simple matter to exorcise the demon.

Afterwards I went with the Sage into the forest, and on the way the Sage told me that he wanted to try another forest, and so we did. We went into a new forest, and the Sage rode alone into the forest, where he stayed about two hours. Here is the proof: when he returned he came by a different way, because he was lost in the forest until he came to a certain house and took a special person to show him the way. When he returned, we went home safely.

Monday, 7 Nisan. He negotiated a deal with a craftsman to build him a structure in his room, in his new house on the Bridge, for £7. 10s. 0d.

Wednesday, 9 Nisan. Today the Sage gave me one guinea to buy myself a cloak. I paid £1. 3s. 3d. *I had to argue with him as before he had given me one guinea. How much aggravation I had over this, as I knew he had much money; and a word to the wise is sufficient.

Thursday, 10 Nisan. Today I went to R. Cosman to beg him for clothing for Passover, that is, I went with the Sage's knowledge. R. Cosman gave me £1. 16s. 0d. to buy some old clothes, which I did, and I spent more than £5. 0s. 0d. on myself.

The total that I received before Passover: £1. 10s. 0d.; two and a half guineas; one guinea from the Sage; and £1. 16s. 0d. from R. Cosman. |fo. 28b| These are the expenses I had for myself for Passover, from the money that I received:

Wig, 16s. 0d.; shoes, 12s. 0d.; stockings, 3s. 0d; shirt, 7s. 0d.—£1. 18s. 0d.

Repair, 1s. 0d.; *Collier's clothes, with expenses, 24s. 0d.—£1. 5s. 0d.

Cape, £1. 3s. 0d.; waistcoat, 6s. 0d.; hat, 12s. 0d.—£2. 1s. 0d.

---

ordered them to engage in study next to him, and also taught them how to write an amulet.

I had to argue with him as before he had given me one guinea one guinea was £1. 1s. 0d., so presumably ZH was trying to get Falk to give him the difference.

Collier's clothes, with expenses possibly the widow of their landlord Collier had given ZH an item of her late husband's clothing, which he sent to be repaired.

Nestukh, 1s. 0d.; pawned items, 16s. 0d. with interest—17s. 0d.

Laundry money for the whole year—£1. 12s. 0d.

Wednesday, the first day of the new moon of Iyar. For a reminder, on this day the Sage went, may it be fortuitous, to begin the construction of the new house on the Bridge. But he wasted his time building a house that has nothing to do with his rituals, and he spent a lot of money [on something] that has nothing to do with his rituals.

Sunday, 19 Iyar. For a reminder, on this day R. Cosman went from here to Paris *with the French ambassador. On the sabbath he asked the Sage's permission, which he gave him, to complete his work. Before he left here, he also gave him much money to begin his work. According to my reckoning, he had from R. Cosman £200. 0s. 0d., besides what he had from the Little One, for I saw with my own eyes that *whatever the Sage saw and coveted, he would buy right away, and there also were many expenses for the two houses.

Tuesday, 21 Iyar. I went with the Sage from the house on the Bridge into the new forest, where I had been with him before, on Sunday, 6 Nisan. I stayed at the inn, while the Sage rode on a horse into the forest. But he told me that if he did not return within three-quarters of an hour, then I had permission to leave the inn with the chaise for the City of London, and he would meet me on the road. Just as the end of the three-quarters of an hour came, the Sage returned to the inn, and we immediately returned home safely.

Sunday, 25 Iyar. For a reminder, on this day I sent a letter with R. Neta of Zamość to my esteemed father, may he live long, *to the Jewish community of Kalisz.

Monday, the first day of the new moon of Tamuz. For a reminder, how Falk insulted me on this day in the new house on the Bridge in the City of London, and how he insulted me on sabbath night in Schatz's house. *Also on the sabbath, 7 Tamuz, a bit.

Nestukh perhaps an attempt to transliterate the German *Nesseltuch*, meaning muslin.

with the French ambassador possibly indicating that Cosman travelled at Falk's bidding to the French king. The references to the journeys by members of Falk's inner circle are indicative of the various missions undertaken on his behalf.

whatever the Sage saw and coveted ZH criticizes Falk's insistence on purchasing whatever he saw and desired.

to the Jewish community of Kalisz [See above, note to fo. 25*a*, p. 127, on the practice of sending letters care of the Jewish community.]

Also on the sabbath, 7 Tamuz [This in fact suggests that the whole entry was written later than the given date of Monday, the first day of the new moon of Tamuz.]

|fo. 29a| For a reminder: *on Monday, 2 Tamuz, the merchant Krumbold came to me and showed me a written note from *R. Laze the windbag *that he had collected in my name in Rotterdam in the amount of £130. 0s. 0d. The merchant wanted me to sign, but I responded to him in a disparaging manner. On Tuesday I sent a letter to R. Laze the windbag.

Friday, 13 Tamuz. Good news! Today he finished the construction in the camp, that is, only from wood. He made a beam in the holy camp, also a domain all round, near the beam (that is, in a drawing on paper), and also great holy names upon them. He also made on the two windows of the holy camp two plaques covered with holy names on both sides, very beautifully executed, as well as a domain of holy names, as wide as a page of paper, greatly embellished, with holy names. Moreover, the entire camp was covered, outside and inside, with a linen cloth, with nothing else inside it. When it was six o'clock in the afternoon, he ordered me that within half an hour everyone must leave the house, and so I did. I prepared myself as he had ordered. The Sage entered the camp with two tallow candles, and he stayed there until half an hour before the sabbath, and then returned. We went home, and I did not know what he had done. I was inside the camp only on Sunday, and I did not see any change, I found it just as it had been—only I saw that the table in the holy camp was covered with a tablecloth, and on it was ink and a quill.

Wednesday, 18 Tamuz. For a reminder: at five o'clock in the afternoon, *it rained and hailed here, in a really unnatural way. The hailstones were almost like pieces of ice, as big as a walnut. This was a wondrous thing, because it was so very hot, more than I can tell.

Saturday night. He returned home from the house on the Bridge, and he had practised only a little bit the entire week. He went to the camp only at midnight, to recite *Tikun ḥatsot*, and there still was nothing more in the camp than on the afore-

on Monday, 2 Tamuz [Since ZH dates the entry as 'Monday, the first day of the new moon of Tamuz', this was presumably added in the evening as that would already have been 2 Tamuz.]

R. Laze the windbag [See note to fo. 3a, p. 75.]

that he had collected in my name [Presumably, that Laze had taken credit for which he said that ZH would serve as guarantor.]

it rained and hailed here ... unnatural way [The combination of rain and hail in the summer months, while not a usual occurrence, is more likely to happen in England than in the continental climate of eastern Europe to which ZH was accustomed; but ZH seems always to have been on the lookout for unnatural occurrences that could be attributed in some way to Falk.]

Tikun ḥatsot [A kabbalistic liturgy recited at midnight to mourn the destruction of the Temple in Jerusalem.]

mentioned Friday. It remained so the entire week, and here is the proof: that on the aforementioned Wednesday I brought a gentile, a carpenter, into the camp |fo. 29b| to see where the rain had entered the camp. On 17 Tamuz he was not in the synagogue, but remained here on the Bridge, even on the holy sabbath day, 21 Tamuz; he said that he had to stay here. And, indeed, he practised within the camp from half an hour before six o'clock. He practised for about half an hour, returned, and said that he had already accepted upon himself the start of the sabbath.

Sunday, 21 Tamuz. The Sage bought books from the esteemed master *David Haes for three guineas that were worth five guineas. That night the Sage took the holy names, and he himself brought all the books home. He stayed at home until Monday night, when he returned to the Bridge.

On Wednesday, 18 Tamuz, the Sage had surely received a note from the Little One that his promissory note, which he received twice each year, had fallen due.

On Monday, 9 Tamuz, the Sage had given me 5s. 6d. for shoes.

Friday, 27 Tamuz. The Sage gave me 4s. 6d. to buy a waistcoat, and also a pair of stockings, for 2s. 6d.; all in all, he gave me 7s. 0d.

For a reminder: the Sage practised in the camp today for about a quarter of an hour, just half an hour before the sabbath. He returned, and stayed here on the Bridge this sabbath, too. This day the carpenter set up *the weighing table in the camp.

Wednesday night, 4 Av. I was melting the lead for the weighing table; while doing so I left the room. The Sage entered the room, took an iron ladle, and wanted to remove the dross from the molten lead. He had forgotten, however, that the ladle had been in the water and was still wet; the moment he stuck it into the lead, there was a reaction. The whole room was full of lead, as was the Sage's clothing, the hat [*indecipherable*] on his head, and his hair. Nonetheless, he suffered no harm from this, which was a great miracle, since this could have killed him.

And indeed, on Friday, 5 Av, the Sage went to the house, and on the sabbath he recited the traditional blessing thanking God for deliverance from disaster.

Sunday, 21 Tamuz the correct date on Sunday would have been 22 Tamuz.

David Haes possibly David b. Anschel Has; see C. Roth, 'Membership', 184.

the weighing table presumably a flat table on which a scale could be placed. [If the scale was needed for Falk's alchemical endeavours, it might have been necessary to bring in a carpenter to ensure that it was absolutely horizontal so that there would be no distortion of weights.]

|fo. 30a| *Sunday, 7 Av.* For a reminder, *R. Isaac, the son of Hannah, the wife of R. Hayim [?] R. Bendayt of Kalisz, left here. He had been here about fifteen days, and he purchased goods together with one *R. Abraham of Lissa.

Tuesday, 16 Menahem Av. R. Cosman came back to London, and he visited him and her in their two houses.

On Friday, 27 Tamuz, I had received from the rebbetsin, with his knowledge, *six cubits of linen for two shirts, each cubit for 1s. 2d. I paid the tailor from my own pocket, for which my expenses were 3s. 0d., *and the linen was purchased for 8s. 9d.

Tuesday night, 2nd day of the new moon of Elul. He started to do something related to his rituals. He began alone in his camp, at two o'clock in the morning, and he ordered me, R. Mann, and R. Itzik of Zamość to stay upstairs in the special room, and *we studied whatever we wanted. After two hours the Sage came upstairs and *brought holy names with him, copied in his house, and he told R. Mann to write on it what he would tell him. R. Mann did so and signed his name, and on the other side he had R. Itzik sign his name as well, as testimony. Within the holy names was something hard, surely some gold that was worth a lot. And thus it was for hours, the Sage stayed with them in the upstairs room for about an hour. The room was clean, with a nice tablecloth, and two candles on it.

*On Monday, 29 Menahem Av, the Little One had been imprisoned for a debt of £12. 0s. 0d. and he sent me a letter imploring the Sage to help him with eight guineas so he could be released from prison. But this was to no avail, for afterwards other debts fell due, and it was not possible to have him released for so little.

R. Isaac, the son of Hannah, the wife of R. Hayim [?] R. Bendayt of Kalisz [The genealogy here is unclear. Oron suggests that the missing word may have identified R. Hayim as the son of R. Bendayt, but does not comment on why R. Isaac is identified as the son of his mother, rather than as the son of his father which is more customary Jewish practice except in certain liturgical situations.]

R. Abraham of Lissa [ZH mentioned a Jew from Lissa on fo. 2a (see p. 72); but he does not say now whether this is the same person; one wonders how many Jews from Lissa would have visited London.]

six cubits of linen [A cubit was approximately 18 inches.]

and the linen was purchased for 8s. 9d. [The arithmetic here is not clear: 6 cubits of linen × 14 pence = 84 pence = 7s. 0d.; ZH does not say why the total would have been 8s. 9d.]

we studied whatever we wanted [Presumably, from the kabbalistic or standard religious works that Falk kept in his house.]

brought holy names with him possibly referring to amulets, examples of which he had in his house.

On Monday, 29 Menahem Av [That is, the previous day.]

Tuesday night, 8 Elul. The Sage ordered that R. Mann and R. Itzik should come, and they did. After midnight we went to the aforementioned special room and we studied. The Sage stayed in the camp until six o'clock and then returned. He ordered them to go to the synagogue, and they went in peace.

———

Friday, 10 Elul. The Sage was grieved, and he fasted. I urged him to eat, but he refused. I sat with him in his room, and we drew what belonged to the camp. Three-quarters of an hour after midday there was a great commotion in the camp. The Sage went to the camp, but he did not stay for even half of a quarter of an hour, and he returned |fo. 30*b*| to the first room. He ordered that no one should come down, and no one go up, and he sealed the entrance to the camp. When we had been seated in the room for half an hour, there were two great commotions, one after the other, and then the Sage ordered me to tell everyone to leave the house, and I stayed alone with the Sage in the house. The Sage immediately went and immersed himself in nine *kabin* of water, even though his legs were swollen and he was in danger; nevertheless, he did nine *kabin*, and he went into the camp. He ordered me to stay downstairs for about three quarters of an hour, and then he ordered me that immediately after this time I should come. He made a sign at the entrance to the camp and said, *'It has already passed.' He returned from the camp and we went home; this was one hour before the sabbath.

———

Sunday night, 13 Elul. The Sage told me that if he knew the whereabouts of R. Barukh, he would use some ploy to bring him because he needed him, and he immediately succeeded in this.

For a reminder: on Saturday night, 12 Elul, *the madness returned to the boy Isaac, the son of R. Simhah Levy, because the Sage *had been obliged to cancel what he had begun for him the first time. The Sage had said so to R. Mann on Tuesday, the

---

'It has already passed.' [Presumably, some evil that Falk was trying to avert.]

the madness returned to the boy Isaac ZH discusses Isaac the madman, about whom he had written six months earlier (see entry for 24 Adar II on fo. 27*b*, p. 135); it seems that the cure he had effected had apparently been only temporary. According to ZH, Falk had foreseen that the cure would not be permanent, and a week earlier he had said as much to R. Mann. Nonetheless, Falk promised that the youth's condition would not be as serious as before. [The boy is referred to here as the son of R. Simhah Levy, whereas earlier he was referred to as R. Simhah Segal; the two names may be considered synonyms since 'Segal' is an acronym for *segan levi* or 'deputy levite' and is often used as a surname by descendants of the biblical tribe of Levi.]

had been obliged to cancel what he had begun for him the first time Falk had been forced to cancel [or perhaps reverse?] his earlier adjurations of the dybbuk in possession of the boy (the *kelipah*). [The text goes on to explain that this had happened only eleven days previously.]

second day of the new moon of Elul, when he cancelled. The Sage had said that he would see a wondrous thing, that the youth would be mad, but not as much as before, and so it was.

Monday night, 14 Elul. The Sage told me that he had had an argument with R. Cosman, for he had already taken from R. Cosman the sum of £360. 0s. 0d., and moreover he told me that R. Cosman did not have enough to complete the job; for that reason he wished to leave this place before Hanukah. He also told me other things.

Sunday, 19 Elul. At dusk the Sage went to his room at Collier's on the Bridge, and he ordered that R. Mann, together with R. Itzik of Zamość and R. Jacob Barbariski, stay in his house on the Bridge. The Sage told me that he might have to deal with his things in his room until midnight, but he practised only until ten o'clock. *He returned from his camp happy, wearing his *kitl*. We returned to the house, and *found students busy studying.

Thursday, 23 Elul. Early in the morning, the Sage went to his room at Collier's on the Bridge, where he practised for about half an hour and returned home. From there, I went with him to the forest.

|fo. 31a| Today I went to the forest with the Sage, and he practised in the forest for about two and a half hours. I was sick, Heaven forfend, and the Sage returned; I left the forest with him. He went around the forest and came home by a different route. He also went to *the nobleman's country house in the village of Upton but he merely looked at the house and we came home safely. *He stayed at the house until nearly eight o'clock at night. R. Mann and R. Itzik of Zamość were in the house on the Bridge, in the downstairs room. The Sage had ordered, before going to the forest, that no one should go upstairs until we returned, and they did as he had asked. When we came to the house on the Bridge, the Sage went upstairs, opened his camp, and looked into it and closed it up, saying that his time had not yet come; he had told me

He returned from his camp [ZH reports (Sunday, 19 Elul) that Falk went to his 'room' but returns from his 'camp', which may shed some light on the relationship between the two.]

found students busy studying [ZH does not identify 'the students'; perhaps he is referring to the young people mentioned earlier as having been sent to Falk for an education. Presumably they were studying Torah.]

the nobleman's country house in the village of Upton this is where Theodore Stephen de Stein (Baron von Neuhoff) had lived before he was imprisoned for debt.

He stayed at the house [The preceding text suggests that he had left the nobleman's country house because ZH reports that they 'came home safely', but since the text that follows says that 'R. Mann and R. Itzik of Zamość were in the house on the Bridge', and continues 'When we came to the house on the Bridge', Falk's movements here are not entirely clear.]

that his time was until ten o'clock at night. Then *I went to the landlord Collier's place to hear what was new, and *the gentile told me that there had been *a great commotion upstairs inside the camp at noon, which was the time that the Sage had begun to practise in the forest. I went with the Sage to the water, where he stayed for about two hours, standing all the time and gazing at the water. Before we had left the house, the Sage had lit the candles in his room near his camp and he ordered R. Mann and R. Itzik of Zamość to recite psalms, and they began. He also lit a large wax candle, just as he had lit a wax candle within the camp. The Sage stood by the water for about an hour, and he ordered me to go to the house and tell R. Mann and R. Itzik of Zamość to recite psalms, that is, Psalm 119 and the fifteen 'Songs of Ascent' [Pss. 120–34], and repeat them over and over until the Sage's return, and so they did. And as they were reciting Psalm 120 for the third time, there was a great commotion within the camp. When I returned with the Sage they told him, and he said that this must have happened during verse 3, 'What can you profit, what can you gain'. The Sage was happy, and he forthwith entered the camp wearing a *kitl*. He practised for about half an hour, returned, and blessed God that he now had at his disposal *the whole camp from Collier's house, inside his camp, that he had not been permitted to touch, and not even to see, for the past three years. He was enveloped by joy, and he immediately set up the camp with holy names, as necessary. The Sage also revealed to me that he had been compelled to cut the rope that had been made with such perfect beauty and that belonged to the *nine camps, in order to practise with it here on the Bridge. He ceased, and sealed the camp, and he said that he had to leave the house on the morrow, God willing, on Friday before noon, and so he did.

Friday 24 Elul. On the way the Sage lost the scabbard of the sword with which he had practised. When we came to the house he realized this; he had not tarried from the forest to the house.

|fo. 31*b*| The Sage went to the house before midday, and he had a reason for that.

I went to the landlord Collier's place to hear what was new ZH went to the house on the bridge to hear if anything had happened in their absence. The 'landlord Collier' was apparently the son of the original landlord, who had died; see diary entry for Tuesday night, 14 Shevat, fo. 26*b*, p. 132 above).

the gentile told me [Presumably, a reference to Collier.]

a great commotion upstairs . . . practise in the forest [The commotion could have been an explosion; ZH seems to imply that the event that occurred was somehow related to what Falk was doing in the forest at that time.

the whole camp from Collier's house, inside his camp, that he had not been permitted to touch [The relationship between the camp and Collier's house is not clear, nor why it was that Falk had not been permitted access to it.]

nine camps [ZH does not elucidate.]

Sunday, 26 Elul. The Sage immersed himself in nine *kabin*.

Monday. After the afternoon prayer, the Sage went to his room in Collier's house. Then he summoned me and told me to take the holy names *that had been placed in front of the inner gate of the camp, and he remained about one hour. He returned and paid £3. 13s. 0d., for renting the house, but *he did not want to pay what I owe the gentile Collier.

Tuesday. Early in the morning, after eight o'clock, I went with the Sage to Collier's house and waited there in his camp for about half an hour. *When he returned we went home *to prepare for the holy festival, although the Sage had sworn last Sunday that he wanted to come home only at prayer time, and after the prayer he wanted to return in a party-chaise to the Bridge. Nevertheless, he did not keep to his vow, and a word to the wise is sufficient.

On the eve of Rosh Hashanah *he argued with me over the walls of the sukkah, and swore to me that I had profited more than 3s. 0d. from them, but I had not profited even a single penny. I could not control my anger, and I cursed him.

He had expenses for the holy festival of Rosh Hashanah of about £6. 0s. 0d. for food and drink and other things: to redeem pledges and also *worthless charities, more than fifteen guineas, but to me he gave not a penny, he only redeemed my black garment, for 4s. 6d., for his own respect.

|fo. 32a|

5511 [1750/1], here in London, may it be propitious

Tuesday, 6 Tishrei. After midday the Sage went with Gedaliah to the Bridge, and the Sage was in his camp. He intended to go to his room at Collier's; moreover, *he had

---

that had been placed in front of the inner gate of the camp [Another small clue as to the disposition of the camp.]

he did not want to pay what I owe the gentile Collier [ZH does not clarify why he had a separate debt to Collier.]

When he returned [ZH does not say where Falk had gone while he was waiting for him.]

to prepare for the holy festival [i.e. to prepare for Rosh Hashanah, which would begin just a few days later. 'Preparations' could well mean the recitation of the traditional penitential prayers or *seliḥot*, but of course Falk may have made more esoteric preparations.]

he argued with me over the walls of the sukkah ... but I had not profited even a single penny [ZH had presumably purchased wood to make the walls of the sukkah that would be needed for the festival of Sukkot a couple of weeks later, and Falk was accusing him of being less than honest in his accounting.]

worthless charities ZH calls them this because of Falk's refusal to give him any money.

he had sent his box perhaps the equipment he needed for his esoteric practices, since he intended to remain for a few days [or perhaps simply the regular possessions he would need for that time].

sent his box with Gedaliah to Collier's, and then regretted this, saying that he was afraid, for *he might have to spend Yom Kippur in the forest. Accordingly, he did not go to Collier's, but returned to the house at 35 Prescot Street, and I do not know what he did.

Wednesday, 7 Tishrei. I went with the Sage to the house on the Bridge, and I bought two wax candles, each costing 10*s*. 0*d*. The Sage entered the camp—this was at eight o'clock at night—and he stayed about half an hour. He called me and told me to summon R. Mann, and also R. Itzik of Zamość, and also that I should go to the house to bring two pairs of candlesticks, two tablecloths, and candles. He ordered me to clear the upstairs room and put the candles on the table; they would engage in study until he gave a sign. I did his bidding, and the Sage practised in his camp, wearing a *kitl*, for about three hours, before returning to the house at 35 Prescot Street, while R. Mann and *the other person remained with me until dawn and then they went to the synagogue. As for myself, the Sage sent word that I should remain in the house and not come out until he bade me, for two reasons: the first, because of his rituals, to which I was accustomed; and the second, because of [*indecipherable*] the trickery in connection with R. Cosman. I stayed alone in the house until eight o'clock at night.

Wednesday night, 8 Tishrei. The Sage came with Gedaliah and bathed and also immersed himself in nine *kabin*. Afterwards he entered the camp, wearing his *kitl*, and he practised for about two hours. He returned to the house at 35 Prescot Street and ordered me to come to the house early in the morning, for he intended to go to the forest, *even though it was the eve of Yom Kippur.

**Eve of Yom Kippur.* After leaving the synagogue early in the morning, I went to the forest with the Sage, and he walked round the forest before entering his domain. Afterwards, when he had entered his domain, he ordered me to remain in our domain with the horses. He entered the domain and engaged in his rituals for more than an hour and a half, and we returned to the house at 35 Prescot Street. He also revealed to me that there had been an accident in which he had almost cut his cheek, for he had

---

he might have to spend Yom Kippur in the forest [Yom Kippur would take place four days later.]

the other person [Presumably R. Itzik of Zamość, since no one else is mentioned.]

even though it was the eve of Yom Kippur [Strictly speaking, the eve of Yom Kippur would be on 9 Tishrei.]

Eve of Yom Kippur. After leaving the synagogue early in the morning [The morning service on the eve of Yom Kippur traditionally starts very early, at six o'clock or even earlier, because of the long penitential prayers recited on that day.]

held the sword in his mouth with the blade the wrong way round and a branch had hit it, and his mouth would have been slashed except that He [the guardian of Israel] neither slumbers nor sleeps [Ps. 121: 4].

|fo. 32b| Even when he returned from the forest, the Sage did not want to enter the inn near the forest, as we normally did. Rather, he went to the village of Stratford, to the Three Birds Inn, where there was a little garden. The Sage stood near the water, and he told me that this was *the boundary of the water.

Also, I forgot to write that on Wednesday night, when the Sage came to me with Gedaliah, he had forgotten his keys, and also the key to the camp. He sent me to bring the keys, but it was almost nine o'clock, and *nine o'clock was the time to enter the camp. He had no choice but to utter a holy name so that the camp gate opened of its own accord, and when I returned from the house with the key, the Sage came out of the camp wearing a *kitl*—wonder of wonders!

Sunday, 11 Tishrei. The Sage gave me 5s. 6d. for shoes.

Before nightfall, the Sage ordered me to go to R. Mann and R. Itzik and tell them that they must come tonight. I went to the house on the Bridge, and at nine o'clock the Sage came, and R. Mann and R. Itzik were there. The Sage began to engage in his rituals at one o'clock in the morning, wearing his *kitl*. R. Mann and R. Itzik stayed with me for the night in the kitchen, until nearly seven o'clock, when they went to the synagogue, while the Sage remained in the camp until half past seven, then he sealed the camp and I returned with him safely to house at 35 Prescot Street.

Eve of the holy festival of Sukkot. After we left the synagogue following the morning service, the Sage sent me to the house on the Bridge to seal the camp gate with blank paper above his seal. Then he ordered me to wait afterwards at that house for about a quarter of an hour, and I did his bidding.

Tuesday, *the fifth of the intermediate days of Sukkot. The Sage sent me, R. Mann, and R. Itzik Zamość, as well as the youth R. Leib Danziger, to the Bridge and gave us something written, a kind of prayer, as well as holy names, on which he ordered us to

the boundary of the water [It would seem quite obvious that the edge marked the boundary, so perhaps the term 'boundary' here had esoteric connotations.]

nine o'clock was the time to enter the camp [Perhaps nine o'clock was deemed a significant time because nine is understood to symbolize completeness; also the Hebrew word for truth, *emet*, has a *gematriyah* of nine.]

the fifth of the intermediate days of Sukkot [In Jewish communities outside Israel the first two days of Sukkot are religious holidays, and these are followed by five days known in Hebrew as *ḥol hamo'ed*, termed in English 'intermediate days' but literally 'the weekdays of the festival'—they are still festive days, but the normal restrictions on work associated with religious holidays do not apply. They are

concentrate intensely. He ordered R. Mann to seal the camp gate |fo. 33a| with the paper that he had given me; I looked inside, and saw that there were dots in it. He ordered us to recite what was written while R. Mann was sealing the door, and after completing the sealing we should repeat from the beginning, reciting together what was written, and so we did. It was three o'clock in the afternoon.

On Tuesday night, the night of Hoshana Rabba, the Sage ordered that the sukkah be cleaned. The table was covered with a clean tablecloth, with four candles on it, and also four large wax candles near it. I also saw paper and a quill with ink on it. He practised there this night, and I did not know what he practised, I only heard him singing, and he also kindled the large lamp.

Saturday night was the night following the festival of Simhat Torah. The Sage went to the Bridge with Gedaliah and practised there in the camp till nearly midnight, and he returned to the house at 35 Prescot Street.

Thursday, 29 Tishrei. An argument erupted between me and the Sage because of Itzik, because of the lawsuit with Leib Plotzker. The Sage cursed me and my father, and I answered him in kind. Then he swore that I would die, and that quickly, because I deserved to die. He then said that if he had not acted on my behalf I would already have been dead; moreover, he said that he wanted to take revenge, and if the Holy One, blessed be He, would help him, he would destroy half of Poland, beginning with my father. I was tormented on that account, and I went to R. Cosman and told him about this. R. Cosman spoke with the Sage on Friday night, and the Sage made an excuse, saying that when he was angry he did not know what he was saying. On the contrary, he thought well of me, if the Holy One, blessed be He, would help him. With these words R. Cosman charmed me, otherwise it would have been my intention *to leave him.

Wednesday, 5 Heshvan. R. Cosman left for France; the Sage gave him permission for six weeks but no more, for several reasons.

Friday, 7 Heshvan. At midday the Sage ordered me to go to the Bridge, to clean the room downstairs, and also to kindle a fire inside. I did his bidding, and then |fo. 33b|

---

followed by another two days of religious holidays (Shemini Atseret and Simhat Torah), hence 'intermediate days'. The fifth of these intermediate days occupies a special place in the calendar; known as Hoshana Rabba ('The Great Salvation'), it has a ceremonial liturgy that marks the end of the season of divine judgement—one more chance to invoke God's mercy, even after the Day of Judgement on Yom Kippur. Perhaps this is why Falk conducted an esoteric ceremony on that day.]

to leave him [Presumably, to leave the service of the Sage.]

the Sage came with Gedaliah. The Sage first went to his room to sleep, and stayed there about half an hour. Then he came downstairs and practised alone in the parlour, and I do not know what he practised, I only heard that he ran downstairs at a great speed. I was amazed that he could run so fast because he is very fat, and because his leg was swollen. Afterwards he went to his camp, wearing a *kitl*, but he did not stay very long. He returned and sealed the camp, as was his custom, and he went to the house at 35 Prescot Street. He ordered me to wait here almost until the sabbath, and then to extinguish the candles that he had lit on the table in the parlour. I stayed about six minutes after he left, and I sat in the parlour and studied **Sefer malakhim*. I heard a commotion in the camp, and I ran after the Sage and told him, but he said that there was no time to go back because it was nearly the sabbath. So I returned alone, stayed almost until the sabbath, put out the lights, and went home.

From here I began to write in a red notebook, as I went to Holland, and I did not want to take this notebook with me. *The events until after 9 Av are written there, and now I shall write here, because that notebook is already full.

Wednesday, 13 Menahem Av, 5511 [1751], at nine o'clock in the morning, I brought the chaise to the Sage's house on the Bridge, and I went with the Sage *to the house of the *rabanit*. The workmen, the carpenters, began to build there on the Bridge, outside *not bayit. When we came to the house the Sage allowed R. Hertz the painter to complete a *tent over the superstructure to keep the rain out, and he also ordered the carpenter to finish the walls of the superstructure. When I was with the Sage in the house, and R. Moses Segal was there, too, the Sage gave me his watch. He told me to observe his seal that was hanging on a chain, and the chain was closed. I took the watch and placed it in my pocket, as people normally do, with the chain outside.

Sefer malakhim the 'Book of Angels'; a work by this name was composed by R. Judah Hehasid (published in Dan, 'Demonological Stories' (Heb.)). ZH may possibly be referring to another work, a magical book on the adjuration of angels (?).

The events until after 9 Av are written there [i.e. the events until after the Fast of the Ninth of Av were noted in another diary, now lost. Some nine months are thus missing from the narrative.]

to the house of the *rabanit* from here to the end of the diary ZH refers to Falk's wife by the Hebrew term *rabanit*, rather than 'rebbetsin', which derives from Yiddish, which he had used previously. [Perhaps the change is connected to the fact that she appears now to be separated from her husband and living in her own house.]

not bayit apparently a place name. The first word might possibly be an acronym for two English words connected to the second word in a hyphenated construction: '-House'.

a tent over the superstructure by 'tent' ZH might mean a roof (possibly a tiled roof). [This would be consistent with *ohel* as a protective structure. However, perhaps ZH uses 'tent' advisedly to suggest a canvas, to be stretched above the 'superstructure' (possibly, exposed rafters), to keep the rain out while the roof was being tiled.]

Another seal hung from this chain, as did the watch-key and another thing, all closed, as is the usual practice; I did not give it such close attention, for I thought it [the watch with the chain] could |fo. 34a| not possibly be lost, or [only] the entire chain [with everything on it] could be lost. Then the Sage summoned me to his room and *entrusted a certain completely sealed object to me. After that, at two o'clock in the afternoon, I went with the Sage and R. Cosman to the river, to see if the building had been finished. But when we came there the building was still not completed, and the Sage went to his room as before and spoke there with R. Cosman. I saw, however, that the Sage had some great worry on his mind, and while on the way, before we came to the river, the Sage took the aforementioned object from me, and he stayed there, by the river, for about three hours or more. Before we left, I looked at the watch, and all the seals were hanging from the chain. We left there, and R. Cosman went to his house and we went safely to our house. When we reached the house I gave him the watch to his hand, and I saw that the seal that he had cautioned me about had been lost. He was so greatly distressed that he could not go to the Bridge because of that. This was a great wonder, because something else also was hanging from the same link of the chain, and that remained, while the seal was lost; no doubt, this was a supernatural occurrence, and even if I had kept it in the innermost place it would still have been lost. But he was very greatly distressed the entire night.

Thursday, 14 Menahem Av. Today *my Master and Teacher ordered me to go to the house of the *rabanit*, that she should make a list of all the debts and pledges. She did so, and it came to *only £14. 0s. 0d. He was angry with her, and he said to me: 'My son, now I will reveal to you that *this woman is responsible for all my troubles. Because of her and the household expenses I pawned and sold all the gold that I had, and now I am in great danger, Heaven forfend, of losing all that I have.' I answered him, 'My Master and Teacher, why did you heed her?' He said, 'I am incapable of seeing distress and discord, and so to have peace I do what she would have me do—*even sell

---

entrusted a certain completely sealed object to me ZH asserts that the loss of this seal, which hung from the chain together with other items (the watch, the watch-key, and another object), was a miraculous event, and even if he had guarded it in a hiding place ('the innermost place') it still would have been lost.

my Master and Teacher from here to the end of the diary ZH refers to Falk as his 'Master and Teacher' (a title generally used by a disciple for his rabbi), instead of as 'the Sage'. The reason for the change is unclear.

only £14. 0s. 0d. He was angry with her [It is not clear what ZH means by 'only', since he goes on to say that Falk was angry with his wife about the amount.]

this woman is responsible Falk accuses his wife of wasting money, thus causing him to fall into serious debt. He was accordingly forced to pawn or sell the gold (apparently referring to the gold tablets that were to be used in the plating of other metals).

even sell the Torah scroll on the sabbath [This would of course be totally against Jewish law.]

the Torah scroll on the sabbath.' I remained silent, and a word to the wise is sufficient. He declared that if the Holy One, blessed be He, would save him this time, then he intended to leave here before Rosh Hashanah with R. Cosman, so that no one should know his whereabouts until he had finished his affairs, God willing. And I began to weep at hearing that a holy man, may there be many like him in Israel, should be in such danger. But he said, 'My son, Heaven forfend that I should leave you—wherever I go, you shall go with me.'

Thursday night, 15 Menahem Av. My Master and Teacher ordered me to stay there on the Bridge and said that I had to be with him, but that I should serve him wholeheartedly and willingly, to which I agreed, and I stayed with him.

|fo. 34b| *Friday, 15 Menahem Av.* My Master and Teacher was waiting for R. Cosman, who promised to bring the money to buy *the gold and silver for a cover for the Torah scroll and for other ceremonial items. *This day was the time to consecrate them within the domain of the camp, and R. Cosman had already promised to be ready this day, and he surely did whatever was humanly possible. R. Cosman came at four o'clock in the afternoon and wept, saying that he could not, but he had a great obligation, without any doubt whatsoever, for Tuesday. When he heard this my Master and Teacher began to sob and scream bitterly. He called me, and said, 'My son, my son, I am marked for death, Heaven forfend, because *I must bring thirteen gold tablets on Monday night, and I am afraid. They must be engraved with drawings and holy names, but I still do not have the gold. If I do not bring these tablets, everything will be lost, and I, too, will be in danger.' And his appearance changed and he said,

the gold and silver for a cover for the Torah scroll [The cover for a Torah scroll—like other ceremonial textiles such as the curtain covering the ark and the pelmet above it, and the cloth covering the desk from which the Torah was read—was (and is) richly embroidered with gold and silver thread, and sometimes also with pearls.]

This day was the time to consecrate them [ZH does not say, but 15 Av is the summer equinox which probably had esoteric significance for Falk. After that day the nights become longer, and since the night is an appropriate time for studying Torah one may speculate that perhaps the 15th could be considered an appropriate time for dedicating ceremonial textiles relating to the Torah. Some consider 15 Av as the proper time to start spiritual preparations for Rosh Hashanah as each day from then on brings us closer to the month of Elul, when such preparations begin in full force.]

I must bring thirteen gold tablets Falk had to prepare, by the following Tuesday, thirteen gold tablets inscribed with divine names. However, since the gold tablets had been sold because of his pressing financial circumstances he could not fulfil this commitment, thus placing himself in great danger. [Thirteen is of esoteric significance in the Jewish tradition, representing the blending of diversity into oneness: the letters comprising the word *eḥad*, 'one', have a combined numerical value of 13, as do the letters of the word *ahavah*, 'love'. See e.g. <http://www.betemunah.org/thirteen.html>.

'Go immediately and bring me a coach and I will go home.' I went, and meanwhile he remembered that *Friday night is the night of his seal, and he had to remain on the Bridge. When I returned with the coach, I found him sobbing bitterly, and I fell on his neck and wept with him, and comforted him. He told me that he had no time, and *he had to be in the appointed place on *29 Menahem Av. Now, however, he had to prepare everything and build a building called *the domain of *not bayit*, and also [bring] chairs and tables, as well as mirrors and silver vessels; all that would cost more than £500. 0s. 0d. and still he has nothing. He wept and wailed and said, 'What shall I do with my people, for they, too, are in danger like me!' He implored R. Cosman, saying to him: 'Listen to what I bid you, and I beg you not to abandon my wife and faithful servant, lest, Heaven forfend, they become dependent on charity.' So R. Cosman left the house, broken-hearted and despondent, saying 'Perhaps God will have mercy', and that he still had another commitment from a certain merchant, but the latter had gone today to the city though perhaps he would return today. R. Cosman left, and it was raining heavily. Then my Master and Teacher summoned me. He ordered me to sit with him and write what he would tell me. I began to write today, Friday, 15 Menahem Av, 5511. Then I wrote down *a riddle, all in Aramaic. It was a wondrous thing, *and I do not have permission to copy, only this I remember, that I wrote that the sanctity of his sword has greater power than **matranota demalka*, and what it did was not with its owner's permission. Moreover, I understood that about the time of 8 Tamuz, *when he disappeared, it was a *teimah

Friday night is the night of his seal ['Friday night' means the start of the sabbath; the meaning of 'the night of his seal' is unclear.]

he had to be in the appointed place [Either Falk did not say or ZH does not tell.]

29 Menahem Av [This is the day before the first day of the new moon of Elul, which marks the start of the penitential period leading up to Rosh Hashanah; this may have had some esoteric significance.]

the domain of *not bayit* [The word *bayit* normally means a house, and since it is used here to refer to something that had to be built it is reasonable to assume that this is its meaning here too. '*Not*', however, is written in a way that indicates that it is an abbreviation but there is no clue as to what it might stand for.]

a riddle possibly ZH characterized Falk's incantations thus as they were written in Aramaic, a language with which ZH was unfamiliar.

and I do not have permission to copy i.e. in the diary, and the following is from his memory alone. In addition to the quotations from what he had written at Falk's behest, ZH also includes his own thoughts. The dictation appears meaningless to ZH, who also states that it was written 'in Aramaic', possibly because of the two-word phrase in Aramaic, *matranota demalka*. He marks the words that are incomprehensible to him with a superior line.

matranota demalka an Aramaic term meaning 'the king's consort', i.e. the queen, in an apparent reference to the *sefirah* of Malkhut.

when he disappeared ZH may possibly be alluding to an event that took place a month previously, when Falk vanished from home for some time.

teimah in Hebrew, the term *teimah* (*taf, yod,*

*3546, that is, he disappeared from the world. They cause this to themselves, and also *it was 1000 *shavu'ah meyerosav. The sign that *what happened on the night of 13 Menahem Av in the window, when we were in *not bayit*. This was the sign from the sword, *that he gave permission to *release them because |fo. 35a| he had learned from *hane'elamim umeha'elmim*, that they would not become corporeal, and because of רוסאש* them, *on the Wednesday before. Consequently, the seventh day is the seventh day and corporeality remains. He also ordered me to write: 'The Lord lives, *for I have already opened the gate in the mountain and have not yet locked it. If I come there, I shall break it and we shall also be lost. The Lord lives, even though you are in your sanctity.' *I have forgotten what else I wrote, except that at the end I wrote that *I would not be silent nor would I be still until I had separated the

mem, heh) could be understood as a transposition of the letters of *mitah*, death. [According to the Even-Shoshan dictionary, the word *temah* (properly spelled without the *yod* that ZH uses) is a talmudic expression for 'wonderment'. The word preceding *teimah* is indecipherable.]

3546 the Hebrew word *teimah*, spelled as above, has the numerical value 455; ZH possibly jumbled the order of the numerals to maintain its esoteric nature. [In fact the total is 455, but 3546 may still represent an esoteric manipulation.]

it was 1000 it was a wonder; the two words *elef* (= 1,000) and *pele* (wonder) have the same numerical value of 1,000. [The 'wonder' would be that he 'turned' the sword, i.e. changed its direction, by changing the order of the letters in the phrase.]

shavu'ah meyerosav I cannot offer an interpretation of this phrase.

what happened on the night of 13 Menahem Av ZH refers to what happened on this night, when he lost the seal that was suspended from the chain. We learn from this passage that he blamed this on the sword that 'flew' and turned about. This entire passage describes the construction of the new house (*bayit*); it is unclear whether it was a residential house (*bayit*) or a synagogue (*beit keneset*).

that he gave permission to release them the sense might possibly be that the loss of the divine names was alluded to by the sword, which apparently flew through the air (as it had in the past). This was therefore an allusion to Falk, who received a 'sign' that permission had been granted (to the forces of evil?).

release them the names?

hane'elamim umeha'elmim the meaning of these words is unclear; possibly 'that they would not become corporeal'.

רוסאש possibly *she'asur*, that it is forbidden (by reversing the letters); or *she'asru*, that they forbade (by transposing the letters).

on the Wednesday before possibly referring to an occurrence on Wednesday, 13 Av, when Falk gave ZH a chain from which Falk's watch and his seals ('and one other thing') hung. Charms also hung from the chain, but only the seals were lost, i.e. were prevented from becoming corporeal.

for I have already opened the gate in the mountain possibly an attempt by Falk to write a spell against the powers of evil.

I have forgotten what else I wrote the entire passage is written in fragmentary and incomprehensible language. ZH apparently tried to dredge up from his memory Falk's dictation to him, but he himself writes that he forgot much; Falk's forbidding him to commit the dictation to writing in the diary explains why much is missing.

I would not be silent ... into two kingdoms the

universe from the world into two kingdoms. Then my Master and Teacher took what I had written, folded it, and sealed it with his writing. This was *one hour before the beginning of the sabbath, and he ordered all of us to go downstairs. Then he summoned me, and gave me orders, saying that if he should not return, Heaven forfend, till a quarter of an hour before the sabbath, then I should write on a bit of paper the following, in square letters: *לא שהשבת לכולהון; לא כי אליהו השבית שבת; לא כי לנו המנוחה עד משמר מוצאי שבת; לא כי לה' המנוחה. And then I should knock three times with my finger at the camp gate and seal this writing on the gate, and so I did. I went back downstairs, and the aforementioned went out immediately, and called us to go upstairs and pray, and welcome the sabbath in joy. After praying the Master and Teacher recited kiddush over wine and recited the blessing over bread, *but he did not eat the bread, and left it on the table. From this night on he did not taste any food, he only drank tea and coffee until Thursday, 21 Menahem Av. I implored him to eat something, but he replied that he had a great reason for this, in particular refraining from eating any kind of bread. In short, we really had *great mourning on this Shabat

language of an oath taken by Falk to do something; possibly alluding to the separation of the domain of *tevel* ('universe'), meaning evil, abomination (based on Lev. 18: 23) from that of *heled*, meaning 'world'.

one hour before the beginning of the sabbath the instructions that ZH received on the eve of Shabat Nahamu (the Sabbath of Consolation after the fast of the Ninth of Av marking the destruction of the Temples in Jerusalem) included the writing of divine names, knocking three times with a finger on the entrance door, writing additionally on the names, and placing them on the entrance door of the occult assembly (the new premises) by the river. [The time immediately before the beginning of the sabbath is an auspicious time in the Jewish tradition.]

square letters i.e. the form of letters used in printing, rather than the cursive script of handwriting.

לא שהשבת...לה' המנוחה Falk's text here seems to have cryptic implications; its surface meaning appears to be 'There is no repose for us, because there is no repose for the Lord, for Elijah did not *hishbit* the *shabat* [*hishbit* being apparently related to the word for resting on *shabat*, the sabbath, but incomprehensible in context] until the departure of the sabbath' (i.e. Saturday night). Perhaps the explanation is that at this time (1751), Falk was a crypto-Sabbatian. Hints to this effect can be found in ZH's reconstruction of what Falk dictated to him, with the requirement to place superior dots above several letters—an established technique to hint that the combined numerical value of the letters so marked was of significance. One phrase Falk wanted to treat in this way was *lo shehashabat lekhulehon*, with the letters marked having a combined *gematriyah* of 814, equivalent to that of *shabetai tsevi* (Sabbatai Zevi). Similarly, the words *tishbi* and *shabat* could be understood as anagrams hinting at *shabetai*, [This is a somewhat condensed version of the rather fuller explanation in the Hebrew edition.]

but he did not eat ZH tells of Falk's fast for seven days, during which he ate nothing, and consumed only liquids. This fast had an occult reason which was most likely related to his working on the gold tablets. [According to Jewish law it is forbidden to fast on the sabbath except when it is also Yom Kippur.]

great mourning on this Shabat Nahamu supposed to be the 'Sabbath of Consolation', on which the *haftarah* (reading from the

Nahamu, may the Lord preserve us from experiencing further torment of this kind.

On *Friday, 14 Menahem Av, R. Cosman had brought the gold tablets. They were so thick that it was not possible to cut holy names through from one side to the other, and we were forced to wait until Monday to make them thinner with grindstones.

Monday, 18 Menahem Av. My Master and Teacher went into the street with R. Cosman, and I, too, rode with them to *the house on the water. It was my Master and Teacher's intention to consecrate the new house, but when we came there it was still not finished; all the same, my Master and Teacher practised there, and then we returned to the house on the Bridge.

Tuesday, 19 Menahem Av. My Master and Teacher completed those thirteen tablets with the holy names incised on them, and at night, after midnight, he entered the camp and ordered us to go downstairs. He instructed me to close the chain downstairs before the steps, and so I did. He ordered us not to sleep, Heaven forfend, and at *five o'clock after midnight on Tuesday night, he summoned me and told me to go to the house of the *rabanit* and stay until she gave a message through |fo. 35*b*| R. Isaac, and so I did. R. Isaac came at seven o'clock and said that I should ride immediately to R. Cosman, to inform him that he must come to the Bridge before midday. So R. Cosman came at eleven o'clock, my Master and Teacher spoke with him upstairs in his room, and then R. Cosman left. My Master and Teacher ordered me to accompany him to the street entrance, so I went with him. And when we got to just before the camp gate, there was a great commotion in the camp. R. Cosman ran outside, and I went back upstairs. But my Master and Teacher was quite upset about this, and said that this was the reason why he had ordered me to accompany him, since R. Cosman was in great danger. My Master and Teacher revealed to me that *R. Cosman had abandoned his disgusting ways and now undertook to be an honest man. He had sold

---

Prophets) is Isa. 40: 1–26, which begins with the word *nahamu* ('Comfort, O comfort My people'), after the three-week period of semi-mourning that culminates in the fast of the Ninth of Av.

Friday, 14 Menahem Av should read 15 Menahem Av.

the house on the water [The Hebrew edition glosses this as 'most likely the house on the Bridge', but that seems unlikely given the reference at the end of the sentence.]

five o'clock i.e. 5 a.m., Wednesday, 20 Menahem Av.

R. Cosman had abandoned his disgusting ways this passage alludes to the psychological transformation of R. Cosman (Cosman Lehmann: see Appendix A), who was known to be frivolous and had a bad reputation despite coming from a distinguished family. Cosman apparently became embroiled in business affairs (or perhaps affairs with women). He went from France to England, where he joined Falk's circle. In London he performed various tasks for Falk and was his contact with the outside world, that is, with the non-Jews who took an interest in Falk and his share in the manufactory in Upton he owned in partnership with gentiles. All this was out of piety, for supernatural things had happened to him, and he had been in danger even in his house, and R. Cosman had proof of these matters.

Wednesday, 20 Menahem Av. R. Cosman brought the gold to complete the gold chain, that cost a total of £360. 0s. 0d., and my Master and Teacher practised the whole week, day and night, in the camp, without tasting any food. Similarly, on that day R. Cosman also brought the *taipitin to form the partition of the domain of *not bayit*, and that cost another £12. 0s. 0d.

And today I took four *lamps with a Star of David that had been pawned for the last six years for nine guineas, and I redeemed them for the principal, without any interest at all.

Thursday, 21 Menahem Av. On this day and on Friday, the eve of the sabbath, my Master and Teacher practised with the gold chain, and on Friday he also practised with the silver chain, which was 38 oz. of silver *three times against the egg balance. He warned us, saying: 'If, Heaven forfend, one of you should take the slightest amount from the gold, he deserves death. It is better that the parings left from the cutting of the letters be lost than that any man's hand touch it, for one cannot be saved from the great and irreversible danger that awaits anyone who sins in this.'

Friday, 22 Menahem Av. Before six o'clock in the evening my Master and Teacher ordered us all to go downstairs. He entered the camp, stayed for about half an hour and left safely, and we went home. On the way he told me that he was greatly distressed, for he was in great danger, and *he stayed at home on the sabbath. On the sabbath day he was called to the Torah *for the fifth section of the portion of 'Ekev'.

---

his activities. He also supplied Falk with the gold tablets that the latter used for his metal-plating activities. Cosman's ties with prominent members of Christian society are documented in the letters of General Charles Rainsford (see Hills, 'Notes on the Rainsford Papers', 127–8). According to ZH, Falk sensed the dangers awaiting Cosman, and therefore ordered ZH to accompany him.

taipitin carpets or rugs used to cover walls.

lamps with a Star of David possibly lamps with a painted or embossed Star of David symbol. [Or possibly the brass *Judenstern* oil lamps in the shape of a Star of David that were fashionable in Germany from the eighteenth century on.]

three times against the egg balance [Not clear. Perhaps this relates to the fact that the *beitsah* (egg) is the smallest unit of weight used in the Talmud.]

he stayed at home on the sabbath [Meaning presumably that he did not go to Friday night prayers, since ZH tells us that he was called to the Torah the next day, which meant that he did go on Saturday morning.]

for the fifth section of the portion of 'Ekev' [Each weekly reading from the Torah is divided into seven sections, and a different

And on the sabbath, before the afternoon service, *he said not to let R. Moses Segal come before him, for he had a specific reason—not, Heaven forfend, because of any enmity. I understood the reason, and my Master and Teacher was greatly distressed the entire sabbath.

|fo. 36a| *Saturday night.* My Master and Teacher went with the *rabanit* to the house on the Bridge and stayed there. My Master and Teacher took her there deliberately, as one taking leave of his loved ones before his departure, Heaven forfend.

Sunday, 24 Menahem Av. R. Cosman, together with Mordecai of Dresden, visited my Master and Teacher, and at five o'clock they dined together, as if it were *the final meal before a fast. They stopped before six, and there was such grieving, may the Lord preserve us, quite as if it were the destruction of the Temple. At six o'clock Jacob Barbariski came, and he [Falk] had cleaned the gold and silver holy names on the chain. He ordered me to draw the bath for him, and so I did. Before midnight R. Cosman left there in great sorrow, and my Master and Teacher spoke with him privately and gave him something written, and, between them, *it was like the departure of the soul from the body.

|fo. 36b| *First, I gave R. Laze of Hamburg three guineas. And the following Friday, 2 Heshvan, on account, 2*s.* 0*d.*; a gold ring, for half a guinea, *first principal, 10*s.* 6*d.*; another half a guinea, close to the sabbath, 10*s.* 6*d.* On Thursday, 8 Heshvan, I gave him 2*s.* 0*d.* On Monday, 12 Heshvan, 33*s.* 0*d.* On Thursday, 15 Heshvan, *18 shillings: 1-6. On Friday, 16 Heshvan. I gave him 4*s.* 0*d.* and afterwards 7*s.* 0*d.*, so 11*s.* 0*d*; nine parcels of books for 4 shillings and a half, first principal 4*s.* 6*d.*

person is called to read each one. [In fact the people honoured in this way do not normally read themselves but merely recite the blessings before and after, while the text itself is chanted by a specialist on their behalf.] The fifth section of 'Ekev' covers Deut. 10: 12–11: 10, which includes a summary of the reasons for and results of obedience to God; this may or may not have been coincidence; people are not normally consulted as to which portion they should be called to but it is sometimes possible to indicate a preference.]

he said not to let R. Moses Segal come before him [The meaning here is unclear.]

the final meal before a fast in the sense of a large meal, as the final meal before a fast would be.

it was like the departure of the soul from the body ZH figuratively depicts Cosman's departure; he may have been sent on some dangerous mission by Falk; the meaning of this parting is unclear.

First, I gave R. Laze of Hamburg three guineas what follows is a list of expenditures and loans. [ZH does not say why he prepared such a list at this time.]

first principal [Perhaps meaning 'first instalment'.]

18 shillings: 1-6 ['1-6' is not clear; 18 shillings would correctly be written 18*s.* 0*d.*, but perhaps ZH meant 18 pence, which would indeed be one shilling and six pence, or 1*s.* 6*d.*]

On Monday night, 21 Heshvan, for sending a letter: 2*s*. 0*d*. On Friday, 24 Heshvan, I gave him 2*s*. 0*d*. On Saturday night, 25 Heshvan, I gave him half a guinea, 10*s*. 6*d*. On Monday, 27 Heshvan, I gave him 9*s*. 0*d*. On *Tuesday, 25 Heshvan, I gave him *eight and a half shillings: 6*s*. 6*d*. On Sunday, 11 Kislev, 16 pence: 1*s*. 4*d*.; *8 pence, I had to give 11 shillings as above re Friday, 16 Heshvan: 1-6. On Monday, 18 Kislev, 1*s*. 6*d*. On Wednesday, 20 Kislev, I had to give 18*s*. 6*d*. for expenses, and also for guarantees for the money that I loaned to add to [the account of] that Laze. *I received from R. Laze 4*s*. 0*d*., an additional 6*d*., and an additional 2*s*. 6*d*.: 8½. On Thursday, 21 *Adar II, I gave him 3*d*. On Sunday, 24 Adar II, I gave him 1*s*. 0*d*. Also for a letter from Italy—2*s*. 0*d*., and money for post from Portsmouth to here: 1*s*. 6*d*.

|fo. 37*a*–*b* blank|

|fo. 38*a*|

*1. For a woman experiencing difficulty in labour: give her milk from another woman and she will give birth quickly. Tested.

2. Another remedy: take the herb called marjoram, cook it in wine, and give her to drink, but it must be cooked in an earthenware vessel. Tested.

3. For a headache: take two or three radishes, crush them in a mortar, and take one quart of wine vinegar. Place in an earthenware vessel, and boil until only one half remains, then give it to the person to drink. Tested.

4. For sleep: take horseradish and cook in a little water, then chop up in a grinder and spread on the person until he sleeps. Tested and proven.

5. For a man who cannot urinate: take nine herrings and burn to ashes, or take butter and put together with the burnt herring, boil in water, and give him to drink. Tested and proven.

Tuesday, 25 Heshvan [Presumably, Tuesday, 28 Heshvan; this could actually be an error in the printed Hebrew edition, since the letter *heh* used to indicate five and the letter *ḥet* used to indicate eight are easily confused in poor light.]

eight and a half shillings: 6*s*. 6*d*. [This is an obvious error; eight and a half shillings should be 8*s*. 6*d*.]

8 pence . . . 1-6 [The arithmetic here is not clear.]

I received . . . 8½ [Because of the half-shilling mentioned at the end, the total would appear to be 9*s*. 0*d*., not 8*s*. 6*d*. (written by ZH as '8½').]

Adar II [A second month of Adar is added to the calendar in a leap year.]

1. For a woman experiencing difficulty in labour numbers have been added to this list of folk remedies and charms; many of the terms used are variants in Hebrew transliteration of the original German or Yiddish.

6. For epileptics: take an owl, put it in a pot, cover with a bowl, and keep it inside until it dies. Invert the bowl frequently. Then take the heart and the front [part of the] feet, make them into a powder, and give the person to eat often from the bowl, without cleaning it. I have tested this tradition received from King Saul, may he rest in peace.

7. For toothache: take nine peppercorns and garlic, crush them finely, and apply to the tooth for the whole night.

8. For a person hard of hearing, take sulphur, and take the smoke into the ear.

9. For gout: take a bone from a corpse and wood from gallows, make a charm, and hang it from the neck.

10. To remove lice from the head: take fat from a dog, boil it in red wine, and smear it on the head.

11. That a nursing woman should have milk: take grape leaves and boil in goat milk, and give her to drink. I have tested this.

12. For a person who has a wound or *tuberculosis on the neck: take dogs' faeces, burn it in a vessel, and give him to eat and drink.

13. To know if a sick person will live: take milk and put it in his urine; if it sinks, he will not live, but if it floats, he will live.

14. For a person who has a swollen body: let him take a quart of bearberries, together with the leaves, burn them to ashes, add two measures of wine, and let him drink.

15. For a person who is hoarse: take garlic and mix with water, drink it, and eat the garlic.

16. For the liver: take galbanum and burn it in front of his nose so that the smoke will enter his nose, and also take bread, while still warm, and place it on his belly.

|fo. 38b|

17. Another one: take heated black wool cloth and place it on his head while he is lying down.

18. To make a woman barren: let her drink the gall of a hare, or the urine of a deer, and she will be barren all her life.

19. To sell merchandise: take a thief's thumb and carry it with you, and you will sell all your merchandise.

tuberculosis on the neck [The term ZH uses, *shahefet*, is understood today as tuberculosis, but the phrase 'on the neck' suggests he probably meant something different— perhaps a swelling?]

20. *To make ink like gold: take an egg and remove its white, fill it with mercury, stop up the hole; put it under a chicken sitting on her eggs and the ink will acquire the appearance of gold.

21. To cause a person not to wake from his sleep: take the gall of a hare, and place a little in the sleeper's mouth; he will not awaken until someone urinates straight into his mouth.

22. For a cricket in the ear or other worms: take butter and much salt and mix them together, boil them in an earthenware vessel on the fire, and put drops in the ear, as hot as the person can bear, and it will come out immediately.

23. For jaundice: take wood and put it in water, and let him drink, and it will be beneficial; or take a live pigeon or a tench and tie it on his belly until it dies, and do so three times; but *he must vow not to eat until his dying day. Another one: take the hide of a kid just after skinning, while still warm, and place on the whole body, or the belly and the waist, and he will be cured.

24. For worms in the stomach: let him urinate in an earthenware pot. Put wormwood into it and cook well; while still hot, place on his belly the whole night and the worms will die.

25. For [*indecipherable*] fever: take a rope with which a thief was hanged, and hang it around his neck.

26. For a person who urinates blood: let him boil fat in water and drink for seven days.

27. For pregnancy: smear the woman's womb with bear fat.

28. To make a person laugh: put a frog's eyes in new wax, and tie them to the arm with new wool.

29. So that a sick person will sleep: take a goat's horn, set it on fire, and have the patient inhale the smoke until he smells of it.

30. *To determine whether a cow is kosher while it is still alive: stop up its nostrils forcefully, and if it immediately shakes it head, it is not kosher; otherwise it is kosher.

To make ink like gold i.e. to make gold-coloured ink.

he must vow not to eat he must vow not to eat a pigeon or a tench.

To determine whether a cow is kosher while it is still alive [The determination would normally be reached only after the examination of the state of internal organs after slaughter. Obviously there would be significant financial advantage if it could be done prior to slaughter.]

31. For dizziness: roast clover, and eat it in the morning on an empty stomach.

32. To make a person vomit: take saffron, mix with lukewarm water, and have him drink.

33. To make a person hated by everyone: take from his hair and place in his faeces while still warm, and immediately he will be hated by everyone.

34. If you want your wife to tell you what she has done all her life, take a frog's tongue and place it on her when she is sleeping and she will tell you.

35. For headache: cook oats in strong vinegar and lay the mixture on the person's forehead from ear to ear until he sweats.

36. A woman who hates her husband should take a calf's eye burnt to ashes, and spread on his foreskin during intercourse.

|fo. 39a|

37. To make a person tell you while he sleeps what he has done his entire life: take a goose's tongue and place it on his heart.

38. For a man who is impotent: take onion seed and fat, grind them in a mortar, mix with wine, and give him to drink.

39. To make a person sleep: take a dead man's tooth and place it beneath his head, without his knowledge.

40. To open a lock without a key: take a scorpion, burn it, and sprinkle it on. Another one: place a thief's finger on it.

41. For a bed-wetter: take a cock's comb, burn it, and give him to drink. Another one: take the inner skin of a gizzard, burn it, and give him to drink.

42. To cause all the diners to sleep: take the needle with which shrouds were sewn, and stick it into the tablecloth.

---

*From the book *Kabalat ma'aseh*, 4: 13. Against wild beasts, one should recite the verse 'You must be wholehearted with the Lord your God' [Deut. 18: 13]. *And these are the holy names: תית יעי ואה המה הליך. There were *thirteen who never died: Enoch;

From the book *Kabalat ma'aseh* I have not found any book by this name, or even the more accurate *Kabalah ma'asit* ('Practical Kabbalah'); possibly the term is simply ZH's appellation for a book of charms. (In fact the entire passage is copied from the book *Yalkut ḥadash*.)

And these are the holy names ZH forms five names from the initial letters of the five words in the verse cited.

thirteen who never died the phrase ZH uses is 'never tasted the taste of death'. [In fact fifteen people are listed; ZH may say 'thirteen' because it ties in with his two references to v. 13.]

*Eliezer; [Eved-]melekh the Ethiopian, who saved the prophet Jeremiah from the pit [Jer. 38: 7 ff.]; Batyah daughter of Pharaoh; Serah daughter of Asher; the seven sons of Korah; Elijah, of blessed memory; Moses; and R. Joshua the son of Levi.

*All the letters in order—mercy; and in reverse order—strict judgement.

*A rainbow without rain is strict justice; and with rain, mercy.

*Eliezer, Abraham's servant, is King Og of Bashan.

'From the dens of lions' [S. of S. 4: 8]—this is Edom; 'from the hills of leopards' [S. of S. 4: 8]—this is Ishmael, for the Holy One, blessed be He, went round offering them the Torah, but they refused.

*147 psalms correspond to the years of the patriarch Jacob, may he rest in peace.

*Moses recited eleven psalms, corresponding to the eleven tribes, that is, excluding the tribe of Simeon because of the events at Shittim [Num, 25: 1–15]:

>A prayer of Moses, etc.,
>You return man to dust' [Ps. 90],
>corresponding to
>'May Reuben live and not die' [Deut. 33: 6],
>since he repented;
>'O you who dwell in the shelter of the Most High' [Ps. 91],
>corresponding to Levi, who dwelt in the shade of the Holy One,
>blessed be He, in the Temple Courts.
>'A psalm. A song; for the sabbath day.
>It is good to praise' [Ps. 92],
>corresponding to Judah [after whose birth his mother said],
>'This time I will praise the Lord' [Gen. 29: 35].
>'The Lord is king, He is robed in grandeur' [Ps. 93],
>corresponding to the tribe of Benjamin,
>who is in the shade of the Holy One, blessed be He;
>'God of retribution, Lord' [Ps. 94],

Eliezer Abraham's servant, as identified in the Midrash.

All the letters in order—mercy; and in reverse order—strict judgement *Yalkut ḥadash*, Amsterdam edn., fo. 60b. 'All the letters' refers to all the letters of the Hebrew alphabet.

A rainbow ... mercy *Yalkut ḥadash*, fo. 61b.

Eliezer ... Bashan *Yalkut ḥadash*, fo. 16a.

147 psalms ... may he rest in peace *Yalkut ḥadash*, fo. 93b.

Moses recited eleven psalms ... *Yalkut ḥadash*, fo. 94a. [The text that follows is perhaps supposed to be a list of the eleven psalms that Moses recited, but only seven are actually mentioned. As ZH explains later, the list comes from *Yalkut ḥadash*, fo. 92. Each psalm cited relates to a different tribe, and the logic of the connection is explained.]

corresponding to the tribe of Gad,
which brought forth Elijah, of blessed memory,
who overcomes *the destructive agents of the nations of the world;
'Come, let us sing joyously to the Lord' [Ps. 95],
corresponding to Issachar,
who is occupied with the singing of Torah.
R. Joshua ben Levi said:
Up to here I have received a tradition,
from this point on go and think for yourself.

And indeed my Sage answered right away that in Psalm 96,
'Sing to the Lord, etc.' corresponds to Joseph, of whom it is said,
'Like a firstling bull in his majesty' [Deut. 33: 17].
This is all in *Yalkut ḥadash*, fo. 92.

|fo. 39*b* blank|

|fo. 40*a*|

[Signed]

Zevi Hirsch

the son of *our teacher and rabbi,
the rabbi, Isaac Eisik Segal, *shtadlan*
of the community of Kalisz.

---

the destructive agents i.e. demonic forces.

our teacher and rabbi, the rabbi an honorific normally applied to outstanding rabbis.

shtadlan A communal representative invited to intercede with the authorities of the state.

PLATE I Hayim Samuel Jacob Falk, the Ba'al Shem of London
Attributed to Philip James de Loutherbourg. Oil on canvas. Unsigned. 29.5" × 24.5", London, c.1777
Private collection, London. Reproduced by permission

PLATE 2 Falk's tombstone in the United Synagogue's Alderney Road Cemetery, London
Photo by Michal Oron

PLATE 3 Inscription on a plaque affixed to Falk's tombstone

[= Samuel Jacob Hayim]

The distinguished elder, the perfect sage, the mystical adept, our teacher
Rabbi Samuel son of Rabbi Raphael of saintly memory
his name was known in the furthermost places of the land and distant islands.
For the forty years he was here he upheld the flag of Torah and service of the Almighty.
He taught and adhered to the Torah and its commandments and laws.
When he died he disbursed all this wealth and worldly goods to different charities
in the merit of which the Creator of Heaven and Earth
will bind his soul in paradise with other righteous souls
and will reward him together with the deceased of Israel with future resurrection.
Passed away with a good name on Thursday, 4 Iyar and was buried with honour
and eulogized on the following day, Friday, the 20th day of the Omer
in the year 5542 from the Creation [1782]

Photo by Michal Oron

[Hebrew/Yiddish cursive manuscript — illegible at this resolution]

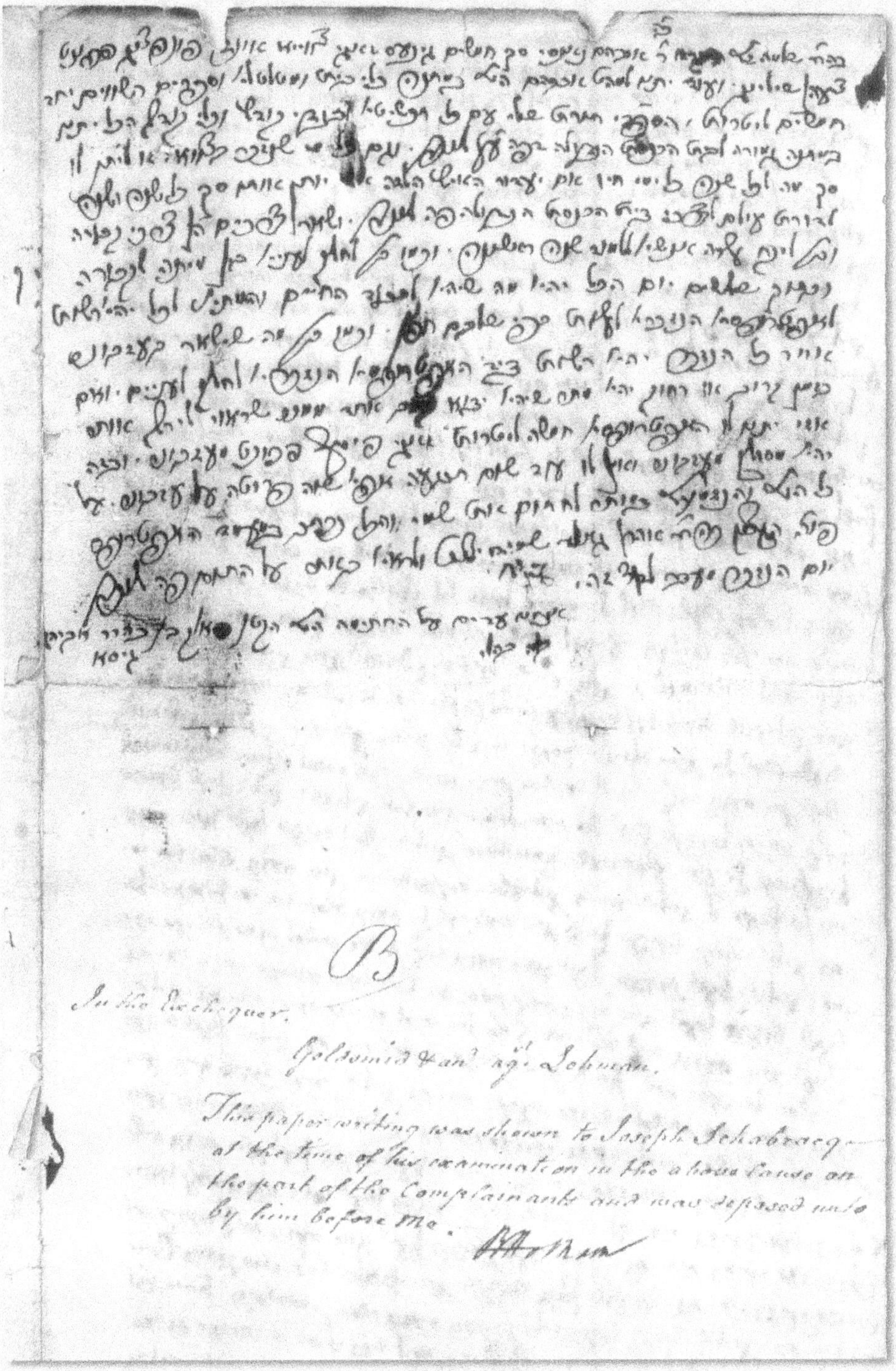

B

In the Exchequer

Goldsmid & an'r ag't Johnson

This paper writing was shown to Joseph Schabracq
at the time of his examination in the above Cause on
the part of the Complainants and was deposed unto
by him before me.

PLATE 4 An extract from Falk's will
Reproduced with permission from the National Archives

PLATE 5 A page from the diary of Zevi Hirsch of Kalisz
Reproduced with permission from the London Metropolitan Archives and United Synagogue

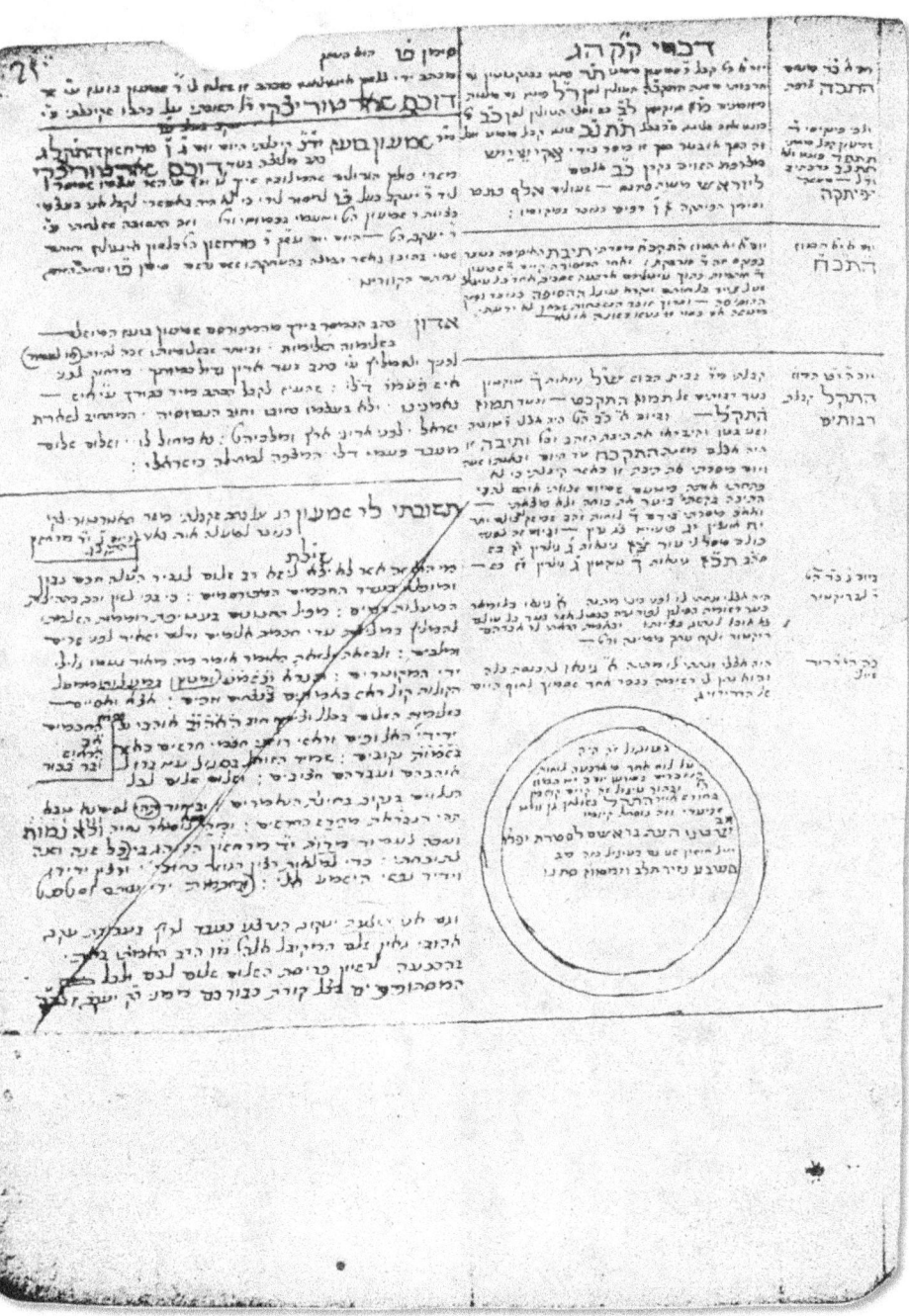

PLATE 6 A page from the diary of Samuel Falk (fo. 25a)

Reproduced with permission from the London Metropolitan Archives and United Synagogue

PLATE 7 Tombstone of Theodor Stephan de Stein von Neuhoff (1694–1756), briefly king of Corsica

Photo by Michal Oron

PLATE 8 Stone commemorating leaders of the London Jewish community buried in the United Synagogue's Alderney Road Cemetery, London

Photo by Michal Oron

THE DIARY OF SAMUEL FALK

|fo. 1a|

BY THE
BA'AL SHEM DR FALK

---

*For a reminder: the desirable Portuguese woman, for whom Jacob worked, got married. This was on Wednesday, 12 Tishrei 5537 [25 September 1776].

For a gift, *24 כלשמר sent with Mendel, *in the week of the Torah portion of 'Vayera', *5542. I sent 2s. 6d. with Jacob to Rachel the sick woman; *2 *sht.* with Reuben, 2 *sh.*, in the week of the Torah portion of 'Toledot', also by [?] 2 *sht.*

For a reminder . . . 12 Tishrei 5537 this entry is in a handwriting different from that of the diary; the three lines following this statement were erased.

24 כלשמר sent with Mendel the meaning of the Hebrew word is unclear. [One may assume from other gifts mentioned that it was a gift of money; however, it is not clear whether this was a gift that Falk was sending with Mendel (and if so, to whom), or whether it was a gift that someone else had sent Falk via Mendel. Mendel is not identified here but he is mentioned on fo. 2a, diary entry for Sunday, 10 Elul 5533, as having come from Leiden. Later we learn that he was apparently part of Falk's circle, since he is mentioned in the latter's will as his servant.]

in the week of the Torah portion of 'Vayera' [A different portion of the Torah is read in the synagogue each week, in a set sequence. The first few lines are read on a Saturday afternoon and repeated on Monday morning and again on Thursday morning, and the entire portion is read on a Saturday. The name of the portion is derived from the first word or two. It is quite common to measure time by association with the Torah reading in this way. The week of the Torah portion of 'Vayera' would have been around October time; the week of the Torah portion of 'Toledot' would have been two weeks later.]

5542 [This entry apparently refers to a date nine years later than the next entry; the reason is unclear, but it could be an error.]

2 *sht.* . . . 2 *sht.* the abbreviation 'sht.' could refer to *shetarot*—bills. [However, since Falk does not use the term elsewhere, and since this entry also includes a reference to 'sh.', and all other gifts mentioned are in shillings, perhaps it is reasonable to assume that the references here are to shillings too.]

[The remainder of the folio (ll. 7–18), which

|fo. 1b| *Friday, 13 Elul 5532* [11 September 1772]. For a reminder: *in my pocket eleven guineas, beside thirty *rekhavim*, sixty-two ducats. In one pocket twenty-five *rekhavim*, forty-three guineas. In the expenses pocket: fifteen guineas, a quarter, two *rekhavim* in silver, twelve and a half gulden.

*Emmanuel
*שיח פעמי

Monday, 8 Shevat 5535 [9 January 1775]. From the destruction of the Second Temple, for our sins, till today, *1,707 years have passed.

|fo. 2a| *Friday, 28 Nisan 5532* [1 May 1772]. *R. Aberley, who is known as a heretic, came to take leave before departing on a journey. I did not see him, but I sent 3s. 0d.

mentions an occurrence on 11 Heshvan 5517 (4 November 1756) followed by an incomprehensible esoteric formula, has not been translated.]

in my pocket [Falk mentions a variety of currencies. It is not clear what they relate to—for example, he mentions 'a quarter' but does not say of what. *Rekhavim* is a Hebrew term, so perhaps this is a coded reference. 'Ducat', the presumed meaning of Falk's *tokton* (i.e., *dokton* = ducat) was a gold or silver trade coin minted in several countries. Gulden were Dutch coins. One may assume that the variety of currencies indicates the extent of Falk's contacts.]

Emmanuel 'Emmanuel' appears twice in Falk's diary. The second occurrence (fo. 33b) describes him as a 'servant of the king of France', a designation that has puzzled scholars such as Neubauer, Adler, and Roth. Schuchard believes it to be a reference to Emanuel Swedenborg (see above, Introduction, Section III, n. 26), but the dates of the relevant entries in the diary postdate Swedenborg's death (1772). Another person by this name was Emmanuel Saint Priest, an adviser to Louis XV and Louis XVI. Professor Michael Harsegor has informed me that 'the minister Emmanuel' was a seasoned diplomat in the Near East and in the Mediterranean lands, and was also known for his ties with Freemasons.

[Following the name 'Emmanuel' four sets of apparently meaningless three-letter abbreviations have not been represented in the translation. Seemingly they had occult meaning because when set out as three vertical columns instead of horizontally two of the sets thus constructed were in alphabetical order and the third is in reverse alphabetical order.]

שיח פעמי Falk sometimes signed his name with his initials S[amuel] J[acob] H[ayim]—שיח (lit. 'conversation, speech') followed by the word פעמי (lit. 'steps, times'), a coded version of the name 'Falk' (see below, fo. 21b).

Monday, 8 Shevat 5535 [Once again, the year of this entry is out of sequence—perhaps an error on Falk's part.]

1,707 years have passed [Falk's calculation of 1,707 years from the destruction of the temple is unclear. The First Temple was destroyed in 586 BCE and the Second Temple was destroyed in 70 CE. It is also not clear why he chose to mention it on 8 Shevat, a date with no significance for the destruction of the temple, which occurred on 9 Av; perhaps he saw occult significance in the six-month difference.]

R. Aberley R. Abraham of Hamburg, who was known as 'R. Aberley'. See Katz, *The Jews in the History of England*, 119, 205–9; Roth, *The History of the Great Synagogue in London*, 20,

with Gedaliah. *This is the third time, etc. He told Gedaliah that he had asked *R. Shimon, *What is a *bat kol*, and why was it not called a *ben kol*? and R. Shimon *answered like a wise man.

*The world—whence was it created? R. Eliezer teaches: from its centre, as it is said: 'Whereupon the earth melts into a mass, and its clods stick together' [Job 38: 38]. But R. Judah says, 'From the sides: "He commands the snow, 'Fall to the ground!'"' [Job 37: 6]. R. Isaac Napaha says, 'The Holy One, blessed be He, cast a stone into the ocean, from which the world was then founded, as it is said: "On to what were its bases sunk? Who set its cornerstone?"' [Job 38: 6]. R. Judah says, 'From Zion, perfect in beauty' [Ps. 50: 2].

Tuesday, 10 Elul 5533 [29 August 1773]. Abraham, the teacher of R. Tuvyah, came to me at night, and took the midday meal with me, something that no one merits; and a word to the wise will suffice. While speaking of various things he asked about paths in

---

29, 48, 138. [Though born in Hamburg, R. Aberley, a jeweller by trade, was a warden and leading spirit of the Ashkenazi community of London; see <http://www.jewishencyclopedia.com/articles/439-abraham-of-hamburg>.]

This is the third time [It is not clear what this might refer to, though from a halakhic perspective something that is done three times is considered to be an established custom (*ḥazakah*).]

R. Shimon [R. Shimon is not identified; perhaps it is R. Shimon Boas, the son of R. Tuvyah Boas; for more on this family, see Appendix A.]

What is a *bat kol*, and why was it not called a *ben kol*? a *bat kol* is a heavenly voice. The question asked here is: Why is the idiom 'daughter of a voice' rather than 'son of a voice'?

answered like a wise man R. Shimon's rather complicated answer, presented in three columns, drawing on more than twenty texts (mostly biblical) in which some reference to *bat kol* or its component letters appearing in adjacent words in longer phrases can be discerned, is given in full in Falk's diary. Translation would be meaningless so the text has been omitted; briefly stated, the response is based on biblical verses containing the words *bat* (literally, 'daughter') and *kol* ('voice'). Falk ends 'page 1' with a brief excerpt from the Babylonian Talmud (*Ber. 3a*) describing an occasion on which a *bat kol* was heard. The first reference is to 1 Kgs 7, in which the word *bat* appears twice (verses 26, 38), but Falk cites only the first verse. In the following passage, in table form, Falk employs kabbalistic techniques of word permutation to find new meanings in these two words. These include replacing one word with another whose letters have the same numerical value; combining the first letters (or the middle letters, or the last letters) of the words in a particular verse to derive a new meaning; some of his allusions are misleading, and sometimes he changes the order of words without explanation but presumably so as to meet kabbalistic ends.

The world—whence was it created? ... 'From Zion, perfect in beauty' see BT *Yoma* 54b. [Falk is misquoting here. In the Talmud, the first statement here attributed to R. Judah is attributed to R. Joshua and the second is attributed to 'the rabbis'.]

Tuesday, 10 Elul 5533 [10 Elul 5533 was in fact a Sunday, as Falk correctly states in the next entry.]

the sea, and I immediately answered him, telling him the basics in brief, for he touched upon *the matter in his name חמר, from 'Abraham' אברהם, in the name of the Zohar. *There are six who frequent the paths of the sea, and their sign and source is חמר.

Sunday, 10 Elul 5533 [29 August 1773]. R. Abraham the teacher came to me as instructed by R. Mendel on Friday, for Mendel had been sent from Leiden to The Hague to tell him that he must see me. So he came, and *where there is talking, there is no lack of transgression. I sensed in him that he had been ordered to deceive me in a way known to them, *so that they should have an illumination to reveal. Blessed be the One who watches to protect, and thus I immediately answered him that, thank God, this year He gave me lodgings and strength, for I cannot deliver into your hand what I summoned you for, that is, to order you to leave with all haste for The Hague. Then I will prepare you, together with another person, *a wanderer, *to hide something in Hague bush, at my source. Afterwards he dined with me at midday: boiled *hokhit*, fried pudding, cheese, butter, and fruit—berries. While talking we went from one topic to another, until he asked, 'What are *the paths of the sea?' and I answered him, '*This is a fundamental of the sabbath, as it is said, *and these are the seven of all.'

the matter in his name חמר from 'Abraham' אברהם the numerical value of the letters that spell 'Abraham' אברהם is 248, the same as that of חמר, which means 'matter'. [Equating two words in this way is a standard kabbalistic technique for explaining meanings.]

There are six who frequent the paths of the sea and their sign and source is חמר [Neither the reference nor the reasoning here is explained. The text that follows (ll. 61–6) being incomprehensible permutations of letters, has not been translated.]

where there is talking, there is no lack of transgression based on Prov. 10: 19.

so that they should have an illumination to reveal i.e. esoteric knowledge.

a wanderer [The meaning is unclear; perhaps a traveller, or a guide familiar with the territory.]

to hide something in Hague bush, at my source the reference to 'hiding something' in 'Hague bush' might be a reference to an area of 'bush' or a thicket in The Hague, or alternatively bush could be a coded reference to a location in the Hague associated with an unidentified Busch family. [The reference to 'my source' is unintelligible in either context, though if the reference here to Bush is to the Boas family (an explanation offered in a note to fo. 4*a*), 'my source' could perhaps allude to them as a source of support for him.]

hokhit the word is not entirely legible, but perhaps refers to hake (*Hecht* in German).

the paths of the sea this question is puzzling, because this phrase does not appear in the sources (mention is made of the 'paths of the heavens', but that is something else).

This is a fundamental of the sabbath, as it is said the text after 'it is said' comprises two phrases that are unidentifiable and incomprehensible and have been omitted from the translation. [They do not appear to relate to the question of the 'paths of the sea' nor to identify a fundamental of the sabbath.]

and these are the seven of all Falk lists the seven 'words' that he derived, using techniques of numerical value and acrostics, from the word חמר. [The meaning of the phrase 'seven of all' is unclear.]

*And the *ḥashmal*, the seven, and אדון ,חג"ש זס"ש חמר הגל, the above-mentioned acronyms; therefore, according to the scholars, *ḥashmal* איש זייני יקרא ממקור חבלו as mentioned above; and a word to the wise will suffice.

By virtue of the inheritance of Mendel, in Adar I 5540 [February/March 1780], I was obliged to keep a letter as testimony, which was written בפ"ק, as the rabbi commanded in this matter, and בפ"ק has written to him. Therefore, I gave this addition to be written in a different script, and thus he did. Indeed, our Master and Teacher, the great *gaon*, the fortress and watchtower, the pious and the humble, *the illustrious ורסה, urged us, in accordance with the request from Paris of our esteemed teacher and master *R. David Tevele, with the official seal of the head of the rabbinical court of our community, the community of London the capital city and of the country, may our sublime citadel be established. ———

|fo. 2b| **Friday, the 26th inst.* *Jacob asked me for a quarter of a guinea, and *I gave him five shillings. ———

And the *ḥashmal* the meaning here is unclear; presumably, the Hebrew terms here further derive from or are related to the esoteric numerical permutations mentioned above. The relationship between *ḥashmal* and איש זייני יקרא ממקור חבלו is similarly unclear. [*Ḥashmalim* (sing. *ḥashmal*) are angelic entities; see Ezek. 1: 4; but the relevance here is again unclear.]

By virtue of the inheritance of Mendel...may our sublime citadel be established this passage, which was composed in 1780, is written at the bottom of the page, in a different script. It was apparently written several years after the other passages on this page. A considerable portion of this passage is barely legible. It might be a will written by Mendel, who apparently belonged to Falk's circle, and who is mentioned in the latter's will as his servant.

בפ"ק usually an abbreviation of 'in a small notebook' (*bepinkas katan*); however, judging from the usage of these letters in the rest of the diary, this is probably a coded reference to a person called Jacob, since the Hebrew letters comprising that name (יעקב) have the same numerical value as בפ"ק (= 182). [Hereafter in the translation the abbreviation בפ"ק has been abandoned in favour of 'Jacob'. The name יעקב, viz. Jacob, also appears in the text, apparently a reference to a servant in Falk's household; perhaps Falk used both terms to refer to the same person.]

the illustrious ורסה the identity of the person referred to is not known.

R. David Tevele David Tevele Schiff, the chief rabbi of London; see Katz, *The Jews in the History of England*, 276; see also above, Introduction, Section IV. [It is not known what he was doing in Paris, but perhaps it is because the request came 'from Paris' that Falk emphasizes that it came 'with the official seal of the head of the rabbinical court of our community, the community of London'.]

Friday, the 26th inst. [The previous entries were for Elul 5533, but 26 Elul was not a Friday. Perhaps the reference is to 26 Marheshvan 5534, corresponding to Friday, 12 November 1773, viz. more than two months after the last entry. This would correspond with the next entry, which is for Tuesday night, 17 Marheshvan (meaning that the date on Tuesday daytime would have been the 16th, which ties up). Both entries were presumably written after the events to which they refer.]

Jacob apparently a servant in Falk's household.

I gave him five shillings [A quarter of a guinea was actually 5s. 3d.]

Tuesday night, 17 Marheshvan 5534 [3 November 1773]. The gout began in my left hand—and on Wednesday night, the 18th inst., *Jacob came to my room to wake me, because Mendel was indisposed on Sunday night. Monday night, the 23rd inst., my right foot began to feel very bad. Nevertheless, it was bearable. This night it was Mendel who woke me, even though he was indisposed, because Jacob did not come as he normally did. And at midday on Tuesday, I got out of bed, and at night Jacob came again to wake me. On Monday, the eve of the new moon of Kislev 5534, *I began to put *tefilin* on my arm, thank God. On Monday night, the new moon of Kislev as aforementioned, Jacob did not come to wake me as was customary, and Mendel woke me in his stead. *On Monday night, the 9th Mendel again woke me because Jacob did not come. And on the aforementioned Tuesday, I washed my left hand for the first time, and I also washed with lye.

---

*Tuesday, 3 Tevet 5535 [6 December 1774]. I dreamed that I was standing in front of the window with my wife, *peace be upon her, and I was in a state of confusion and sensed some evil. And then I heard a great commotion from the members of my household as she jumped from the window and broke her neck. I looked out of the window, trembling, and saw that *her head was beneath her body. Soon the members of my household came in to seize me and I knew not why. Then I understood that in her malice, peace be upon her, she had informed against me, and for that reason she threw herself from the window. And lo, it was but a dream; may it be propitious.

*And on Tuesday night, 4 Tevet, I dreamed a dream.

*I began to make the seal of a man in the water on Thursday, 21 Menahem Av

---

Jacob came to my room to wake me . . . because Mendel was indisposed Falk apparently relied on one of the servants or a member of his circle waking him during the night for prayers.

I began to put *tefilin* on my arm, thank God [Presumably he had not been able to do so for some days because of the pain from the gout.]

On Monday night, the 9th [Falk appears to have lost track of the dates. If the previous Monday was 'the eve of the new moon of Kislev' the date was in fact 29 Heshvan, and if the new moon of Kislev started on Monday night 30 Heshvan, the following Monday was not in fact the ninth of the month.]

Tuesday, 3 Tevet 5535 [More than a year has apparently elapsed since the last entry.]

peace be upon her the phrase 'peace be upon her' indicates that his wife was already dead at the time of the dream in December 1774.

her head was beneath her body the words following 'her body' have been erased but can be reconstructed as 'because of sins'.

And on Tuesday night, 4 Tevet Falk notes that he had another dream on Tuesday night but does not record its content. [The first dream, which Falk records as being on Tuesday 3 Tevet, was presumably in the early hours of Tuesday morning; the second dream was in the evening, which would already have been 4 Tevet.]

I began to make the seal of a man in the water [The text that follows describes an event that had apparently occurred some thirty years previously. Its meaning is unclear, as is the reason it is mentioned so much later. In fact

*5504 [19 July 1744], and the entire act was completed on Monday night, 11 Elul 5504 [8 August 1744]; three hours after midnight *it was completed and sealed, in the forest and in the camp in the forest; and a word to the wise will suffice. Then I testified to the signature of *Jacob son of Sazbona, and the youth Abraham. *In the element of *se'ah*, that is, 60, man, the water, for a reminder.

*A gold breastplate was sold, *because of our sins, by *Hirsch and Mendel, on Thursday, 24 Shevat 5521 [29 January 1761]. Its weight was 19 oz., 19 dwt., at £3. 18s. 0d. per ounce, for a total of £67. 15s. 6d. I have a sketch of the shape, which I drew as a reminder. God willing, may the Lord grant that I make it again; at least I have it drawn on paper, as mentioned.

Selections from the new moon of Heshvan 5542 [19/20 October 1781]. 'How great is the good that You have in store for those who fear You.'

|fo. 3a| From *the introduction by Rabad, of blessed memory.

the date may be in error since the thirty-year difference is due solely to the omission of a single letter *lamed*.]

5504 [The equivalent civil dates for 5504 have been calculated according to the Julian calendar used in England at that time; if in fact the year should have been given as 5534, as explained above, the equivalent dates for Av and Elul respectively would be 29 July 1774 and 18 August 1774.]

it was completed and sealed, in the forest and in the camp in the forest [It is not clear what is meant by an event being 'completed and sealed', but Hebrew often uses two verbs for effect. It is perhaps also why Falk had to say 'in the forest and in the camp in the forest', but perhaps the emphasis was important to him.]

Jacob son of Sazbona [Perhaps the servant Jacob who was mentioned earlier.]

In the element of *se'ah*, that is, 60, man, the water *se'ah* is a measure of volume. In Hebrew it comprises the letter *samekh*, which has a numerical value of 60; *alef*, the initial letter of the word for 'man' (*adam*); and *heh*, the initial letter of 'the water' (*hamayim*).

A gold breastplate [Presumably, a breastplate for a Torah scroll.]

because of our sins [This is a figure of speech used when something bad happens.]

Hirsch and Mendel [This is presumably Zevi Hirsch and Mendel, another member of Falk's entourage, as mentioned above.]

Selections from the new moon of Heshvan 5542 the quotation is from Ps. 31: 20. [The significance of the date is unclear; Oron suggests that one of Falk's esoteric permutations in the text that follows may suggest that he actually made the calculations in the previous year, but does not explain the relevance of this. The significance of Falk's writing vocalization and cantillation signs above some of the letters in that verse is also not explained. The next twenty lines (ll. 107–27) have been omitted: they comprise numerical permutations of the letters of various verses cited—some biblical and some based on the *ma'ariv* prayer for the evening of Shavuot, as well as other incomprehensible esoteric manipulations.]

the introduction by Rabad referring to the introduction to *Sefer yetsirah* that is attributed to R. Abraham b. David of Posquières (known as Rabad) but actually written by R. Joseph Ashkenazi. See Scholem, 'The True Author' (Heb.). In the lines that follow, Falk makes several numerological manipulations

*In thirty-two paths: *(15) 'Let there be lights' [Gen. 1: 14]—*two times אור ['light'] has the same numerical value [414] as ית״ד* ['peg']. And know that with the thirty-two paths as mentioned *God says three times יהי ['Let there be']: this is לשון הסכמה* [i.e. wording signifying assent], *with a numerical value of 516. The three instances of יהי together have a numerical value of 75. And there are corresponding signs [in the numbering of the said introduction] ג (= 3), ז (= 7), ט״ו (= 15), that together have a numerical value of 25. In section 3, יהי אור ['Let there be light']; in section 7, יהי רקיע ['Let there be an expanse']; in section 15, יהי מאורות ['Let there be lights'].

Question of *R. Abraham Nanshikh, in Heshvan 5542 [October 1781]: *What is it that I have heard, that instead of *ḥasin kadosh berov*, one should say *gadol* instead of *berov* ברוב, which in *gematriyah* has a numerical value of 210. And in יד החזקה יד

based on words in the said text. [The last two lines of the paragraph are unintelligible and have been omitted.]

In thirty-two paths [There is a kabbalistic notion that the act of Creation was achieved by using the twenty-two letters of the Hebrew alphabet and the ten *sefirot* that represent different elements of the divine, hence 'thirty-two paths'.]

(15) [The significance of fifteen, represented here by the Hebrew letters *tet* and *vav*, is not clear; perhaps it somehow connotes the divine, since 15 can also be rendered by the letters *yod* and *heh*, both of which figure in the Tetragrammaton.]

two times אור ['light'] [Presumably referring to the two 'lights', the sun and the moon.]

ית״ד ['peg'] [The significance of the term is not clear, but perhaps it relates to the pegs mentioned in connection with the construction of the Tabernacle (Exod. 35: 18).]

God says three times [In the Torah portion of 'Bereshit', Gen. 1: 1–6: 8.]

לשון הסכמה [A term signifying assent; the significance is not explained.]

with a numerical value of 516 [The significance is not explained.]

And there are corresponding signs Falk links the word יהי (which has a numerical value of 25) with certain sections of the introduction to *Sefer yetsirah*, viz. sections 3, 7, and 15 (significant because the chapter numbers themselves, added together, total 25), each of which contains the word יהי.

R. Abraham Nanshikh R. Abraham Nanzig, also known as Abraham b. Solomon Hamburger, came from Nancy in Lorraine [hence the alternative appellations 'Nanshikh' and 'Nanzig']. He was a frequent visitor to Falk's house, and a beneficiary of his will. He was a warden of the Hambro Synagogue, a member of the London *beit din* (rabbinical court), and the author of a book in Hebrew entitled *Alim literufah* (London, 1785). See Duschinsky, *The Rabbinate of the Great Synagogue*, 76; Roth, *The History of the Great Synagogue in London*, 192, 270; and William Rubinstein's *Palgrave Dictionary of Anglo-Jewish History*, which describes him as a 'rabbi and medical ethicist'. [The title of Nanzig's publication should perhaps correctly be *Aleh literufah*, a work advocating a precursor of vaccination against smallpox; see <http://www.jewishgen.org/JCR-UK/susser/roth/chthirteen.htm>.]

What is it that I have heard the question pertains to one of the words in the mystical *Ana bekho'aḥ* prayer composed by R. Nehunya b. Hakanah, which is recited during the

הגדולה [lit. 'the strong hand the great hand'], the numerical value of *the initial letters is 210. And the [initial letters] of יד רמה [lit. 'the exalted hand'] are י"ר [= 210]. That is, 3 [= ג] times י"ר = יג"ר. The total of י"ר and י"ר [210 + 210] has the numerical value of 420 [כ"ת]. Then, as it is said, כת יג"ר, and three times י"ד [14 + 14 + 14] [has the numerical value of] מ"ב [42, signifying the 42-letter name of God] and the initial letters י"ר and the name יג"ר have *the total numerical value of הסתי"ו; and a word to the wise will suffice.

|fo. 3b| *Tuesday, 24 [Sivan] 5522* [15 June 1762]

*ITEM 1

*Cosman's list. First, things that I gave as a gift to *my friend מקבע, for a total of £11. 12s. 0d., as well as a coffee pot and a tea pot, that I left out of the total.

morning service and also during the service that inaugurates the sabbath; see the notes to Zevi Hirsch's diary, fo. 13a. R. Abraham claims that he heard that the word *berov* in the fifth stanza of the prayer ('Powerful Holy One, in Your abundant goodness guide Your congregation') was to be replaced by *gadol*, thus changing the meaning from 'abundant goodness' to 'great goodness'. Falk's answer apparently relies on a source interpreting the meaning of the divine name of forty-two letters (to which the forty-two words in this prayer are understood to correspond). This response is reminiscent of the thought expressed by R. Moses Cordovero, in his *Pardes rimonim*, sha'ar 21, ch. 12: 'According to one opinion, these letters [i.e. the first forty-two letters in Gen. 1], employing the methodology of *temurah* [the interchanging of letters in accordance with specific systematic rules], form the divine name of forty-two letters: אבגיתץ קרע שטן נגד יכש בטר צתג חקבטנע יגל פזק שקוצית, which are to be divided into three *yadot* [i.e. 'hands', each of which, in rabbinic terminology, is a 'language of redemption', used in relation to the Exodus from Egypt; the word יד has the numerical value of 14, and the three *yadot* therefore total 42]: *yad yemin* [the 'right hand' that Falk later identifies with the 'great hand'], *yad ramah* ['upraised hand'—see Exod. 14: 8], and *yad haḥazakah* [the 'mighty hand'—see e.g. Exod. 13: 9].' Thus, Falk bases his response on this anonymous view presented by Cordovero, while advancing reasons of his own for this division.

the initial letters the numerical value of the initial letters in the second word in each of the phrases יד רמה, יד הגדולה, יד החזקה, (ה' ה' ר': *heh, heh, resh* = 5 + 5 + 200 = 210).

the total numerical value 42 + 14 + 210 + 210 = 476 = (ה)סתיו.

ITEM 1 [This is the first of nine numbered items, although what follows this one—unlike what follows the other eight—is hardly a single item. After Item 9 (on fo. 5a), Falk writes that all the nine items are in a chest that he has buried in Holland; the relevance of Item 1 to the other eight is a mystery. Perhaps 'Item 1' should have been the amulet with which fo. 5a starts.]

Cosman's list Apparently a first list of things given to Cosman Lehmann, on whom see Appendix A.

my friend מקבע the name מקבע, sometimes given as מבקע, and also סכל ['the fool'], appears a number of times in Falk's diary, as a coded allusion to Cosman. The letters of מקבע allude to the Hebrew spelling of Cosman (קושמן/קוסמן) as follows: the letters *mem* and *kuf* appear both in Cosman's name and in this allusion; the other two consonants in his name (*samekh, nun*) have the numerical

1. Tea kettle
2. Coffee pot
3. Some small pans
4. Some more small pans
5. Rice bowl
6. Small frying pan
7. Bowl containing a stove
8. A stove, 14 parts
9. Big bowl containing all the above
10. Lid for the bowl so that it can be used for cooking

All ten items were in one big bowl together with fifteen lids and a grate; with the latter sixteen items in total, not including the fourteen parts of the stove.

Wednesday, 26 Nisan 5532 [29 April 1772]. A second list, of items for sale: seven pots with lids, two pots without lids, one tea pot, one strainer, a board with a knife for cutting meat, and other household utensils: £14. 9s. 0d.

*A Second List

1. Coffee kettle
2. Tea kettle
3. Some small pans
4. Ditto for milk
5. Rice bowl
6. Small frying pan

value of 110 = סכל. The letter *ayin* may possibly owe its inclusion in the code word to its place in the order of the Hebrew alphabet (following *nun* and *samekh*); the letter *beit* represents the *vav* in Cosman's name. This identification is based on the entry for 24 Shevat 5533 (fo. 32*b*). [To make it easier for the reader, 'Cosman' is hereafter used throughout instead of the coded form.]

Wednesday, 26 Nisan 5532 [29 April 1772] this list is dated some ten years after the last. [An incomprehensible phrase following the date, apparently relating to a book of Falk's given to a printer for 3s. 0d., has been omitted.]

A Second List Falk's second list offers an interesting insight into his vocabulary and knowledge of languages. For example, he combines the English words 'coffee' and 'tea' with the Yiddish (or German) *Kessel* ('kettle'), writing them all in Hebrew transliteration replete with spelling mistakes. For 'rice' he transliterates the English term [perhaps he knew the food only in English], whereas the word he uses for strainer is the German term *Sieb*, and the word he uses for pasta is the Yiddish *lokshn*.

7. Bowl containing all the above
8. Stove in 14 pieces
[?] Strainer for pasta
9. Bowl for anything
10. Bowl for anything
11. Bowl for anything
12. Lid for item 7, as big as that bowl
13. Lid for no. 11, as nice as all the items
14. A second lid, over everything, and everything is the best, as stated
15. Lids for all the bowls

A total of twenty-one pieces, apart from the fourteen parts of the stove and six lids (not counted in the second list from here). Also three grates, one-third of copper; seven copper dishes; also a spoon for soup, a spoon for tasting, *tongs for the fire, some small copper pans for anything.

|fo. 4a| *I copied this from the translated Pentateuch of the cantor of Leiden in the month of Menahem Av 5540 [August 1780], *a gift, two gulden, five pence.

*Five times did the patriarch Abraham rise early to pray for his sons: on Hoshana Rabba, on the Ninth of Av, on Yom Kippur, on Rosh Hashanah, and on Purim.

*The seven commandments imposed on the sons of Noah were: civil law; the prohibitions on blasphemy, idolatry, incest, murder, robbery; and eating a limb of a live animal.

tongs the word Falk uses is *siyung*, possibly from the Yiddish *tsvange* (my thanks to Shmuel Ram for this suggestion).

I copied this from the translated Pentateuch of the cantor of Leiden the page on which this is written was pasted onto fo. 4. ['This' presumably relates to the text about Abraham that follows.] The translation was into Yiddish. [Falk does not say here whether he was visiting Leiden or the cantor was visiting him, but since the subsequent entry for 28 Menahem Av says that he left Leiden on that day, it becomes apparent that it was Falk who was visiting the cantor.]

a gift, two gulden, five pence [Perhaps the translated Pentateuch was a gift from the cantor to Falk, or perhaps 'a gift' relates to the sum of money mentioned. This is not clear.]

Five times did the patriarch Abraham rise early to pray for his sons there are in fact only three occurrences in Genesis of the phrase 'Abraham rose early' (viz. of Hebrew words with the root *shin-kaf-mem*), so it is not clear what Falk intended by this. [Of course, the festivals mentioned did not exist in Abraham's time.]

The seven commandments [These are the so-called Noahide laws, Torah-given precepts applying to all mankind; their relevance here is unclear. Following this statement, eight esoteric word combinations have been omitted, viz. eight groups of letters

|fo. 4b| *Thursday, 21 Elul 5540* [21 September 1780]. *I copied all that is written here from Sunday, 22 Elul 5537 [24 September 1777]. Through R. Abraham Nanzig I purchased books from R. Shimon for the aforementioned three ducats. Given to R. Shimon—two ducats, to R. Eliezer—two ducats. A book, one ducat. R. Akiva, two gulden.

Sunday, 17 Elul 5540 [17 September 1780]. I gave R. Abraham Nanzig a present, five ducats; to R. Munish Menahem, twenty gulden; to my servant Baer, who wrote something, a present, three gulden; cakes for R. Shimon, one ducat; cakes for R. Eliezer, one ducat; *for a boat from the *nivleh* of the day of his oath, two gulden and two pence; servants.

*Thursday, 20 Elul 5540 [20 September 1780]. *I went from Rotoles to Menirza.

On 28 Menahem Av 5540 [29 August 1780], I travelled by carriage from Leiden and arrived at *the Bosh house as night was falling. The expenses for the coachman, the members of my household, and *the sages of Holland in the Bosh house: two gulden and two [*not specified*]. Jacob received on account two ducats; and in London, five shillings; *and for prayer, sixteen pence.

comprising different combinations of the same five letters—*beit*, *ḥet*, *resh*, *dalet*, *lamed*—seemingly meaningless, and unrelated to the previous text, but obviously significant to Falk.]

I copied all that is written here apparently from an earlier notebook. [The references to money are unclear; there is no earlier mention of three ducats.]

for a boat from the *nivleh* of the day of his oath the relevance of the boat here is unclear. The meaning of *nivleh* is similarly unclear: it could be a curse, or perhaps the intention is *mehanevelah*, 'from the contemptible person'.

Thursday, 20 Elul 5540 [The seeming inconsistency with the day and date in the previous entry (Sunday, 17 Elul) is because 17 Elul started on Sunday evening and finished on Monday evening, so Thursday during the day would indeed have been 20 Elul. From the next entry, which in fact recorded an event from the previous month, it becomes apparent that Falk made a trip to Holland ('I travelled by carriage from Leiden'). The entries are therefore out of order.]

I went from Rotoles to Menirza 'Rotoles' is possibly Rotterdam, but 'Menizra' cannot be identified.

the Bosh house possibly meaning 'the Boas's house'. If so, then the reference is to Falk's friend Tuvyah Boas.

the sages of Holland in the Bosh house [Possibly the reference to 'sages' means that Boas had rabbinical scholars living with him or visiting him, and Falk felt duty-bound to support them; or similarly it could be a barbed reference to penniless scholars that Boas was supporting and whom he felt similarly bound to support. Boas is known to have supported such people; see Appendix B.]

and for prayer, sixteen pence [This could be a reference to the established custom of a mourner paying a poor person or scholar to say Kaddish for a dead person if the mourner is unable to fulfil the obligation himself (thereby also fulfilling the obligation of giving charity), but in context this is not obvious.]

|fo. 5a|

*AN AMULET

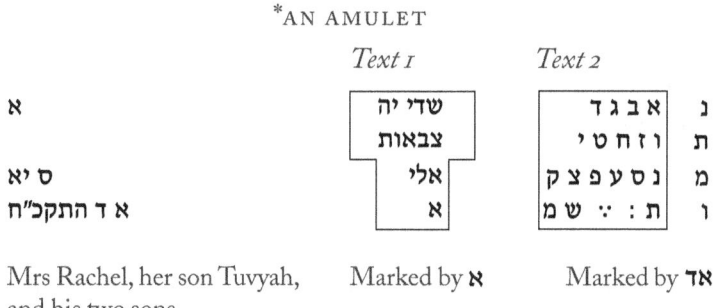

	Text 1	Text 2
א	שדי יה צבאות אלי א	נ א ב ג ד ת ו ז ח ט י מ נ ס ע פ צ ק ו ת ׃ ֶ ש מ
ס יא		
א ד התקכ״ח		
Mrs Rachel, her son Tuvyah, and his two sons	Marked by א	Marked by אד

Text 1 is written on one side of a smooth stone, one of nine. These two texts, *whose principle is ז״ם, are written and drawn on the stone, one text on one side, and the second text on the other side. This stone is concealed in a chest of gold encrusted with pearls and sealed with a key, a chest with a Star of David seal.

That is, there is only one crown on it; the chest is wrapped in paper, and on the paper is written as follows; and a word to the wise will suffice. A stone from seven: nine: eleven: smooth stones that were worthy of having holy names, inscribed in the top stone before it was buried in the place that had been decreed in the year 5516 [1755/6], on which was written the divine name of seventy-two letters, *and the secret of ט״יז, equivalent to ז״ך.

*ITEM 2

> אלהים מחול גרמה וגרמי
> מתקוי כי הסוקך נידח בתקיא
> ואתה הרחמן מָחול זְסולח
>
> טבעת זו נצררה בניר ועל הניר נכתב ככתוב
> למעלה בזה הלוח ונחתם בחותם המזוזה
> ואז נצטנעה בלב של זהב כנזכר למעלה וד״ל

From the chest, the aforementioned Text 1 continuing to the back of the page, this

---

AN AMULET Text 1 contains divine names, which Falk marks with the letters א ד. Text 2 contains most of the letters of the alphabet, in alphabetical order: the first line contains four letters, the second, five, and the third, six, while the fourth line contains three letters and two vocalization marks, a *sheva* and a *segol*. The notations to the right of Text 2 contain a reference to the year 5528 (= 1768), and the text beneath seems to be a reference to Tuvyah Boas: 'Tuvyah and his two sons'. [The possible meanings of other notations are not specified.]

whose principle is ז״ם [No explanation is given.]

and the secret of ט״יז, equivalent to ז״ך the numerical value of the first phrase is 27, represented by ז״ך, meaning 'pure'.

ITEM 2 the meaning of the text in the upper, enclosed box is unclear; the third line can

diary records the matter of Boas of The Hague and שיונה*, with R. Tuvyah and his two sons, may they live long, *from 8 and 11 Tamuz 5428 [summer 1768].

And what was in the book of meditations at the entry 'Daily' is eternal, *in a gold vessel, no. 32, with a chain on it; and a word to the wise will suffice. This vessel was wrapped in paper upon which was written: 'a ring that was concealed beyond the sea, and returned because of the known sins'.

ITEM 3

Three parts of the head of a *sword, for when it was sanctified the blade was entirely separated from the hilt. That is to say, all the silver on the hilt was broken into about thirteen parts. In the year 5509 [1748/9] all three parts were found scattered by the heat that it gave off. Then they all came together, and *what was lost from the table. They came to the domain of my forest, inside the tent, *during the act of shields of the forest, and they were concealed in the gold box that was like a half-shield. And in the said month of Tamuz, I repaired the sword once again in the hilt that had been scattered, as mentioned—and in the *war of the *rehatim* the parts of the hilt were scattered again

seemingly be understood as: 'And You are the Merciful One, who pardons and forgives.' The text of the lower, open, box reads: 'This ring was wrapped in paper, and on the paper was written as written above on this tablet, and sealed with the seal of the *mezuzah*, and then it was concealed in a heart of gold, as mentioned above, and a word to the wise will suffice.'

שיונה unclear word: possibly ושיוכה, 'concerning'. Alternatively, Falk may be referring to The Hague suburb of Scheveningen, where the Jewish cemetery was situated.

from 8 and 11 Tamuz 5428 [summer 1668] [Possibly there is an error here, since the amulet refers to 5528 (1768), which would be consistent with the rest of the text; this suggests that the letter *kuf*, which would have added 100 years to the date, was accidentally omitted. Following this statement there is a complicated mystical text that has not been translated (ll. 208–12).]

in a gold vessel, no. 32, with a chain on it the text that follows seems to comprise unclear references to various objects that Falk apparently wrapped in paper and placed in a chest. [Perhaps 'gold vessel . . . with a chain on it' should be understood as a gold ring on a chain, and 'no. 32', written with the two letters *lamed* and *beit*, which spells *lev* (meaning 'heart'), as an inscription. This would tie up both with the ring mentioned in Item 2 above and with the reference later in the sentence to 'a ring that was concealed beyond the sea, and returned because of the known sins', though perhaps it was returned not because of 'known sins' but because of 'one known as a sinner'? This latter version might explain the reference above (fo. 4*b*) to 'a boat from the *nivleh* of the day of his oath', since the ideas of 'beyond the sea' and 'the contemptible person' both seem relevant here.]

sword the Hebrew word used for what in context is obviously a sword is in fact *sheluḥah*, the feminine form of a Hebrew/Aramaic word meaning 'agent, emissary'.

what was lost from the table [The reference is unclear.]

during the act of shields of the forest [The reference is unclear.]

war of the *rehatim* this 'war' is mentioned again in the diary. The date would lead us to believe that Falk is referring to what would later be

and the blade was left bare. So I cut a branch to make a hilt for it, and it is still in the wooden hilt made from that branch to this day; and a word to the wise will suffice. After the war of the *reḥatim* I sought the pieces of the hilt but found only eight and the knob. These are the princes of evil: by casting lots six were left to be hidden, and three to be concealed in the sea. And *the significance of the three is that they are the three that were wrapped together with leather, and on it is the following inscription: '3. Three pieces that were forbidden after the sanctification of the sword by the scattering in which they were scattered during the war of the *reḥatim* by the power of the man of war, by a temporary measure.'

ITEM 4

Here are three parts of the sword, out of the six mentioned in Item 3, and they are the first; *the part of the key that is called concealment; and the second covered the tip of the blade of the sword, so that it should not cause harm and be thrust in the ground; and a word to the wise will suffice. And on the sides that are wrapped, that is, on the paper, the following is written: '4. Silver covered the head of the sword, *that contains with the concealment of the key in the large *raḥat*, etc.'

ITEM 5

Here is the silver rod; that is, it is the shaft of a silver pen. It was inside, and on the shaft was impaled a staff, on the top of which was a silver top like a myrtle, like the top of the gold staff presently in my possession. The said staff was hidden; and a word to the wise will suffice. And within this shaft is the sixth piece of those mentioned in Item 3 in that shaft; and it is the knob of the sword; and a word to the wise will suffice. They are wrapped in paper, and on the paper the following is written: '5. Silver, *the staff that was sanctified in the holy long war, in the planting of his holy staff, until the fall of the knob of the sword in the war.'

ITEM 6

The mouthpiece of the holy shofar, from which nine blasts issue in one melody, is made of soaked waxed paper, and God's name was uttered during the invocation. While our mouth is issuing *the warning, the mouth of this ram's horn is inserted in

known as the Seven Years War. The numerical value of רהטים *reḥatim*, is 264, the same as that of יעקובואיטים (Jacobites).

the significance of the three [In the Jewish mystical tradition, three is understood to signify strength and permanence; perhaps Falk is hinting at that here.]

the part of the key that is called concealment [The meaning is unclear.]

that contains with the concealment of the key [The meaning is unclear.]

raḥat [The singular of *reḥatim*.]

the staff that was sanctified in the holy long war [The phrase 'the holy long war' may suggest that Falk was aware of the religious context of the Jacobite campaigns.]

the warning perhaps referring to the blowing of the shofar as a warning. [Alternatively, the Hebrew word Falk uses, *hazharah*, could be a

the mouth of this shofar-trumpet, and from this object *the Appellation is uttered while this shofar is being blown. During the sacrifice of the *rehatim* *the slaughterer was seized and adjured to stand trial. After he had been tried and was found innocent, he was obliged to leave this shofar at the place of the altar, and a word to the wise will suffice.

But the fools did not know that this was made by the slaughterer, and because of this [?] it is divided into thousands of thousands of pieces, and on Rosh Hashanah they were seized, and they are mentioned in the paper. The following is written on the paper: '6. Mouthpieces of shofar-trumpets, from the shofar of the congregation with a shaft on which was penned the great and holy divine name, on the shofar that was left on earth to play its part.'

ITEM 7

Here are *three tablets from the rope, in three readings, from time to time. That is to say, they are on a rope, with *the names written once, and duplicates were never written; only four times the same names on four tablets: those three tablets that are here and the fourth that was hidden by me. There are also *thirty-two tablets that are called 'hidden tablets'. These three tablets were wrapped in paper on which the following was written: '7. Three pure copper tablets'. (The meaning of these pure copper tablets is as explained on the fourth tablet in my possession.)

ITEM 8

These four gold stars are *from seven, from nine, from eight—the matter of זט״ח. Their names are from the pearl rope, on the outer face of which was inscribed on the חז״ט* silver stars, that together are the matter of twenty-four, the well-known twenty-four; and a word to the wise will suffice. And the twenty-four gold stars were wrapped in paper, on which the following is written: '8. Four gold stars that were invalidated from the staff of *the exiled one. After their great action, He shall rule, in Whose hand is all, and Who decrees all.'

misspelling of *hatsharah*, meaning 'declaration'.]

the Appellation an alternative name of God.

the slaughterer was seized and adjured to stand trial [The reference is unclear.]

three tablets from the rope, in three readings, from time to time [The meaning is unclear.]

the names [Possibly the reference is to names of God, which are regarded as having mystical powers.]

thirty-two tablets that are called 'hidden tablets' [On the significance of thirty-two, see note on 'thirty-two paths of wisdom' on fo. 3*a* above.]

from seven, from nine, from eight—the matter of זט״ח the three letters are equivalent respectively to 7, 9, and 8. [Added together, they total 24, which seems to be a significant number as it occurs again below.]

חז״ט a rearrangement of the three letters just mentioned. [It is not clear why this is necessary.]

the exiled one [The reference is unclear.]

ITEM 9

They are *the four silver stars mentioned in Item 8, and on their wrapping the following is written: 'four silver stars from seventy-two stars, which by the holy four were sanctified [—].'

These nine items are inside the gold chest containing *the main group, *the seal of the assembly, with *four stones the like of which never existed before, or of such size. Since 5519 [1758/9] they have been buried in the soil of Holland, for they were buried there in Adar 5518 [spring 1758]. They are not buried [there any longer]; and a word to the wise will suffice. Since 5522 [1761/2] they are fortunately in *the forest of Harderwijk, and *their clothing and sceptre are in the forest of The Hague, *which is invalidated, for it is planted, and there is no confusion in it, as far as I understand. And the chest was buried in the forest of Harderwijk as mentioned, with these nine items inside, for good fortune. And to this day, *wherever my footsteps may lead me, this chest is sealed with the seal of my sign from the day it was buried, as mentioned. *And now that I have been privileged to build only nine camps, and all the more so to build *a house for the flock that shall be for the benefit of all Israel, I do not wish to leave it in that ground, [despite its having been] beneficial for all, and beneficial for Israel, by my many sins. Therefore I desired to bury it in the soil of The Hague forest, if Shimon's domain had not been invalidated by his changing his house; and a word to the wise will suffice. The domain of Boas's has been sold to another, and I have no permission to enter there to do anything; and a word to the wise will suffice.

But everything comes from the Lord, blessed be He who decrees, for this, too, shall be for the good, as happened in the month of Menachem Av 5527 [1767], *when I cancelled the action of R. Tuvyah and his sons, may they live long, as is written in my

the four silver stars mentioned in Item 8 [In fact only gold stars were mentioned in Item 8; the significance of the discrepancy is unclear. Oron comments that she does not understand the text that follows so it has not been translated.]

the main group of sacred objects, as described above.

the seal of the assembly the seal of the members of Falk's circle.

four stones [Perhaps precious stones.]

the forest of Harderwijk Harderwijk is in the north-west of Holland. The forest there apparently belonged to Shimon Boas.

their clothing and sceptre [A sceptre would normally be a mark of royalty, so perhaps the context is a pretender to a European throne seeking refuge.]

which is invalidated ... as I understand [The meaning is unclear.]

wherever my footsteps may lead me, this chest is sealed with the seal of my sign [Falk seems to be emphasizing that the chest is safe, irrespective of where he personally is located.]

And now that I have been privileged to build only nine camps [It is not clear why building 'only nine camps' should be a privilege, nor is the nature of a 'camp' ever really explained.]

a house for the flock that shall be for the benefit of all Israel possibly referring to a synagogue.

when I cancelled the action [The reference is unclear.]

book; and a word to the wise will suffice. *I sent all my belongings from them in all innocence, and God's plan for me turned out for the good, for R. Shimon changed his residence and pitched his tent elsewhere; *Boas's house was sold and the person with whom I had made my deposit, who was *Zelig of Harderwijk, peace be on him, died. *All of this was from the day I began to cancel the power of the soil of Holland, in the year—End of passage.

|fo. 5b| *Monday, 12 Tamuz 5528* [27 June 1768]. End of passage—the year 5526 [1765/6]. In order to reconvene the assembly once more in the first place until today, Monday, 12 Tamuz 5528, but I was not successful in that matter; and a word to the wise will suffice. For this meeting, and the reason for its disbanding, I committed myself today, Monday, 12 Tamuz 5528, to deposit my gold chest, which contained the objects listed in the nine items on the other side of the page, with R. Tuvyah and his two sons, R. Shimon and R. Abraham, the firstborn, as customary, as written below: R. Shimon

I sent all my belongings ... and God's plan for me turned out for the good Falk seems to imply that he moved the chest from the forest of Harderwijk because he had some sort of a premonition that Boas would sell his land.

Boas's house was sold Falk goes on to mention yet another thing that happened—'that the place of ? was torn', but the meaning is unclear; perhaps 'part of the foot'?

Zelig of Harderwijk [No details are provided as to Zelig's identity and his relationship with the Boas household is not specified.]

All of this was from the day I began to cancel the power of the soil of Holland, that was in the year of—End of passage [Falk seems to imply that everything that happened was because of something he had instigated, but he gives no reason for having done so. He also does not state the year, though perhaps it was 5526 [1765/6], as suggested by the date at the start of the next entry.]

Monday, 12 Tamuz 5528 [27 June 1768] Falk now appears to record what happened two years previously, possibly in Holland. [The meaning of the first sentence is not very clear but thereafter the text becomes quite lucid.] In the first passage, Falk relates how he asked R. Tuvyah (Tuvyah Boas) and his two sons R. Abraham and R. Shimon to act as signatories for the gold chest whose contents Falk itemized in the preceding pages. His account emphasizes the unusual way in which the signing was done: the first to sign was R. Shimon (the younger son), who signed on the first two lines. Then R. Tuvyah his father signed on the fourth line, and finally R. Abraham, R. Tuvyah's firstborn. At the end of the whole passage Falk provides a diagram illustrating the procedure: a rectangular 'chest', above which are the signatures in the order described and below it the names of the signatories. Alongside the signatures are the initial and middle letters of words from biblical verses. The letters alongside R. Shimon's name are the initial letters of Jer. 33: 26, with the additional notation 'said י"י' ('the Lord said'), which prefaces this prophecy, in the preceding verse (v. 25). Alongside the name of R. Abraham, who signed last but who appears in the third line, appear the letters המפנו י"י צבאות. The last part of this is a name of God: the Lord of Hosts; I have not succeeded in finding the verse connected with these letters. The fourth line has Tuvyah's name, along with the initial letters of Ps. 89: 51.

wrote on lined paper, and in sections, simply. And in the proper order, what was written on the tablets: R. Shimon wrote until the third line, the fourth line was written by R. Tuvyah himself, and he signed his name, as did R. Shimon afterwards, and then after him R. Abraham. By rights, R. Abraham should have signed his name first, but I did not want to let him write the matter that was in the third tablet, so as not to lead him astray in his thoughts, Heaven forfend, *for why should they have faith if their forefathers did not believe—and a word to the wise will suffice. But as for R. Shimon, I have no choice; and a word to the wise will suffice. And after they finished, *before my Torah scroll, that was covered with a kerchief, that is, they did not notice and I was relieved. For this purpose I wrote it; and a word to the wise will suffice. It can testify, and it will testify, that I folded the paper on which they had written, as mentioned, and I stuck it under the strap around the coffer in which the gold chest was placed, as mentioned. The three signed with their signatures and departed in peace, together with *Boas's son-in-law, son of the money-changer from Berlin, to whom R. Tuvyah had given his youngest daughter; and a word to the wise will suffice. *His young man was also with him. All this was in שיונר*, in the house of יגיר*, *where my home is today.

for why should they have faith if their forefathers did not believe Solomon Schechter, in 'The Baalshem—Dr Falk', presumes on the basis of this rhetorical question that Falk converted to Christianity and interprets it as veiled advice to Boas's two sons. However, he distorts the following sentence ('But as for Shimon, I have no choice, and a word to the wise will suffice'), mistranslating it, as if Falk were saying that he, Falk, and not Shimon Boas, had no choice in the matter. For further discussion of Falk's rumoured conversion to Christianity, see the Introduction, Section IV, n. 12.

before my Torah scroll perhaps Falk adjures them in front of the Torah scroll. [However, this explanation does not seem to square with the rest of the text, viz. that it 'was covered with a kerchief, that is, they did not notice and I was relieved'.]

Boas's son-in-law Tuvyah Boas gave his youngest daughter Belia in marriage to Ber Moses Levin of Berlin, and they married in 1769 (see van Zuiden, *Proeve eener genealogie*). However, this passage describes an event that took place in 1768, when they were not yet married. Falk could thus be talking about the husband of one of Tuvyah's other daughters (though he does refer to her as 'the daughter of his old age'), but most of them were married into families from Frankfurt and not Berlin, such as the court Jews Beer and Kahn, so the facts do not quite fit. It is perhaps more likely that since the couple were already betrothed, Falk referred to the future son-in-law as if the marriage had already taken place; this is not uncommon, since the Hebrew phrase used, *ḥatan*, means 'bridegroom' as well as son-in-law, and is thus the standard way of referring to a man engaged to be married to one's daughter.

His young man [Presumably a servant.]

שיונר possibly a place name (Scheveningen?). See above, fo. 5a, at שיונה.

יגיר the term could be a misspelling of מגורים, meaning 'residence', or possibly a misspelling of the surname Jaeger. [It is not known to whom this might refer.]

where my home is today [The reference is unclear.]

R. Shimon came today with R. Mendel, and then he left me and brought his father *and his son R. Abraham, and his young man, as mentioned. Then they sent the young man with the son-in-law to observe, that is to say, when we carried out our actions, as mentioned. Then they departed in peace, and I, too, departed in peace, because my lodgings were there. On Wednesday I returned there, and from there, at six o'clock in the evening, I rented a coach with four horses, ordered it to come at midnight, and so it was. *It came close to בית תיקשרי, half an hour before, also by night. *Then I, too, went after him and travelled together with Mendel and Meyer to the inn that was about half way, where I had arranged to spend the night. I gave instructions to await me the whole night; and so it was. I arrived there between one and two o'clock in the morning, and *I told the innkeeper that her clock was wrong, for it was only a little after midnight, and so it remained, etc. In the morning we set off, arriving at ten o'clock in the morning, and I had to pay for the coach from six o'clock yesterday evening till ten o'clock today, Thursday, 8 Tamuz—fifteen gulden, and the coachman behaved completely unreasonably, *twenty-two gulden and six pence, and I spent it in The Hague. *Know that all the aforementioned was on the table, covered, without a candle except for the wax candle we needed for sealing. Nevertheless, *as I knew, I came to this room, I lit a tallow candle, and I placed it on the stove; and a word to the wise will suffice.

New moon of Nisan 5523 [15 March 1763]. Know that all the items mentioned earlier and what was done with them *are unfolded as a scene before you. This was on the day and the eve of the new moon of Nisan 5523, *in the room of the forest of assembly in

and his son R. Abraham [Presumably, his father's son Abraham, viz., his own brother.]

It came close to בית תיקשרי, half an hour before, also by night בית תיקשרי appears to be a place name. [The meaning of the rest of the sentence is unclear.]

Then I, too, went after him [It is not clear to whom 'him' refers.]

I told the innkeeper that her clock was wrong [It seems that Falk arrived late but chose to cover this up by telling the innkeeper that her clock was wrong.]

twenty-two gulden and six pence, and I spent it in The Hague [This is not clear. Perhaps the coachman was 'completely unreasonable' and demanded more money, but this would not explain what Falk spent in The Hague unless he meant that he paid him the extra later in The Hague.]

Know that all the aforementioned was on the table [The subject changes very abruptly. Perhaps 'all the aforementioned' refers back to the nine items, but this is not specified, and nor is a table mentioned.]

as I knew [The reference is unclear. Following the end of the sentence, esoteric manipulations of names relating to the Boas family have been omitted (ll. 316–19).]

are unfolded as a scene before you [Presumably, Falk is emphasizing that he has provided a detailed description, though it is unclear for whom this description is intended.]

in the room of the forest of assembly in the domain of 5518 [1757/8] 'forest of assembly' is Falk's usual term for the place where his circle used to meet, apparently the 'camp' in Epping Forest. [The meaning of 'in the domain of 5518' is unclear. Perhaps the location of his

the domain of 5518 [1757/8], at the end of *the preparatory watch for the recitation of Kaddish; and a word to the wise will suffice. *When all the powers of the assembly were gathered in the said forest in 5504 [1743/4], etc. To this day, the day of the new moon of Nisan 5523, I committed myself to extract powers from the gold chest: *the powers of the assembly, the power of the world, the power of *the *rehatim*, the power of the pits, the power of the tooth, the power of the staff, and the force of all the powers, that is the power of the **lul*, the necessary, and *the colours, that has never been known to any beings of our times; and blessed be the Lord.

This entire operation was for the reason hinted sensed with the **gushit* intellect, that there was no choice but to behave in this way, *since the prosecuting חרך was weakened because I did not properly נשותי with שכזוט בהעולה until the end of the watch on the eve of the holy sabbath, 15 Shevat 5523 [29 January 1763], as mentioned in **Sefer hama'aseh*, *in the story of the judge who delivered a judgment that *we need not desecrate the sabbath for all the worlds before me, on the eve of the sabbath, the 15th inst., *and this was only Leib Kruka, the perfect one.

---

camp was later changed, or perhaps this somehow relates to the burial of the gold chest (see Item 9 above, on fo. 5*a*); or perhaps it should be '5528' as in the first note on this folio.]

the preparatory watch for the recitation of Kaddish [Presumably a kabbalistic practice that Falk followed.]

When all the powers of the assembly were gathered... in 5504 [1743/4] a reference to events many years previously, perhaps at the beginning of Falk's activities among his circle.

the powers of the assembly... the perfect one the entire passage is unclear.

the *rehatim* apparently a coded reference to Jacobites; see note to fo. 5*a*, above.

lul a small room.

the colours [According to some kabbalistic theories, each element of the sefirotic system represents an emanation of the divine, and each emanation is associated with a different colour.]

gushit human (*enoshi*) intellect? [But since *gushit* is an adjectival form deriving from *gush* ('block'), this cannot be more than a conjecture.]

since the prosecuting חרך was weakened because I did not properly נשותי with שכזוט בהעולה [The meaning of the Hebrew terms Falk uses is unclear, but it would seem that his wonder-working abilities were diminished because of something he did not do properly.]

Sefer hama'aseh [The reference is unclear.]

in the story of the judge who delivered a judgment possibly an allusion to a folk tale.

we need not desecrate the sabbath for all the worlds before me [The meaning is unclear.]

and this was only Leib Kruka, the perfect one [Since 'Kruka' is Yiddish for Kraków, this could be a reference to a 'Leib of Kraków', or perhaps to Aryeh Leib ben Shaul Lowenstam of Kraków, who was born in Kraków in 1690 and died in Amsterdam in 1755. This was before the time of which Falk is writing here, but the reference could be to something from the past. Why this Leib should have been referred to as 'the perfect one' is not clear. Esoteric texts following this passage, from line 334 to line 372, have been omitted, including all fo. 6*a* and the start of fo. 6*b*, which begins in that section.]

|fo. 6b| *Sunday night, 13 Kislev 5541* [10 December 1780]. By meditating upon *Ana bekho'ah*, I discovered *the alphabetical element within it, except that the letters הסמ are in a different order המס.

|fos. 7a–8a blank|

|fo. 8b| *Take heed, I have warned you, of the words of the living God, for His great name's sake, and they called to Him with all their full heart, from today, *Thursday, the new moon of Adar II 5535 [2 March 1775], that He should have mercy on us, and not rebuke us as befits our bad deeds; and He should not shorten the years of our lives, as we deserve; also, for He is a merciful Father, He will surely answer us on the day we call Him. *Amen, for eternity, *selah*, for ever.

|fo. 9a| *These are the spare books, of the books in the house of my tabernacle, that are therefore in a chest here in The Hague, the capital city, from Tamuz 5533 [summer 1773], *that are marked at the end of each line so, with the letter ס at the beginning of the list, and at the end of the books, for a reminder, today, Wednesday, eve of the new moon of Elul 5540 [30 August 1780]; may it be propitious.

4. *Ḥelkei zohar*
5. *Tikun hazohar*
6. *Avak soferim*
7. *Ḥelkat meḥokek* by Alshekh, and the eight sections, in a single volume

Sunday night, 13 Kislev 5541 [It is not clear why this passage should be out of sequence unless perhaps Falk got the date wrong. Esoteric texts in ll. 374–81 at the end of this text have been omitted.]

Ana bekho'ah a mystical prayer composed by R. Nehunya b. Hakanah, which is recited during the morning service and also during the service that inaugurates the sabbath; see further the notes to ZH's diary, fo. 13a.

the alphabetical element all the letters of the alphabet are included in the divine name of forty-two letters that can be formed from the forty-two words in this prayer.

Take heed the text that follows, written in 1775, appears to be a sort of sermon.

Thursday, the new moon of Adar II 5535 [2 March 1775] [The significance of the date is not clear. Normally the new moon of Adar is regarded as initiating a time of rejoicing.]

Amen, for eternity, *selah*, for ever Falk represents this phrase by an acronym; I am grateful to Professor Liebes for explaining it. [Esoteric text constituting the rest of l. 385 has been omitted.]

These are the spare books each entry in the list of books is preceded by a Hebrew letter-number (beginning, inexplicably, with 4), with a small circle above the letter. For details concerning these books and those in the following list, see Appendix E, 'Falk's Library'.

that are marked at the end of each line so, with the letter ס [In the continuation of the sentence Falk says that the letter *samekh* is also marked 'at the beginning of the list, and at the end of the books', but in fact it appears only at the end of each line.]

8. Further, *Ḥavatselet hasharon* by Alshekh, on Daniel
9. *Kaftor vaferaḥ* and the book *Kavanot ha'agadot* from *the year ישר"ש יעק"ב יציץ ופרח ישראל
10. *Magid mereshit*, responsa
11. *Mishnat ḥasidim*
12. *Sefer karnayim* and *Dan yadin*, from the bookseller
13. *Asarah ma'amarot*
14. **Esrim ve'arba*, in red
15. *Pa'amon verimon*, *Asis rimonim*, and *Pelaḥ harimon*, that are in a single volume
16. *Kav hayashar*, with Yiddish translation
17. *Shulḥan arukh* by Rabbi Isaac Luria, of blessed memory
18. *Shomer emunim*
19. *Si'aḥ yitsḥak*, grammar
20. *Ḥozeh tsiyon* with Psalms, *a commentary based on *pardes*
21. **Gefen yeḥidit* written in clear language
22. Pentateuch with Targum
23. *Emek yehoshua*, questions and answers on the weekly Torah portions
24. *Sefer hahigayon* by Maimonides

For a reminder: in the month of Menahem Av 5537 [summer 1777] I checked the list of these books here at Boas's house in The Hague.

For a reminder from the new moon of Tamuz 5540 [3–4 July 1780]: to buy the books listed here, with God's help, each according to its marking:

1. Mishnah, vocalized, *with the *Kaf naḥat* commentary: by the sage R. Obadiah of Bertinoro, and by the sage the author of the Tosafot.
2. *Ir giborim* on the Pentateuch, by the sage Ephraim Luntshits.

---

the year ישר"ש יעק"ב יציץ ופרח ישראל the phrase is a quotation from Isa. 27: 6; numerical manipulation may indicate the year of publication as 5468 [1708]. For *Kaftor veferaḥ* see Appendix E, list 1, no. 6; also list 2, no. 10.

Esrim ve'arba in red *Esrim ve'arba* ('Twenty-four') is a reference to the Hebrew Bible, which is composed of twenty-four books—here in a red binding.

a commentary based on *pardes* [A Hebrew acronym referring to the traditional method of exegesis incorporating four approaches: literal, allegorical, comparative, and esoteric.]

Gefen yeḥidit an ethical treatise.

with the *Kaf naḥat* commentary: by the sage R. Obadiah of Bertinoro [Falk may have been mistaken, since *Kaf naḥat* is a commentary by Isaac b. Solomon Gabbai

These are the books that are always with me when I travel long distances, so that they are there wherever I am. *And I wrote on the first pages a mark for myself:

1–2. *Or torah*, with errata
3–4. *Tohorat aharon*—laws of ritual slaughter
5–6. *Yalkut ḥadash labekiyut*—*Yosher levav*, kabbalah
7–8. **Mafte'aḥ hazohar*—*Mareh mekom hadinim*
9–10. *Mikhlol yofi*—*Musaf he'arukh*
11–12. *Sha'arei orah*—*Sifra ditseni'uta*
13–14. *Sefer hashorashim*—*Pa'ane'aḥ raza*
15–16. *Me'ah berakhot*—*Neḥmad vena'im*
17–18. *Sefer masoret*—*Seder olam raba*

Menahem Av 5537 [summer 1777]

19–20. *Likutei hapardes*—*Matsat shimurim*
21–22. *Magen david*—*Mesilat yesharim*
23–24. **Ḥibur yafeh mehayeshu'ah, lamed-ḥet*—*Mavo she'arim*
25–26. *Sefer leḥem yehudah*—*Mo'ed david*
27–28. *Kol ya'akov*—*Siftei yeshenim*
29–30. **Sefer haḥinukh*
*40–41. *Apiryon shelomoh*—*Derekh tevunot*
42–43. *Hadrat melekh*—*Vayakhel mosheh*
44–45. *Ḥelkei avanim*—*Ḥizuk emunah*
46–47. *Mishmerot kehunah*—*Magal ha'omer*
48–49. *Mikdash melekh*—*Ne'edar bakodesh*
50–51. *Sefer nitzaḥon*—*Arugat habosem*
52–53. *Emek yehoshua*, see *the list

appended to the 1614 Venice edn. of the Mishnah; but since the second reference here to a sage is to one of the tosafists, authors of the classic medieval commentaries on the Talmud known as the Tosafot, his intention is not clear.]

And I wrote on the first pages a mark for myself [It is not clear how this relates to the double numbering system that follows. Perhaps he means that he wrote something inside so that he could identify them as belonging to him.]

Mafte'aḥ hazohar*—*Mareh mekom hadinim index to the Zohar with an index to the laws mentioned.

Ḥibur yafeh mehayeshu'ah followed by the abbreviation *lamed-ḥet*, possibly referring to the book *Leshon ḥakhamim uleshon paz* ('Language of the Sages and Finely Refined Language: Epistles in Pure Language, with Added Charms and Cures'; pub. Zolkiew, 1747).

Sefer haḥinukh Falk's copy of this book was apparently in two volumes, thus the listing as two books.

40–41 [The interruption in the sequence of numbering from the last entry is not explained.]

the list the first list, on fo. 9*a*.

Those up to no. 29, except for those marked with a circle, were with me in Menahem Av 5537 [summer 1777] here in The Hague; and a word to the wise will suffice. Items 40 to 52 were with me in 5533 [1772/3], and also all those mentioned until item 29, even those marked with a circle, as mentioned.

*A bag in the ship's sail, carefully written down in Av 5537 [August 1777]. A bag of good white undergarments and a white *arba kanfot*; a bag of good black garments and a black *arba kanfot*; a bag of formal dress clothes, nightclothes, and three mesh shirts; a bag of kerchiefs and other linen, two *scarves and the good hat; a bag of six shirts marked with the letter *samekh* in blue; and a new *box, four pairs of black stockings, and also white ones, besides the big ones; two white camisoles; a large garment for the sabbath with a belt, a black belt, and the good *roquelaure* in the bag; and all the other things mentioned above from the year 5537. *He has dealt bitterly with me for my sins.

|fo. 10a| *Elul* 5537 [late summer 1777]

1. *Four screws in the lower circle; they are like a kind of fork to join the tent's square roof from above, which are four pieces of wood inserted in the roof, as mentioned, which is of *linen. In the corner where the letter *gimel* is sewn, you have to insert the corner of the square, where the letter *gimel* is carved into the two poles of the corner, and from there proceed in the order *dalet*, *beit*, *alef* to the other three corners. And four circles ⊙ like this, to insert in the aforementioned screws underneath the poles, so that the part of the circle with two holes will enter the tent, in which the ends of the curtains attached to the roof are hanging. And four nuts to close the four screws that are in the four corners of the roof. And in each of

A bag in the ship's sail [Possibly, a bag made of sailcloth. Since the garments listed after this appear to be recorded by the bags in which they were kept, perhaps the bag listed first was the one in which all the others were stored.]

arba kanfot [A four-cornered garment with ritual fringes in each corner, worn by Jewish men (normally as an undershirt but sometimes as an outer garment) in fulfilment of a biblical commandment.]

scarves...hat the terms that Falk uses are *halstuch* (from the German) and *mutsh* (from the Dutch *muts*). I am grateful to Shmuel Ram for helping me with these terms.

box 'box' is a term for riding breeches that derives from the English term 'box cloth' [a particularly densely woven and felted woollen cloth that is almost waterproof and hence used for this purpose].

roquelaure a French term for a short coat with a wide opening at the neck.

He has dealt bitterly with me for my sins [The reference here is unclear.]

Four screws in the lower circle the items listed here, all with their dimensions, were used by Falk to build the structure that he called *ha'ohel* ('the tent'), near London Bridge, which served for prayer or for meetings of his circle. [The choice of this term is possibly linked to the biblical term *ohel mo'ed* ('tent of assembly').]

linen [Perhaps meaning 'canvas', which would be the more usual material for a tent.]

the aforementioned screws, insert two rods of the screens, and their closure is the four, whose shape is as follows: 🔩. And four more screws to lead the curtains, together with the four that are in the corner of the roof from above, if need be. And the eight rings in the screws here, to bear the ends of the rods of the screens ℧; and if they are of this shape: ⌒ long and thin, all the better.

2. Another four, like the screws of the corners mentioned in item 1, shorter than all of them, like the dimensions of this drawing, with four nuts. As I understand, these screws are the finest to fasten the aforementioned square of the tent. They also contain:

3. Wheels in the long cord, in which two ropes are fixed, with which to raise and lower the tent, that is, always *from the side where the table is—the east.

   That is to say, in this wall, because two pulleys are inserted in the pole on the side of this wall, to raise and lower the tent easily, and a word to the wise will suffice. (And there should be two copper wheels in the screw to insert into this wall, in order to pull the ropes of the tent and tie them with them); (or two rings, of the iron rings, of the length that I have at home, the big ones. For a reminder, what is written in these two lines is what should be).

4. Four squares in the screw to insert in the wall, coated with tin; a rod to easily pull the holy rope.

5. Another four squares, as in item 4, without the tin rod, to turn the holy rope etc., if someone wishes to do so.

6. A cord in two wheels, one higher than the other, that is to say, in the shape of item 1, if someone wishes. I took from there to my home.

7. A bag for all that is required, if needed.

8.*The tent on the west side is five widths double, which are in all ten widths: five inside, in which the pole is inserted from below, and five on the outside, on them. And at the south-east corner, four widths; at the north-east corner, four widths; and in the middle of the eastern wall of the tent, one width, to be raised and lowered as usual.

   1–1. The lengthwise measure of the western pole

   2–2. And the measure of the pole to the south of this. Everything mentioned here is to be found in the Harderwijk tent

from the side where the table is—the east
  [Presumably the layout was supposed to echo the layout of the Temple.]
**The tent on the west side ... ** a description of the tent, the drapes, the curtains, etc. [The level of detail here is reminiscent of that in the biblical description of the sanctuary in the Torah portion 'Terumah', e.g. Exod. 27: 9–19.]

3–3. And like that, the measure of the eastern pole, that is, the poles of the square of the roof

4–4. And, similarly, the measure of the northern pole of the aforementioned, and they are marked 1–1, 2–2, 3–3, 4–4

The main thing is to fasten the roof of the tent once more: the bolts, four big ones, for the roof of the tent, upon its erection, the four big ones, two for the middle of each pole of the roof, to hang the curtains outside, joined with the roof bolts; and the short bolts, to hang the red ropes; and a word to the wise will suffice. And each of them has a male and a female connection. Eight rings of the bolts for the rods of the screens in the middle of the poles. And four females as in the fork, to hold the aforementioned rods in the corners of the roof; and four pockets to reinforce the roof, the corners of the roof, if need be, under the bolts. This assemblage *was tested for the main thing *on a sabbath eve in Elul 5537, for a reminder, separated from item 1; and a word to the wise will suffice.

|*fo. 10b; fo.11a blank|

|fo. 11b| *Proverbs 1: 17: כל בעל כנף ('every winged creature'): the initial letters of each word have a total numerical value of 42, the last have a total numerical value of 140, for a total numerical value of 182 בפק; the second letters total 120, for a grand total of 302; and *their element: שבן בפקע or מן מקבע*.

was tested for the main thing [Perhaps meaning 'was tested thoroughly', though since the first line of the paragraph says 'that the main thing is to fasten the roof of the tent' perhaps this refers back to that.]

on a sabbath eve [Presumably to make sure that the structure did not collapse on the sabbath.]

[fo. 10b: The entire folio contains a single cryptic line; its meaning is not explained in the Hebrew edition so it has been omitted.]

Proverbs 1: 17 ... *Thursday night, 26 Kislev 5538* Falk now lists charms he derives from biblical verses. Similar charms appear in his *Sefer segulot vegoralot* (Book of Charms and Fortunes), the manuscript of which is among the holdings of the archive of Jews' College London (see Neubauer, *Catalogue of the Hebrew Manuscripts in the Jews' College, London*, no. 128) and now held in the London Metropolitan Archives. Lots that fell to the members of Falk's circle are recorded in Falk's handwriting; these are letters derived from biblical verses chosen by lot and then manipulated using an esoteric methodology that he explains.

their element apparently a reference to a new arrangement of the order of the letter-numbers so as to form 'words', such as שבן בפקע, which when rearranged gives בפק נע שב.

מן מקבע with a numerical value of 302 = שב (the grand total, as explained in the text).

Deuteronomy 32: 11: יפרוש כנפיו ('He spread His wings'): the initial and final letters form the letter combination שכוי, with the numerical value שול [= 336]; the middle letters: פר פני, with a numerical value of תך [= 420]. *שול תך כשתול, with a numerical value of שנות [= 756].

Psalms 68: 14: כנפי יונה נחפה בכסף ('there are wings of a dove sheathed in silver'). And behold, the initial letters have the numerical value of ונבכים.* *Here. The second and third letters, rearranged: פן ספן הנוכח; the final letters rearranged: ההי פה* (הנוכח).

Zechariah 5: 9: והנה כנפים ככנפי החסידה initial letters פרח, last letters ימה, with a numerical value of 115.

Lamentations 4: 16: פני יי חלקם ('The Lord's countenance has turned away from them') *(see Genesis 31): the initial letters form the word פיח ('soot'); the last letters rearranged, form the word ימה ('seaward'); ש*: קו נחל, that is to say, ונקהל; *in order and combined with ל"א, has a numerical value of למ"ש; and without ל"א, a numerical value of שמד ('destruction').

1 Kings 6: 15: עד קירות הספן צפה עץ מבית ('He also overlaid the walls on the inside with wood'): the initial letters of this verse, rearranged: מעץ העקד ('from wood speckled' or 'bound'); *the last letters: התנצת ('shall you be victorious'). מבית ('on the inside') has a numerical value of נבת [= 452].

Mishnah *Kinim 1 [mishnah 1]: חטאת העוף נעשית למטן (['the blood of a bird] that is a sin-offering is sprinkled below'): the initial letters rearranged: נחלה ('land inheritance'); last letters rearranged: תפתן, or rearranging these two letter-combinations: *עולת העוף נעשית למעלה. הנחלת פתן ('[the blood of a bird] that is a wholly burnt

---

שול תך these two 'words', rearranged, form the word כשתול ('as planted'), which has a numerical value of 756, that of the word שנות ('years of') [The significance of these phrases is unclear.]

ונבכים the numerical value of the initial letters = this word ('and the depths of'), without the final *mem*, which is written above the line.

Here Falk apparently erred here; he might have thought to write the initial and last letters of the words in the phrase from Psalms, but then changed his mind.

ההי פה these letters mean 'that one, here', which could be understood as הנוכח, 'the one who is present'.

(see Genesis 31) presumably for similar content (namely, falling into disfavour).

ש possibly the remaining, or the second and third letters, which produce the following seeming 'words'. (Falk adds the remaining letters of the Tetragrammaton, ו ה, to the count.)

in order and combined with ל"א the numerical value of these words: פיח (98) + ימה (55) + ונקהל (191) + ל"א (31) = 375 (למ"ש); and without ל"א, these words total שמד = 344.

the last letters rearranged, without the word עד, which entered, in its entirety, the calculation of the initial letters.

Kinim the last word of the original mishnaic text is למטה.

עולת העוף נעשית למעלה from the continuation of *Kinim* 1: 1.

offering is sprinkled above'): the initial letters rearranged: הנעל ('the sandal'); the last letters in order תפתה ('seduce'), *or נתעלת הפה or, rearranged הנתעלתפה.

Mishnah *Ḥulin* 12 [*mishnah* 1]: (see there) שלוח הקן אינו נוהג אלא בעוף שאינו ('the sending [of the mother] from the nest applies only to birds that are not—'): *the middle letters = קול; the initial letters and the last letters of these two words, rearranged = הנחש ('the serpent'), which has a numerical value of שסג [= 363]; *the ascending letters: עדת ('congregation of'). The single word עוף ('bird') has a numerical value of וקן ('and the nest') [= 156]. מרז*, the descending letters form the word קול.

(ותרנגולים) * מזומן כגון אווזין ('at one's disposal, such as geese [and fowls]'); and a word to the wise will suffice: the numerical value of the single word מזומן is קמ"ג [= 143], of אווזין, 80 [פ], and its ascending letters rearranged are כזבח זס, which in turn has a numerical value of ק"ד [= 104], *that is, פקד. The ascending letters of קמ"ג = נדר ('vow').

*Exodus 9: 5: פיח כבשן ('soot of the kiln') has a numerical value of עת צח שעב ('time') [= 470].

---

or with the addition of the initial letters.

the middle letters of the two words שלוח הקן, rearranged = קול ('voice' or 'sound').

the ascending letters the letters following each of the given letters שסג (called 'ascending letters' because the numerical value of the letters of the Hebrew alphabet increases (or 'ascends') as the alphabet progresses), rearranged, are עדת.

מרז the meaning of this word is unclear. It might be derived from וקן, with the *vav* ascending (as explained above) to *zayin*, the *kuf* ascending to *resh*, and the *nun* descending to *mem*. ['Descending' because the numerical value of the letters of the Hebrew alphabet decreases (or 'descends') as the letters are taken in reverse order.]

(ותרנגולים) מזומן כגון אווזין from the continuation of *Ḥulin* 12: 1.

that is the combination of ק"ד + פ = פקד.

Exodus 9:5 Should be Exodus 9:10. [The esoteric phrase that follows (l. 514) has been omitted as incomprehensible, as have ll. 515–24. The latter comprise nine 'sentences' that contain letter and word combinations derived from esoteric numerical calculations and the like, together with several words from the above biblical and mishnaic phrases, but are similarly incomprehensible.]

Thursday night, 26 Kislev 5538 [25 December 1777]. *As is the custom, I sent a *kalk hoen*, that is, a type of dark brown goose, and cash; and a word to the wise will suffice, with Gedaliah to Cosman, on condition that he roasts it and sends me with Jacob the first two little joints, tied and with a seal.

And Jacob was [?], and I sent to enquire whether he had brought *the said deposit, and he replied that he knew nothing about a deposit. I replied via Gedaliah that he would be forgiven if he brought the deposit, then I would speak with him. On Monday night, the night of the new moon of Tevet, R. Jacob came to me. The deposit was tied as I had instructed, and I received it via Gedaliah. I did not agree to meet Jacob then but told him to come on Tuesday at ten o'clock in the morning.

After Gedaliah had left, I summoned R. Mendel to my room and had him write *a rhyme from my signs, nine lines, etc. I ordered him to come the next day and stay downstairs until R. Jacob arrived and then to come and take the said rhyme and give it to R. Jacob to sign the paper on which the rhyme was written and then seal it with four angles inside four circles. And so he did in front of R. Mendel and Gedaliah, on the covered table in front of me, in the room that is *in front of the hut of the successful ones. Then he gave it to R. Mendel to pass it by hand, and he did as I bid him, and then they ate breakfast in the said room. R. Jacob thought that he would be meeting me after that meal, but he had not deserved that yet.

Thursday night, 26 Kislev 5538 [25 December 1777] [Much of the text that follows is a description of a ceremony involving *goralot* (lots used in fortune-telling). It is perhaps no coincidence that it was Christmas as it was the custom among some east European Jews to avoid Torah study on Christmas.] Apparently, after the lots had been written, they had been sent to Jacob as a deposit for safe keeping; but the latter had seemingly had a disagreement with Falk so that when Falk sent a messenger to him to bring what had been sent for safe keeping, Jacob was evasive. Falk therefore sent his adopted son Gedaliah (in fact, his wife's son) to represent him and say that he would forgive Jacob if he returned the deposit. A few days later Jacob did indeed bring the deposit, but Falk did not agree to see him, and ordered him to come the following morning at ten o'clock. The sealing of the lots was done the next day, but even after this Falk did not permit Jacob to come before him. The following evening, R. Mendel and Gedaliah took branches and pegs (the reason for this is not specified), marked letters on them and added a seal, and placed them in a black chest.

As is the custom, I sent a *kalk hoen* a type of fine bird suitable as a Christmas gift—a goose, as Falk says, though Shmuel Ram has suggested that it could be turkey (from the Dutch for turkey, *kalkoen*).

the said deposit [Perhaps meaning the 'proof of delivery' that he had requested, viz. the first two little joints?]

a rhyme from my signs 'Rhyme' is a valid translation of Falk's term *ḥaruz*, though in medieval Hebrew the term had the additional meaning of something that is rearranged to convey something new. The reference here is to the charms derived by manipulating the texts of the nine 'signs' or 'formulas' above.

in front of the hut of the successful ones [The reference is unclear.]

Tuesday night, 1 Tevet [31 December 1777]. I sent R. Mendel with Gedaliah to open the dark hiding place and take out four pegs that Cosman had hidden there in the company of him and of Jacob on Sunday night, 1 Kislev 5538 [1 December 1777]. And the custom and the actions you will find in the rhymes of *the night of dew and rain 5538, as written above, on the aforementioned night of 4 Kislev [4 December]. And after R. Mendel had taken out the said branches and pegs from the hiding place, in order, one after the other, so as to *mark them with letters אבגד, he similarly put them in my black chest and then closed the chest and the gate of the hiding place. Then he emerged from the darkness behind him till he was outside, as I had instructed him through Gedaliah. Then Gedaliah sealed the gate of darkness with the silver seal that I have; and a word to the wise will suffice. And he came to my home with R. Mendel, who carried the said chest.

And he put it on the table of my downstairs room. And then R. Mendel went to his home in peace. The whole subject of 'every winged creature', without 'is adjured', and *all the words written on them in the chest were identified with a mark and are not in the nine rows of rhymes that Jacob wrote on my instructions and were signed by him and read by both of them.

|fo. 13a|

ITEM 1

*My reply to the fool Cosman, Tuesday, 16 Adar I 5540 [22 February 1780], concerning his letter of Monday 15th inst. And my reply to the fool from Thursday, 18 Adar I 5540 [24 February 1780], concerning his letter of Wednesday, is below in Item 2.

the night of dew and rain ... 4 December outside the Land of Israel, the words 'Give dew and rain' are added to the Amidah prayer from the night of 4 December (or on the 5th before a leap year).

mark them with letters אבגד [These are the first four letters of the alphabet. Since they were to be taken out 'in order', perhaps the order was signified by the letter of the alphabet.]

all the words written on them [Following this sentence, starting on fo. 11b and including all of fo. 12a (ll. 550–92), Falk presents esoteric manipulations to create charms by combining letters using various methods. The notes in the Hebrew edition point out that this passage was most likely written in Tevet 5538 (1777/8), and explain all the techniques but since they are too complicated for English-speaking readers to follow they have been omitted. The techniques used include, for example, manipulating separately the second, third, and last letters of the names of the months that mark the solstices and equinoxes to form new words and then calculating the numerical value of these new words, or sometimes of two, three, or four times the value of the words thus generated and attributing meaning to the words derived from these calculations. Esoteric techniques are also applied to phrases in particular Torah portions, though the significance of these particular portions is not explained.]

My reply to the fool Cosman the text that follows is what Falk sent, in cryptic language. The first four items constitute a single unit, the initial letters of which are כנחש ('as a

Greetings

1. שמור ['guard']: initial letters כנחש
2. חלק ['a part/smooth']: last letters קמת
3. נייר ['paper']: the second [letters]: מלכי ['my king']
4. ככתם: the remainder: תוי ['to mark']
5. עד—initial letters עבת, which has the numerical value of בשבחך בעמי
6. כי—last letters, דלת ['door']. וחד לדת
7. כנחש, second letters, מבנדר; numerical value, רוח ['spirit']
8. שדי, fourth letters תר זה ; together, חרורת.
9. חמד
10. בברק
11. מרורתו
12. יהלוך, initial and last letters, מבכי; second letters, להמות
13. הלמות or בתמם

*ITEM 2

*Job 39: 5: 'Who sets the wild ass free? Who loosens the bond of the onager?' Prov. 17:

serpent'); the final letters are the equivalent of קמת ('you rose') (combining the two *reshim*, each = 200, to one *tav* = 400). Items 5–13 are a second unit. The word combination בשבחך בעמי ('with your praise among my people'—not a biblical citation) is constructed from the initial letters of the following words: כי ('for'), שדי ('the Almighty'), בברק ('with lightning'), חמד ('pleasant'), כנחש ('as a serpent'), עד, בתמם ('until', 'ever'), מרורתו, יהלוך (these two words, with an additional *mem* (*mimerorato yahalokh*), appear in Job 20: 25: 'through his gall, strikes'). The numerical value of this combination is עבת (= 472). The last letters of items 5–11 are also calculated by different methods, as Falk chooses. ד = 4 + י = 10 + ש = 300 + י = 10 + ד = 4 + ק = 100 + ו = 6, for a grand total of 434 = דלת, or, transposed = לדת. The second letters from items 7–11 are נ ד מ ב ר, and rearranged: מבנדר. The fourth letters (including item 12), ש ק ר ו ו produce the following combination: ש + ק = 400 = ת; ר remains unchanged; ו + ו = 12 = זה, which together form the combination תר זה. The combination of רוח and תר produces the combination חרורת. The initial and last letters of the words in 12 and 13 produce the word מבכי ('from weeping'); and the second letters, להמות or הלמות. Items 8 and 9 are taken from Isa. 32: 11, and items 10–12 (with minor changes) from Job 20: 25.

ITEM 2 the first version of the letter that Falk sent to his friend Cosman. The letter is written in cryptic language, and is composed of bizarre words or, more correctly, letter combinations obtained from calculations involving initial letters, last letters, second letters, and numerical equivalents. Falk combines these 'words' with fragmentary biblical verses and incomplete citations from rabbinic and medieval literature, thus generating 'sentences' without logical meaning. In my attempt to decipher the text I at times succeeded in locating the sources he used, but the logic behind the joining together of all the words into a single unit escapes me. [The esoteric texts in ll. 612–23 have been omitted as untranslatable.]

Job 39: 5 ... Ps. 37: 14 the connection between these three verses is unclear. Ps. 37: 14

19: 'He who loves transgression loves strife; he who builds a high threshold invites broken bones.'

Ps. 37: 14: 'Concerning them it was said, "The wicked draw their swords"' etc., till the end of the verse. וקלע לידו נרו. Final letters: ליום ['for the day'], that is to say, *ומלי נחיך = עקד(ו).

*Onager [*arod*]—it is permitted in the world to go only the distance of the *sabbath bounds; three *eyes in the forehead, because of the middle and small one, it is called the eyed one; and a word to the wise will suffice—and iron, *'I will hoe with him, and I will hoe with you'—a matter of digging.

continues, 'bend their bows, to bring down the lowly and needy, to slaughter upright men'. The numerical value of the initial letters of the continuation of the verse, וקלע לידו = 256 = נרו ('its/his light').

ומלי נחיך which has the numerical value of 174 = עקד(ו).

Onager Falk's explanation of the word relies on that of Rashi on the verse in Job. Yehuda Liebes wrote, in a review of the Hebrew edition of this book in the *Haaretz* newspaper: 'Among the many (and difficult to decipher) warnings on the need to maintain secrecy, Falk states here ... that he is about to repeat the counsel of the serpent: "Only I will speak before the Lord the advice given to Eve." It seems to me that the reference is to the verse in which the serpent prophesies to Adam and his wife that their eyes will be opened and they will be like God (Gen. 3: 5). Following this declaration, Falk then discusses the matter of the *arod*, the animal identified here (according to various sources) as a "wild serpent" or as a "wild ass", but its main identification might not be set forth here. The *arod* might be Falk himself, the spiritual man, who stretches the boundaries of the permitted within the realm of religion. The *arod*, of whom it is said (Job. 39: 5): "Who sets the wild ass free? Who loosens the bond of the onager?", is portrayed here as loving freedom, and also crime and strife, hating bonds, bounding and leaping, who digs down, but is only permitted to go afar within the "sabbath bounds". From another aspect, as well, the *arod* seems to resemble the seer and mystic (and possibly an Indian fakir), because it is depicted here as having three eyes in its forehead, with a small middle one, after which it is called "the eyed one". At the end of this description Falk urges his friend to continue to delve further into this and the many other allusions here, which I did not fully examine. Possibly, however, the verse that is used here to encourage searching and delving into the meaning of these matters will also be seen to contain an allusion to Falk's inner thought and the depths of his soul, and perhaps also to the spirit of freedom. For this is the wording of the verse, in whose letters Falk, in a certain way, also found the words "do not forget": "They search out iniquities, they have accomplished a diligent search, even in the inward thought of everyone, and the deep heart." [The esoteric manipulations of ll. 631–2 at the end of the paragraph have been omitted.]

sabbath bounds [The distance that a Jew is halakhically permitted to walk on the sabbath beyond a settled area—about one kilometre.]

eyes in fact Falk's term is *aniyim*, which translates as 'poor ones', but the relevance is unclear; in context *einayim*, meaning 'eyes', makes more sense. Falk's spelling is in any case often poor.

'I will hoe ...' based on Mishnah *BM* 5: 10. [The meaning of this is unclear.]

|fo. 13*b*| *I sent this letter from here, London, to my bosom friend R. Shimon Boas, with a letter written by R. Jacob in his own name on Friday, 9 Adar II 5540 [16 March 1780]. My friend, from me, whose soul is bound to you *from the day of your fate. Do not await the answer of my thoughts, all the more so since it is late in coming. Lest you say, the soul has done this to me, for he did not want to rejoice with his beloved ones at the proper time, Heaven forbid. For this occurred due to carelessness, and was not intentional. And it is well known to all who are wise-hearted and loyal that your joy is my joy. And may the Holy One of Israel grant that in stillness and quiet we shall be saved, together with *the legion of myriads. Greetings from the man of faith, who signs with the seal of his plan.

|fo. 18*a*| *18 Iyar 5533* [11 May 1773], which is Lag Ba'omer, fell on Tuesday, eleven days before *the end of the watch of Tamuz 5532 [1772]; for the order of the entire watch of Tamuz begins at the *molad* of the Sivan preceding it and it ends at the *molad* of the Sivan of the following year. Thus, the watch of Tamuz 5532 began in Sivan 5532, and it ended in Sivan 5533, as mentioned in the watches of *ma'aseh merkavah*; and a word to

I sent this letter words from the preceding section (see parenthetical note) are incorporated in this letter. On Shimon Boas's ties with Falk see the extensive discussion in Appendix A. [The preceding section is divided into three columns. The first column contains biblical references, the second words from the Bible and their permutations, and the third the numerical values derived from the permuted words. The words in the first main column are to be read vertically, from top to bottom. The words in this column, too, are followed by the new 'words' derived from the initial letters and by other methods from the words in the first main column. As elsewhere, Falk employs various pseudo-mathematical techniques based on the numerical value of the letters and those that follow or precede them, referred to respectively as 'ascending' or 'descending' letters. Since these texts are meaningless to English readers even when translated they have been omitted. Falk continues his narrative, with the paragraph starting 'I sent this letter', towards the end of the folio, at l. 667. However, the text that follows, starting at l. 673 and continuing over fos. 14*a*–16*b*, once again comprises esoteric manipulations of words and phrases and has been omitted; fos. 17*a*–*b* are blank, and the first lines of fo. 18*a* (ll. 750–2) have been omitted for the same reason as elsewhere.]

from the day of your fate [The reference is unclear.]

the legion of myriads [The reference is unclear.]

the end of the watch of Tamuz 5532 . . . ends at the *molad* of the Sivan of the following year [Falk explains how 'the watch of Tamuz', which evidently lasts for a year, is calibrated, but does not explain its significance. In the Jewish calendar, the order of the months he mentions are Iyar, Sivan, Tamuz. 'The watch of Tamuz' in a given year starts at the first appearance of the *molad* (new moon) of the month of Sivan immediately preceding it and continues until the *molad* of Sivan of the following year. The paragraph concludes with incomplete phrases and unclear texts all relating to the esoteric manipulation of words and phrases (ll. 764–8).]

ma'aseh merkavah mystical doctrine concerned with the vision of the divine chariot (*merkavah*) in the book of Ezekiel.

the wise will suffice. In brief, who is he who does not give thanks to the Creator of all. As it is said, 'The Lord has given and the Lord has taken away, blessed be the name of the Lord now and for ever' [Job 1: 21]. Amen, for eternity, *selah*, for ever. It is of the essence of His loving-kindness that He kept His promise and *destroyed the Accuser in the watch of Tamuz 5532, which fell on Tuesday, 18 Iyar 5533, which is eleven days before the end of the watch of the past Tamuz of 5532, that will conclude on Friday, 28 Iyar 5533 [21 May 1773], as is customary in the watches of the *ma'aseh merkavah*; and a word to the wise will suffice.

*These are the four quarters of the lottery ticket in London, of the four kinds of signs that Reuben Zamość bought for me on Saturday night after the sabbath, the night of the new moon of Kislev 5542 [17 November 1781] for fourteen shillings, may they prove lucky; and I gave Reuben half a crown as a gift. *And these are the signs:

1. 2,000   365
2. Sign   45   God have mercy upon me, for You
3. Sign   377   Live and endure for ever, do not fell me
4. 600   76   In my old age, God

|fo. 18b| *A page for a reminder *of the evil that shall become good, Amen, for eternity, *selah*, for ever, from the new moon of Kislev 5532 [8 November 1771].

*Kislev page pushed in: the sale of seven whole *trees, for my sins, by Gedaliah. God be blessed, the eighth tree in its entirety remains in my possession to this day. And know that from the silver of the menorah, 203 oz., 3 dwt.; and its gold, together with 226 oz., 15 dwt., from the money of the seven abovementioned trees, that [*incomprehensible words omitted*]. And in the four items 1, 2, 3, 4, you will find the sum from the weight of the silver of the seven trees, and you will understand it.

destroyed the Accuser in the watch of Tamuz 5532 [The reference is unclear.]

These are the four quarters Falk records the signs for the four lucky numbers in the lottery tickets that he has bought.

And these are the signs what follows are coded allusions to the numbers of the lottery tickets that he purchased. Line 1 alludes to the number 2365. Line 2 alludes to the number 45. Line 3 alludes to the number 377. Line 4 alludes to the number 676.

A page for a reminder a record of the sale of various objects.

of the evil that shall become good [The reference is unclear.]

Kislev page pushed in probably meaning that this page was inserted here, since the preceding page refers to matters connected with a date a decade later (1782) than the time frame of this page (1772).

trees possibly a coded reference to very expensive gold or silver objects.

*The sum of the money from their sale, and all as I received it, is as follows:

*From the total of items 1, 2, 3, and 4, I spent	1. 421 oz. 15 dwt.; 5s. 6d. every tree, £115. 18s. 0d.
All the pledges mentioned on the pledges page	2. 303 oz. 15 dwt.; 5s. 6d. every tree, £83. 10s. 0d.; this is all.
And the repayment of the debts, as mentioned below	3. 209 oz. 15 dwt. from the trees, totalling 429 oz.; £115. 7s. 0d.
	203 oz. 3 dwt. from the menorah total weight: 153 oz., I received £314. 0s. 0d.

*PAGE OF PLEDGES

1. The menorah, £54. 0s. 0d., for a total of eleven months, interest of *202 per month, sold, £62. 18s. 0d.
2. Eight crowns eight, on the trees: £28. 0s. 0d., including interest: £30. 6s. 0d., sold.
3. Trumpets and two cups, including interest for nine months, £6. 0s. 0d., sold.
4. A gold watch and a gold chain, £20. 0s. 0d., including interest for nine months, £22. 14s. 0d.
5. A pair of candlesticks, *in the pocket, £7. 0s. 0d., including interest, £7. 17s. 0d.
6. A pair of candlesticks from the table: £26. 0s. 0d., including interest, £9. 15s. 0d., sold.
7. The ring of R. Moses, may he rest in peace, £9. 2s. 0d., including interest, £11. 3s. 0d.
8. Two gold watches, 2 hundred, including interest, £2. 2s. 0d., 12.
9. A second pair from my table, £26. 9s. 0d.; and interest for five, £9. 12s. 0d., sold.
10. Four brown *busby, that are, 17 parts, £22. 0s. 0d., and high interest for eleven months, *£26. 0s. 0d.

The sum of the money [Despite Falk's claim that the figures would be understandable, the list is difficult to follow.]

From the total listing of the redemption and sale of pledges.

PAGE OF PLEDGES [Many of the entries here are difficult to follow as units are not specified and other information is missing.]

202 [No unit is given.]

in the pocket their location [perhaps a coded reference].

busby [Apparently a reference to a bushy, tall wig (a usage noted from 1764), though later the term came to be applied to a form of military headdress.]

£26. 0s. 0d. the notation '29' in the original is superfluous.

11. A pitcher and a bowl, eight guineas, and including interest, £9. 6s. 0d., sold.

12. A stand for a candlestick cup, £2. 10s. 0d., including interest: £2. 11s. 8d.

On Monday 18th inst. I began to sell, though Gedaliah, the pledges recorded above, for my sins, according to the numbers listed above, *until 11 Shevat 5532 [16 January 1772].

|fo. 20a| This is a record of the debts that were repaid from the total from Kislev 5532 long-passed [winter 1771].

1. ביראיור*, of two years' standing, £19. 6s. 3d.
2. Baker, of two years' standing, £25. 16s. 6d.
3. Grocer, £7. 8s. 2d.
4. Glazier, 17s. 10d.
5. Doctor's bill
6. *Hivir
7. Wolsey, apothecary, 16s. 4d.
8. Candles, £13. 12s. 0d.
9. Simmons *kar bindir, 7s. 6d.
10. Coalman, £15. 15s. 4d.
11. Butcher, £11. 13s. 0d.

On the eve of the holy sabbath, 5 Tishrei 5533 [2 October 1772]

12. *Kutsche machen, £6. 8s. 0d.

---

until 11 Shevat 5532 [ll. 829–34 comprise further information on items sold, all of it difficult to follow. Among the items sold was 'a pony, sold to Burley, may he be cursed, for £15. 0s. 0d', with no explanation as to who Burley was (perhaps this should have been 'Burleigh', a famous noble family) or why he should be cursed, though perhaps he is the coachman mentioned in item 15 on fo. 20a). Other items mentioned are two furs, some vessels, and three trumpets with two pipes. The proceeds include a mention of *tet*, glossed in the Hebrew edition as 'possibly a form of currency', perhaps an abbreviation for thaler, a silver coin used throughout Europe at that time.]

ביראיור I do not know the meaning of this term. [Perhaps a spelling pronunciation for 'brewer'?]

Hivir the meaning of this term is unclear. [Perhaps a name?]

kar bindir possibly meaning 'carpenter'.

Kutsche machen maintenance of a coach (from German).

*Thursday, 5533

    13. Blacksmith for the horses, £5. 13s. 0d.

    14. *Sheital, £6. 10s. 0d.

    15. Burley the coachman, may he be cursed, £16. 14s. 9d.

    16. From a pledge falling due, £3. 5s. 6d.

    17. *Zin ḥov yashan, £1. 6s. 3d.

Sunday night, 7 Tishrei 5533 [1772]

    18. *Zinkim, £25. 0s. 0d.

Tuesday, 7 Marheshvan 5533 [3 November 1772]

    19. Hurtle the coachman, £1. 15s. 6d.

|fo. 20b| 5532 *Iyar* [spring 1772]. On Monday night, 26 Kislev 5532 [2 December 1771], I informed my maidservant Suki that from that day on I would pay her only £4. 0s. 0d. per annum.

Tuesday, 9 Iyar 5532 [12 May 1772]. Suki received a total of 3s. 0d. owing from her old account, and a guinea that she received today on account of the rent, כמז"ט*, *25 Kislev, £1. 4s. 0d. And in Nisan 5532 [spring 1772], *as mentioned, a gift of 4s. 0d to cover the cost of the work involved in having a gown made from a dressing gown of mine that I had given her as a gift.

    Jacob my servant—I paid him his wages today, Tuesday, 9 Iyar 5532 [12 May 1772], for the two months that will fall due on Thursday, 11 Iyar. This was a matter of some contention because he had been released completely from my service on Monday, 11 Adar II 5532 [16 March 1772], and he had received what he was owed with compensation for dismissal as is customary. But afterwards he asked me to allow him to stay a

---

Thursday, 5533 [Since the eve of the sabbath is Friday, which technically begins on Thursday night, this could simply be a reference to a transaction which preceded that mentioned earlier.]

Sheital possibly a person's name (a David Sheital is mentioned below).

Zin ḥov yashan an old debt; Falk mixes German and Hebrew words.

Zinkim the term is followed by an abbreviation that could mean 'landlord', but as no property is specified and the name does not appear elsewhere it could refer simply to a member of Falk's circle [or perhaps to the purchase of zinc for alchemy purposes].

כמז"ט should perhaps read במז"ט, 'for good fortune'.

25 Kislev [This was the first day of Hanukah, so perhaps the money was given in the tradition of Hanukah.]

as mentioned [It is not clear where.]

few days until he could find lodgings for himself, and I agreed on that condition. But he, the blackguard, stuck like a plague until Tuesday 9th inst. Then I argued with him, and I gave him £1. 0s. 0d for the two months as mentioned, as well as a Purim gift for two years, 11s. 0d. He thanked me and took my blessing, and left my service, for the benefit of all Israel, Amen, for eternity, *selah*, for ever, with a new dismissal from today.

*Meyer, my manservant—his wages that were due him from the new moon of Sivan 5531 [14 May 1771]: (*a*) £4. 0s. 0d annually; he received till today, Tuesday, 9 Iyar 5532, £3. 5s. 0d; and (*b*) as written in the resignation that he gave me today, and that was finished on the new moon of Sivan 5532 [2 June 1772], may it be propitious; then I have to give the balance of his wages, 14s. 6d, as mentioned.

Wine—in the month of Iyar 5532 [spring 1772]. *I transferred a barrel full of wine from last Passover to my small cellar, as well as nine bottles of this wine, and of the aforementioned wine, £3. 0s. 0d. And of R. Jacob's wine, three bottles, all sealed. They were put away by my servant Meyer. And empty bottles are tied at their neck with a white thread, to indicate that they are for Passover wine. A total of twenty-three bottles, etc.

On Friday, 5 Iyar 5532 [8 May 1772]. Gedaliah rudely asked me in the following words: 'Give me a shilling that I need'; and a word to the wise will suffice, and I gave him a shilling. On Tuesday, 26 Iyar, he asked politely, and I gave him a shilling.

Wednesday, 9 Sivan 5532 [10 June 1772]. *Jacob my son-in-law—the wedding day of Jacob, *ass doctor, son of the sister of my friend Cosman, *who is leaving these parts for now. I sent two *silver vessels *with Meyer my servant, and he received from *Mardoch half a crown as a gift. The above vessels weigh 10 oz. 3 dwt. And for the fashionable vessels, I paid £3. 14s. 6d.

Meyer, my manservant who is also mentioned in Falk's will as a beneficiary.

I transferred a barrel full of wine ... and of the aforementioned wine, £3. 0s. 0d. [The relevance of the money here is not clear since Falk seems to be sending the wine to himself.]

Jacob my son-in-law Falk refers to Cosman's nephew as 'my son-in-law'. As scholars have noted, Falk had no children of his own, though he had adopted his wife's son, Gedaliah.

ass doctor apparently, a veterinarian.

who is leaving a possible reference to Cosman's mission from England to France and Holland (we know of this trip and Cosman's stay outside England from the letters of General Rainsford, who was a Freemason; see also Appendix A, section 2).

silver vessels I do not understand the term used to explain what the vessels were for.

with Meyer my servant [The reference seems odd because Meyer had apparently left Falk's service a month earlier, but perhaps the gift was sent in advance of the wedding.]

Mardoch the reference is unclear.

Thursday, 2 Marheshvan 5533 [29 October 1772]. Today I paid Suki her wages from 8 Sivan 5532 [9 June 1772] to the coming 8 Kislev 5533 [4 December 1772], the sum of £2. 2s. 6d. as a gift for trimming candles last Yom Kippur *for good, and her dismissal was written in Gedaliah's notebook as a reminder.

*To Meyer my manservant I paid the balance of his wages for sixteen months, the total today being £1. 5s. 6d., and that includes the total of what he received, all in all £5. 7s. 0d., that is £4. 0s. 0d. Today, Tuesday, the new moon of Marheshvan 5533 [27 October 1772], I gave him 3s. 0d. as a gift.

*R. Eliezer Cohen, the cantor from Pisen, received my blessing on the said new moon. I gave him as a gift fifteen of my surplus books, that is to say, duplicates, and also two guineas. He left here in peace for the boat to Danzig in the week of the Torah portion of 'Lekh lekha'.

In the month of Tishrei 5533 I paid the blacksmith, as mentioned in the above list. The carriage maker I paid, too, as mentioned there.

The farrier was paid.

WINE, PASSOVER 5533 [1773], NINE BOTTLES, INSCRIBED ON THE CORK '5533'

And more of that wine mixed with sugar, twenty bottles, and on them is written שפך*. And of the wine that I made on the intermediate days of Passover from a quart of red raisins in four jars, from today, sixteen bottles; a total of forty-five bottles of wine from the said Passover.

Thursday, 12 Sivan 5533 [3 June 1773]. Gedaliah counted *the portraits of France in front of Jacob and Mendel: a total of 81 papers, 8 big ones, 19 big ones, 8 medium ones, 36 medium ones and 4 small ones that were in the booth, 6 black ones engraved in copper, and I also have some small ones:

|fo. 21a|

1. *Twelve pages, amounting to a principal of £8,280. 0s. 0d, the principal to be paid without interest in the year 5525 [1764/5], and they are from a lottery. The interest to be paid each Tamuz, £414. 0s. 0d.

for good [Perhaps meaning 'for good will'.]

To Meyer my manservant [As already mentioned, Meyer had apparently left Falk's service a month earlier.]

R. Eliezer Cohen…from Pisen [Perhaps Posen, as in Appendix A.]

שפך presumably meaning 'for Passover'. [Perhaps because the term, which means 'pour out', appears in the Passover Haggadah, in a liturgical text that calls on God to 'pour out' his wrath on those who do not acknowledge him.]

the portraits of France [Seemingly an allusion to promissory notes, though the categories are not clear.]

Twelve pages these and the numbered items that follow list monies due to Falk as recorded on 'pages', possibly IOUs. The repeated mention of them as 'from a lottery' is because Falk's wealth came mainly from winning lotteries and success at games of chance.

2. Fourteen pages, amounting to a principal of £9,640. 0s. 0d., the principal to be paid without interest in the year 5526 [1765/6], and they are from a lottery. The interest to be paid each Tamuz, £483. 0s. 0d.

3. Fifteen pages, amounting to a principal of £10,400. 0s. 0d., the principal to be paid without interest in the year 5527 [1766/7], and they are from a lottery. The interest to be paid each Tamuz, £506. 0s. 0d.

4. Twenty-four pages, amounting to a principal of £16,640. 0s. 0d., the principal to be paid without interest in the year 5528 [1767/8], and they are from a lottery. The interest to be paid each Tamuz, £833. 0s. 0d.

5. Twenty-eight pages, amounting to a principal of £19,600. 0s. 0d., the principal to be paid without interest in the year 5529 [1768/9], and they are from a lottery. The interest to be paid each Tamuz, £1,000. 0s. 0d.

6. Eleven pages, here in *their home, amounting to a principal of £42,000. 0s. 0d., the principal to be paid with interest in the year 5550 [1789/90], and they are from the East India Company of glorious France, and the interest will be paid in two parts each year: in Tevet £1,050. 0s. 0d., and in Tamuz £1,050. 0s. 0d.

Know that the total of listed items together is six, as you see before you: 1, 2, 3, 4, 5, 6. They make up 104 pages, whose principal comes to a sum of *£106,600. 0s. 0d., that is, one hundred and six thousand and six hundred pounds.

And fortunately I bought them for myself for four thousand and eighteen pounds sterling in London currency £4,018. 0s. 0d., on Friday, 20 Tevet 5519 [19 January 1759], that is, £3,402. 0s. 0d. in bank notes I deposited with R. Tuvyah, may he live long with his family, on the new moon of Marheshvan 5519 [1–2 November 1758]. For then, three months before receiving the aforementioned notes, the money was here, the notes in his hand. And when receiving the 104 said pages, the notes as above, this was 20 Tevet as mentioned, I found the sum of £4,018. 0s. 0d., less £616. 0s. 0d. that was required to make up the aforementioned sum of £4,018 0s. 0d. And for security, as is proper, I received a receipt signed by R. Tuvyah and his two sons, exalted in all, *may they live long; and besides the receipt I also received the list of items, the pages marked also by their signatures; and a word to the wise will suffice.

For a reminder: Item 6 of the eleven aforementioned pages, which was in their home for several years—R. Shimon [Boas], may he live long, begged me to make an exchange with him, giving me one page instead of ten pages, for that page is the total of my ten pages. I did what he wanted and exchanged with him today, Monday, 22

---

their home the Boas residence.

£106,600. 0s. 0d. [Arithmetic may not have been Falk's strong point. The total is actually £106,560. 0s. 0d. The error recurs below.]

may they live long in the diary this is followed by an acronym possibly meaning, 'with all the great Children of Israel'.

Menahem Av 5524 [20 August 1764]. From this day on, the said Item 6 is only eleven pages, as mentioned, for until Monday, 22 Menahem Av 5524, the said Item 6 was of twenty pages from the day of acquisition: and a word to the wise will suffice.

The principal is £106,000. 0s. 0d., which is the total of five to here. And the interest is £5,330. 0s. 0d., which is

7. Six pages, amounting to £22,000. 0s. 0d. as principal. I purchased them for a total of £884. 0s. 0d. today, Sunday, 24 Menahem Av 5525 [11 August 1765], and the pages amount to the sum of £1,000. 0s. 0d., according to what my friend R. Shimon has stated. For this, too, I hold in my hands a bill of acquisition from him, and the interest will be paid each month of Nisan, may it be propitious.

For a reminder: my dear friend R. Shimon told me that *from the day of the month of Nisan all seven items will no longer pay interest at 5 per cent, but only 4½ per cent.

|fo. 21b|	Parchment notes	Mark 1, 2	*Of the king
	Parchment notes	Mark 2, 3	Of the king
	Parchment notes	Mark 3, 3	

Together, eight promissory notes on France, and five on his majesty the king of France, amounting to a principal of £86,600. 0s. 0d. in French money, and three remaining notes on the East India Company of France amounting to £42,000. 0s. 0d. in French money, for a total of £128,600. 0s. 0d., for a reminder, as in the promissory note of R. Shimon before his brother R. Abraham, may he rest in peace, here in The Hague, *Boas, in the house on the bridge, today, Monday, 8 Elul 5532 [7 September 1772], may it be propitious.

For a reminder: the first six items amount to a total of £106,600. 0s. 0d., plus Item 7, £22,000. 0s. 0d., for a total of £128,600. 0s. 0d.

This *I sent with Mendel in his writing to R. Shimon the son of R. Tuvyah today, Monday, 16th inst., writing in my name דימעפלי*:

Hayim Samuel Jacob di Falk *Valk Tradiola: the second letters yield my signature דימעפלי, *which is the same as פעמ"י ד"לי as in Scripture; and further, מיד פעלי.

from the day of the month of Nisan [Perhaps meaning 'from the first of the month of Nisan'.]

Of the king a list of the purchases and sales of promissory notes of the king of France.

Boas apparently a reference to the Boas family residence.

I sent with Mendel in his writing [This and similar references elsewhere to sending things written by others might seem to suggest that Falk was aware that his orthography was poor.]

דימעפלי Falk's signature, following a code he goes on to explain.

Valk according to Elhanan Reiner this is how Falk's name was sometimes pronounced. Falk uses his name twice to write his code name: פעמי דלי.

which is ... מיד פעלי Falk mentions two additional names derived from the letters of his name: דימעפלי = פעמי דלי, מיד פעלי.

*Hayim—*yod*; Samuel—*mem*; Jacob—*ayin*; di Falk—*peh*—the second letters forming פעמי; Tradiola—*dalet*; Valk—*lamed*; Laniado—*yod*—third letters forming דלי.

|fo. 25*a*|

*CONCERNING THE JEWISH COMMUNITY OF THE HAGUE

**Sunday, 24 Menahem Av 5425*, *France. And according to my notebook R. Shimon received from me £884. 0*s*. 0*d*. and not £852. 0*s*. 0*d*. as recorded; and a word to the wise will suffice. *The matter of the note.

On the said Sunday R. Shimon received from me £600. 0*s*. 0*d*. in banknotes, as well as interest for the year 5525, amounting to the sum of £230. 0*s*. 0*d*., as well as money in cash: forty-seven ducats, thirty-two pence. *And a half amounting to the sum of twenty-two pounds and a few shillings, amounting to a total of £852. 0*s*. 0*d*.; he received that from me, and *uber that amount he delivered to me stocks from France worth in the principal £22,000. 0*s*. 0*d*. in French currency—that makes £1,000. 0*s*. 0*d*., and he marked the note **zayin, vav*, pages mentioned previously.

**Sunday, 11 Tamuz 5528.* I delivered *the chest of the meeting as mentioned in this notebook on the page pasted in. And after the delivery R. Shimon confirmed four seals within circles, four around each circle on the drawing of each seal, and it is called the circle of the meeting, as mentioned in the note of the meeting, and *blessed be

---

Hayim—*yod* Falk's presentation of the derivation of these names from the second and third letters of his full name.

CONCERNING THE JEWISH COMMUNITY OF THE HAGUE [The reason for the heading is unclear since little of the text that follows appears to relate to it at all.]

Sunday, 24 Menahem Av 5425 [Presumably in fact 5525, corresponding to 11 August 1765.]

France Falk describes transactions that took place in France.

The matter of the note [The reference is not clear.]

And a half [The reference is not clear.]

uber a reference to some sort of banking activity, perhaps meaning 'over, beyond' (German *über*).

zayin, vav [The two Hebrew letters, which on their own could stand for 7 and 6, are highlighted with a curly superior mark; the meaning is unclear, as is the connection to 'pages mentioned previously'.]

Sunday, 11 Tamuz 5528 [Falk originally recorded the year as 5428; he then wrote the correct date, as here, but without deleting the original entry.]

the chest of the meeting [Perhaps meaning 'at the meeting', or 'for the meeting'; or perhaps meaning 'the chest with the collection'—the Hebrew words are similar (*aseifah, osef*) and orthography was not Falk's strong point.]

blessed be He who remembers forgotten things [God is referred to in this way in the liturgy for the Additional Service on Rosh Hashanah; the phrase used there is actually 'who remembers all forgotten things', so Falk has slightly misremembered.]

He who remembers forgotten things. For here I knew not the matter, *whether this covering was done differently or not.

Thursday, 19 Tamuz 5530 [12 July 1770]. I received interest from *R. in Boas's home three hundred and thirty guineas, twenty ducats for interest due in Tamuz 5529—and for Tamuz 5530—and on Sunday the 22nd inst. R. Tuvyah and his two sons came to see me, and they brought the gold chest etc. That chest had been in their possession from 5528 until today. I had delivered that chest as it was on the hour and the day that I had received it, for I did not open it, for the reason that since the day I ordered them to bring the chest, I had sought its power in the forest and did not find it—and then I delivered to them four gold ingots, weighing altogether 18 oz. 13 dwt, 23 gr.—and on that day, in front of them all, he further delivered to me ninety-seven guineas, three gulden, seventeen pence, for a total of four hundred and twenty-seven guineas, one hundred ducats, three gulden, and seven pence.

Tuesday, 24 inst. R. Leib Doctor came to see me, and in the presence of his son I gave him a gift of a guinea, that is, for prescribing the pills in a little box. *For all the world I cannot do as he commands, and indeed I showed *R. Abraham Doctor, and he took the value of its money; and a word to the wise will suffice.

25th inst. R. David Sheital came to see me. I gave him a gift of a guinea for a dowry fund, and *he gave me a list in a village near the coast in Harderwijk.

whether this covering was done differently or not [The meaning is not clear.]

R. [No further identification is offered.]

For all the world [The meaning of this sentence is unclear.]

R. Abraham Doctor Dr Abraham Gomez Argas, also known as Dr Philippe de la Cour, mentioned as a beneficiary in Falk's will (see Appendix F). The relationship to R. Leib Doctor, mentioned previously, is not specified; the entry suggests that perhaps they were father and son. ['Doctor' would seem to have been an indication of R. Abraham's occupation, since we know that his surname was in fact Argas.]

he gave me a list in a village near the coast in Harderwijk [The meaning is unclear.]

> בעיגול זה היה
> על לוח אחד מארבעה לוחות
> הנזכרים בעיתין יום ה' יט תמוז
> הנ"ל ובתוך עיגול זה קיים קושמן
> בחודש אייר התק"ל בשולחן גן ויט
> שביערי וזה נוסחת קיומו
> וא"ב] שטנו העת בראשם לסטרת יפלו
> ועל חושין שני גם בעיגול כזה כתב
> משבע נזיר תלב וזממוז מתנו

　　　　*In this circle, which was
　　　　on one ingot of the four ingots
　　　mentioned in the entries for Thursday, 19 Tamuz,
　　　as mentioned and within this circle Cosman confirmed
　　　in the month of Iyar 5530 on the table of *White Garden
　　　that is in my forest and this was the formula of his confirmation
　　　　　　[*combinations of 21 letters]
　　　and on the second *ingot, also in such a circle, is written:
　　　　　　[combinations of 21 letters]

　　*Item 9 is a translation into English of what was written by my hand, this letter that R. Shimon Boas sent to me by the noble *Duke Czartoryski, that is to say, my answer to his letter that I received through R. Jacob, who wrote this.

In this circle the text inside the circle is some sort of amulet.

White Garden the term Falk uses is a combination of Hebrew and English, with 'white' in Hebrew transliteration preceded by *gan*, the Hebrew for 'garden', thus following the Hebrew word order (noun + modifier). [In other words, the location cannot be identified from the moniker Falk uses.]

combinations the letter combinations on the two plaques, with twenty-one letters on each, possibly allude to the forty-two-letter name of God.

ingot gold ingot.

Item 9 [The reference is unclear. A further reference occurs in the next entry.]

Duke Czartoryski Prince Adam Czartoryski (1739–1823), born in Gdańsk (then Danzig) in Podolia, travelled to England, France, and Austria in 1768, revisiting England in 1772 in the hope of finding financing and support for his struggle to liberate Poland [then partitioned between Austria, Prussia, and Russia]. In 1781–2 he served as president of the Lithuanian Tribunal, the highest appeal court for the nobility of the Grand Duchy of Lithuania. The wealthy banker Shimon Boas maintained close contacts with members of various royal houses in both western and eastern Europe. These probably led to Boas meeting Czartoryski and bringing Falk and his talents to the prince's attention. The prince, desirous of meeting Falk, used Boas's

Tuesday, 6 Marheshvan 5533 [2 November 1772]. I received today from R. Shimon Boas, my bosom friend, a letter of recommendation for Duke Czartoryski, one of the great nobles of Poland who holds hands with royalty, etc., by the noble himself, who delivered it to R. Jacob, who wrote this, to deliver to me, for it was not possible for me to receive him myself as requested by R. Shimon. I have my own reason, and a word to the wise will suffice. And this is the answer that I sent by R. Jacob, today, Friday 10 Marheshvan, in the English language as mentioned, with the seal of my name in it, as you will find in its copy, where it is listed as Item 9, and the impression in the gold seal is inside a square.

> Sir, as to the letter placed in your hands by the renowned Shimon Boas, who is perfect to the epitome of perfection, all the more so in his perfection he has merited to stand before you, and to recommend in his letter such a great lord as yourself, coming from afar to your humble servant who has been so bold as to receive the letter from your honour by a man of our trust rather than in person as was his duty as good manners dictate, he who is committed to the remnant of Israel.
>
> Before the lord of the land and its kings, please forgive him, and greetings from your servant, who awaits pardon as an Israelite.

Tuesday, 14 Marheshvan 5533. My answer to R. Shimon as mentioned, for the letter that I received from the noble Czartoryski as mentioned above, verbatim:

> *I am ever mindful of the Lord's presence
> Who is he who did not go forth to offer his greetings to the exalted, wise, discerning nobleman, singled out among the flock of renowned scholars? For there is a golden tongue in my mouth, uttering many praises of virtues. He offers entreaties with a fine pen, aspiring to perfection to wax eloquent for the wisdom of the youthful and the weak; he sings before noblemen and kings. And for such and such does one say, how pleasant are the perfumed

good agencies to that end, bringing Falk a letter of introduction from Boas. However, as becomes clear from the diary, the meeting never took place. Falk was apparently apprehensive about the encounter, and waited for some divine omen indicating whether or not he should receive the prince. As Falk notes in his diary, he interpreted his ill health as such a sign, and therefore sent his stepson Gedaliah in his stead with a letter. (I am indebted to Dr Ruth Schoenfeld, who translated these details for me from *Polski Słownik Biograficzny*, vol. iv (Kraków, 1938), 249–57.)

I am ever mindful of the Lord's presence at the time this was a standard salutation at the start of a letter. It derived from the phrase in Ps. 16: 8, *shiviti hashem lenegdi tamid*, represented in Hebrew by the acronym שיל״ת. The letter itself was erased and has been reconstructed. [Some unintelligible phrases in ll. 1024–7 have been omitted, as indicated by ellipses.]

pillars of my hands! And the renowned and famous Shimon [...] I will go forth and conclude with the epitome of peace in its entirety, together with my obligation to the beloved, the wise ones, *the father, the head, and the firstborn son, my beloved friends, the champions, the heads of the nobles [...]. And from now, let us say, may we live *and not die; *may we merit to commemorate 14 Marheshvan, that I will observe every year to rebuke me, in order to fulfil the will of the one who imposes my obligation, and the will of my friend, my bosom friend, may he hear me. (With the wisdom of my hand this was signed), and as mentioned. *And I, too, the worm Jacob, bound as a slave to hasten in the constant service of *my beloved, the perfect brilliance, the divine kabbalist, the genuine rabbi, I have come in humility to write, I am taking my leave with the final salutation, Peace be you and to all who take shelter under your honour's aegis. From me, the humble Jacob, may I be remembered for good at this time.

|fo. 26a| In my chest that is in the Jewish community of The Hague, the capital, in the house of *my friend, wonderful and outstanding among the flock of sages, lie the items as mentioned in detail on this page as a reminder on 1 Tamuz 5533 [22 June 1773]. And thus I begin:

*The hangings of the tent in my forest first, in seven parts, marked *A*, 4 wide parts and 3 parts *A*, 2 wide parts, total: *22 wide parts.

The curtains of the tent, each as wide as nine parts *B*, each 6 yards wide *B* 3½ yards each. *A* 7 yards long—four, about ¾ of a yard each or more; total: nine wide pieces.

Eight new shirts of mine are lying in a linen wrapper there—and *a beam of the tent of linen, one large sabbath garment and one small one, whole ones, are also there—and one torn—

the father ... firstborn son the father Tuvyah and his firstborn son Abraham.

and not die the Hebrew word is a chronogram that alludes to the Jewish year. [The phrase 'may we live and not die' derives from Ps. 118: 17.]

may we merit to commemorate 14 Marheshvan ... to rebuke me [It is not clear why the date should be commemorated, nor why doing so would be a rebuke to Falk.]

And I, too, the worm Jacob an addition to Falk's letter written by Jacob. [The phrase 'the worm Jacob' comes from Isa. 41: 14.]

my beloved ... rabbi a reference to Falk.

my friend i.e. Shimon Boas.

The hangings of the tent [The descriptions that follow are difficult to understand. Perhaps they are supposed to be reminiscent of the very explicit instructions for the cloth furnishings of the Tabernacle in Exod. 26: 1–14.]

22 wide parts [It is difficult to follow the arithmetic here but 22 may be a coded reference to the 22 letters of the Hebrew alphabet and therefore an allusion to completeness.]

a beam of the tent of linen [Perhaps 'from a beam', meaning 'hanging from a beam'.]

And fourteen wool hangings for the windows are there, too—and their rods of iron—also the rods of the tent screens, in four parts, that together comprise sixteen joints closed together of iron—also eight rods from the first tent are there—

A leather wrapper containing all the tent components—and they are, in detail, a double wheel with a red cord, for hanging the tent from the beam of the house; a double wheel belonging to the said cord, also for the beam of the house; twelve bolts known as *schireifin for the beam of the tent. Twenty-four things belonging to the said twelve bolts; the cords of the curtains, also in the wrapper. A double wheel of wood, to draw the said tent cord; four chains for hanging the tent, covered with linen, also on their wheels; a large *drill to bore a hole, for inserting the wheels in the beams of the house; one bundle of metal and a chain and other things there as well, eight to bind everything; and in one bundle are eight bolts in which are the rods of the screens.

And besides what is in the said wrapper, what is not needed is placed in the said chest. Everything is wrapped in paper, and what is in it is written first. Four bolts for bolting the corners of the wood beams, two bolts for connecting the curtain cords, and everything that is not so necessary is bundled up, such as the double wheel actually included in this, along with another bundle of items, including wood, a *ya'arat for cooking water for drinking and other things, large, and another ya'arat for cooking coffee; small *rulbikot, that are a *shishilis and a *toller from pottery mentioned below;*munfakh of red leather, an iron pan for frying; a knife to cut meat and vegetables, or *dairy; a shishilis; a deep plate; a plate—another old one; within a pottery tea kettle, a *vessel from Japan, from Levy; a pottery colander.

A large white garment for the sabbath, and ditto a small one; likewise, within a white wrapper, *two cravats. Two scarves from Damascus, these are two linen scarves. White leather, also *the stiff paper from the cache; and a word to the wise will suffice.

|fo. 27a| *These are duplicate books from the library in my home in London the

schireifin screws, from the Dutch *schroeven*.
drill the term Falk uses is *ingibir*; in Yiddish *einboiren* means to drill a hole.
ya'arat from the context, a pot for cooking liquids.
rulbikot meaning unclear.
shishilis from the German *Schussel* ('pan').
toller from the German *Teller* ('plate').
munfakh meaning unclear. [Perhaps, given the context, the reference is to 'bellows'.]
dairy Jewish dietary laws require meat and dairy dishes to be cooked and served in different utensils.
vessel from Japan, from Levy from a person named Levy in Japan. [Or perhaps the reference is to a utensil of Japanese porcelain.]
two cravats [The Hebrew term, which is of course unvocalized, is unclear. Oron's reading was *kroitim*, which she understood as derived from the German *kreuten*, and therefore meaning herbs. Given that the discussion here relates to clothing, *kravitim*, intended as a reference to 'cravats', is perhaps more logical.]
the stiff paper from the cache [The reference is unclear.]
These are the duplicate books a list of the duplicate copies of Falk's that he stored in a chest in Shimon Boas's house. On this list, see Appendix E.

capital; accordingly, these are the books in the chest in the house of R. Shimon Boas. For a reminder, recorded here, *Shiyunah, 18 Tamuz 5533 [9 July 1773].

1. *Avak soferim* on the Torah
2. *Ḥozeh tsiyon* with Psalms, [a commentary] according to *pardes*
3. *Ḥavatselet hasharon* on Daniel, by Alshekh
4. *Magid mereshit*, responsa
5. *Shomer emunim*, the acceptance of the faith
6. *Si'aḥ yitsḥak*, grammar
7. *Pa'amon verimon*, kabbalah
8. *Kav hayashar*, with a commentary in Yiddish
9. *Asarah ma'amarot*, kabbalah
10. *Sefer *pat vakar nifraḥ*, kabbalah
11. *Kaftor vaferaḥ*, kabbalah
12. *Ḥelkat meḥokek* on Job, by Alshekh
13. *Mishnat ḥasidim*, kabbalah
14. *Arba'ah ve'esrim*, in a red binding
15. The Zohar, in three volumes
16. *Tikunei zohar*
17. Pentateuch, in five volumes: Genesis, Exodus, Leviticus, Numbers, Deuteronomy, with the commentaries of Rashi, Rashbam, Ibn Ezra, the Ba'al Haturim, a commentary on Targum Yerushalmi and on Targum Pseudo-Jonathan, *Toledot aharon*, *Mesoret ketanah ugedolah*, and *Totse'ot ḥayim* (5524), a gift from *Kalman Levy

*אעמל

*56. Small *Gefen yeḥidit lashon*
57. Small *Shulḥan arukh* by Rabbi Isaac Luria, of blessed memory

Shiyunah a suburb of The Hague [possibly Scheveningen].

pat vakar nifraḥ Falk's erroneous rendering of *kaftor vaferaḥ*, which he corrected himself in the next line. The notation 'What is this' appears next to this entry.

Totse'ot ḥayim *Totse'ot ḥayim*, on the Torah [by Ḥayim Boskowitz, 5524 = 1764].

Kalman Levy [Perhaps the same Levy mentioned on the previous folio as having given Falk an item of Japanese porcelain.]

אעמל meaning unclear. [The superior dots that Falk marked over the letters, not reproduced here, would normally suggest that the letters are to be understood as numerals.]

56 [Items 18–55 missing.]

Gefen yeḥidit lashon [On fo. 9a, this appears as *Gefen yeḥidit lashon tsaḥ* ('written in clear language').]

Shulḥan arukh by Rabbi Isaac Luria [A kabbalistic compendium, following the order of the *Shulḥan arukh*.]

|fo. 28a| *__Tent of Harderwijk, from the year 5520__ [1759/60]: it was square, at 2 yards 12 inches, and its foundation is large; and a word to the wise will suffice. On Wednesday, the day following Passover, that is 23 Nisan of the said year, it was put out of service. Its roof measurement was 230.

Tent of East Ham, from the year 5527 [1766/7]: its roof measurement, including the pockets in which the poles are inserted, each pocket about 2¼ inches wide, was 2 yards 16 inches long and 2 yards 9 inches wide.

Tent of The Hague, the home of Boas, from Tamuz 5531 [*c.*June 1771]: its roof measurement, including the pockets in which the poles are inserted, 1 yard 28 inches long and 1 yard 25 inches wide, two poles at 1 yard 4 inches long, and it should be 5 foot, and the two others at 1 yard 18 inches long, and it should be 5 foot 10 inches; diameter of the pole: 1 inch, and it should be 1 inch and a half width of the pole: 3 inches, and it should be 2 inches.

*BRANDY, FROM 24 NISAN 5538 [21 APRIL 1778], AND READY FOR LAG BA'OMER 18 IYAR 5538 [15 MAY 1778]

Cloves	¼ oz.	2*d*.
Cinnamon	¼ oz.	3*d*.
Cardamom	¼ oz.	4*d*.
*Musk filir	¼ oz.	2*d*.

Tent of Harderwijk, from the year 5520 [1759/60] Here and in the paragraphs that follow Falk gives the dimensions of 'tents' [or some of the dimensions, sometimes without specifying the unit] in various locations in England and Holland. His use of the term 'tent' is unclear [though it echoes the biblical usage of 'tent of assembly'], but it would seem to refer to a structure constructed by members of his circle for their meetings. [In the Hebrew edition it was suggested that these were portable structures, but the fact that Falk gives a date for each structure suggests that each was purpose-built for a particular meeting and then put out of service. The Hebrew edition mentions a further four such tents—one in an unspecified location (5532); two in 'Boas's place' in The Hague (5532 and 5531, i.e. listed in reverse chronological order; and another one in Harderwijk (5531)—but they have not been included here because the information is in any case incomplete.]

BRANDY . . . LAG BA'OMER [Presumably the ingredients were combined on the first date given and left to mature until Lag Ba'omer, a minor holiday just over a month later. (In fact in a comment following a second recipe (ll. 1151–70) that has been omitted, Falk gives the date the concoction was ready as 20 Iyar, in fact two days after Lag Ba'omer.) The entries for some ingredients conclude with an indecipherable cryptic allusion that has been omitted here. It is noteworthy that Falk gives the cost of each ingredient; this is not usual in a recipe but is in line with his general concern for his finances.]

Musk filir possibly musk *Pulver* (German) = musk powder. [But musk has an unpleasant

	Ground nutmeg	¼ oz.	4d.
	Oregano	¼ oz.	3d.
	*Calamus	¼ oz.	1d.

And something else called savory, one piece

	Saltpetre	½ oz.	½d.
	*Wine stone	½ oz.	½d.
	Wild rod, i.e. violet	½ oz.	½d.
	*Angelica stem	½ oz.	½d.

|fo. 30b|

JOTTINGS

From this page, jottings from Adar I 5532 [spring 1772] that I copied from other books.

Cakes

Little cakes that my servant Jacob learned from the daughter of R. Shimon my friend in the year Tamuz 5532 [summer 1772], and when I returned to my home in London I made them for myself. To bake the said cakes, there must be fire below and fire above. Here is the recipe, including the method of preparation and the measures and weights.

(A silver cup of) butter, ½ lb.
(8 cups) fine flour, ½ lb.
6 eggs
3½ cups water, ½ lb.

First boil the water and the butter in an earthenware bowl. When they begin to boil, take the bowl off the fire, quickly put the flour in the water and the butter and mix well together to make a dough in this bowl. And it seems to me that you then leave the dough to cool in the bowl, and then mix the eggs into the dough, also in that bowl. Then begin to bake the cakes in the following way. Fill the tins half-full with this dough and place them in the above pan with fire below and above, as mentioned, and

---

scent and no culinary uses; perhaps the intention is 'ground muscat', 'muscat' being a food ingredient related to nutmeg.]

Calamus a semi-aquatic plant with fragrant leaves deemed to aid digestion.

Wine stone [A by-product of fermentation that is deposited in wine barrels as a white powder that acts as a preservative; more commonly known today as cream of tartar.]

Angelica stem This is followed by the comment *mitah meshunah*, literally 'a strange death'; however, since that phrase would be meaningless in this context, and given that Falk's spelling was poor, perhaps he meant *midah meshunah*, 'a strange measure'.

then the cakes will come out puffed up and beautiful, that is, hollow within. They are good to eat, will be tasty, and will give you pleasure when you recite the blessing over them.

Wednesday, 27 Av 5518 [31 August 1758]. And on Wednesday, 7 Iyar 5520 [23 April 1760], I made wine as mentioned—see above.

1.	Cloves,	½ *lot
2.	Cinammon,	½ lot
3.	Wine stone,	½ lot
4.	Saltpetre,	½ lot
5.	Sugar,	3 *revi'it
6.	Brandy	2 revi'it
7.	Cardamom	¼ lot
8.	Muscat	a pinch
9.	Ginger	a pinch
10.	Oregano	a pinch
11.	Calamus	a pinch

A recipe for brandy that I learned from R. Moses Resona also in 5518 [1778] has only items 1–6, combined in this way. After the cloves and the cinnamon have been ground together very finely, take the saltpetre and the wine stone together and pound well in a mortar. After the pounding, burn them together in the mortar until they come together like a piece of white *halun*. Then grind them to a powder, and then mix this powder with the spices, and leave them in a *malbek*, in whose spout some cotton wool has been inserted in order to refine it from the waste of the spices, and from the powder that is in the *malbek* with the spirits. That is, the *malbek* should be well covered so as not to lose the potency of the spirits and its spices. *Viol vorshil* in English is Fleur de Luce in every sense.

Wednesday, 27 Av 5518 ... of the page [The dates in the section that follows do not seem to relate to each other.]

lot a unit of weight [in use in many European countries from the Middle Ages to the early twentieth century. Most often it was defined as 1/30 or 1/32 of a pound, making it equivalent to approximately ½ oz.]

revi'it [A halakhic measure of the amount of wine needed for kiddush, approx. 3 fluid ounces.]

halun possibly alum (aluminium sulphate) [which is used as a preservative]. Falk describes the mixture as being similar in colour to an alloy of white aluminium.

malbek from the context, it seems that this is a type of funnel or filtering device.

Viol vorshil apparently the name of an alcoholic drink (Fleur de Luce). This term originated in France as a name for the lily (*fleur-de-lis*), which was the symbol of the Bourbons from 1594. This name might have been given to a type of whiskey or cognac.

In Elul 5531 [autumn 1771] I bought through my manservant Meyer in The Hague a lottery ticket, no. 3695, for seventy-five gulden, and it will be included in the sum that I *had to give for the total expense mentioned.

*A further 15s. 0d. by Gedaliah to Moses Levi, may he rest in peace, so that I shall have another ticket, and so it was. In the intermediate days of Sukkot 5532 [autumn 1771] I received another ticket for the aforementioned, no. 2104: may it be propitious!

On Monday, 10 Nisan 5532 [13 April 1772], I received care of Gedaliah a lottery ticket, no. 2013; may it be propitious! And from the wheel of fortune came ninety gulden, but I received only £7. 0s. 0d. from the widow of Moses Levi, may he rest in peace.

For a reminder: on the night of Shemini Atseret 5532 [22 Tishrei / 30 Sept. 1771]. *I dreamt that I met Jacob my manservant in a vineyard, as I understood in the vineyard of my house (from which I am absent now), with a basket full of grapes. Then I came from the room also, to pick grapes for myself. He was frightened at seeing me. I asked him, 'Why are you frightened—because you are stealing grapes?' He answered me, 'God forbid, I wanted *to bring you the grapes.' And thereupon I awoke from my sleep, and lo, it was but a dream; may it be propitious.

*CLOTHING, 5532 [1772]

For a reminder, on Thursday, 24 Sivan 5529 [29 June 1769], I bought 16 yards of silk damask at £5. 0s. 0d. per yard, and on Wednesday, 26 Nisan 5532 [29 April 1772] I ordered a caftan to be made from it by Hayim *the thief, for Jacob found that when he was cutting the sleeves he wanted to cut another two, etc. Through Gedaliah I bought lining, 12 yards of *kalamanka* at 18d. per yard, a total of £18. 0s. 0d., and while the cutting was being done, a tip of 1s. 0d., and a second time of 6d. And the cost of the work, silk included, was 9s. 0d., and the tip, 1s. 6d.

had to give possibly meaning that he won a sum equal to what he had invested, and so gained nothing.

A further 15s. 0d. . . . to Moses Levi, may he rest in peace [The meaning here is unclear. If Moses Levi is dead, how could he be given something? Perhaps this a reference to the widow of Moses Levi, who is mentioned below.]

I dreamt . . . may it be propitious Falk recounts his dream, but also interprets it. In the dream he appeared to catch his manservant Jacob stealing from him (Falk apparently greatly feared theft, and possibly also treachery, by members of his household), but he learns in the dream that everything Jacob did was out of concern for his master, as we realize from the ending of the dream: 'and lo, it was but a dream, may it be propitious'. See Appendix B, 'Falk's Dreams'.

to bring you [The Hebrew text actually reads 'to bring him', but it is not uncommon for Hebrew (and indeed other languages) to replace 'you' with the third-person form of address in more formal contexts.]

CLOTHING, 5532 [Most of the calculations in this paragraph are wrong.]

the thief Falk uses the term presumably because the tailor tried to cheat him out of a piece of fabric, as he goes on to say.

kalamanka a head covering, or perhaps a type of cloth. [In context, a head covering seems

*PRAYER *MY CLOTHING, MENAHEM AV 5528 [SUMMER 1768]

Through Gedaliah, black *lifin*, 31 yards at 4s. 6d. per yard, a total of £6. 19s. 6d.; *shlon, 8 yards, 15s. 0d. I had a *rokolor, a *rok, and a camisole made for myself. The tailor's wages: £1. 15s. 0d.; brown *kamelot from Holland. For Gedaliah I had a *rok* and a camisole made, 10 yards. The tailor's wages 18s. 0d. From the aforementioned *kamelot* I had a caftan and a camisole made for myself, about 18 yards. The tailor's wages, including a tip, 3s. 0d., total: 15s. 0d.

Shlon for the four aforementioned garments of *kamelot*, each one a yard at 20 pence per yard.

*Tsamut for two *boxin* for me; one, 2½ yards, at 8s. 1d.; 2½ yards for the other, at 6s. 0d., a total of £1. 15s. 0d. Two hides, through Hayim and Gedaliah, 4s. 0d.; four *gartel. [?] Half a yard of *shlon for two *boxin*, 1s. 0d. Buttons, *toz and a half, 1s. 0d.; also the tailor's wages.

To make the upper *lilikh, length: 3 yards and a half; and the lower ones, 2 yards 3 quarters, to be chosen by the one doing it, etc.

Cakes. From Adele, in 5526 [1766] flour, fire, 4 eggs, 3 lb. butter, a little milk, rose water.

*Sequestration of my roof *ayin-heh* by the wicked one, Leib of Portsmouth, on Tuesday night, 28 Elul 5527 [27 September 1767], for our sins.

unlikely; perhaps Falk was referring to kalamkari, a block-printed cotton textile from India that was popular in England from the eighteenth century; see <https://en.wikipedia.org/wiki/Kalamkari>.]

PRAYER Falk writes that on Lag Ba'omer in 5531 (2 May 1771) he gave the cantor of his prayer house verses from the Song of Songs to chant. He records in his diary those verses that allude to his name and to the year, as ever using various techniques to derive significant allusions. For example, by taking the second letters of words from S. of S. 6: 9 he arrives at יום ח״י אייר, 'the 18th day of Iyar', which is the calendrical date of Lag Ba'omer; similarly the second letters of S. of S. 4: 7 produce the same numerical value as his name, פעמי. [Falk's full text here is too esoteric to make sense in translation and has been omitted; the above is a summary of salient points from the Hebrew edition to demonstrate the explanations there of the techniques used.]

MY CLOTHING A list of items purchased and garments made.

lifin [The reference is unclear.]
shlon a type of lining fabric.
rokolor a short coat with a large collar; from the French *roquelaure*.
rok abbreviation of *rokolor*.
kamelot perhaps camel-hair cloth.
Tsamut for two *boxin* *Tsamut* is possibly a type of velvet (from the German, *Samt*); *boxin* is possibly from the English: box cloth—a densely woven and felted cloth [almost waterproof], and used in riding clothes. [How the two materials would work together in riding garb is not clear, but perhaps the velvet was used for decoration, e.g. on the collar.]
gartel belt (Yiddish).
shlon for two *boxin* a type of lining cloth (see above) for two pairs of riding breeches.
toz possibly meaning 'a dozen'.
lilikh sheets; from the Yiddish.
Sequestration of my roof *ayin-heh* a description of events that occurred in 1766, possibly referring to the placing of a lien on

To Hannah I lent half a guinea in Elul 5531 [autumn 1771].

|fo. 31a| Shellac   ½ lb, two gulden
          Vermilion, which is called   6 oz., one gulden and five pence
            cinnabar
          *balsamo detolio   1 lot, three pence
          *Venetian turpentine   2 oz., three pence

The weights and the currencies are from Holland, *for it was made in my presence in the home of R. Shimon son of R. Tuvyah, may they live long, of The Hague, by an old man and by Gedaliah, and these materials were bought by the aforementioned man, Wednesday, 25 Sivan 5519 [20 June 1759].

You have to put the turpentine in an earthenware or, even better, a copper frying pan, heat, and when you see bubbles in it, remove the frying pan from the fire. When it cools a little, put the cinnabar in the pan, mix quickly with the turpentine, and immediately place the shellac on both of them while stirring strongly, that is, on the fire once again. And when you feel that these three things have been well mixed, remove the pan once again from the fire and put the balsam quickly into the pan with the other ingredients and mix the four things together well, like dough for bread, and this is varnish that can be used to seal anything. And when it is like dough, remove it from the pan and make tubes between two very smooth tablets of wood, or even better, of copper, or by a mould; and the wise man will act according to his wisdom. The polishing of the tubes must be on the fire with hands from a distance, so that they will receive the heat of the fire, and you will be able to smooth every tube like glass, etc.

For varnish that will adhere strongly to paper: reduce the weight of the cinnabar, since it is the cinnabar that breaks the varnish and serves to stabilize the varnish in which it is put. Therefore put in instead of 6 oz. of cinnabar as mentioned, only 1½ oz. of cinnabar, etc. And for black varnish: instead of the cinnabar, add to the aforementioned ingredients a cask of *kin ros for a halfpenny, that is, you have to clean the kin ros as follows: put the cask of kin ros as mentioned into a paper dudkah, and

---

Falk's prayer house; this conjecture is suggested by the letters *ayin-heh*, which might possibly represent *avodat hashem*, the service of the Lord.

balsamo detolio a plant with a strong fragrance [used in the preparation of oily and sticky oleoresins; the word *balsamun* does not occur anywhere else in the book]

Venetian turpentine derived from the larch tree.

for it was made [Falk does not actually say what the product is; at one point he says 'this is varnish that can be used to seal anything' but as the description continues it is not clear that the product is varnish at all; perhaps these are formulas for different products Falk needed for his work.]

kin ros ... dudkah ... Cailomium meaning unclear.

press it firmly into the *dudkah*. Then light a fire around the *dudkah* until it turns to embers, and when it has turned to embers, extinguish the *dudkah* by covering it, for if not, nothing will remain of the *kin ros*, etc.

> *Cailonium* known as *harash*, 6 lot
> Shellac, ½ lb.
> Cinnabar, 6 lot
> *Puder or *kayrayt*, 4 lot
> Turpentine, 6 lot

This is medium varnish. The *kayrayt* requires grinding, and afterwards drying in a pan on the fire. If you use **haishtish iseterlas*, which is as gold, in place of the cinnabar, you will have lacquer like gold etc.

Two-fifths of saltpetre—one-fifth of potash, one-fifth of sulphur, grind them well, that is, each one by itself, and then mix them. And when it is necessary to cover, place them on a copper sheet under which is camphor with a fire, or on some fire; and a word to the wise will suffice.

|fo. 31*b*|

*PLASTER FOR EVERYTHING, FROM JACOB THE *PARNAS* OF ASTOR

> Wax, 1 lb.
> Bone marrow, 1 lb.
> Butter, fresh without salt, 1 lb.
> White rice, 1 lb.

Melt everything by itself except for the fat, and then melt the wax, the butter, and the rice together, until they are combined together when melted, and then place the fat in them before the three aforementioned begin to be cooked, for when the cooking begins all four things must be together. And when it comes to a first boil, remove them from the fire. That is, you must mix them together constantly when they are on the fire, and also after their removal from the fire, until they are completely cool, and then, before they cool completely, you must place them in an earthenware vessel and leave them there. That is plaster for everything; and a word to the wise will suffice. And do

---

Puder or *kayrayt* possibly *poeder krijt* ('powdered chalk' in Dutch).

haishtish iseterlas possibly some material of a golden colour. [Perhaps isinglass, a material made from the dried swim-bladders of fish and used for gluing. It is also used for preserving parchment and for coating goldbeaters' skin, a parchment traditionally used in making gold leaf.]

PLASTER FOR EVERYTHING, FROM JACOB THE *PARNAS* OF ASTOR [The meaning here is not clear, since these ingredients seem unlikely to produce anything like plaster. Similarly the identity of Jacob is not obvious; *parnas* would normally be a synagogue warden but the reference to 'of Astor' is unclear.]

not forget to clean the fat from its skin and other blood. And do not allow water or salt to come into them, God forbid.

JACOB'S CAKES

Copied letter for letter from the language and writing of Jacob, who learned from my friend Cosman in 5538 [1777/8], to pass the time; and a word to the wise will suffice.

Take ¾ lb. of semolina, and ½ lb. choice butter, and put in 1 oz. of white sugar, no more. Put into it 1½ oz. of sesame. Mix everything together, and knead everything together. Then roll the dough to make a cake.

CAKES FROM 5539 [1778/9]

A pack and a half of flour—3½ lb. butter—½ lb. sesame for 5*d.*—cinnamon—rose water—about *shilfeh hopin*.

FOR SHAVUOT: CAKES FROM TUESDAY, 25 IYAR 5539 [11 MAY 1779]

My cakes: a pack and a half of semolina; 3½ lb. butter; sesame; rose water; cinnamon.

And theirs: a pack and a half of semolina; 2½ lb. butter; rosewater and cinnamon; 1½ lb. sugar.

|fo. 32*a*|

RECOLLECTIONS THAT I BEGAN TO WRITE DOWN TODAY, WEDNESDAY, 3 IYAR 5532 [6 MAY 1772]

Barukh the cantor: Barukh led the prayers on Monday, 13 Elul 5526 [18 August 1766] and I persuaded him with many entreaties to receive my gift of ten guineas.

On 15 Elul 5526 [20 August 1776] it was arranged by Mendel that whereas Gedaliah had agreed to pay half a guinea to hire a carriage when needed, he Mendel has now agreed with the owner to pay £1. 13*s*. 5*d*. per week, and thus it has remained.

On Wednesday, 28 Tamuz 5528 [13 July 1768], I sent a wedding gift to the son of R. Johanan the worthy: six silver jugs, at 5*s*. 8*d*. per ounce [?] : 6 oz., 11 dwt., a total of [?]

I also sent by the said R. Johanan to the person who dealt with the burial of my mother, may she rest in peace, *in the community of Fürth, a gift, a pretty pearl, weighing 10 oz., and a half of silver at 6*s*. 0*d*. per ounce, amounting to [?]

To R. Moses the ritual slaughterer, *who began to deal with her burial but did not

---

shilfeh hopin unclear; perhaps a small measure. [The problem here may be Falk's orthography; he may have meant the Hebrew word *hofen*, which is the volume that can be contained in the palm of the hand when the fingers are curled towards the palm.]

in the community of Fürth from Falk's mention of the gift that he sent to the person who arranged for his mother's burial in Fürth and of the sum of money that he sent to this community for its poor, we understand that his family lived there after having left Podhajce in Poland and moved to Germany.

who began to deal with her burial Falk writes

act, I gave him, too, a gift, about a guinea and a half, and to his brother in Fürth I sent with the said R. Johanan, besides what he had received from the money I sent as charity to Fürth to distribute to the poor.

Lopez Pineira came to see me today, Sunday, 17 Menahem Av 5528 [31 July 1768], and I gave him a gift of two guineas.

*R. Isaac the cantor came to me on Monday, 15 Adar II 5527 [16 March 1767], to collect the ten guineas that I had vowed to give after I had paid my entire donation and the expenses for the burial of my wife, may she rest in peace, and also the donations in return for which blessings were recited in her memory in all three communities, as mentioned in the letter that I received from their charity officers. Regarding the other expenses as mentioned there, today I fulfilled my vow to donate ten guineas as charity to the community. And when R. Isaac the cantor received the said ten guineas, he told me that the warden R. Meyer intended to make me a *ba'al bayit* in the community, as is the custom, in return for the said ten guineas. And I answered him, 'Heaven forfend that my name should be mentioned in such a matter, for I am a *ba'al bayit* for all the world.' I warned him sternly against such a thought, all the more so against action; but, nevertheless, I am grateful. Therefore I gave him two guineas as a gift, and as I understand I owed him one guinea for Purim; and a word to the wise will suffice.

Re R. Barukh the cantor, who is mentioned at the top of the page. He came to see me on Monday, 28 Nisan 5527 [22 April 1767], and began to weep copiously, and he asked me for a loan on the security of his pledges, eighteen guineas. So immediately I vowed to give him twelve guineas, and the following day he came to me and I had mercy on him and gave him eighteen guineas, as a gift and not as a loan, and certainly not on the security of pledges, Heaven forfend. And how he rejoiced, as he said to me, 'Say little and do much'; and a word to the wise will suffice.

*With the aforementioned R. Johanan I sent the community of Fürth £5. 0s. 0d.

that although R. Moses did not complete the arrangements for his mother's burial, he nevertheless sent R. Moses a gift of money. [Perhaps his role was to arrange the *taharah* (ritual purification of the corpse) prior to the burial rather than to arrange the burial itself, in which case a gift of money would not have been unreasonable.]

R. Isaac the cantor ... and a word to the wise will suffice here Falk writes, inter alia, about the charitable donations that he made after his mother's death in 1767. In return for the large sums of money that he gave to the community (the entry here speaks of a contribution of ten guineas), he was considered an honorary *ba'al bayit*, or member of the community, with the communal rights that such a status conveyed. Here Falk relates the prestigious offer and his refusal to accept the post. In the opinion of Yehuda Liebes, Falk's response that he was a 'citizen of the world', meant that he saw himself as a cosmopolitan individual. Such a self-appraisal was clearly compatible with the world-view of the Freemasons of the time. This world-view appears explicitly in what the character Falk says in Lessing's play *Ernst und Falk*; see Introduction, Section V, above.

With the aforementioned R. Johanan ... £19. 19s. 0d. in this passage too Falk details

for the burial society, £5. 0s. 0d. for the charity fund, £5. 0s. 0d. to be distributed in the hospital for the poor, and £4. 10s. 0d. for the tombstone, to the brother of the aforementioned R. Moses the ritual slaughterer, a total of £19. 19s. 0d.

*Silver salver: my large salver, weighing 38 oz. 14 dwt., through Gedaliah, at 7s. 0d. per oz. Total: £13. 11s. 0d. Sabbath eve, 6 Tamuz 5526 [Friday, 13 June 1766].

*The big bottle of rum [?] R. Johanan, 5 quarts 1 pint.

*A dream, Sunday night, 25 Adar 5528 [14 March 1768]. After coming from the new bridge, I went to bed. I dreamed that Cosman was standing before me, without breeches; he looked to me as someone who has just got out of bed, and I was sitting on a chair. I saw that his nakedness was so hard that it stood by itself, and he was making it erect with the movement of his mouth and body, till he had to take his saliva in the palm of his hand, that is, silently, very quickly. He began to stretch his nakedness until it lengthened and became more than a quarter-yard long, and as thick as my arm. He then began to cast his filth to the south of me and the north of me, going around in a half circle, three or four times, like an arrow, to a distance of three or four yards, without stopping. For the filth welled forth and subsided like a flowing fountain. Then the nakedness subsided in its hardness, so that the robe came down to half a yard. Only God knows its meaning.

*A dream, Tuesday night, 27 Kislev 5529 [7 December 1768]. I dreamed today that my wife, peace be upon her, was lying asleep on two chairs in front of the window of my room, the place of falling, and I was lying in my bed. In my sleep I experienced weakness or fear, and then I awoke and I remember no more. Only God knows its meaning.

*Levy of The Hague: on sabbath eve, 20 Tevet 5519 [Friday, 19 January 1759], sale of the gold that Levy sold me: from the double seal—8 oz. each, and a simple seal—

donations that he sent to Jewish institutions in Fürth [though as elsewhere his addition is inaccurate] including the burial society (which he calls *ḥevrat hakaberanim*, the society of gravediggers, instead of the traditional *ḥevra kadisha*, literally, holy society) and the hospital for the poor. [In fact the term *ḥevrat hakaberanim* (or *ḥevrat hakavranim*) is attested in Alsace; see <http://judaisme.sdv.fr/perso/slpicard.htm>.]

Silver salver ... Sabbath eve [On the basis of earlier entries the salver was either pawned or sold, probably the former, to buy provisions for the sabbath.]

The big bottle of rum [The meaning is unclear.]

A dream, Sunday night the dream that Falk relates might have a meaning beyond the obvious erotic symbolism. In *On Sabbatianism and Its Belief* (Heb.), 98–9, Yehuda Liebes writes of a masturbation ritual that was practised in the circle of Wolf Eybeschuetz and among Frankist groups. As Marsha Schuchard has observed, this was a pseudo-ritual conducted in Masonic groups to cleanse the body of waste matter.

A dream, Tuesday night the description of a dream Falk had portraying his wife's death. Falk had a similar dream in 1774 (see Appendix B, 'Falk's Dreams').

Levy of The Hague ... and to whom shall I reveal it? Falk complains about gold that was

8 oz., for a total of 24 oz., and also additional gold calculated as follows: 24 oz. for one hundred and ten ducats; 30 oz. for two hundred and forty-eight ducats, three gulden, five pennies; with each 30, 100 dwt. more—a total of one thousand one hundred and four ducats, two and a half gulden for 145 oz. And today, for our sins, 29 Tamuz 5528 [14 July 1768], I discovered the theft, really one by one, and to whom shall I reveal it?

*Upper *lilikh*, at 3½ yards, with a length of 4 yards and a width of 2 yards 12 inches; and lower ones, at 2¾ or 3 yards length, with a width of [?].

I had four tunics made to measure in The Hague from 18 yards, that is, two tunics were made from each 9 yard length, a total of four tunics, as mentioned, including cuffs for all four, 25 inches, and they were ready on Thursday, 16 Elul 5530 [6 September 1770] though the work was begun in Tamuz 5530 [July 1770].

Tunics, 5532 [1772] here, 3 Tamuz [4 July], made by a seamstress from Paris, there were twelve tunics, made from sixteen widths of fine linen, each width was 3 yards 15 inches long; as mentioned in the black notebook, the linen was from nine camps; and a word to the wise will suffice. And cambric—I gave 44 inches, and I bought from the seamstress cambric for five more tunics, to complete the twelve tunics. And for the said cambric I gave her a thaler, which is two guineas and two shillings, and for their sewing, nineteen gulden, four shillings, and including the other expenses, she received a total of twenty-three gulden and four pennies plus a tip of a *thaler, *for my expenses; and a word to the wise will suffice.

|fo. 32b| *23 Marheshvan 5533* [19 November 1772]. *Hinshort*.

Tuesday, 5 Kislev 5533 [12 December 1772]. I sent Gedaliah to the Isaac house in my forest, to prepare my room with a carpet *to receive Duke Czartoryski of Poland, who

stolen from him. He has discovered the theft after making his calculations, but there is no one to whom he can complain as he discovered the loss only nine years after the event.

Upper *lilikh* *lilikh* are sheets. [Falk seems to have had upper and lower sheets made, but the dimensions are difficult to fathom.]

thaler a Dutch coin.

for my expenses [This appears to be Falk's memo to himself of his outgoings.]

Hinshort meaning unclear. The word is connected to games of chance or to the place where such gambling is conducted. [The text that follows (ll. 1391–4) seems to relate to a ticket that gave Falk some chance of winning a large sum but it is too obscure to be understood and has been omitted.]

to receive Duke Czartoryski Falk describes the meeting, already mentioned in the diary (see fo. 25a above) he was to have with Duke Czartoryski and his indecision as to whether he should go ahead with it. As noted above, Falk waited for a sign from heaven: if he recovered from his weakness (i.e. illness) he would go to the meeting, and if he didn't he would remain at home. He writes that this thought was immediately followed by his being in pain, with his foot greatly swelling up. Accordingly, he was forced to remain at

was recommended by R. Shimon Boas, and to wait for me from one o'clock in the afternoon till two o'clock, and if I were not to come within that time, it would be for naught. Indeed, I got myself ready to travel, and while preparing I said, God, if it is for the good that I travel to meet the duke, may I recover from my weakness very much, and if not, I shall bear my rebuke—then shall I know what is good. My leg began to swell immediately, and I was almost unable to rise from my chair. Then I sent to cancel the coach that was hired for my journey. Gedaliah received the duke there, and was with him for two and a half hours, and each of them went on his way; and a word to the wise will suffice.

And yesterday, for a reminder, re R. Jacob: I heard from R. Jacob that he wrote on the new moon of the aforementioned Kislev what he had heard from me that day, that I had said: 'My son, know that in this year something good should happen to me, if, Heaven forfend, a *catastrophe does not befall him next year.' And he said, 'Who will be affected by that catastrophe?' I answered him, 'The good will happen to me, and the catastrophe, to another.' He asked me if he was included. I answered him, 'Why should you think of yourself in these matters?', etc.

And on Sunday, the 10th of the aforementioned month, I said to R. Jacob that *I had erred in saying to you that something bad would happen, Heaven forfend, or good, as mentioned; and a word to the wise will suffice.

Monday, 23 Tevet 5533 [18 January 1773]. The aforementioned prince sent R. Shimon Boas's letter with R. Jacob to *Solly Nordah, and the prince received through the aforementioned Solly £200 by a secret arrangement of the prince who had come with R. Jacob to Nordah's home, and R. Jacob stayed in his home.

Monday, 23 Tevet 5533, Nordah received R. Shimon's letter from the prince; and a word to the wise will suffice.

R. Jacob was in the prince's home, and said that yesterday he had delivered to Solly Nordah a letter of credit of R. Shimon Boas. Solly was willing to give him the

home, and sent his adopted son Gedaliah in his stead.

catastrophe the Hebrew term Falk uses translates literally as 'breach'; the meaning 'catastrophe' is based on BT *Ber. 19a*.

I had erred Falk appears to retract the prophecy he had told R. Jacob.

Solly Nordah a man's name; or possibly an allusion to Falk's name: Solly might allude to Samuel; and the numerical value of Solly, סאלי (with an additional letter *alef*) = 101, which is the same as the Hebrew for 'Laniado'; and the numerical value of Nordah, נורדה = 265, which is the same as that of the Hebrew for '*mem heh* [honorific acronym] de Falk'. These calculations are mere speculation. [The notes in the Hebrew edition do not comment on the significance of 'Laniado', but a search of the internet suggests that 'Solly Nordah' could be a coded reference to Solomon b. Abraham Laniado, who was a preacher in Venice in the eighteenth century; see <http://www.jewishencyclopedia.com/articles/9630-laniado>.]

sum he wanted, and for that R. Jacob immediately returned with the prince's doctor in the coach to the house of Solly Nordah, and the prince's doctor received £200, and brought it to the prince, without R. Jacob.

Thursday, 11 Shevat of this year. I instructed R. Jacob not to speak with or to enter the house of *Fornis Rafin of Moscow, and *he gave me his word that he would do as I said, but he did not keep it, and he was in his house and spoke with him, and did not stay. And as far as I know, he received a gift from the said Fornis Rafin. And on that day he wrote a letter to R. Shimon in his name about all the events, a copy is in his hands, and as mentioned; and Gedaliah brought the letter to the post; and a word to the wise will suffice.

Wednesday, 24 Shevat. The famous prince travelled from here to Kalisz in peace, where *he secretly met Cosman on *Thursday night the 26th, at about four o'clock in the night. According to the letter that he wrote to R. Jacob, when they parted from this secret meeting the prince tarried and kissed Cosman; and a word to the wise will suffice.

Wednesday night, 25 Nisan 5535 [25 April 1775]. I dreamed a dream about my father, peace be upon him, the rabbi, R. Joshua Raphael Falker Falk. Suddenly he came to me

---

Fornis Rafin of Moscow Falk may have deliberately distorted this name; the reference is to Prince Repnin. According to Boris Orlov (private communication) Repnin was the name of a Russian aristocratic family, several of whose members served as diplomats. I received additional information on this family from Joel Raba, who found that Prince Nikolai Vasilevich Repnin, who served in the military and was a diplomat, was a prominent scion of this family. Prince Repnin participated in the Russo-Turkish War (1768–74), and in 1775–6 was the Russian ambassador to Turkey. I wish to thank Professor Raba and Dr Orlov for their assistance.

he gave me his word ... but he did not keep it Falk tells of an act of subterfuge by R. Jacob. Falk ordered R. Jacob not to enter the house of Fornis Rafin, who had arrived on a mission from Moscow, but R. Jacob broke his promise and secretly came to the house of the Russian emissary. Falk conjectures that he did so because of a gift (money?) that he had received from the Russian emissary. This episode is apparently related to economic and monetary affairs in which several leading financiers were involved, including R. Shimon Boas, the prominent banker from The Hague.

he secretly met Cosman [The Hebrew term used, *lehamtik sod*, based on a phrase in Ps: 55: 15 that translates as 'sweet was our fellowship', suggests great intimacy.]

Thursday night the 26th [The date is correct, even if Wednesday was the 24th Shevat; Thursday was then the 25th; but since the Jewish day starts in the evening, Thursday night would have been the 26th.]

from his land and I was amazed, since *for some thirty-five years I had heard nothing of him. I understood that it was because of hearing of my great fame that he came to me here in London. And when I saw him he embraced me and kissed me; and I am not sure what happened next, for I have forgotten. I remember only that his face was handsome, his beard white, and his visage that of a philosopher, that is, pensive, not happy or sad, just pensive. He marvelled at my wisdom. And there were students with me, learning, standing and watching. And then he went upstairs to my synagogue for it was time for afternoon prayers, so I understood. And then, when he had gone upstairs to the synagogue, I said to the students who were in my room above: 'Beware of his silence and do not let him deceive you by his standing silently as if lifeless, for none is greater than he in Torah and in the sharpness of his tongue and his voice.' And then fear seized all the hearers, *for they already knew. In the dream I knew nothing of his death, nor of the explanation; but may it be propitious.

BISCUITS OR CAKES THAT COSMAN TAUGHT R. JACOB

Cakes that my friend Cosman taught R. Jacob in Kislev 5538 [1777], here in London.

Take ¾ lb. of semolina flour and ½ lb. of choice butter, and put in 1 oz. of white sugar, no more. Add 1½ oz. of sesame. Mix everything together, and knead them together. Then roll the dough to make a cake. I copied this from the letter of my friend R. Jacob verbatim, etc., letter by letter.

And on Friday, the eve of the holy sabbath, 4 Iyar 5538 [1 May 1778], I let Rebecca make me fourteen cakes of double the above amount in honour of Shavuot for ten gulden. To bake as well, a total of 20*d*., including rosewater, £1. 0*s*. 0*d*.

|fo. 33*b*|

ITEMS COPIED IN NISAN 5540 [SPRING 1780] AND MISCELLANEA

*Sunday night, eve of the new moon of Adar 5539 [spring 1779]

---

for some thirty-five years I had heard nothing of him since Falk wrote that this took place in 1775, it suggests that he began his wanderings in 1740.

for they already knew [Presumably, they already knew that Falk's father had died. At the end of the paragraph two lines of text were erased.]

Sunday night, eve of the new moon of Adar 5539 in this passage Falk relates his conversation with Cosman about a loan of £6,036, a sum that Falk represents esoterically as follows:

(1) the letter *vav* in Hebrew for 'and these' (ואלו) stands for six (thousand), and the last two letters of this word have the numerical value of 36. The numerical value of the word גם, 43 (*gimel* = 3 + *mem* = 40), is the same as that of ואלו (*vav* = 6 + *alef* = 1 + *lamed* = 30 + *vav* = 6). (2) An additional signification is to be found in the first three letters of אלוהים ('God'), with the letter *vav* being written twice, above the line and on the line, and twice also in the word ואלו. [The corresponding text has not been translated as

Tuesday night, 7 Tamuz 5535 [5 July 1775]. *Rachel travelled with her son Leib at my bidding to the Isle of Wight from Portsmouth to hide seals that Cosman had carved in flint, expenses three guineas, and another three guineas for [something unfathomable], and four shillings.

Our master, R. Jacob the Sharp, פ"י*—on *Thursday, 25 Shevat 5538 [22 February 1778] I noted as a reminder the day of his burial, which was on Friday, 8 Tevet 5516 [12 December 1755], *and Jehu was a *kohen tsedek*.

*ON ROOTS, TU BISHEVAT

*Master of the Universe, Merciful One, forgive me that I forgot to observe Your commandment on the night of the sabbath, 15 Shevat 5540 [22 January 1780], the commandment to couple the *ilan* with *peri de'ilan ets peri*, for the verse 'You have proffered him blessings of good things' [Ps. 21: 4] yields the name of the month of Tevet, for those knowledgeable in esoteric matters and numerical manipulations of *gematriyah*;

it is convoluted, as these notes suggest—not even the direction of the loan is clear. The next paragraph, Falk writes, is copied from a small notebook that he found, dating from 1772/3 (see above, from fo. 32*b*, 'Tuesday, 5 Kislev 5533'). Once again the text is too obscure to permit translation, though it should perhaps be noted that he mentions 'my friend R. Monash' and also 'Montrier' which Oron suggests is a place name, perhaps Montreux. The full extent of the text omitted is ll. 1446–62.]

Rachel travelled with her son Leib Rachel is mentioned as a beneficiary in Falk's will. [Given that they sailed from Portsmouth, Leib is perhaps the 'Leib of Portsmouth' mentioned earlier?]

פ"י possibly an abbreviation for *parnas* (warden) and leader, or *parnas* and intercessor [viz. representing the community to the authorities].

Thursday, 25 Shevat 5538 [In fact 25 Shevat was a Sunday.]

and Jehu was a *kohen tsedek* unclear meaning in this context, especially since this seeming quotation is not a biblical verse; *kohen tsedek* ('of the priestly class') might allude to R. Jacob's family name, Katz (which is an abbreviation of *kohen tsedek*). [The text that follows (ll. 1458–61), comprising esoteric numerical manipulations, is too obscure to be translated.]

ON ROOTS, TU BISHEVAT ['On roots' perhaps relates to Tu Bishevat (15 Shevat) being the date of the new year for trees. Kabbalists deemed it to have mystical significance and therefore created liturgies, such as the one Falk records here, with a view to stimulating the supernal roots to supply energy to the world as earthly roots support trees.]

Master of the Universe... this is an invocation in which Falk asks for divine forgiveness for having forgotten in the year 5540/1780 a mystical obligation apparently associated with the new year for trees to bring about the coupling of the *ilana* (literally, 'tree'; an appellation for the *sefirah* Yesod) with *peri de'ilanei ets peri* (literally, 'the fruit of the tree', 'the fruit tree'; an appellation for the *sefirah* Malkhut; the reference is to the coupling of Yesod with Malkhut). Falk expounds the name of the month of Tevet as being an anagram of the initial letters of the verse he cites from Ps. 21: 4.

*Whether for reproof or for mercy, for it is said,
'Whether for correction or for his land' [Job 37: 13], for it is said,
'your royal sceptre is a sceptre of equity' [Ps. 45: 7]
'You have proffered him blessings of good things' [Ps. 21: 4],
    initial letters, Tevet
'Whether for correction or for his land'—initial letters אלאל
'your royal sceptre is a sceptre of equity'—initial letters שמשם

For a reminder, from Friday, 26 Shevat 5539 [12 February 1779], lest my letter be cursed, that I sent Cosman today to the prince *Emmanuel, servant of the king of France, to teach him to write his name in square script [?] and was no more here, that is, I copied what I found, *and I know not its meaning.

|fo. 37b| *22 Menahem Av 5541* [13 August 1781] in the week of the Torah portion 'Re'eh'. *Take the liquor from Meyer, for our sins, for that made it necessary for me to say after him, may he rest in peace.

And the markings of the wine bottles *from the aforementioned 22, *four bottles, marked *AA, AB, AC, AD*

Whether for reproof or for mercy this wording is produced from the second and third letters of the verses that follow. [The final line, l. 1472, is obscure and has not been translated.]

Emmanuel, servant of the king of France Schuchard understands this as a reference to Emanuel Swedenborg. Since the date given here is 1779 and Swedenborg died in 1772, this does not seem likely; it is more probable that the reference is to Emmanuel Saint Priest (see above, note to fo. 1b).

and I know not its meaning the text that follows, on fo. 34b and the following pages (fos. 35b and 36b), is in a different handwriting. The text of ll. 1476–86 on fo. 34b is an incantation; the word- and letter-combinations in this passage figured earlier in the diary, as part of Falk's numerological calculations; they derive from permutations of the first and last letters of the words in selected biblical verses using various esoteric techniques. [The result is obscure and has not been translated. Fo. 35a is blank; fo. 35b, ll. 1487–90 has not been translated, being an incantation derived from miscellaneous words and letter permutations. Fo. 36a is blank.] Fo. 36b is a monorhyme poem composed of portions of the following biblical verses: 'they dug a pit for me' (Ps. 57: 7); 'for there is the portion of the revered chieftain' (Deut. 33: 21); 'allotting them their portion by the line' (Ps. 78: 55); 'The head upon you is like crimson wool' (S. of S. 7: 6); 'judgements' (Deut. 33: 21); 'The Lord has done what He purposed' (Lam. 2: 17); 'and His decisions for Israel' (Deut. 33: 21). [The result is obscure and has not been translated (ll. 1491–4).]

Take the liquor . . . may he rest in peace a heading for the list of bottles that follows.

from the aforementioned 22 [Presumably, a reference to the date, 22 Av.]

four bottles, marked *AA, AB, AC, AD* [For simplicity, the Hebrew letters Falk used here and below have been replaced by their English equivalents. The significance of the labelling system is unclear.]

11 Elul, in the week of the Torah portion 'Ki Tavo': four bottles, marked *BA, BB, BC, BD*

19 Elul, in the week of the Torah portion 'Nitsavim': three bottles, marked *AA, AB, AC*

26 Elul, Sunday: three bottles marked *AD, BA, BD*

5 Tishrei, Monday, 5542 [1781]: three bottles, marked *AA, BC, BD*

12 Tishrei, Monday, the aforementioned: three bottles, marked *AB, AC, AD*

29 Tishrei the aforementioned, Monday: four bottles, marked *BB, BC, BD, AD*

9 Heshvan, Sunday of the week of the Torah portion 'Vayera': four bottles, marked *AA, AB, AC, BA*

16 Heshvan, Sunday: four bottles, marked *AD, BB, BC, BD*

23 Heshvan, Sunday of the week of the Torah portion 'Toledot': three bottles, marked *AC, AD, BA*

1st day of the new moon of Kislev: three bottles, marked *AC, AD, BA*

8 Kislev, Sunday of the week of the Torah portion 'Vayishlaḥ': three bottles, marked *AC, AD, BA*

15 Kislev, Sunday of the week of the Torah portion 'Vayeshev': three bottles, marked *AB, AC, AD*

Total so far: 44

*6 Tevet, the first day in the week of the Torah portion 'Vayeḥi': four bottles, marked *AA, AB, AC, AD*

24 Kislev, Tuesday of the week of the Torah portion 'Mikets': four bottles, marked *BA, BB, BC, BD*

26 Tevet, Tuesday: three bottles, marked *AA, AB, AC*, sealed

5 Shevat, Sunday: three bottles, marked *BA, BB, BC*, sealed

16 Shevat, Thursday: three bottles, marked *CA, CB, CC*, sealed with 'o' *Monday 21 the aforementioned three bottles marked

26 Shevat, Sunday: three bottles, marked

12 Adar, Monday: three bottles, marked *CA, CB, CC*, sealed

---

6 Tevet [The entries here are out of order; 6 Tevet should come after 24 Kislev, not before.]

Monday 21 the aforementioned three bottles marked [If 16 Shevat was a Thursday (Falk is correct on that), 21 Shevat was not Monday. The way in which the bottles were marked is not mentioned, either here or in the entries that follow.]

|fo. 38*b*| *Coffee pot and milk jug, weighing 33¾ oz.

*Two boxes for *etrogim*

A big bowl and a teapot, weighing 18½ oz.

Three platters

Two canisters, weighing 32 oz.

*A myrtle on a chain, weighing 15 oz.

Two goblets and two boxes for *etrogim*, weighing 10 oz.

Fourteen coins, weighing 39 oz.

Four *ets ḥayim* and *taz*, weighing 12 oz.

Six pairs of small handles, weighing 1½ oz.

|fo. 39*b*|

DUE DATES OF IOUS DATING FROM THE MONTH OF MENAHEM AV 5534 [SUMMER 1774] UNTIL THE END OF 5538 [AUTUMN 1778]

The earliest due date fell on the eve of Sukkot 5539 [5 October 1778]; the others are given below in order. 'Rd.' means that the pledge has been redeemed.

No.	Date and item	Redeemed	Principal	Interest
1.	10 Menahem Av 5532		£10. 0s. 0d.	
2.	Thursday, 11 said Menahem Av		£10. 0s. 0d.	
3.	Thursday, 11 the aforementioned, for six knives and six *Passover books	Rd.	£2. 0s. 0d.	12s. 0d.; and a word to the wise will suffice

Coffee pot and milk jug, weighing 33¾ oz. [The list is not headed, but the fact that weights are given suggests that these may have been items of silver that were to be pawned or sold.]

Two boxes for *etrogim* citrons; one of the four plant species used in the rituals of the Sukkot festival. [When an *etrog* is not actually being used it is kept in an ornamental box, often of silver.]

A myrtle on a chain a pendant, or perhaps a spice-box. [Perhaps an ornamental pomander, which could have fulfilled both functions.]

ets ḥayim the term for each of the two wooden (or silver) staves on which the Torah scroll is rolled in the synagogue.

taz [Falk writes 'taz' but given the context he perhaps meant *tas*, which is a term for a Torah shield, though given the weight involved the reference was probably to the small silver labels used to indicate which Torah is to be used in a particular week. Some weeks have special readings in addition to the regular one, in which case a second scroll should be rolled to the correct position in advance and labelled in this way to indicate that it is ready.]

Passover books perhaps referring to the Passover Haggadah. [Or perhaps to prayer-books for the festival, known in Hebrew as *maḥzorim*, but which Sephardi Jews (a significant community in London at this time) refer to in English as 'books'.]

No.	Date and item	Redeemed	Principal	Interest
4.	[No entry given]			
5.	Inkwell, from the new moon of Elul 5532	Rd.	£13. 0s. 0d.	£3. 13s. 0d.
6.	*Etrog* box belonging to the community, from Kislev 5538	Rd.	£2. 0s. 0d.	
7.	Wednesday, 10 said Kislev, silver watch	Rd.	£1. 1s. 0d.	5s. 3d.
8.	*Saturday night, 12 said Kislev, *the large platter for	Rd.	£2. 10s. 0d.	9s. 2d.
9.	In the said Kislev, my *etrog* box for	Rd.	£20. 0s. 0d.	5s. 0d.
10.	Saturday night, 21 said Kislev, milk can and tea canister for	Rd.	£4. 0s. 0d.	14s. 8d.
11.	Friday, 26 said Kislev, *bucket for the big one, *tuz*	Rd.	£3. 0s. 0d.	11s. 0d.
*13.	Thursday, 1 Tevet 5538, candlesticks from forest for	Rd.	£2. 13s. 0d.	7s. 0d.
14.	Tuesday, 7 said Tevet, coffee can for	Rd.	£5. 0s. 0d.	18s. 0d.
15.	Wednesday, 15 said Tevet, a chain and a pair of cuffs *from my stage, and a cane for	Rd.	£10. 0s. 0d.	
16.	Monday, 12 Shevat 5538, *another pair	Rd.	£1. 8s. 0d.	4s. 3d.
17.	Monday, said 12 Shevat, *14 ring and *hodes*, on their chain, and two goblets	Rd.	£7. 12s. 0d.	£1. 8s. 0d.

Saturday night, 12 said Kislev [The date appears to be in error.]

the large platter for [This entry and those that follow appear unfinished. Perhaps the amount originally followed directly (e.g. for '£2. 10s. 0d.') and the 'Rd.' column was added later.]

bucket for the big one [The reference is not clear.]

tuz [Perhaps meaning *tas*, as explained in the note to fo. 38*b*.]

13 the items are numbered in the diary and there is no item 12.

from my stage [The reference is not clear.]

another pair [Presumably of cuffs.]

14 ring [The two Hebrew letters used to indicate '14', *yod* and *dalet*, are the same as the word for 'hand', *yad*. The Hebrew word for 'ring', *taba'at*, is singular, so perhaps Falk was simply referring ungrammatically to a ring for the hand.]

hodes perhaps *hadas* ('myrtle')—a sort of jewellery, pendant; possibly referring to the spice holder used in the Havdalah ceremony marking the end of the sabbath [or a pomander, as mentioned in the note to fo. 38*b*, which would fulfil both functions].

No.	Date and item	Redeemed	Principal	Interest
18.	Wednesday, 14 said Shevat, four *ets ḥayim for	Rd.	£2. 6s. 0d.	8s. 4d.
19.	Friday, new moon of Adar 5538, canister for	Rd.	£1. 6s. 0d.	2s. 2d.
20.	Thursday, 6 said Adar, teapot for	Rd.	£2. 2s. 0d.	6s. 0d.
21.	Friday, 2 Iyar 5538, two spoons for	Rd.	£1. 0s. 0d.	2s. 2d.

*|fo. 44a|

Wednesday, 7 Nisan 5539 [24 March 1779], a further pledge of an inkwell by Gedaliah and by me, total	Rd.	£16. 0s. 0d.	5s. 8d.
Chain, *pair of cuffs from the stage and the cane, 13½ yards, from pottery	Rd.	£10. 0s. 0d.	£2. 8s. 0d.
Vessel for wine and two spoons (I gave Gedaliah for his needs, as mentioned in the small notebook, a gift of three and a half guineas)	Rd.	£2. 10s. 0d.	10d.
Forest candlesticks and watch	Rd.	£3. 13s. 0d.	[Indecipherable]

Thursday, 8 Nisan. For a reminder, Meyer the manservant received one guinea on account for his wages.

*And I, Mendel, also on account for my wages, received 25s. 0d.

REDEMPTIONS

Thursday, 8 Nisan 5539 [25 March 1779]. Began to redeem the pledges from what Gedaliah had pawned in Menachem Av 5532 [summer 1772], as follows:

Date and item	Redeemed	Principal	Interest
Teapot for 5s. 0d.	Rd.	5s. 0d	2s. 3d
Two watches, one of gold and one of silver	Rd.	£3. 5s. 0d.	£1. 6s. 0d.

ets ḥayim see note to fo. 38b above.

fo. 44a fos. 40–43 are missing from the diary.

pair of cuffs from the stage and the cane, 13½ yards, from pottery [The meaning here is unclear; perhaps the Hebrew words understood here to mean 'stage' and 'cane' represent something else entirely, given the mention of '13½ yards', and perhaps the word understood to mean 'pottery' is someone's name.].

And I, Mendel apparently Mendel's confirmation that he had received this sum.

Date and item	Redeemed	Principal	Interest
Pledges from Abraham Feier for 4 guineas 1 shilling. And an *exceptional gift that he brought in addition to the pledges, half a guinea; *total £6. 5s. 6d.	Rd.	£6. 5s. 0d.	6d.
Rusted metal chandelier from Gedaliah's list, as mentioned in above redemption list	Rd.	5s. 0d.	9d.
Sunday, 2nd intermediate day of Passover, to Lang Shimon, a gift			Two guineas
Abraham *Toctor, two guineas; and a word to the wise will suffice			Two guineas
Monday, new moon of Nisan, a gift for burning the fleas			Half a guinea

|fo. 44b| For a reminder: the pledges that were redeemed as recorded and marked 'Rd.', are in my possession today, Thursday, eve of the new moon of Iyar 5539 [15 April 1779], may it be fortuitous.

Monday, 13 Iyar 5539. I pawned the double watch and the second watch for £2. 5s. 0d. *R. Aaron Goldsmid, may he live long

|fo. 46a|

1. *Chest with silver
2. Chest with beams of the holy *ma'arakhot, with a circle, of leather
3. Chest, a second one, sacred like chest 2, with a circle, of leather

exceptional gift exceptional, because this was a gift in addition to the payment.

total £6. 5s. 6d. [Falk's arithmetic here seems unreliable: four guineas is £4. 4s. 0d., plus a further shilling would be £4. 5s. 0d., plus a further half a guinea, or 10s. 6d., would give a total of £4. 15s. 6d.]

Toctor possibly Abraham Doctor.

Monday, 13 Iyar 5539 [Falk was mistaken here: 13 Iyar 5539 was not a Monday; the corresponding civil date was Thursday 29 April 1779. Perhaps the confusion was because both Monday and Thursday are days on which the Torah is read publicly in the synagogue.]

R. Aaron Goldsmid, may he live long the continuation of the sentence is unknown as fo. 45 is missing. On Aaron Goldsmid, see the Introduction.

Chest with silver thus begins a list of five chests that Falk intends to move (see below) to the house of Aaron Goldsmid.

ma'arakhot Falk might be referring to the chests containing the walls of the tent, that he calls the 'holy *ma'arakhot*', since these chests contained items connected with Falk's place of prayer (= the tent).

4. Chest, also round, but shorter than chests 2 and 3, and there—a word to the wise will suffice—of leather

5. Chest, of wood, covered with animal hide

---

21 Tamuz 5540 [24 July 1780]. Today I informed my bosom friend, his esteemed excellency R. Aaron Goldsmid, that tomorrow, on Tuesday, 22nd inst., I will send the five chests marked 1–5 to his house in a cart, as he wrote the signs on the chests in his handwriting, in full, in his language, and on Wednesday, 23rd inst., R. Aaron sent me though his son Gershom, may he live long, £20. 0s. 0d. as a loan, and it has been paid.

Sunday, 9 Heshvan 5542 [28 October 1781]. Today I received a loan of £50. 0s. 0d. from *the warden and R. Aaron Goldsmid, that is, through his son Gershom, may he live long, against a promissory note that I sent with Gershom, sealed with my wax seal and with my signature, thus פעמי, S[amuel] J[acob] H[ayim].

---

3 Kislev 5542 [20 November 1781]. Today *I sent two goblets of good Dutch silver with a combined weight of 5½ oz. and a few pennyweight with Mendel to R. Leib the son of R. Samuel Firstrag and his mother, the righteous Bertka, may she rest in peace; he is to be the son-in-law of my beloved friend, his esteemed excellency R. Aaron Goldsmid. And may the Lord God fulfil their joy in accordance with their good will, on Wednesday, 4 Kislev, their wedding day, may it be fortuitous.

On Sunday 8 Kislev [25 November 1781] and again on Tuesday night, 11 Kislev I received *R. Leib the son of R. Eleazar Kann, my friend, who came here to London from Ostend with my bosom friend, our master, the rabbi, R. Abraham Nanshikh, may God bless him, and they drank coffee and had some sweets. I sent the said Leib my friend a gift with Mendel for his journey to The Hague: a roasted *kalk hoen* and a cooked chicken for 9s. 7d.; a smoked tongue, well cooked; a bowl full of aniseed and good *cronish*; six good *popish*; six of my cookies; *half a pound plenitas.

---

the warden [The reference is unclear.]

I sent…to R. Leib the son of R. Samuel Firstrag Falk records a gift he was sending to R. Leib 'Firstrag' (Pressburg), also known as Baron Lyon de Symons, on the occasion of his marriage to Polly, the daughter of Aaron Goldsmid. Leib (Lyon) was a first cousin of Simon Geldern, and his father Samuel Pressburg was a banker in Vienna; see Roth, *Records of the Western Synagogue*, 19.

R. Leib the son of R. Eleazar Kann perhaps a member of Falk's circle.

cronish…popish unclear.

half a pound plenitas 'plenitas' is from the Latin for 'fullness', perhaps meaning for good money. [It is not clear whether 'half a pound' refers to weight or monetary value.]

Thursday, 23 Shevat 5542 [7 February 1782]. I delivered into the hands of R. Aaron Goldsmid my friend eighty ducats to be a pledge, by the hand of R. Abraham Nanshikh, which I gave as a gift. And on the same day I received in return by the hand of R. Gershom his son, may he live long, thirty-six guineas, **dalet-shin*, *and also for the eighty ducats, and they are worth five guineas, and also for eleven ducats, and so they are.

And to the said R. Aaron I delivered two **sheginshun* from the total of £132, and those I defrayed to the said R. Aaron, the £50. My promissory note, too, is still in his hands, and the remaining £45 are still mine in the hands of R. Aaron my friend as a deposit, and a word to the wise will suffice.

|fo. 47*b*| *A Monsieur
                    Monsieur Philip Benjamin
                    in de Klynne Mark strat
                    tot Harderwijk

|fos. 48–55*a* blank|

|fo. 55*b*| **Tuesday night, 10 Shevat 5539* [27 January 1779]. Cosman came to me unannounced from France. Had I known of his coming, I would not have let him into my presence, because of the *children of demons. And on Wednesday he sent me a letter that he had to follow a certain noble from here to the country. And on the night of 18 Shevat as well he came to me. And on Saturday night he came to me, too. And after the whole thing I revealed to him that *she had emerged six times in the world:

dalet-shin an acronym that could mean 'guarding fee' (*demei shemirah*) or 'rental fee' (*demei sekhirut*).

and also for the eighty ducats ... and so they are [The meaning here is unclear.]

sheginshun apparently a form of currency.

A Monsieur Fo. 47*b* is written in Dutch and in Yiddish. My thanks to Professor Chava Turniansky for her assistance with the translation. The address reads 'of Small Market Street'. Falk adds a note to himself, 'The address of Feif in Harderwijk, Tamuz 5537 [summer 1777]'. [The significance of the address is not explained. 'Feif' may be Falk's way of referring to 'Philip'.]

Tuesday night, 10 Shevat 5539 [27 January 1779] [This entry appears to be out of chronological order.]

children of demons The children of demons are those born in impurity. [Perhaps this is a reference to children conceived through intercourse at a time when the mother was ritually impure, or perhaps it is connected to the earlier account of Cosman masturbating, which is also considered impure because of the spilling of holy seed.] This is perhaps why Falk would have refused to see Cosman if he had known of his arrival. In the year recorded, 1779, Falk might have changed his previous attitude to Cosman and therefore refused to see him.

she had emerged the Na'amah referred to is a she-demon. The entire passage is unclear.

in the time of Abraham, peace be upon him—the first time; in the time of Isaiah—the second time; in the time of Ezekiel—the third time; after the destruction of the Second Temple—the fourth time. And she was in the world four days, and wrought great destruction. And Abraham, peace be upon him, saw this with me, and they did not speak together because of the story of Na'amah; and a word to the wise will suffice.

RECOLLECTIONS FROM MONDAY, 8 MARHESHVAN 5541 [6 NOVEMBER 1780]

Ps. 102: R. Abraham Doctor my friend showed me in Psalm 102, verse 19. Ps. 109: 'May this be written down', and I did not understand its meaning; and a word to the wise will suffice. Also from Psalm 109 in the matter of the curses in the plural, and then in the singular, etc.—for a reminder to me to explain it to him; and a word to the wise will suffice.

*Roots כתש: 'the hollow which is at Lehi' 'the socket within which the tooth rests'; see there, very profound.

*Weight: 16 oz., weight of silver and gold. This is a pound and an ounce and a half, simple weight from the shops. For a reminder.

|fo. 57b| *Sunday, 3 Elul 5539 [15 August 1779]. Today I received all my wages for two years, till Tishrei 5540, a total of £12. 0s. 0d., and I have no further demands, as signed in the letter of dismissal in the English tongue, Menahem son of Joshua.

RECOLLECTIONS [FROM 5542 (1781/2)]

Shisil received a sabbath eve gift of money that I owed her, till today, Friday, 14 Heshvan 5542 [2 November 1781], amounting to half a guinea and, as a gift for the festivals, one crown.

|fo. 58b| 5532 [1771/2]. *Today Thursday, 11 Iyar of this year* [14 May 1772], the butcher stopped giving meat on credit, and said he would send me the bill for the meat in the coming week, and so I was obliged to ask Gedaliah and the *betulah kikhin* to buy meat for cash.

Roots ... profound see the commentaries by Rashi and R. David Kimhi (Radak) on Judg. 15: 19.

Weight: 16 oz. ... This is a pound and an ounce and a half [This is not clear, since 16 oz. is exactly one pound.]

Sunday 3, Elul 5539 written in a different handwriting: this appears to be a receipt from Falk's manservant in this period, Menahem son of Joshua, on his dismissal from service, for two years' back wages [to Tishrei 5540, which is in fact the next month since the new year commences in Tishrei].

betulah kikhin unclear; possibly cook [or a kitchen maid; *betulah* is an unmarried woman].

Tuesday, 27 Nisan 5540 [2 May 1780]. Mendel received on account 2*s*. 0*d*. to pay the rabbi for his letter of inheritance. Friday, new moon of Iyar, further, to send to his rabbi 1*s*. 0*d*. Sunday, 9 Iyar, to pay [?] 5*s*. 0*d*. Another debt. Friday, the 28th inst., that is to say, he asked for half a shilling, on account. Before Shavuot 5540 [1780], to buy him a pair of *shiterinik, received also half a crown.

Friday, 11 Tamuz 5540 [14 July 1780]. *Mendel held two shillings from my account, for a reminder, also, to Mendel 5*s*. 0*d*.

*Thursday, 6 Tamuz 5540 [9 July 1780]. Mendel held half a guinea of my money, and I did not know whether on account of his pledge, or on account of his salary. He said, as I remember, that he would give *a tithe in Elul 5540. In Holland Mendel received on my account one ducat.

---

*On Thursday night, 5 Marheshvan, I received the money from the son of R. Aaron Goldsmid, then on Wednesday night, the 4th inst., I gave Mendel a guinea for his needs.

On Tuesday, 9 Marheshvan, I gave Mendel money to buy me a lottery ticket from London, may it be propitious, one guinea more.

On Tuesday, 16 Marheshvan 5541 [14 November 1780]—to *Moishele, 5*s*. 0*d*.
Up to Tuesday, 16 Marheshvan 5541, the aforementioned account, £3. 11*s*. 5*d*.

---

*Wednesday, 17th inst., he received on account for Tuesday the 16th, in addition to the aforementioned, one more guinea.

On the night after the sabbath, 21st of the said month of Marheshvan, to buy me a ticket, etc. five shillings, Monday, the 22nd inst., to buy another ticket, may it be propitious, one more guinea.

---

shiterinik unclear.

Mendel held ... 5*s*. 0*d*. [The meaning is unclear.]

Thursday, 6 Tamuz 5540 [6 Tamuz 5540 was a Sunday, so Falk seems to have erred in his record-keeping.]

a tithe i.e. for charity.

On Thursday night, 5 Marheshvan [The timings here are difficult to follow since Marheshvan is four months after Tamuz; moreover, events that took place on the 4th are described as if they took place after the 5th.]

Moishele [Moishele's identity is not explained; perhaps it is Moses Kerem, mentioned on fo. 59*b*.]

Wednesday, 17th inst., he received [Presumably Mendel, but this is not stated specifically. Oron points out that the previous line was erased, so perhaps the answer lay there.]

In short, on Monday, 22nd inst., we added up the total as written on Tuesday, 27th of the said Nisan, and by his hand everything was written, by his accounting and signed in his name, a total of £5. 18s. 0d., for a reminder, the list is in his hand.

Today, Wednesday, 17 Marheshvan, after the aforementioned accounting, Mendel received another guinea.

And on Thursday the 25th I sent with Gedaliah to R. Shimon half a crown. Also to R. Samuel Hazan, half a crown; to Hayim the sick tailor, 2s. 0d.; to the rabbi and preacher, a guinea.

On the night of 25 Marheshvan 5541, after all our calculations, he asked me for another half a guinea to buy a ticket for him, and I gave him, for a reminder.

For a reminder, Mendel received his wages for Tishrei and Heshvan from the year 5542 [1781], £1. 0s. 0d; also on 4 Kislev he received 5s. 0d. on account; and another half a crown in the month of Kislev mentioned below.

|fo. 59a| I bought 4 lb. of tuna, cleaned and then fried, for the upcoming Passover, may it be propitious, for 8s. 8½d., and I gave 9s. 0d. to the trusty Jacob none the less—for a reminder.

|fo. 59b|
*COPIED FROM HARISH'S LIST IN THE NOTEBOOK

Linen from nine camps from the house of [?]: Friday, 4 Iyar 5534 [1774]. Sold by Moses Kerem, seven big pieces of satin from the destroyed camp, in front of witnesses.

*|fo. 60a| *Thursday, 5522* [1762]. For the year 5522, from Sunday, 8 Tevet 5522 Says he who prays בותק וי

COPIED copied from another notebook. This might have been an entry that was written earlier and copied here.

fo. 60a The last page was apparently pasted onto the end of the notebook. I do not understand what the signature refers to.

APPENDICES

APPENDIX A
PEOPLE FEATURING PROMINENTLY IN THE DIARIES

1. *The Boas Family*

The founder of the Boas family, Hayim (Abraham) Boas, was born in 1661 in Schriemm, in the Polish province of Posen (Poznań).[1] Jews probably first settled there in the twelfth century, and in the sixteenth and seventeenth centuries it was a well-known Jewish centre. During the Cossack revolts led by Chmielnicki in 1648 and 1656, some 100,000 Jews were massacred by Cossacks, Tatars, and Ukrainians, and more than 700 communities were devastated. Many of the survivors escaped to Holland, among them Hayim Boas, who settled in The Hague in 1680. His only son, Tobias, was born there on 3 November 1696.

Tobias Boas, referred to in the diaries as 'Tuvyah', became a wealthy banker, playing an important role in the finances of the Dutch republic. Among his clients were Joseph II of Austria and the Polish king Stanisław August Poniatowski.[2] The importance of The Hague as a cultural centre was largely due to the activities of Tobias and his two sons, Abraham and Simeon (referred to in the diaries as 'Shimon'), who were partners in their father's business and maintained international contacts with European royalty in Austria, France, Holland, Poland, and Sweden. Tobias was known in the Jewish world for his patronage of scholars: his house was always open to them, and he was head of the Tiferet Bahurim charitable society for the support of scholarship. He was also active in trying to prevent the expulsion of the Jews from Prague in 1745.[3]

Tobias's two sons continued their father's banking activities. The better known of the two, Simeon, also had far-reaching international connections. On 1 December 1766 Haarlem city council gave him the task of organizing the Jewish community in

---

[1] See Boas, *My Ancestors*; I am grateful to Samuel Aharon Boas, a descendant of this renowned family, for giving me a copy of this privately printed booklet that records the annals of the family. See also Michman, Beem, and Michman (eds.), *Encyclopaedia of Jewish Communities: Holland*: for Tobias Boas, see the index of names.

[2] See Boas, *My Ancestors*; Michman, Beem, and Michman (eds.), *Encyclopaedia of Jewish Communities: Holland*, 25.   [3] See Boas, *My Ancestors*.

the city. Jews could not receive rights of residence there unless they held a certificate signed by Simeon testifying to their moral rectitude.[4]

Samuel Falk became closely acquainted with the Boas family when he passed through Holland on his way from Germany to England. He seems to have been a guest in their home, even leaving some of his possessions there. He also received loans from them, as mentioned in his diary.[5] Simeon Boas's documented contacts with prominent Freemasons in Europe imply that he himself was a member of a Masonic lodge. The Rainsford Papers in the British Museum contain a note written by General Rainsford on 11 November 1777 to the effect that, when in need of money, he appealed to his Jewish friend, the banker Boas. He continues:

> In conversing with one of the Sons, we fell upon the Topick of Dr. du Falk, the famous Cabalist, whom I had heard a great deal of both at *Harwich* from the Capt[ain]s of the Packets,—at *Helvoet Sluys*, and at *Maasland Sluys* and found him in high Repute at all three Places, for the Propriety of his Behaviour and Sanctity of his Manners and, as well, from the respectable Character he appeared in of a venerable Rabbi of great Benevolence and Generosity, but knowing long before that the *Boas*' family had a particular Knowledge and Correspondence with him, I questioned the Son about him.[6]

Simeon Boas was also in close contact with Prince Czartoryski (whom Falk refers to in his diary as 'Duke'), providing him with a letter of introduction to Falk and requesting that he receive the Polish nobleman.[7]

2. *Cosman Lehmann*

Cosman Lehmann is mentioned frequently in both the diary of Zevi Hirsch and that of Falk himself. These references paint a picture of a person closely associated with Falk—organizing his affairs, giving him assistance on various occasions, and even supporting him financially.[8] Zevi Hirsch frequently mentions sums of money that Cosman left for Falk's household expenses. According to the diaries, Cosman participated in all the gatherings at Falk's home and was entrusted with various missions.

On the basis of the available information, we know that Cosman was born in Vienna the son of Hertz Lehmann, and was a cousin of Behrend Lehmann of Hanover. He apparently emigrated in his youth to France, where he became a textile merchant. In Paris he had a reputation for being headstrong, a womanizer, and a libertine. Upon reaching London (probably in the 1740s) he became a staunch admirer of Samuel Falk. Cosman quickly won people over, and seems to have been a born

---

[4] See Boas, *My Ancestors*.   [5] See FD, fos. 5*b*, 26*a*, 27*a*.
[6] Hills, 'Notes on the Rainsford Papers in the British Museum', 124–5.   [7] See FD, fo. 25*a*.
[8] For references and details of Cosman's life, see C. Roth, 'The King and the Cabbalist', 142; Duschinsky, *The Rabbinate of the Great Synagogue, London*, 93 n. 90; Hills, 'Notes on the Rainsford Papers in the British Museum', 124.

diplomat. Zevi Hirsch relates in his diary how he appealed to Cosman to mediate between him and Falk after the two had fallen out.[9]

General Rainsford refers to Cosman in a letter, calling him 'a very upright man' and noting that he had been told the same by others.[10] Rainsford also attests that he was 'in close correspondence' with Cosman and had 'some particular business' between them, the exact nature of which is not specified. It seems that both Rainsford and Cosman Lehmann were Freemasons, and that the latter's frequent journeys overseas (to France, Germany, and Holland) were related to various missions he undertook for his lodge. Rainsford also noted in his letter that at the time Cosman was in Versailles with the Chevalier de Luxembourg and P. de Tin.[11]

Cosman figures in an explicitly sexual dream recorded by Falk in his diary,[12] in which Falk dreamed that he saw Cosman standing by his (Falk's) bed and masturbating. It has been suggested that such acts of masturbation were part of purification ceremonies performed both in Sabbatian and in Frankist circles,[13] and in some Masonic lodges.

After Falk had died and his last will and testament was made public, Cosman Lehmann sued the executors in France (as most of Falk's wealth was invested in letters of credit of the French government), in an attempt to prevent Falk's money going exclusively to his heirs. Cosman claimed that over the years he had given Falk upwards of £20,000, and he should have been remembered in the will. During the deliberations, Aaron Goldsmid (on advice from Simeon Boas) wrote a letter to one Hertz Edelstein, in which he asked the latter to use his influence to ensure that the money would indeed be paid to the beneficiaries of the will.[14] Cosman's claims were not upheld by the court.

3. *Aaron Goldsmid*

Aaron Goldsmid was a member of a family originally from Frankfurt that settled in London in the second quarter of the eighteenth century and was active in the field of finance and banking.[15] Goldsmid accumulated considerable wealth and became one of the leaders of the Jewish community. In Levy Alexander's book about the family (devoted mainly to the lives of Aaron's sons Benjamin and Abraham, later two of the most prominent bankers in the City of London), he refers to Aaron's close

---

[9] See ZHD, fo. 33 a.   [10] See Hills, 'Notes on the Rainsford Papers in the British Museum', 127.

[11] Hills (ibid.) refers to Rainsford's mention of the collaboration between Cosman and the Chevalier de Luxembourg on several Masonic plans.   [12] See FD, fo. 32a; see also Appendix B below.

[13] See Liebes, *On Sabbatianism and Its Belief* (Heb.), 98–9.

[14] Cosman's attempt to receive some of the monies from Falk's estate is mentioned in Duschinsky, *The Rabbinate of the Great Synagogue, London*, 93, and in Hills, 'Notes on the Rainsford Papers in the British Museum', 127. See also below, Appendix F, 'Falk's Will'.

[15] See C. Roth, 'Goldsmid, Aron' (Heb.).

relationship with Samuel Falk.¹⁶ Falk's diary similarly speaks of his ties with Aaron Goldsmid and his sons. In fact, Falk made him both a witness of his will and its executor. Alexander tells fanciful tales of the relationship between Falk and Goldsmid, and of wonders that Falk performed. He also reports that Aaron Goldsmid died suddenly after having opened a mysterious 'packet of papers carefully sealed', which Falk had left in his care with instructions not to open.¹⁷ Goldsmid, Alexander relates, succumbed to his curiosity, opened the packet, and died the same day, to the consternation of his friends and family. The paper he had looked at was found to be covered with 'Cabalistic figures and Hieroglyphics'.¹⁸

4. *Elias Levy*

Elias was the son of Benjamin Levy, a wealthy and influential member of the Ashkenazi congregation in London; thanks to his philanthropy he was also accepted as a member of the Sephardi community in the city. Elias was still young when his father died. In his will Benjamin expressed his desire that his son should receive a Jewish education and become either a rabbi or a doctor. Although he did receive a Jewish education, Elias's predilections were not in accord with his father's wishes. He was drawn to his cousin Judith, the daughter of Moses Hart, who was known for his great wealth. This uncle invested Benjamin's capital in shares in the South Sea Trading Company, and succeeded in selling the stocks before the company collapsed, at a profit of 600 per cent. The match between Elias and Judith was solemnized in 1727. After their wedding the couple moved to a grand house in Wellclose Square. In his business dealings, which included trading in diamonds, Elias could draw on the resourcefulness and good instincts of his wife, who invested a considerable portion of their capital in privateers during the war between Spain and Holland. Upon her brother's death, Judith Levy also inherited a sizeable portion of her family's property, which was now divided between her and her sister. Elias took an active role in the affairs of the Great Synagogue. He was its first warden when this position was created in 1749, and he was one of the trustees involved in the expansion of the cemetery that had been purchased at the time. He also engaged heavily in philanthropy, and was involved in the affairs of the Jewish hospital. Elias Levy died, still young, on

¹⁶ Alexander, *Memoirs of the Life of Benjamin Goldsmid*, 46–50.

¹⁷ Ibid. 45–7. This tale also appears in other scholarly works on Falk that rely on the account by Alexander (see Webster, *Secret Societies*, 187).

¹⁸ In this context, Alexander speaks of Falk's wonders and portrays various events connected with him. He tells of a fire that erupted in London's Great Synagogue which threatened to burn the structure to the ground. Falk arrived at the scene, and wrote the Tetragrammaton on the synagogue door; the fire immediately subsided, and the synagogue was saved from destruction. Alexander also reveals other miraculous acts performed by Falk: how pawned objects marvellously returned to him, and how a catastrophe was miraculously averted when one of the wheels fell off a carriage in which Falk was travelling. The carriage continued its journey, and the wheel accompanied it until the carriage came to a halt.

14 January 1750.¹⁹ Judith later sold the Wellclose Square house to Falk (see gloss to Zevi Hirsch's diary, fo. 1*b*, Prescot Street).

5. *Falk and the Duke of Orleans*

A story connecting Falk with the duke of Orleans, Louis Philippe Joseph, also known as Philippe Égalité (1747–93), appears in several of the studies on Falk.²⁰ According to this narrative the two met in London, and when they parted Falk gave the duke a magic ring set with lapis lazuli, telling him that whoever wore the ring would eventually ascend the throne. According to the tale, the ring was forgotten and lost; years later, however, a Jewish woman by the name of Juliette Goudchaux returned the ring to Égalité's son, Louis Philippe (1773–1850), who did indeed become king of France in 1830.

This story, with its characteristic folk-tale elements, was seized upon by several antisemitic historians as 'proof' of Jewish involvement in world politics.²¹

---

¹⁹ See C. Roth, *The History of the Great Synagogue in London*, 164–5; ZHD, fo. 24*b*.

²⁰ See Drumont, *La France juive*, 275; Webster, *Secret Societies*, 194; Adler, 'The Baal Shem of London' (Berlin, 1903), 7 (Adler mentions in a footnote that Drumont cites an additional source, Gleichen's *Denkwurdigkeiten*); C. Roth, 'The King and the Cabbalist', 142.

²¹ Drumont and Webster cite different sources for this story, but they share the same patent antisemitic bias.

APPENDIX B

FALK'S DREAMS

FALK'S DIARY records several of his dreams. In doing so he follows a trope familiar in works of literature, and especially in mystical writings. Thus, for example, the diary of Rabbi Hayim Vital, *Sefer baḥezyonot*, written in the sixteenth and seventeenth centuries, describes dreams experienced by Vital himself and by others about Vital.[1] Such accounts provide clues to the personality of the writer, and psychiatrists make extensive use of them.

Some of Falk's character traits are indeed disclosed through his diary, and through that of his factotum. The dreams, however, perhaps unbeknown to the writer, reveal something of his inner, and unrevealed, self. Below I quote the dreams included in this translation and endeavour to interpret them.

Dream I

Tuesday, 3 Tevet 5535 [6 December 1774]. I dreamed that I was standing in front of the window with my wife, peace be upon her, and I was in a state of confusion and sensed some evil. And then I heard a great commotion from the members of my household, as she jumped from the window and broke her neck. I looked out of the window, trembling, and saw that her head was beneath her body. Soon the members of my household came in to seize me and I knew not why. Then I understood that in her malice, peace be upon her, she had informed against me, and for that reason she threw herself from the window. And lo, it was but a dream; may it be propitious. |fo. 2b|

This dream clearly expresses the writer's subconscious desire: his relationship with his wife was far from cordial, as we know from Zevi Hirsch's diary. A variation of this dream was recorded at a later date:

Dream II

A dream, Tuesday night, 27 Kislev 5529 [7 December 1768]. I dreamed today that my wife, peace be upon her, was lying asleep on two chairs in front of the window of

---

My thanks to Professor Yoram Bilu for his comments on several of the topics that appear in this appendix.

[1] See Oron, 'Dream, Vision, and Reality in Hayim Vital's *Sefer baḥezyonot*' (Heb.).

my room, the place of falling, and I was lying in my bed. In my sleep, I experienced weakness or fear, and then I awoke and I remember no more. Only God knows its meaning. |fo. 32a|

This dream, which appears near the end of the diary, bears a date earlier than that of the first dream, and may be an earlier, less developed, version of Dream I. The repetition of the subject of the dream—his wife's suicide by throwing herself from a window—attests to Falk's concealed desire to be rid of his wife. The designation 'peace be upon her' indicates that both entries were made after her death.

Dream III

For a reminder: on the night of Shemini Atseret 5532 [22 Tishrei /30 September 1771]. I dreamt that I met Jacob my manservant in a vineyard, as I understood in the vineyard of my house (from which I am absent now), with a basket full of grapes. Then I came from the room also, to pick grapes for myself. He was frightened at seeing me. I asked him, 'Why are you frightened—because you are stealing grapes?' He answered me, 'God forbid, I wanted to bring you the grapes.' And thereupon I awoke from my sleep, and lo, it was but a dream; may it be propitious. |fo. 30b|

This dream reveals something of Falk's fears for his property, and his apparent suspicions that his enemies had designs upon him and his possessions. Further indications of these fears are the lists of household effects in his diary, the marks he made on the bottles of wine in his house, and the lists he drew up of the contents of the chests in his cellar. In the dream, he catches his manservant Jacob stealing. One gains the impression of a suspicious, fearful person, reluctant to trust even his closest associates and believing them to be bent on doing him harm and laying their hands on his property.

Dream IV

A dream, Sunday night, 25 Adar 5528 [14 March 1768]. After coming from the new bridge, I went to bed. I dreamed that Cosman was standing before me, without breeches; he looked to me as someone who has just got out of bed, and I was sitting on a chair. I saw that his nakedness was so hard that it stood by itself, and he was making it erect with the movement of his mouth and body, till he had to take his saliva in the palm of his hand, that is, silently, very quickly. He began to stretch his nakedness until it lengthened [...] and became more than a quarter-yard long, and as thick as my arm. He then began to cast his filth [i.e. semen] to the south of me and the north of me, going around in a half circle, three or four times, like an arrow, to a distance of three or four yards, without stopping. For the filth welled forth and subsided like a flowing fountain. Then the nakedness subsided in its hardness, so that the robe came down to half a yard. Only God knows its meaning. |fo. 32a|

This dream is explicitly erotic: an account of his friend Cosman standing in Falk's room and masturbating in his presence. Does the dream express Falk's desires, or does it merely recall an actual occurrence? Falk's comment on the interpretation of the dream indicates an additional possibility.[2]

Dream V

Wednesday night, 25 Nisan 5535 [25 April 1775]. I dreamed a dream about my father, peace be upon him, the rabbi, R. Joshua Raphael Falker Falk. Suddenly he came to me from his land and I was amazed, since for some thirty-five years I had heard nothing of him. I understood that it was because of hearing of my great fame that he came to me here in London. And when I saw him, he embraced me and kissed me; and I am not sure what happened next, for I have forgotten. I remember only that his face was handsome, his beard white, and his visage that of a philosopher, that is, pensive, not happy or sad, just pensive. He marvelled at my wisdom. And there were students with me learning, standing and watching. And then he went upstairs to my synagogue for it was time for afternoon prayers, so I understood. And then, when he had gone upstairs to the synagogue, I said to the students who were in my room above: 'Beware of his silence and do not let him deceive you by his standing silently as if lifeless, for none is greater than he in Torah and in the sharpness of his tongue and his voice.' And then fear seized all the hearers, for they already knew. In the dream I knew nothing of his death, nor of the explanation; but may it be propitious. |fo. 32b|

Falk dreams of his father, specifying the latter's name in full, describing him as a scholar, learned in Torah and with the appearance of a philosopher. In this dream Falk might be attempting to come full circle, as it were. He had left his birthplace and family while still young. In his flight from Germany he possibly had no time to take proper leave of his family, with the memory of this hasty departure hounding him for many years. The dream seems to be preoccupied with the father's greatness and with Falk's own stature, as he is seen by his father, surrounded by disciples.

---

[2] The act of Cosman masturbating revealed in Falk's dream might possibly have some basis in the reality of Falk's daily life. Despite the erotic nature of the dream, it most likely portrays a common practice among the Sabbatians and Frankists, as among the Freemasons, who gave it their sanction, regarding it as an action that cleansed the body; see also Liebes, *On Sabbatianism and Its Belief* (Heb.), 98–9.

APPENDIX C

THE LETTER OF SUSSMAN SHESNOWZI TO HIS SON

JACOB EMDEN prefaces Sussman Shesnowzi's letter with the following:

Here is a copy of the insane letter by the accursed fool Sussman Shesnowzi, which he wrote to Poland about the repulsive *ba'al shem* of London. I have altered nothing of the text, save a few letters in certain words, as we are commanded to give no respect to the vile and to minimize folly and idolatry.

The notes explain Emden's deliberate distortions, and add references for most of the biblical expressions appearing in the letter.

The letter reads as follows:

[My] son, tender and choice,[1] shall grow and be as a moist garden, my son, the son of my innards, my precious one, my delight, the fruit of the harvest, the wondrous and wondrous young man, the esteemed teacher Shabetai. Now hear, my son, companion of my soul, the wondrous judgements of the Torah of our God, entrusted to one like a son of man[2] who is not a man. *Or me'or hagolah*,[3] a stronghold and killer, the beggar[4] of the champions of Israel, who places himself in the remotest ruins[5] to gather in the dispersed, the dispersed of the Exile of Ariel. It is a religious duty to broadcast his repute to all the Children of Israel, with a voice heard high,[6] a voice ringing out in the desert[7] that very dead one was taken by that *kafra*,[8] that man and that business that

---

Translated from the text as it appears in *Sefer hitabekut* by Jacob Emden (Altona edn.), 126–8.

[1] Following Gen. 18: 7 (*ben* . . . instead of *ben-bakar* . . . —calf).

[2] *Kevar enosh*, instead of *bar enosh* (man).

[3] Emden changed *or me'or hagolah* (with each *or* spelled with the letter *alef*), meaning 'the light of the luminary of the Exile', an honorific, to *or me'or hagolah* (with each *or* spelled with an initial *ayin*); with the latter spelling the word means the male sexual organ.   [4] *Rash*, instead of *rosh*, head.

[5] *Iyim* (spelled with an initial *ayin*), instead of *iyim* (spelled with an initial *alef*), meaning islands.

[6] Following Jer. 31: 14.   [7] Following Isa. 40: 3.

[8] *Kafra*—remains, refuse, sediment (following BT *BK* 101a). See Krupnik (Karu) and Silbermann, *A Dictionary of the Talmud* (Heb.), 428; Melamed, *Dictionnaire araméen–hébreu*, 182, understands this word differently, to mean 'cleaning'.

comes in a light bag,⁹ from a distant land. He is a murderer in Sheshakh,¹⁰ and he has a name in Rakat,¹¹ that is Tiberias, in which five things are to be found. The captain of violent robbers,¹² magnate and counsellor, expert sorcerer and wise in broken potsherds,¹³ a spirit from on high has possessed him.¹⁴ He reveals to the male sexual organ¹⁵ the cunningnesses¹⁶ of wisdom that is hidden and concealed from the eyes of all living,¹⁷ dry and unjust things, verbiage, *bepumi nehora*,¹⁸ destructive things¹⁹ contrary to the Torah.²⁰ These are the vision of the rotting,²¹ plumbing length and width and height. A sage, whose intelligence gives him understanding, who is able to comprehend male sexual organs²² in easy matters and pits,²³ hidden and occult matters, sciences and opinions, in *Sefer yetsirah* and the act of Creation, according to the combination of letters in the Bible, and in the genealogical lists of the thick ones,²⁴ letters and points. He reveals the true secrets of wisdom, to the aura of worm essence,²⁵ such as the angels of household idols²⁶ and heavenly creatures. These are the things that I, the youngest [or: most minor] among the holy congregation that our eyes have beheld, and not another's, great is the sickness of the man and his [imminent] killing.²⁷ He is exalted in his world, the most paltry matters are renewed, plated underneath the everlasting arms;²⁸ he has a monument and name²⁹ in the palace of Molekh³⁰ the Lord of Hosts. He entered in a dream [*beḥalom*], and emerged in a

---

⁹ i.e. someone lacking in worth. An intriguing parallel—linguistically if not in terms of content—would be the American post-Civil War carpetbagger.

¹⁰ Sheshakh = Babylonia, employing the *at-bash* method of letter inversion (in which the first letter of the Hebrew alphabet is replaced with the last letter, and so forth).

¹¹ Following BT *Meg.* 6*a*: 'Great was he in Sheshakh and he has a name in Rakat'; see the identifications of Rakat in the talmudic discussion.

¹² Based on Isa. 3: 3, but *ḥamasim*, spelled with the letter *samekh*, instead of the biblical *ḥamishim* (spelled with a *shin*)—'captain of fifty'.

¹³ i.e. worthless things; based on the continuation of this verse in Isaiah, but with the exchange of the letter *shin* in the biblical *ḥarashim* (artisan work) with the letter *samekh*, to produce *ḥarasim*—potsherds (following BT *BK* 91*b*: 'You have brought up a potsherd in your hand').   ¹⁴ Following Isa. 32: 15.

¹⁵ Again, *or* written with an initial *ayin*, instead of an *alef*, which would have meant 'He brings to light'.

¹⁶ *Ta'arumot*, instead of *ta'alumot*—secrets.   ¹⁷ Following Job 28: 21, which refers to wisdom.

¹⁸ Following BT *Yev.* 17*a*, where the reference is to a city; here, the meaning is 'with a glowing mouth', or something similar.   ¹⁹ *Ḥabalah*, instead of *kabalah*—kabbalistic.

²⁰ *Sotrei torah*—contrary to the Torah—instead of *sitrei torah*—the esoteric knowledge of the Torah.

²¹ *Merkavah*, written with the letter *kuf*, instead of *merkavah*, with a *kaf*, referring to the mysteries of the divine chariot throne (a basic theme in Jewish mysticism).

²² Yet again, *orot*, spelled with an *ayin*, instead of *lehorot*—to teach.

²³ *Maḥamorot*, instead of *vaḥamurot*—in easy and difficult matters.

²⁴ *Avot*, spelled with an *ayin* (with an obvious sexual innuendo), instead of an *alef*—the Patriarchs.

²⁵ *Hilat ha'ayalot*, instead of *ilat ha'ilot*, with an *ayin*, the 'cause of all causes', a kabbalistic-philosophical term: an appellation for Ein Sof, the concealed godhead.

²⁶ *Terafim* (see e.g. Gen. 31), instead of *serafim*—seraphim.   ²⁷ Following BT *Pes.* 110*b*.

²⁸ Following Deut. 33: 27.   ²⁹ Isa. 56: 5.   ³⁰ See e.g. Lev. 18: 21; instead of *melekh*—the king.

dream [*beḥalom*].³¹ The paths of the blind³² are familiar to him, the path of gossip like the paths of earth; the beginning of knowledge,³³ to lock with a bar the door of the sea³⁴ from end to end;³⁵ thick in bans³⁶ and making evil,³⁷ the hard onion,³⁸ murderer and murdered, his is the heavy chair of his whipping,³⁹ he directs the festive gathering of the beauty of his whipping⁴⁰ in his head, with a frontlet for the holy diadem,⁴¹ who stops during his work,⁴²and he shall be remembered for abomination. His name is false for him and he is false⁴³ for his name. He was an obtuse⁴⁴ man, a plunderer⁴⁵ of light, a h[oly] man who delivers curses,⁴⁶ Samuel Falk, may his spirit and soul expire⁴⁷ and ascend as smoke, may he live, the son of Master Raphael the Sephardi, now resident here in the holy community of London, the great city. Indeed, because of his volubility and his speaking in the language of the Jerusalem Talmud,⁴⁸ I could not fully understand him. Later, however, he wrote his commentary and explanation for the most abominable and cursed⁴⁹ Moses David, may his spirit and soul expire,⁵⁰ the aged and venerable defective one,⁵¹ the obliterated one, previously resident in the holy [community of] Podhajce, where he was famed as a *ba'al shed*,⁵² and was surely closely known to the head of the rabbinical court of our community, May God preserve him, and now he dwells in the home of this *k*-⁵³ prevaricator. Having seen his *k*- script, I have copied it verbatim. Here he related in his name new interpretations of the Torah, Majusian⁵⁴ utterers of incantations, and he did not know what he uttered. As the false writer attests of himself, not understanding, none other than the devil

---

³¹ Following BT *Ḥag.* 14*b*, which relates how only R. Akiva emerged unscathed (*beshalom*) from the mystical 'Garden'.   ³² *Samya*, instead of *shemaya*—heaven (following BT *Ber.* 58*b*).
³³ Prov. 1: 7.   ³⁴ Following Job 38: 8–10.   ³⁵ Following Exod. 36: 33.
³⁶ i.e. many people placed him under a ban; instead of *av* (with an *alef*) *beḥokhmah*, first in wisdom.
³⁷ *Vayirah*, with an *ayin* instead of an *alef* (with the meaning of 'and fearing [God]').
³⁸ *Butsila karisha*, instead of *butsina kadisha*—the holy lamp.
³⁹ *Kise kaved malkuto* (the latter word spelled with a *kuf*), instead of *Kise kevod malkhuto*—the throne of glory of his (i.e. God's) kingship.
⁴⁰ *Atseret . . . malko* (the latter word spelled with a *kuf*), instead of *ateret . . . malko* (with a *kaf*)—the crown of beauty of his kingdom (following BT *San.* 42*a*).   ⁴¹ Following Exod. 39: 30.
⁴² By changing the spelling of *otser* and *melakhto*, the meaning could be either 'he reigns during his reign' or 'he stops during his work'.
⁴³ *Na'ah* ('false'), spelled with an *ayin*, instead of *na'eh*, with an *alef*—fit, fine.
⁴⁴ *Tamim*, spelled with an initial *tet*, instead of an initial *tav*, with the meaning of 'perfect'.
⁴⁵ *Buzina*, instead of *butsina*, lamp; see below, n. 119.
⁴⁶ *Me'orer*, with a sound similar to the acronym meaning 'Our master and teacher, the rabbi, Rabbi . . .'.
⁴⁷ Instead of the usual acronym standing for 'May God preserve him'.
⁴⁸ i.e. the language of the Jerusalem Talmud, Aramaic.
⁴⁹ See above, n. 46.   ⁵⁰ See above, n. 47.   ⁵¹ *Hameḥubal*, instead of *mekubal*—kabbalist.
⁵² Instead of *ba'al shem* (see above, Introduction, Section IV).
⁵³ The two instances of *k*-: an abbreviation for *kadosh*—holy, or possibly for *kotel*—murderer.
⁵⁴ Majusian (Magi): Persian fire-priests, and, obviously, idolaters (see BT *Shab.* 139*a*).

M[oses] D[avid].⁵⁵ He is knowledgeable in the speech of demons⁵⁶ like himself, and he did not allow them to be banished. He spoke in delusions, from a spirit of confusion⁵⁷ that swelled within him.

Then he related some demonic acts and fabrication such as this and that.⁵⁸ My son, I have written you these things by the word of the Torah, so that you may show them to the rabbi and preacher of our community, the aforementioned *gaon*.⁵⁹ He will surely understand and deduce one thing from another and comprehend the sacred sayings and acts of that holy man, for his actions, deeds, and stratagems are pertinent to an explanation of the words of this holy man, when he speaks out loud of his holy actions from time to time. How despicable and snivelling⁶⁰ he is, altogether piles of debris,⁶¹ to the shepherd's eye,⁶² and the ear that hears the fullness of swallowed⁶³ novellae and secret matters and shattered⁶⁴ deeds. Know that all the lamps hanging on the walls, that are called *wandleicher*,⁶⁵ of which there are many pairs in each room, are all made of pure, refined silver, are fashioned in the likeness of the heavens, a likeness of the heavenly male sexual organs⁶⁶ in the spouts. The . . . large lamp is one of pure silver, made with double and triple lights one above the other, with eight branches and petals coming out of the sides, of hammered work, in the likeness of sacred, secret letters. And with this lamp he wrought a distortion⁶⁷ and Tofet⁶⁸ in the nature of spiritual illuminations. For he put oil in it on the eve of the sabbath, in the same measure as he did each week. The oil continued to burn for about three weeks, until he annulled with his hands the sanctity of the lamp, and then the lights were all quenched at once, as if they had never burned. This was a novel thing, done by the Master of the Universe, greater than the miracle that had been wrought on the strangled⁶⁹ for eight days.

An event from the new moon of Kislev: on Monday night, the eighth day of last Kislev, we saw with our own eyes a novel act, a suspension of the laws of nature. From Heshvan until now his magnificent visible⁷⁰ excellence shut himself up in his house

---

⁵⁵ This sentence is wholly an addition by Emden.
⁵⁶ Following BT *Suk*. 28*a*.   ⁵⁷ Following Isa. 19: 14.
⁵⁸ Added by Emden.   ⁵⁹ A rabbinic honorific; I have not determined to whom this refers.
⁶⁰ Instead of: 'How good [*tov*] and pleasant [*na'im*]' (Ps. 133: 1).
⁶¹ *Meḥamrim*, instead of *maḥamadim*—'and he is altogether delightful' (S. of S. 5: 16).
⁶² *Ein ro'eh*, spelled with an *ayin*, instead of 'the ear that hears [see the continuation of the letter], the eye that sees [*ro'eh*, spelled with an *alef*]'—Prov. 20: 12.
⁶³ *Nivla'im*, instead of *nifla'im*—wondrous (while maintaining the rhyme).
⁶⁴ *Nora'im*, spelled with an *ayin*, instead of *nora'im*, spelled with an *alef*—awe-inspiring.
⁶⁵ Wall lamps.   ⁶⁶ Again, *orot* spelled with an *ayin*.
⁶⁷ *Ot*, spelled with an *ayin*, instead of an *alef* (see the next note).
⁶⁸ i.e. the place where children were sacrificed to Molekh, instead of *mofet*—a sign and portent (Isa. 20: 3).   ⁶⁹ *Ḥanukah*, spelled with a *kuf*, instead of the festival (spelled with a *kaf*).
⁷⁰ *Nirah*, instead of *nora'ah*—awesome.

on the Bridge, for 'his thigh[71] was shut up tight; no one could leave or enter',[72] for he was shut in, until the Torah portion of 'Vayishlaḥ', without food, drink, or sleep, and needless to say, without lighting fire, which it would not be believed if told,[73] for it cannot be told. In the sixth week of his seclusion he commanded that ten learned men be assembled, [and] that they go to the ritual bath. At midnight we came to his holy abode, and he dressed us in *kitls*[74] and seated us in a room in the house. On Tuesday night, the twenty-sixth, the holy man ordered the destroyed one,[75] the cursed [holy?],[76] his candle[77] Moses David. Afterwards he ordered the said R. Moses, as well as another member of that holy brotherhood, our teacher Jacob, the grandson of our master and teacher, the rabbi, Rabbi Meir Eisen Stadt.[78] R. Moses kindled one large lamp, and R. J[acob] the other. Thereupon R. Moses finished writing in his notebook. He then instructed the entire brotherhood to enter the inner sanctum barefoot. And lo, we beheld the holy man seated on his holy throne, dressed like an angel of God, offered as a sacrifice[79] with a gold headdress,[80] a golden chain around his neck, reaching down to his breast. From this chain hung [an ornament] like a large star, made of silver, and holy names were written upon the star. He sat there, his face covered with a star-shaped veil. His headgear was *nivla'ah*,[81] fashioned of paper, and sacred names were written on it. Fashioned to the hat at each end was a sort of star of pure, refined gold, and [holy] names were engraved upon them as on the Tablets [of the Law]. Who can describe the perfection of the paintings on tapestries draped on the walls from end to end in this chamber, the inner sanctum, with sacred drawings, representing the vision of the rotting;[82] and within the drawings were inscriptions full of the well-known sacred names. And lo, the whole chamber was hung with ropes with combinations of names on them. And we sat there, five men within the rope and five men outside the rope before him. Resting upon the table was a great shofar, which the holy man had made himself of paper with holy handiwork, and in it was a

---

[71] *Yerikho*, spelled with a *khaf*, instead of *yeriḥo*, spelled with a *ḥet*—Jericho.   [72] Following Josh. 6:1.
[73] Following Hab. 1:5.   [74] *Kitl*: the white robe worn on the High Holy Days.
[75] See above, n. 51.   [76] See above, n. 46.   [77] Instead of the customary 'may his light shine'.
[78] The author mentions one member of Falk's circle, Jacob Eisenstadt, the grandson of R. Meir Eisenstadt. We know of two individuals bearing the latter name. One, the author of *Panim me'irot* (c.1670–1744), was the teacher of R. Jonathan Eybeschuetz. According to Liebes, 'On a Christian Jewish Sect' (Heb.), 'R. Meir was initially a follower of R. Leibele Prossnitz, but after R. Leibele was revealed to be a fraud R. Meir withdrew his support from him' (p. 231). The other, known as Meir b. Hayim Katzenellenbogen of Eisenstadt, the author of *Mishteh yayin* and *Ner lama'or*, was active during the seventeenth century, and was a known Sabbatian. For these two individuals, see Liebes, *On Sabbatianism and Its Belief* (Heb.), index. The wording of the text indicates that Sussman referred to the first R. Meir Eisenstadt, who, according to Liebes, was regarded forgivingly by Emden, whose censure of him was couched in quite moderate language; nor does Emden disparage him in this letter.
[79] Or 'sent up in smoke'—*muktar*, spelled with a *kuf*, instead of *mukhtar*, spelled with a *khaf*—crowned.   [80] Following Lev. 8:9.
[81] Either 'swallowed up' or 'evil', instead of *nifla'ah*—wondrously.   [82] See above, n. 21.

trumpet, also made of paper, and everything was inscribed all around with holy names etc. This is the holy man who, in my poor understanding and knowledge, stands tailored[83] in our generation, who knows the pillage[84] of the innermost secrets of our God's Torah, as I saw that the lips of the righteous know what is pleasing,[85] and does great acts for despicable[86] action, for the perfect act, and they are now beloveds and darlings,[87] with life restored[88] to every living soul.[89] The man, famed throughout the province of Volhynia, the destructive one,[90] the restrained[91] man of God who delivers curses,[92] Moses David,[93] may his spirit and soul expire, known as R. Moses *ba'al shed*[94] of the holy community of Podhajce[95]—I shall present before you his unique speech and extensive explanation of that *melila deta'ana hata'un*,[96] who delivers curses[97] [Rabbi] Jonathan,[98] may his spirit and soul expire,[99] the renowned head of the Hamburg rabbinical court, and told him of the great wonders and heresies[100] of the man, that holy man who is like a son of man but not a man, and in his eloquence he said: This person is the most polluted one,[101] the most high obtuse one[102] alluded to in the *tikunim*[103] [paras.] 69, 106a, and 106b: 'R. Simeon bar Yoḥai immediately said: Happy is the generation in which such mysteries have been disclosed, as Hannah said, "He will give idolatry[104] to His king", and then, "will raise the horn of His

---

[83] *Yaḥit*, instead of *yaḥid*—alone.

[84] *Shod*, spelled with a *shin*, instead of *sod*, spelled with a *samekh*—mystery.

[85] Following Prov. 10: 32.   [86] *To'av*, spelled with an additional *ayin*, instead of *tov*.

[87] Following S. of S. 5: 16.   [88] Following Ps. 19: 8.

[89] Following Job 12: 10. This entire sentence consists of flowery biblical (or biblical-sounding) phrases that Emden changes from honorifics to ridicule.

[90] See above, n. 51.   [91] *Muvlag*, insead of *muflag*—most excellent.

[92] See above, n. 46.   [93] See above, n. 47.   [94] See above, n. 52.

[95] This reference to Moses David of Podhajce is one of the most important testimonies to the ties between Falk and Moses David. The letter tells us that the latter visited London in 1759. Emden notes (*Sefer hitabekut* (Altona edn.), fo. 38b) that Moses David fled to London to escape his enemies. In his article 'The Kabbalist Moses David of Podhajce' (Heb.), Chaim Wirszubski unfolds Moses David's annals, on the basis of the testimonies that he collected from numerous sources. Wirszubski also notes the connection between the latter and Falk, and indicates his tendency 'to combine Sabbatian belief with Christianity' (*Between the Lines* (Heb.), 199). See also Liebes, *On Sabbatianism and Its Belief* (Heb.), 81, 223.   [96] Possibly a distortion of 'fruitful statements by the *gaon*' to 'things that maintain the harlot'.

[97] See above, n. 46.

[98] R. Jonathan Eybeschuetz, the head of the Hamburg rabbinical court, whom Emden attacked in his books, charging him with Sabbatianism. As this letter indicates, Emden accused Falk of maintaining close ties with Eybeschuetz. An extensive literature has been devoted to Eybeschuetz, among which is Liebes, *On Sabbatianism and Its Belief* (Heb.), which sheds new light on him and on his son.

[99] See above, n. 47.   [100] An addition by Emden.

[101] *Se'av dese'avin*, with an additional *alef* in each word, instead of *sav desavin*—an appellation in the Zohar and in *Tikunei zohar* for the most supreme one, Adam Elyon, the *sefirah* of Keter (the *sefirah* closest to the godhead), and also to the very elect, i.e. a luminary who is great in Torah learning.

[102] *Otem*, instead of *adam*—man.   [103] i.e. *Tikunei zohar*.

[104] Emden turns the two-letter word *oz* ('power') in this passage, from 1 Sam. 2: 10, into an acronym with this negative meaning.

anointed one".' His impure mouth made of him an anointed one[105] in accordance with his impurity, may his spirit and soul expire.[106]

Thereupon the fool continued at length to describe his marvels and his dealings with lots, and went so far as to praise them as though this was the Urim and Tumim [used by the High Priests for divination], or a case of the wife suspected of infidelity, woe to the silly[107] fool! And after discoursing the fool continued further, the fool has a mouth,[108] and he sealed his death sentence,[109] as follows: Now, my beloved son, his miraculous acts may be retold—where is one who could weigh? where is one who could count?[110] to what is inscribed in a scroll, giving goodly words,[111] and all his own exploits, are great and many, to relate wisdom and knowledge, all that they thought and knew, not like he thought and knew, wondrous things without number,[112] that multiply from day to day,[113] though they know not how to tell it.[114] Now, before concluding to speak, let me reveal one more of those great things that we have heard from this holy man. But in the interests of brevity—for I have little time—I shall content myself with referring to *Midrash konen*,[115] where the matter is dealt with at length. 'Just as the denizens of the world, who do not reside in this world, but are rather in another world, he [Falk] is the one who was born in one of the seven lands.' For the sake of brevity, I shall write a bit of the end of the holy man's words on this subject, that even if the Redemption were to come, the Redemption will not be complete until all denizens of the earth submit and accept the yoke of the Kingdom of Heaven, as stated in the verse, '[All the world's inhabitants] perceive and know, etc.'[116] And he [Falk] is the one who causes all to submit, for he has the power and might to subdue. But enough of this; and the erudite shall comprehend and understand. And for love of brevity I have abbreviated my words, for this is the day [I have hoped for], since I have lived to see the great favour vouchsafed me and many others by the Lord, in so far as all Israel of our provinces in Poland would earnestly and earnestly desire, would long and yearn[117] to hear such words of wisdom, [and witness] such actions and the body and essence of that great and renowned rubbish heap,[118] the holy man. They shall say to him, this is our master and teacher, the lamp of light[119] who goes up in smoke[120] with [holy] names, may he live long, may his spirit and soul expire.[121] For

---

[105] i.e. messiah.　　　　[106] This sentence is an addition by Emden.

[107] A play on words based on the similarity between *sotah* (the accused wife) and *shoteh* (silly one).

[108] Following Prov. 10: 14.

[109] A wordplay based on the two meanings of the word *ḥatam*—conclude, or sign. This paragraph, to here, is Emden's own words.　　　[110] Following Isa. 33: 18.　　　[111] Following Gen. 49: 21.

[112] Following Job 5: 9.　　　[113] Following Gen. 8: 17.　　　[114] Following Ps. 71: 15.

[115] Perhaps the intention is to show what this *midrash* relates about the world and its numerous creatures; see Jellinek (ed.), 'Midrash konen', 36.　　　[116] From the Aleinu prayer.

[117] Following Ps. 84: 3.　　　[118] *Kafra*, instead of *gavra* ('that great man'); see above, n. 8.

[119] An appellation applied to a Torah scholar, and especially to R. Simeon bar Yoḥai; see Liebes, 'Chapters in a Dictionary of the Zohar' (Heb.), s.v. 'Butsina', paras. 20, 55.

[120] *Muktar*, instead of *mukhtar*—crowned.　　　[121] Addition by Emden.

the things that are heard among those living behind the [heavenly] Curtain,[122] unclear matters, that one said thus and another said thus.[123] And I, guided by fate to bring my food from afar,[124] was living here in the holy community of London for some time, have been betrayed by Time,[125] as I am occupied with my business to ensure my sustenance and that of my dependants, with God's help, I hardly have time to catch my breath,[126] and I do not have time for everything.[127] For that reason I have not come constantly to frequent his temple,[128] the sacred temple of the Lord, of that holy man. I was only in the master's house a single day; I leaped over mountains, bounded over hills,[129] to the footsteps of the herald announcing good fortune[130] for my haughtiness and the haughtiness of others[131] in my saying: 'It is a time to act for the Lord',[132] and I set my mind to seek to know the acts, the fruit of the righteous one, that is a tree of life.[133] I am thankful for my lot, that I was pleasing[134] to this holy man, and I was admitted with much respect into the holy brotherhood, the holy congregation who seek his company, the shelter of his wisdom, and who are bound by the drizzle[135] of his deeds, partners[136] in religious deeds,[137] engaging in frequent prayer and supplications to the Creator, who has guided me on the true path. For I have found that the actions of the righteous man and the drizzle[138] of his deeds are all accounted for guilt,[139] and he plumbs the depths of things; for he is of the aspect of the First Temple, to bring merit upon Israel and he has worked wonders that will be of avail in expediting the coming of the Redeemer; for by his sexual organ[140] shall we see the sexual organ of the King Messiah, Zevi,[141] may his name be blotted out,[142] the King Ein Sof. Therefore I have spoken at length, and I have beseeched the holy man, to permit me to put hand to quill and respond to those who ask me, to express good news, and state a little of what I know. Here is the story of that act of villainy[143] and *nora'ut*,[144] it is a small thing[145] of him [i.e. of his greatness]. In actuality, these matters

---

[122] Following BT *Ḥag*. 15*a*.
[123] Following 1 Kgs 22: 20.   [124] i.e. to seek my livelihood; following Prov. 31: 14.
[125] A medieval expression that anthropomorphizes Time and its hardships. The expression appears in Hebrew secular poetry—laments and wisdom poetry.   [126] Following Job 9: 18.
[127] Following Eccles. 3: 1.   [128] Following Ps. 27: 4.   [129] Following S. of S. 2: 8.
[130] Following Isa. 52: 7; Nahum 2: 1.
[131] *Zaḥut*, spelled with a *ḥet*, instead of *zakhut*, with a *khaf*—for my benefit and the benefit of others.
[132] Ps. 119: 126.   [133] Following Prov. 11: 30.   [134] Following Gen. 18: 3.
[135] *Ḥisharon*, a made-up word spelled with a *ḥet*, instead of *kisharon*, with a *kaf*—skill.
[136] Possibly a disparaging addition by Emden, based on Mishnah *Men*. 11: 6 (with the meaning of part, attachment).   [137] A euphemism for sexual intercourse (as in BT *Eruv*. 100*b*).
[138] See above, n. 135.   [139] *Ḥovah*, instead of *tovah*—'[accounted] favourably'.
[140] Yet again, *or* written with an initial *ayin*, instead of an *alef*, which would have meant 'by his light that brings light'.
[141] A reference to Sabbatai Zevi, probably meaning that Falk was the false messiah's successor.
[142] An addition by Emden.   [143] *Nivla'ut*, instead of *nifla'ut*—something wondrous.
[144] Spelled with an *ayin*: a made-up word relating to the male sexual organ, instead of *nora'ot*, with an *alef*—awesome things.   [145] Following BT *Ber*. 33*b*.

are as a drop in the ocean, of all his other revealed and concealed villainous and [sexual][146] deeds. What I read and found from what came to me I already wrote, as it happened.[147] I related them in the proper order[148] as one gathering among the speakers[149] and those who expose[150] his labour in the Torah. From the valiant man who performed great deeds[151] in the holy labour; I will come this far, and not add anything that need not be said. If the reader will proceed according to the order, then he will understand everything, by deduction. In A[vodah] Z[arah][152] I did not find its interpretation; may it be His will, before the Holy One, blessed be He, that for us the scriptural passage shall be fulfilled, to wit: 'For the land shall be filled with devotion to the Lord as water covers the sea';[153] may our eyes merit seeing the habitation of Mount Zion;[154] as on the day we went forth from Egypt show us wondrous deeds;[155] may we be avenged from all our enemies;[156] and may we merit seeing the goodness of the Lord in the land of the living.[157] Amen, may it be His will. Now, my beloved son, after I have told you all these things, that my eyes, and not another's, have seen and my ears have heard, I know that, God be thanked, many will believe my words, and will pay no regard to false words.[158] Therefore, I have unfurled a flying scroll[159] as a rolled garment,[160] and I have opened my mouth wide[161] to tell of the scholar, my master, that holy lamp.[162] You are not one of those frivolous heralds who tells all and sundry of his heresies,[163] his deeds, and his annals. For any person who has no business with the secret things[164] will consider my words as deceit and jest. Therefore, my beloved son, do not reveal them readily to all and sundry. Needless to say, show my account only to humble and wise men, to those adept in concealed wisdom,[165] possessed of sense and despicableness,[166] evil and knowledge.[167] For even here in the community of London nothing is being disclosed to outsiders who are not members of the brotherhood, until an auspicious time.[168] I shall listen to what they say,[169] those great in their wisdom, the elders of my city, and the other great sages of Israel, and I enquired after those endowed with the understanding to know;[170] and I was sick[171] for the sanction and acceptance of all the brotherhood, to restore us, from mental and

---

[146] See above, nn. 63, 64. [147] Following BT *BM* 86*b*. [148] Following BT *Ta'an.* 6*b*.
[149] *Ha'omerim*, with an *alef*, instead of 'gathering among the sheaves', with an *ayin* (following Ruth 2: 7). [150] *Mefa'arim*, with an *ayin*, instead of *mefa'arim*, with an *alef*—who extol.
[151] Following 2 Sam. 23: 20; 1 Chron. 11: 22. [152] i.e. the talmudic tractate. [153] Isa. 11: 9.
[154] Following Isa. 4: 5. [155] Following Mic. 7: 15.
[156] From the blessing recited after the reading of the book of Esther on Purim (following BT *Meg.* 21*b*). [157] Following Ps. 27: 13. [158] Following Exod. 5: 9. [159] Following Zech. 5: 1, 2.
[160] Following Isa. 9: 4. [161] Following 1 Sam. 2: 1. [162] i.e. Falk; cf. above, n. 119.
[163] *Kefirotav*, with the addition of a prefixed *kaf*, instead of *peirotav*—his fruits.
[164] Following BT *Hag.* 13*a*. [165] i.e. knowledge of the occult. [166] See above, n. 86.
[167] *Ra'ah*, with an *ayin*, and *da'at*, instead of *re'eh*, with an *alef*, and *da*, meaning 'see and know', or (based on Ps. 119: 66), possibly 'good sense and knowledge'.
[168] Following Isa. 49: 8. [169] Following Judg. 7: 11; Jer. 8: 6.
[170] Based on the Amidah prayer. [171] *Haliti*, with a *het*, instead of *kaliti*, with a *kaf*—longed for.

physical backsliding.[172] And to hastily sound a warning[?][173] and reveal their holy knowledge and to hear their return to Ramah,[174] that would be to the delight of all. And I, I say to those who know me, when I say that the actions of this holy man are great, and that his intellect and insight greatly facilitate matters for the ignorant, to advance merit before strict judgement. The one who judges him in the scale of merit[175] shall carry away a blessing from the Lord, a just reward from God, his deliverer,[176] may his great hand be raised for wondrous rejoicing in Jerusalem, the eve of the holy sabbath, on the eve of the Passover festival, in the year 'but all the Israelites enjoyed light in their dwellings'[177] by the minor count,[178] these are my words, your father, who delights in your love, Eliezer Sussman.

[172] *Meshuvat*, instead of *meshivat*—restoration [of the soul].
[173] *Lehatra'ot*, instead of *leharot*, to show.
[174] Based on 1 Sam. 7: 17; based on the dual meaning of *teshuvah*—'return' and 'reply'.
[175] Based on Mishnah *Avot* 1: 6.   [176] Following Ps. 24: 5.   [177] Exod. 10: 23.
[178] The letter was finished on a sabbath eve that also was the eve of the Passover festival, a combination that occurred in 1759, a year that corresponds to the numerical value of the letters comprising the Hebrew words of 'but all the Israelites'. See also Wirszubski, *Between the Lines* (Heb.), 83 n. 3.

APPENDIX D

THE LETTER OF JACOB EMDEN

THIS IS EMDEN'S RESPONSE to the friend who sent him a copy of Sussman Shesnowzi's letter; Emden appended it to his reproduction of Shesnowzi's letter in *Sefer hitabekut*.[1]

My response to this despicable letter that that stupid Sussman the writer, who was paid with money for the grain[2] that he received from his acquaintance,[3] who is deserving of ostracism, being placed under the ban, and excommunication. He is deserving of ostracism, being placed under the ban, and excommunication for having opened wide his mouth[4] with such blasphemy and curses that would make the reader's hair stand on end.[5] Should he not be tried as an inciter and one who leads others astray,[6] who plucks saltwort and wormwood,[7] the demonic one,[8] before he flourishes, may his name be utterly blotted out.[9] And lo, his falsification is self-evident.[10] For he frequently prophesied, and if the word of the Lord is with him and if he came on His mission, this is in plain view of all[11] as an army. Why does he perform his actions in secret, like a covert from the tempest?[12] Undoubtedly, it is to cut out the [holy] names[13] that he is hiding,[14] as a wild ass[15] braying among the bushes,[16] huddling among the nettles. Woven falsehood shall come from mendacity.[17] As regards the man who takes the [holy] name,[18] his judgement, deed, and speech are a vagabond,[19] prominent in anguish.[20] Although I never met him, I have a good idea, from several people from Poland[21] who spoke unaware [of what they were saying],

---

[1] See Emden, *Sefer hitabekut* (Altona edn.), fo. 71a.
[2] Following Gen. 44: 2.
[3] This is apparently directed at Falk
[4] Following Job 16: 10.
[5] Following Job 4: 15.
[6] Incites to idolatry; see Mishnah *San*. 7: 10.
[7] Following Job 30: 4.
[8] For related words, see Eccles. 2: 8.
[9] Following Ps. 109: 13.
[10] Following BT *Git*. 89a.
[11] Following Num. 33: 3.
[12] Following Isa. 32: 2.
[13] Following BT *Shab*. 116a.
[14] Following 1 Sam. 10: 22.
[15] Job 6: 5.
[16] Job 30: 7 (Emden combines sources here, joining together fragments of verses).
[17] Based on Isa. 60: 6, but replacing 'from Sheba' with 'from mendacity'.
[18] Followed by an abbreviation possibly meaning 'the name of God has been desecrated here'.
[19] *Na'ah*, spelled with an *ayin*, instead of *na'eh*, with an *alef*—fit, fine.
[20] *Batsa'arim*, spelled with a *tsadi*, instead of *basha'arim*, spelled with a *shin*, following Prov. 31: 23.
[21] This is the only source we possess that states that Falk was born in Poland.

what is his nature and desire: only to take the [holy] name, for he is proficient in practical kabbalah, and to act by the power of the use of [holy] names[22] to dig and find treasures, false language. Afterwards, he was apprehended in the province of Westphalia for he was seized [i.e. arrested] and was almost burnt,[23] if he had not found a place to which he could immediately flee, [swift] as a deer, without suffering punishment as a sorcerer. He took as a wife a harlot, a woman well known for her licentiousness, who had several bastards from gentiles,[24] and he went with her to London, in the land of England, where he found helpers from the fringes of the camp[25] who acted on his behalf among the gentiles (but not a single one of the wealthy members of our people were so tempted, only the poorer classes, who thought to profit from him. They acted successfully on his behalf.) Gentiles with [deep] pockets believed in him; they wanted him to reveal to them unfathomable treasures, whether buried in the land, or sunken at sea.[26] He did so by showing wondrous-seeming things that were only deceitful illusions,[27] before fools who set for Luck a table[28]—strange is his work, astounding is his task,[29] for demons is the rite.[30] They think there is none like him, but this is delusion, an act of chaos.[31] In this manner he succeeded in snaring a very great and rich captain, who gave all his great riches to that man, hoping to be greatly successful through him; now, however, he has become a pauper, and he arises early to come to the door of that *ba'al shed*,[32] to give him something to keep him alive. Notwithstanding all this, that captain who was impoverished by him extols him among the wealthy gentiles, and is effusive in telling of his vast knowledge and the

---

[22] Emden mentions Falk's involvement with magic.

[23] Thus testifying to Falk's trial in Westphalia, and his being sentenced to be burnt to death.

[24] Emden's slanderous description of Falk's wife is a distortion of the truth and is not credible. From what we know from other sources, Falk married a widow or divorcee who had an only child named Gedaliah. Falk adopted him, and also bequeathed his estate to him.

[25] Emden's characterization of Falk's believers and followers as coming from the fringes of society is inaccurate. It is quite likely that the various people who gathered around Falk in his early years in London were indeed marginal in the society of the time, but this was far from the truth in the year in which Emden wrote this. From the 1760s on, Falk acquired a powerful public standing, and he enjoyed numerous ties with distinguished Jewish families in Holland (the Boas family) and in London (the Goldsmids).

[26] Emden states that Falk was known as one who could discover hidden treasures. According to other testimonies that we possess, Falk was indeed reputed to be capable of finding treasure troves (see also the memoirs of the Comte de Rantzow).

[27] We hear of Falk's 'abilities' to 'move objects' from several sources (de Rantzow's memoirs; the diary of Zevi Hirsch of Kalisz). Emden labels such activity as 'deceitful illusions'. Clearly, this telekinetic 'ability' to move objects or to influence them or people is what gave Falk his reputation as a magician and wonder-worker. Was Falk truly telekinetic (in the manner of the modern-day Uri Geller), or was he merely a charlatan capable of mesmerizing his audiences (i.e. a stage magician)?

[28] Following Isa. 65: 11.   [29] Following Isa. 28: 21.

[30] Emden turns this into a rhyme, with the Hebrew words for 'table' (*shulḥan*) and 'rite' (*pulḥan*).

[31] Based on Jer. 10: 15.   [32] See Introduction, Section IV, above.

power of his actions. He has also found many gentiles who shower much money on him, and the *ba'al shed* thereby conducts himself as one possessed of tremendous riches. He is also generous with the members of his band and others, so that he shall have a great name; notwithstanding this, at times his pocket runs empty, and he must make do with the contents of the charity boxes of the storekeepers and merchants. According to all, he is an ignoramus and unlettered in the revealed [Torah]; he knows nothing, but he says that he is a kabbalist and that mysteries have been revealed to him, but [in truth] without understanding and without having any mysteries[33] revealed [to him], without understanding and not knowing anything; all his speaking and writing is so stammering of tongue that they are not understood,[34] and it is poor bread indeed that comes from that oven.[35] That false writer[36] gives false testimony about himself, so that no one else understood anything of his Torah teachings, only the cursed despicable M[oses] D[avid],[37] may the name of the wicked rot, may his spirit and soul expire, he alone understood his demonic language. There is nothing other than this, and this suffices. I was also told by a decent man, a Torah scholar, who was in his synagogue, that he saw that when he was called to the Torah reading at the morning service on the holy sabbath he recited the blessing on the Torah [reading] piping like a swift or a swallow,[38] like moaning doves[39] and the croaking of coarse roosters, whose sound goes unheard.[40] Neither comprehensible speech, nor clearly expressed. The other ugly deeds that should not be done in Israel that were related of him I shall not present here. It was not my wish to speak ill of him, since he is distant from me and I did not know that he had been the misdoing of many.[41] Besides this, the dullard vents all his rage[42] with false titles with spangles of wrath.[43] In truth, may his spirit and soul expire, this is a band against Heaven.[44] And they also made use of him in a deceitful amulet.[45] Since I see that he seeks to confuse the fools in the land of Poland, the simple people who believe anything,[46] by means of his agent who is as himself[47] the fool Sussman, his agent who is full of worry,[48] sin [*hata'ah*] in a row, and *tse'orah*[49] that is planted to establish a new idol and sun image.[50] For he

---

[33] Ps. 44: 22; Job 11: 6. [34] Following Isa. 33: 19. [35] Based on *Genesis Rabbah*, ch. 44.
[36] i.e. Sussman Shesnowzi, the author of the letter about Falk (Appendix C).
[37] Moses David of Podhajce, who was a guest in Falk's home.
[38] Following Isa. 38: 14. [39] Following Ezek. 7: 16. [40] Following Ps. 19: 4.
[41] Emden explains why he decided to write about Falk. [42] Following Prov. 29: 11.
[43] Emden distorts the verse (S. of S. 1: 11) in two places: *ta'arei*, with an additional *alef*, instead of *torei* (wreaths), and *ketsef* (wrath) instead of *kesef* (silver).
[44] The original talmudic phrase (BT *San.* 105a) reads: 'Insolence towards Heaven'.
[45] An allusion to a charm made by Jonathan Eybeschuetz that contained the name Samuel.
[46] Based on Prov. 14: 15.
[47] A well-known principle of talmudic law; see e.g. BT *Hag.* 10b (one example of many).
[48] I have not been able to find the source.
[49] A made-up word derived from the root of distress/causing distress; this is a double distortion of Isa. 28: 25: 'wheat [*hitah*] in a row, barley [*se'orah*] [in a strip]'. [50] The sun god; see Lev. 26: 30.

strays,[51] setting his heart after other gods and is not faithful to the Holy One.[52] Accordingly, it is our duty to publicize this, so that the masses will not be led astray by him. And his despicable friend Moses David[53] will say of him, who is jealous with anger against inquity[54] to his fellow Eybeschuetzer,[55] the foe of faith,[56] and thereby there is no doubt that the despicable Samael[57] is the object of the accursed amulet of that Jonathan[58] who invalidated the crucible for the lie.[59] He found him in a desert poison[60] in an empty, howling waste.[61]

[51] *Tav-tav-vav*, instead of *tav-tet-ayin-vav* (or *tav-tet-vav*).
[52] Based on Hos. 12: 1, with the addition of the word 'not'.
[53] Moses David of Podhajce.
[54] Following Job 36: 33.
[55] Emden's appellation for Jonathan Eybeschuetz, his sworn enemy.
[56] *Tsar emun*, a wordplay from 1 Kgs 22: 26: 'Amon, the city's governor [*amon sar ha'ir*]'.
[57] A name of Satan; Emden deliberately distorts Falk's first name, Samuel.
[58] Jonathan Eybeschuetz.
[59] *Kazav*, instead of *kesef* (silver), a distortion of Prov. 17: 3, 27: 21.
[60] *Eres*, instead of *erets*—region.
[61] Following Deut. 32: 10.

APPENDIX E

FALK'S LIBRARY

IN TWO PASSAGES in his diary (fos. 9a, 27a) Falk lists the books in his library, with the titles of the books in his home, the titles of the duplicate books he possessed, and the names of the books that he always took with him on his journeys. Why did Falk draw up such lists? And why did he include them in his diary? One might say that they are consistent with the other lists he includes in the diary: his household objects (furniture, household and kitchen utensils, and the like); the loans that he took and gave; the items that he pawned; the bottles of wine in his cellar; and the numbers of the lottery tickets that he had purchased.

The practice of making such lists tells us a lot about Falk's personality and concerns. He suffered from excessive worrying; apprehension concerning the loss of his possessions; a lack of confidence (he did not rely on his memory); and the pathological suspiciousness of someone who draws up lists in order to guard his possessions and itemize them. In addition, the list of his books also tells us about the areas of Falk's interest and his spiritual and cultural world.

Most of the books in his lists are kabbalistic texts; the rest include commentaries on kabbalistic tracts (interpretations on the various parts of the Zohar, on *Pardes rimonim* by Moses Cordovero, on Lurianic kabbalah and the like), kabbalistic tomes on ethical conduct, collections of kabbalistic exegeses, and works on prayer, medicine, linguistics, and numerology.

The absence of books on Jewish law and philosophy is striking. There are very few interpretative works on the rabbinic literature (Talmud, Midrash), works by the geonim, the responsa literature, or works of medieval Jewish thought; the primary sources themselves are absent. Moreover, the numerous books among his holdings seem to have had no significant influence upon their owner. Our expectation of finding traces of their content in his writings is not fulfilled. Falk provides us with a list of books that he took with him on his trips—which were probably meant to favourably impress his hosts, and which he might have used in his encounters with Christians who sought to learn from him the secrets of kabbalah.

Several of the works mentioned in his lists were written by Sabbatians, either those who openly professed their views, or crypto-Sabbatians, that is, those suspected of belonging to this sect. Despite their authorship, these tractates cannot be classified as Sabbatian compositions; on the contrary, essays such as these won praise from

Jacob Emden (the leader of the battle against Sabbatianism), and their presence in his library should not lead us to conclude that Falk belonged to a sect that believed in Sabbatai Zevi (either Sabbatian or Frankist, as Schuchard observes). Falk's lists do not include the place and year of publication of his books, which unfortunately hinders their precise identification.

1. *The List of Books Mentioned in Falk's Diary (fo. 9a)*

1. *Ḥelkei zohar* (the parts of the Zohar)—probably the three main volumes of the Zohar, a kabbalistic commentary on the Torah (Pentateuch). Traditionally attributed to the first-century sage Simeon bar Yoḥai; modern scholarship dates it to the thirteenth/fourteenth century and attributes it to Moses de Leon and his circle.

2. *Tikun hazohar—Tikunei zohar*, a kabbalistic work in the style of the Zohar, probably written in Spain in the fourteenth century by an anonymous author, and included as the fourth volume of the Zohar in printed editions.

3. *Avak soferim*[1]—expositions and literal interpretations, in three parts. Part I: 'Em hayeled'—expositions on the Torah; Part II: 'Ugat retsafim'—miscellaneous literal interpretations of the Bible and Mishnah; Part III: 'Em labinah'—nineteen expositions.

4. *Ḥelkat meḥokek*—a commentary on the book of Job, by Moses Alshekh.[2]

5. *Ḥavatselet hasharon*—a commentary on the book of Daniel by Moses Alshekh.

6. *Kaftor vaferaḥ*—we know of three books by this name:
   (i) a commentary on the Song of Songs by David ben Aryeh Leib;
   (ii) a commentary on the non-legal portions of the Talmuds and the Midrashim by Jacob ben Isaac Luzzatto of Safed (this book is also called *Yashresh ya'akov*);

---

[1] The first edition was printed in Amsterdam in 1704 at the press of Nathaniel Foa. The author Abraham Cuenque was a known Sabbatian, and traces of Sabbatian teachings emerge from his work. He was an emissary from the Land of Israel who went to Jewish communities abroad to collect donations for the Jewish community in Hebron. See Benayahu, 'The Letters of R. Abraham Cuenque' (Heb.).

[2] Moses Alshekh was born in Adrianople c.1520. He studied in Salonika, and was a pupil of Joseph Taitatsak and Joseph Caro. After his arrival in Safed (the date has not been determined) he was granted full ordination by Caro (Alshekh in turn granted such ordination to Ḥayim Vital). Alshekh was primarily a halakhist, but also engaged in kabbalah. He was known in Safed as a preacher, and his sermons formed the basis for his commentaries on the Bible. His commentary on Daniel, *Ḥavatselet hasharon* ('Rose of Sharon') appeared in 1563, and his commentary on Job, *Ḥelkat meḥokek*, was printed in 1603. See Pachter, 'Ḥazut kashah' (Heb.); Shalem, 'The Exigetical and Homiletical Method' (Heb.).

(iii) a compilation of the laws of tithes given to members of the priestly class and various other laws by Isaac (Estori) ben Moses Haparhi.³

7. *Magid mereshit*—eight responsa by Hayim Alfandari, arranged according to the legal code *Arba'ah turim* by Jacob ben Asher.

8. *Mishnat ḥasidim*—an abbreviated guide to devotional intent in prayer in the spirit of Lurianic kabbalah, written by Raphael Immanuel Hai Ricchi.⁴

9. *Sefer karnayim* and *Dan yadin*—a kabbalistic work attributed to Aaron ben Abraham of Cardena, with the commentary *Dan yadin* by Samson ben Pesah Ostropoler.⁵

10. *Asarah ma'amarot*⁶—various discourses based on Lurianic kabbalah, by Menahem Azariah of Fano.

11. [*Sefer*] *esrim ve'arba* ('Twenty-four')—perhaps the reference is to the Bible (which consists of twenty-four books), in a Christian printing (in which case this is to be read as *meha'edomim*, based on the identification of Rome with Edom)? or possibly to the Bible in a red binding (= *meha'adumim*)?

12. *Pa'amon verimon*, *Asis rimonim*, and *Pelaḥ harimon*—three different works published as a single volume in Amsterdam in 1708: (i) *Pa'amon verimon*—a commentary by Mordecai ben Jacob of Prague on *Pardes rimonim* by Moses Cordovero; (ii) *Asis rimonim*—an abridgement of Cordovero's *Pardes rimonim*, written by Samuel Gallico; (iii) *Pelaḥ harimon*⁷—an abbreviated version of and commentary on the 'Ha'atsilut' section of *Pardes rimonim*, by Menahem Azariah of Fano.

13. *Kav hayashar*⁸—a work of ethical instruction by Zevi Hirsch ben Aaron Samuel Koidonover.

14. *Shulḥan arukh* by Isaac Luria, of blessed memory—a compendium of laws and devotional exercises based on kabbalah, following the order of the 'Oraḥ ḥayim' section of the *Shulḥan arukh* legal code, compiled from the writings of Luria's disciple Hayim Vital (various editions).

---

³ The book Falk possessed was probably that by Luzzatto (pub. Amsterdam, 1709).
⁴ Raphael Immanuel Hai Ricchi, a well-known kabbalist, was born in Ferrara in 1686. See Wilensky, 'Notes on the Biography' (Heb.), 311–14.
⁵ For Samson Ostropoler, see Liebes, 'Mysticism and Reality' (Heb.).
⁶ The earliest editions of the book are Venice, 1597, and Amsterdam, 1649. Menahem Azariah of Fano (1548–1620) switched his allegiance from Moses Cordovero to Isaac Luria; to be exact, he became a follower of the latter's pupil Israel Sarug. See Avivi, 'The Kabbalistic Writings of R. Menahem Azariah of Fano' (Heb.); Altmann, 'Notes on the Development of Rabbi Menahem Azariah of Fano's Kabbalistic Doctrine' (Heb.), 244.   ⁷ *Pelaḥ harimon* was first printed in Venice in 1600.
⁸ *Kav hayashar* was first printed in Frankfurt am Main in 1706, and again in 1709/10.

15. *Shomer emunim*[9]—dialogues on kabbalistic wisdom, by Joseph Ergas.

16. *Si'aḥ yitsḥak*—a grammar book, by Isaac ben Samuel Halevi.

17. *Ḥozeh tsiyon*[10]—a kabbalistic commentary on the book of Psalms, by Raphael Immanuel Hai Ricchi.

18. *Gefen yeḥidit*—an ethical work in flowery language, rhymes, and laments, by Ze'ev Wolf ben Judah Leib of Rosni.

19. Pentateuch with Targum—Pentateuch with Aramaic translation.

20. *Emek yehoshua*—questions and answers on the weekly Torah portions and halakhic matters, by Joshua ben Judah Leib Falk.

21. *Sefer hahigayon* (*Milot hahigayon*)—explanation of the words and names used by Maimonides in his treatise on logic, in the translation by Samuel ibn Tibbon.

2. The List of Duplicate Books in Falk's House in London, kept in a chest in the house of Simeon Boas (fo. 27a)

1. *Avak soferim* on the Torah—expositions and literal interpretations, by Abraham Cuenque (in three parts), Part I of which is entitled 'Em hayeled'.

2. *Ḥozeh tsiyon* [a commentary] according to *pardes*—a kabbalistic commentary on the book of Psalms, by Raphael Immanuel Hai Ricchi.

3. *Ḥavatselet hasharon*—a commentary on the book of Daniel by Moses Alshekh.

4. *Magid mereshit*, responsa by Hayim Alfandari.

5. *Shomer emunim*—the acceptance of the faith—dialogues on kabbalistic wisdom in a question-and-answer format, by Joseph Ergas.

6. *Si'aḥ yitsḥak*—a Hebrew grammar book, by Isaac ben Samuel Halevi.

7. *Pa'amon verimon*—kabbalah—a collection of elucidated kabbalistic works published as a single volume in Amsterdam in 1708, and named after the first composition: *Pa'amon verimon*, a commentary by Mordecai ben Jacob of Prague on *Pardes rimonim* by Moses Cordovero.

8. *Kav hayashar* with a Yiddish commentary—a work of ethical instruction by Zevi Hirsch Koidonover.

9. *Asarah ma'amarot*, kabbalah—various discourses based on Lurianic kabbalah, by Menahem Azariah of Fano.

---

[9] First printed in Amsterdam in 1736, and afterwards in Zolkiew in 1766.
[10] First printed in Leghorn, 1742.

10. *Kaftor vaferaḥ*, kabbalah—possibly referring to the book of this name by Jacob ben Isaac Luzzatto of Safed.

11. *Ḥelkat meḥokek*, Alshekh on Job—a commentary on the book of Job, by Moses Alshekh.

12. *Mishnat ḥasidim*, kabbalah—an abbreviated guide to devotional intent in prayer in the spirit of Lurianic kabbalah, written by Raphael Immanuel Hai Ricchi.

13. *Arba'ah ve'esrim*, in a red binding; a single-volume Bible.

14. The Zohar, in three volumes.

15. *Tikunei zohar*.

16. Pentateuch—in five volumes, with the commentaries of Rashi, Rashbam, Ibn Ezra, the Ba'al Haturim, a commentary on Targum Yerushalmi and on Targum Pseudo-Jonathan, *Toledot aharon*, *Mesoret kabalah* [referred to in Falk's diary, fo. 27a, as *Mesoret ketanah ugedolah*].

3. *The List of Books That Accompanied Falk on His Travels (fo. 9a)*

1. *Or torah* with errata[11]—on all the open and closed passages (that begin, respectively, on a new line or in the middle of a line) in the Torah, and the plene and defective spellings [i.e. the presence or absence of certain consonants, used as *matres lectionis*, to indicate vowels] in the Torah, by Menahem de Lonzano. Appended to *Shivrei luḥot*, 'a table of glosses and corrigenda on all printed books'.

2. *Tohorat aharon*—a commentary on *Seder hanikur* ('Laws of Porging') from *Sefer ha'itur*, with extracts from other halakhic works, by Aaron ben Moses Meir Perles.

3. *Yalkut ḥadash labekiyut, yosher levav*—kabbalah[12]—extracts from midrashic works, arranged in alphabetical order for the benefit of preachers, by Israel ben Benjamin, head of the rabbinical court in Belz (also entitled *Yalkut yisra'eli*).

4. *Mafte'aḥ hazohar*—possibly referring to the index of biblical verses in the Zohar by Moses ben Mordecai Galante.[13]

5. *Mareh makom hadinim*—alphabetical index of laws in the *Shulḥan arukh*, by Meshullam Feibush ben Israel.

---

[11] Printed in the book *Shetei yadot* (Venice, 1618). See Elitzur, 'Different Readings' (Heb.).
[12] Published in several editions, including Lublin, 1648, Prague, 1657, and Wilhelmsdorf, 1673.
[13] Published in Venice, 1636. There is another work by the same name: *Mafte'aḥ hazohar*, by Abraham b. Raphael Rovigo (Amsterdam, 1710).

6. *Mikhlol yofi*.[14]

7. *Musaf he'arukh*—the *Arukh*, a classic medieval lexicon of the Talmud and Midrashim by Nathan ben Jehiel of Rome, with glosses, the addition of roots of words, and an explanation of non-Hebrew words, by Benjamin Mussafia.

8. *Sha'arei orah*—a kabbalistic commentary on the names and appellations of the *sefirot*, by Joseph Gikatilla.[15]

9. *Sifra ditseni'uta*—a part of the Zohar, at the end of the Torah portion of 'Terumah'; the reference might possibly be to the edition published with the commentary by Isaac Luria.

10. *Sefer hashorashim*—the first dictionary of biblical Hebrew, by Jonah ibn Janah, originally written in Arabic and translated into Hebrew by Judah ibn Tibbon.

11. *Pa'ane'ah raza*—short literal interpretations, in the order of the Torah, employing the techniques of *notarikon* (acrostics) and *gematriyah* (numerology), by Isaac ben Judah Halevi, the grandson of Samuel of Falaise.

12. *Me'ah berakhot* ('One Hundred Blessings')—a guide to the blessings that a person should recite during his lifetime, for all occasions, written and collected by Shalom Shakhna ben Nahum Koidonover of Vilna.

13. *Nehmad vena'im*—an astronomical text (including the determination of the new lunar month), by David Gans.[16]

14. *Sefer masoret*—an explanation of the Masorah (traditions defining the Bible text), by Joseph ben Samuel ibn Dios.

15. *Seder olam raba*—a history book, from the Creation to the time of Hadrian, attributed to the *tana* (mishnaic sage) Yose ben Halafta.

16. *Likutei hapardes*—there are several books by this name, all consisting of collections of early legal rulings and responsa. One, which is named *Likutei hapardes* [*shel rashi*], was put together by Abraham Hakohen; each of the others is a separate edition of one of the parts of the book of collections by Judah al-Harizi entitled *Refu'ot hageviyah*.

17. *Matsat shimurim*[17]—a kabbalistic guide to the laws of *tsitsit* (ritual fringes) and *tefilin*, by Nathan ben Reuben David Tevele Shapira.

18. *Magen david*[18]—a kabbalistic interpretation of the letters of the Hebrew alphabet, by David ibn Zimra.

---

[14] The reference may possibly be to *Mikhlol yofi*, a commentary on the book of Ecclesiastes by Elijah b. Moses Loanz (Amsterdam, 1695). Loanz was a known *ba'al shem*, who engaged in practical kabbalah. See Tishby, 'Documents Written by the Hand of R. Moses Loanz' (Heb.).

[15] First edition, Mantua, 1561.   [16] Jessnitz, 1743.   [17] First edition, Venice, 1660.

[18] First edition, Amsterdam, 1713. See Scholem, 'Identification of the Book *Magen david*' (Heb.).

19. *Mesilat yesharim*[19]—a book of ethical instruction, by Moses Hayim Luzzatto.

20. *Ḥibur yafeh mehayeshu'ah*—a book of ethical instruction, containing many stories from the Talmud and other early sources, by Nissim ben Jacob of Kairouan.

21. *Sefer leḥem rav* [listed in Falk's diary, fo. 9a, second list, no. 25, as *Sefer leḥem yehudah*]—there are two books by this name: one, by Judah ben Abraham Zarco, consists of poems and rhetoric; the other is an essay on Maimonides, by Judah Ayash.

22. *Mo'ed david*—possibly the book by David Oppenheim on *Mo'ed*, the second of the six orders of the Talmud.

23. *Kol ya'akov*—there are several books by this title: (i) homilies on the Torah, by Jacob Castro; (ii) a Passover Haggadah according to the Spanish rite, translated into Dutch by Jacob ben David Lopez Cardozo; (iii) homilies and interpretations, by Jacob Koppel ben Zevi Hirsch Margaliot;[20] (iv) homilies, laws, and linguistic studies of the *Mishneh torah* by Maimonides, by Jacob Saul ben Hananiah.

24. *Siftei yeshenim*—explanations of words from the works of early commentators and grammarians, by Wolf Meir of Prague.

25. *Sefer haḥinukh*—a classical educational work based on the 613 commandments, by Aaron Halevi of Barcelona.

26. *Apiryon shelomoh*—there are several books by this name: (i) a kabbalistic work by Abraham Sasson;[21] (ii) a kabbalistic work by Solomon Alkabets; (iii) literal interpretations, following the order of the Torah, by Solomon ben Israel of Zolkiew.

27. *Derekh tevunot*—a guide to the study of the Talmud based on the rules of logic, by Moses Hayim Luzzatto.

28. *Hadrat melekh*[22]—a commentary on the kabbalah by Shalom ben Moses Buzaglo.

29. *Vayakhel mosheh*—there are two books by this name: (i) homilies by Moses Alfalas; (ii) introductions and an index to kabbalah, by Moses ben Menahem Graf of Prague.[23]

30. *Mishmerot kehunah*—a work on the Talmud, including proverbs, dicta, and ethical teachings, by Hayim (Hiya) Kohen de Lara.

---

[19] First edition Amsterdam, 1740. See Ben-Menahem, 'Four Editions' (Heb.), 479; Tishby, '*Mesilat yesharim*' (Heb.).

[20] The book *Kol ya'akov* by Jacob Koppel, containing kabbalistic expositions, was published in Venice in 1658, and in Amsterdam in 1708 (with an appended lament on the Chmielnicki massacres of 1648/9).

[21] Published in Venice in 1608.

[22] Published in Amsterdam, 1766; London, 1770–3. The book contains a commentary on passages from the Zohar, a commentary on the kabbalistic *Idrot* works, and a commentary on passages from the book *Ets ḥayim*.

[23] Published in Dessau, 1699 and Zolkiew, 1771.

31. *Magal ha'omer*.²⁴

32. *Mikdash melekh*²⁵—a kabbalistic commentary on the Zohar, by Shalom ben Moses Buzaglo.

33. *Ne'edar bakodesh*²⁶—*Idra raba* and *Idra zuta* from the Zohar with an introduction by the publisher, Moses Hagiz. A later edition also contained *Sifra ditseni'uta*, *Tefilat eliyahu* (The Prayer of Elijah), and *Sefer yetsirah*.

34. *Sefer nitsahon*—there are several books by this name: (i) the best known is the anti-Christian polemic by Yom Tov Lipmann Muelhausen; (ii) a book by Joseph Kimhi; (3) a casuistical book on faith, by Matityahu ben Moses Hayitshari.

35. *Arugat habosem*—there are two books by this name: (i) a medical book, by Judah Harofe ('the physician'); (ii) a kabbalistic commentary on the Song of Songs, based on the Zohar and on Lurianic kabbalah, by Moses ben Hillel Osterer.²⁷

36. *Emek yehoshua*—questions and answers on the weekly Torah portions and halakhic matters, by Joshua ben Judah Leib Falk.

[Note: The list in Falk's diary, fo. 9a, under the heading 'Menahem Av 5537 [summer 1777]', includes titles that are not mentioned here, viz. *Mavo she'arim* (no. 24; assuming this is a separate work), *Helkei avanim* (no. 44), and *Hizuk emunah* (no. 45).]

4. *The List of Books That Falk Intended to Purchase (fo. 9a)*

1. Mishnah, vocalized, with the commentary *Kaf nahat*, by Obadiah of Bertinoro. [It is not clear whether this is a commentary by Obadiah of Bertinoro, or the commentary by Isaac b. Solomon Gabbai appended to the 1614 Venice edn. of the Mishnah.]

2. *Ir giborim*—a book of homilies arranged in the order of the Torah, beginning with an exposition on the suppression of the evil inclination, by Ephraim Solomon ben Aaron of Luntshits (Łęczyca).

---

²⁴ I have not found any book by this name.   ²⁵ Published in Amsterdam, 1750.
²⁶ On the Torah portion of 'Naso' in the Zohar and *Idra zuta*. First edition, Amsterdam, 1723.
²⁷ Published in Zolkiew, 1745.

APPENDIX F

FALK'S WILL

THE LITERATURE OF WILLS is a special genre within the broader context of the ethical *hanhagot* literature. Even many wills of a private nature contain ethical instruction, along with recollections and stories going back over the generations transmitting family history and traditions, together with requests and even demands that the remaining family members should maintain these customs. Beginning in the eighteenth century the will also assumed a public character as some hasidic leaders saw it as an 'instrument' for disseminating the views of the spiritual luminaries of the new movement. Thus we see different wills that, like books of ethical instruction, seek to educate the writer's contemporaries, to preach to them, and to delineate the path they should follow in life. They are written in flowery language, at times in rhyme, with an abundance of biblical verses. The general philosophy they espouse sees this world as a lengthy corridor through which one must pass to reach the desired goal. Wills of this type usually tell us about the world of the writer, his way of life, his family, and the cultural environment in which he lived.

The English version of Falk's will, which was probated and bears a seal confirming its execution, is located in the National Archives at Kew in London. This version was translated from the Hebrew soon after the will was written, by the notary public Joseph Schabracg, on 6 May 1782. The will was probated by Dr Andrew Coltee, and was signed by the notaries who authorized the translated version on 18 May. I asked the staff of the National Archives to find the original Hebrew version of the will, written in Falk's hand, and they promised to look for it, despite their doubts as to whether it still existed.

My elation at the news that it had been found can easily be imagined, as can my joy at receiving a large chest that was sent from Hayes in Middlesex. The chest, which contained the wills of English residents, written in the month of May in the years 1755 to 1785, was filled with paper scrolls, each tied with ribbon and bearing a numerical designation, and each undoubtedly attesting to the profoundest desires of the writer as he bequeathed his material and spiritual possessions to those he held dear.

The search in the chest for Falk's will did not take long. Following the numerical designation that I possessed, I found it, rolled as a scroll and tied with a ribbon, and placed together with the other wills written at that same time. Its contents, however, proved somewhat disappointing. I read the document, again and again, but I could not find any spiritual or cultural message to the members of Falk's circle, his disciples, or his followers, those who in his early years in England had endangered their standing and good name in Jewish society by their loyalty to Falk.

I found nothing on a personal level relating to any of Falk's followers and admirers who participated in the prayers and ceremonies that he conducted in his place of worship. I had hoped to find some trace of spiritual content, of the things that one wishes to pass on to family and friends after one's death. I had expected to discover in his will something that would confirm and explain the admiration of Falk expressed in Masonic writings, which extol him as the 'Unknown Superior'. I had looked forward to finding even a single sentence that contained some spiritual message to his contemporaries, his friends, his heirs—but to no avail.

On the one hand there was the mysterious figure of Falk, whom the different testimonies that I had gathered depicted as a man with many faces: fraud, charlatan, scoundrel, miser, and ignoramus. On the other, he was also portrayed as a distinguished, honoured individual, possessing knowledge in many areas, skilled in the occult, a healer of the sick, who performed wonders and miracles, exalted the name of Israel among the gentiles, showing them the proper path, with a just and all-encompassing world-view couched in the spirit of the prophets of Israel; a Jew proud of his Jewishness, which he publicly proclaimed; a person to whom renowned individuals flocked.

None of these traits come to light in the will, but it does reveal another aspect of Falk's character that can perhaps also be deduced by reading closely between the lines of the diaries: namely, the social ties and friendships that he forged with people and his loyalty to his friends, along with his aversion to communal factionalism and his unwillingness to belong to any ethnically defined community (this may be at the core of his refusal to accept the distinguished position that he was offered as a warden (*parnas*) of the Great Synagogue). Falk distributed all his property among the institutions of the London Jewish community, both those administered by Ashkenazim and those controlled by Sephardi Jews.

Falk's will is of indisputable importance, since it casts light on his attitude towards the beneficiaries and heirs mentioned in it, as well as towards those whom it omits. On the basis of this will we should totally reject Schuchard's forceful assertion that Falk became an apostate from Judaism in the last five years of his life, founding a new quasi-religion that combined Christian, Jewish, and Masonic elements. If there was a shred of truth in this hypothesis, Falk would have bequeathed a portion of his great wealth to his acquaintances and friends in the Masonic lodge to which he belonged, or have ordered that certain sums from his estate be given to the institutions of the Masonic community. There is no mention of these institutions in his will; he did not leave them a single penny.

This exclusion stands in striking contrast to Falk's outstanding generosity to all the institutions of the Jewish community in London, as well as to the separate communities in the city—the Spanish and Portuguese congregation and the Ashkenazi community. The executors of his will were his friends from the Goldsmid family: the head of the family Aaron, his son Gershom (who went by the English name of George), and his son-in-law Judah Leib (with the English name Leon), the son of Samuel.

Falk's Hebrew will repeatedly emphasizes the sums he is bequeathing, giving the amounts in Yiddish as well, in order to remove all doubt and to prevent error.

According to the will, Falk bequeathed huge sums of money to Jewish communal institutions (of both the Sephardim and the Ashkenazim): this was to be given on a permanent basis from existing funds. He left the largest amount to the central institution of English Jewry, the Great Synagogue. Nor did he discriminate against other institutions: he gave considerable sums to the two Ashkenazi synagogues (the Hambro Synagogue and the New Synagogue), as he did to the Sephardi synagogue (the English translation reads 'the Portuguese', but it was one and the same). He also made significant bequests to the study halls that served, respectively, the Ashkenazi and Sephardi communities, and the four charitable societies that were active in the London community—Hebrath Talmud Torah, Hebrath Gidul Yethomim (the Orphan Aid Society), Hebrath Malbish Arumim (which provided clothing to the poor), and Hebrath Meshibath Nefesh (the Jewish Friendly Society)—received a fine inheritance. The fact that he gave identical amounts to all these institutions reveals his sincere desire to give his wealth to the needy, without discrimination or preferential treatment. His beneficence was based on his knowledge of how they helped the indigent, most of whom at this time were penniless immigrants from eastern Europe.

While providing for the institutions of Jewish society in London, Falk did not forget the inhabitants of Fürth, the city where his family had settled in his youth and where he had made his home. The Jewish communal organization in this city had cared for the members of his family after Falk himself had fled Germany, and Falk, who had maintained ties with his relatives, was grateful to the community, which cared for his mother during her lifetime and also ensured that she received a dignified funeral. Just as he had contributed to the Fürth congregation during his lifetime, so he arranged for it to be supported from his assets after his death. He also made a standing bequest of 10 pence per year to the 'High Priest' of the Great Synagogue (the de facto chief rabbi of English Jewry), whoever he might be (I have been informed that this bequest is still in effect today).

After listing his public contributions, Falk then specifies the names of his personal heirs from among the members of his household and his friends and acquaintances. To some he gave one-off gifts, while others were to benefit from fixed allowances for their entire life:

1. 'my Step-Son Gedaliah'. Intriguingly, none of the works on English Jewish history mentions him. According to the two diaries, Gedaliah was concerned with household matters, assisted his stepfather with his overseas contacts, and performed many missions on his behalf, as a sort of 'foreign minister' who, in practice, enjoyed the status of a blood relative (some sources state that he had been adopted by his stepfather). The lack of any reference to a personal relationship with this son or his family, with the exception of the unembellished mention of the tie between them, and the sum of the inheritance, is quite puzzling. (Falk left him a fixed annual stipend for life in the not inconsiderable sum of 10 guineas.)

2. I have not been able to determine the identity of '**the learned Mr. Joseph Sheknopzh**', who was given a generous stipend in the will.

3. '**Mr. Mendle, Reader**', the cantor in the synagogue that Falk maintained in his home.

4. '**my Servant Mendle**', Falk's personal servant (referred to as Mendel in the diary) during the last years of his life.

5. '**Mr. Hirsh Bristol**', whom we know as Zevi Hirsch of Kalisz, Falk's servant, and the author of the diary that documents his life between 1747 and 1751. Hirsch wandered about after leaving Falk's household before finally settling in Bristol. He was appointed cantor in this city, was an employee of the community there, and also taught students.

6. '**Mrs. Rachel, wife of Meyer**'. This woman is mentioned in Falk's diary as setting out on a mission for him and performing a 'magical mission'. Falk most likely recalled her loyalty when he included her in his will. (Perhaps 'Meyer' is the beneficiary listed as no. 8.)

7. '**Mr. Aaron Under Reader in my Synagogue**'. I have not succeeded in identifying this beneficiary.

8. '**my Servant Meyer**'.

9. '**Mr. Moses Priest in the new Synagogue**'. I have not succeeded in identifying this beneficiary.

10. '**Mr. Abraham Doctor**', i.e. Dr Abraham. This was probably Dr Abraham Gomez Argas, also known as Dr Philippe de la Cour: we learn of his relationship with Falk from the diary of Zevi Hirsch: see fos. 3*b*, 4*a*. (He is also mentioned in Falk's diary (fo. 25*a*).)

11. '**Mr. Levi Kroka**', who is mentioned in Falk's diary (as 'Leib'), fo. 5*b*.

12. '**Mr. Monish at The Hague**'. I have not succeeded in identifying this beneficiary.

Perhaps a reference to R. Munish Menahem, mentioned in Falk's diary on fo. 4*b*.

13. **'Mr. Susman at Amsterdam'**. This might be the same Sussman Shesnowzi whose letter to his son (see Appendix C above) was published by Jacob Emden.

14. **'Mr. Mordecai the son of Lima Dresden'**. I have not succeeded in identifying this beneficiary. He is apparently mentioned in Zevi Hirsch's dairy, fo. 36*a*.

15. **'Mr. Jacob Son of Lima Dresden'**. I have not succeeded in identifying this beneficiary (presumably the brother of Mordecai, above).

16. **'Abraham Nancy'**, who is mentioned in Falk's diary on fos. 3*a* and 46*a* (as 'R. Abraham Nanshikh'), and fo. 4*b* (as 'R. Abraham Nanzig').

Falk's will was approved by the court but executed only after a legal battle, conducted in France, when one of his close friends who is mentioned in both diaries, Cosman Lehmann, sued the executors, claiming that all of Falk's property was rightfully his. Cosman argued in his suit that over the course of many years he had given Falk monies from his private capital, and that therefore all of Falk's capital had come from him. However, this claim was rejected at the legal proceedings in France and the executors were able to distribute Falk's substantial estate to all the beneficiaries mentioned in the will in accordance with his wishes.

Examination of the will lays to rest the various claims by putative 'relatives', 'grandchildren', or 'great-grandchildren', which cropped up towards the end of the twentieth century, by individuals attempting to trace their lineage to Falk after his name had reappeared on the pages of history. (These seeming relatives include the widow of Professor Cecil Roth, who wrote an article for a Jewish newspaper published in New York in which she states that she was Falk's granddaughter. Her husband, by contrast, writes in one of his books that she was a member of the Collins family, which is descended from Zevi Hirsch of Kalisz, Falk's factotum.)

The sums mentioned in the will, both the one-off bequests and the sums bequeathed on an annual basis in perpetuity, reveal Falk's great wealth, and his loyalty to those who visited his home. He was generous to those who had been his friends and intimates, his admirers, his personal attendants, and the religious functionaries in his synagogue.

The will is concerned exclusively with the distribution of Falk's wealth among his heirs and beneficiaries. Once again, we are faced by the dilemma of the importance of this episode and the documents connected with it for Jewish historiography, with the multifaceted enigma of Falk's personality remaining unresolved.

As in the diaries, a picture emerges from Falk's will of the Jewish institutions in

London, along with the names of his friends and followers; moreover, the will attests to the importance ascribed by Falk to his burial in a Jewish cemetery, in accordance with the requirements of Jewish law and custom. He had designated sums to ensure that he would receive a dignified burial, and that the learned would visit his grave and pray for his soul.

These desires, committed to writing while Falk was of sound mind, with monies allotted for their fulfilment to ensure that they would not remain merely pious wishes, totally contradict the allegations that have been voiced concerning his presumed conversion to Christianity, his alienation from Judaism, and his involvement in the founding of a new religion that blended Christian ideas with kabbalistic Jewish concepts.

Further corroborating evidence is proved by a passage from a rare book published in the first half of the nineteenth century, *Sefer afar ya'akov* by Rabbi Jacob ben Joseph Eichhorn, which incorporates personal memoirs and testimonies such as the following characterization of Falk:[1]

I heard from my esteemed and illustrious father-in-law, the late Rabbi Zalman Revesz, that when he was in the Jewish community of London the capital he, too, encountered the circles of the great, wonderful *ba'al shem* who was in London then. He was a great and wonderful light, and his demeanour and actions were as those of one of the great princes, the *partemim*;[2] his origins are unknown. He did not grant an audience even to the greatest of nobles, and he scarcely granted an audience to the royal house. He was a great kabbalist from the land of inner Western [i.e. Germany], who came to London for various wondrous reasons (that it would be inappropriate to discuss at length here), and he established his domicile in the community of London. On Rosh Hashanah my late father-in-law was the shofar blower in his prayer service, and before his blowing my father-in-law asked that he relate to him the mystical significance that he should contemplate during the blessings for the blowing, and during the performance of the commandment. The *ba'al shem* replied that he should contemplate that this is the commandment of the Lord, may He be praised, that He commanded us to perform on this day, and that it should be done to please the Lord, may He be praised. The *ba'al shem* possessed wondrous knowledge of [such] mystical meditations, as I heard related by the rabbi, the author of *Sefer haberit*,[3] who had also been in the London community at that time, and was greatly honoured. He perused the books that the *ba'al shem* had left after his passing, for he [Falk] was a great and marvellous man, even though he had never spoken with him during [the latter's] lifetime, for he had not granted him a personal audience; only once, and no more, he had addressed a query to him in a letter, and he had

[1] Oron, *Et-mol*, 13.

[2] i.e. nobility; this term, taken from Esther 1: 3, 6: 9; Dan. 1: 3, is obviously used to emphasize Falk's exalted standing.

[3] Pinhas Elijah Hurwitz, whose book *Sefer haberit* ('The Book of the Covenant') was first published in Bern in 1797, and later reprinted in many editions.

answered his query. After his [Falk's] death, he [Hurwitz] saw his writings, and this was wondrous in his eyes, for as the author of *Sefer haberit* he, too, was a great kabbalist, as is known.

This testimony, written by a proponent of ethical teachings who heaped abuse on Sabbatai Zevi, Jacob Frank, and their followers, only strengthens our conclusion: Samuel Falk—Dr Falk, or the 'Ba'al Shem of London'—was born a Jew, died a Jew, and was buried as a Jew in a Jewish cemetery.

THE TEXT OF THE WILL
Translated from the Hebrew

God be praised

On this day the second of the month of Ayr [Iyar] in the year 5542 finding myself of sound mind and understanding I do again confirm what I yesterday the first of Ayr / April 14th, 1782 according to the Christian reckoning / signed with my own hand that after my Decease / which Heaven defer / Mr. Aron Goldsmid his Son Mr. George Goldsmid and his Son in Law Mr. Judah Lion Son of Samuel of blessed Memory shall be my Executors. And whereas in the Writing which I signed yesterday it is mentioned that what I might in writing or by word of Mouth further order my Executors to do should all take place I therefore direct as follows / the first of all things is to fear the Lord / that my executors shall give every Year yearly for ever £100, say one hundred Pounds Sterling to the behoof of the Great Synagogue of the holy congregation here in London which is called by the name of the Duke's place Synagogue. They shall also give to the Hambro Synagogue of the holy Congregation here at London every Year yearly for ever £15, say Fifteen pounds Sterling. They shall also give to the New Synagogue here in London every Year yearly for ever £15, say fifteen pounds Sterling. They shall also give to the holy Congregation of the Portuguese Synagogue here in London every Year yearly for ever £15, say fifteen Pounds Sterling. They shall also give to the Beth Hamedrash [study hall] of the holy Congregation of the German Jews here in London every Year yearly for ever £10, say ten Pounds Sterling. They shall also give to the Beth Hamedrash of the holy Portuguese Congregation of the Jews here in London £10, say ten Pounds Sterling every Year yearly for ever. They shall also give to the four Charitable Societies here in London that is to say to the Society called Talmud Torah[,] the Society called Gidul Yethomim[,] the Society called Malbish Arumim and the Society called Meshibath Nefesh to each of the said Societies every Year yearly for ever £5, say five pounds Sterling that is to say to the said four Charitable Societies together £20, say twenty Pounds every Year yearly for ever. They shall also give to the Congregation at Furth / whom the Lord protect / every Year yearly for ever £20, say twenty pounds Sterling. They shall also give every Year yearly for ever to the High Priest of the Great Synagogue that is to say to the high Priest for the time being whosoever he may be Ten guineas Say ten Pounds ten Shillings. To my Step-Son Gedaliah they shall also give every Year yearly during his Life Ten guineas Say ten Pounds ten Shillings. To the learned Mr. Joseph Sheknopzh they shall give every Year yearly during his Life three guineas say Three Pounds three Shillings. To Mr. Mendle Reader in my Synagogue they shall give during his Life five guineas every Year yearly say five pounds five Shillings. They shall also give out of my Estate as a present to my Servant Mendle Ten Guineas Say ten Pounds ten shillings as a present. They shall also give as a present out of my Estate to Mr. Hirsh Bristol Ten guineas say ten pounds ten Shillings. They shall also give as a present out of my Estate to Mrs. Rachel wife of Meyer of blessed Memory Ten guineas say ten Pounds ten Shillings. They shall also give as a present out of my Estate to Mr. Aaron Under Reader in my Synagogue five guineas say five Pounds five Shillings. They shall also give as a present out of my Estate to my Servant Meyer Five guineas say five pounds five Shillings. They shall also give out of my Estate as a present to Mr. Moses Priest in the new Synagogue Ten guineas say ten Pounds ten Shillings. They shall also give out of my Estate as a present to Mr. Abraham Doctor ten guineas say ten Pounds ten Shillings. They shall also give as a present out of my Estate to Mr. Levi Kroka Ten guineas say ten pounds ten Shillings. They shall also give as a present_____ out of my Estate to Mr. Monish_____ at the Hague one hundred_____ Dutch Guilders say one hundred guilders hollands. They shall also give as a present out of my Estate for Mr. Susman at Amsterdam Five guineas say five pounds five Shillings. They shall also give as a present out of my Estate to Mr. Mordecai the son of Lima Dresden ten guineas say ten pounds ten Shillings. They shall also give as a present out of my Estate Six guineas say Six pounds six shillings to Mr. Jacob Son of Lima Dresden. They shall also give as a present out of my Estate to Mr. Abraham the Son of Shelomo of blessed Memory usually called Abraham Nancy the Sum of Fifty guineas say fifty two pounds ten shillings and they shall moreover give as a Present to the said Mr. Abraham Furniture House Utensils and Books to the amount of Fifty pounds in the whole. My Books of Torah with all their Ornaments Holy Dresses and Holy Utensils_____ shall also be faithfully given_____ to the Great Synagogue of _____ the Holy Congregation here in London as a present and as those who are remembered or mentioned in this Will to whom the Specified Sums are to be given every Year during all the Term of their Lives shall die such his sum shall be given every Year yearly for ever to the behoof of the Great Synagogue in London. And as to what further may be requisite either for the Burial or to take ten Men to learn the first Year or to give Money to the poor between the Decease and the Burial and in the thirty days of Mourning be it what it will to the honour of the Living and the Dead it shall all be left at the Option of the Executors aforesaid to do as they shall think proper. And also whatever may be left of my Estate after all that has been mentioned shall remain in the hands of the aforesaid Executors at their Option to divide it to the poor. And if in a short or a long time be it when it will any Relation of mine should come who is entitled to have inherited me the Executors shall give him Five pounds say five pounds out of my Estate and therewith he shall be cut off from my Estate and shall have no further Claim whatever not even for a farthing upon my Estate. To all the foregoing I now come to sign my Name and all has been written in the presence of the Executor Mr. Aron Goldsmid whom the Lord protect and in testimony I now sign my Name. Done on the day on the other side written.

/Signed/
We are Witnesses to the above signature
Falk the son of Abraham Gisa
Belah Behilah

The foregoing is a faithful Translation, out of the Hebrew Language,
of the Will of Dr. Samuel Falk hereunto annexed,
Translated by me the underwritten

London 6 May 1782
Quod attestor
Jos. Schabracg
1782

GLOSSARY

ba'al shed possessor of, or one possessed by, a demon

ba'al shem, pl. *ba'alei shem* or *ba'alei shemot* literally, 'master(s) of the [divine] name'; a wonder-worker who employed the names of God (or of his angels), through certain techniques, for various theurgic purposes

Ein Sof (literally 'the Infinite') the kabbalistic 'concealed God' or God transcendent

etrog, pl. *etrogim* citron(s), one of the four different plants (the 'four species') which are used in the rite of the festival of *Sukkot

Fast of Esther the fast-day preceding *Purim in commemoration of the fast observed by Queen Esther and the Jews in Shushan (see Esther 4: 16)

Frankists followers of Jacob Frank (1726–91), the head of a mystical antinomian sect among Polish Jews, who hailed him as the messiah

gematriyah a method of explaining a word or group of words according to the numerical value of its constituent Hebrew letters, each Hebrew letter having a specific numerical equivalent; numerology

genizah a repository for unfit holy books and other ritual items, or the act of depositing (burying) such items

Haggadah a book which gives the set form of words to be recited at the *seder* ritual on the first night of Passover (and in the diaspora, also on the second night). It consists of the recital of the story of the Exodus from Egypt (based on excerpts from the Bible, Mishnah, and Midrash) integrated into a prescribed festive meal, interpolated with blessings, prayers, and other rituals

Hasidei Ashkenaz groups of Jewish pietists who appeared chiefly in the Franco-German communities of the Rhineland in the twelfth and thirteenth centuries

Heshvan *see* Marheshvan

Holy One, blessed be He an appellation for God

Hoshana Rabba the seventh and last day of *Sukkot

intermediate days those days during the seven-day festivals of Passover and *Sukkot on which work is permitted

kabbalah the traditional term used for the esoteric teachings of Judaism and for Jewish mysticism

kefitsat haderekh the miraculous 'shortening of the way', i.e. travelling from place to place at miraculous speed by means of a magical incantation

kelipah a late term for demonic forces, or the forces of evil in general

kitl the white robe worn by male worshippers during the prayer services on *Rosh Hashanah and *Yom Kippur, and on some other ritual occasions

Lag Ba'omer the thirty-third day of the counting of the *omer (18 Iyar), which is celebrated as a minor festival

Lurianic kabbalah a system of *kabbalah based on the teachings of Rabbi Isaac Luria (Ha'ari; 1544–72)

Malkhut (literally 'Kingdom') the tenth and last *sefirah* in the hierarchy of the *sefirot*, representing the feminine principle in the divine world; also known as the Shekhinah (the Divine Presence)

Marheshvan a month of the Jewish year, frequently shortened to Heshvan

Menahem Av an alternative designation for the month of Av incorporating the idea of consolation (*menahem*, 'consoling'), because of the ideas of consolation expressed in the readings for the sabbaths of consolation that follow the fast-day of the *Ninth of Av marking the destruction of both temples in Jerusalem, the first of which is known as *Shabat Nahamu

Midrash rabbinic commentaries, usually on specific books of the Bible, consisting of exegesis, homilies, and legends

menorah candelabrum

minhah the afternoon prayer service

merkavah the divine chariot-throne, a basic theme in Jewish mysticism

Ninth of Av a traditional day of mourning commemorating the destruction of the temples in Jerusalem, observed by fasting and other mourning rites; the culmination of a three-week period of semi-mourning

notarikon a technique using the initial (or subsequent) letters of the words in specific biblical verses to create other words or phrases, for the purposes of meditation or incantation

omer (literally, 'sheaf') an offering brought to the Temple on 16 Nisan (the second day of Passover), and by extension the name of period between the festivals of Passover and Shavuot. There is a biblical injunction to count the forty-nine days between 16 Nisan and Shavuot (based on Lev. 24: 9 ff.), which is referred to as 'counting the *omer*'

pardes the four traditional methods of biblical exegesis; an acronym of *peshat* (literal meaning), *remez* (allusion, e.g. *gematriyah*), *derash* (homiletical interpretation), and *sod* (esoteric interpretation)

Purim festival which celebrates the deliverance of the Jews from the Persian minister Haman's plot to kill them, as told in the book of Esther

Sabbatians followers of, or disciples and believers in, Sabbatai Zevi (1626–76), who was proclaimed the Jewish messiah by Nathan of Gaza in 1665

Shabat Nahamu (literally, the 'Sabbath of Consolation') the sabbath after the fast of the *Ninth of Av, so called because of the first word of the *haftarah* portion from Isaiah which is read in the synagogue on that day: 'Comfort [*nahamu*], oh comfort my people.'

Rosh Hashanah Jewish New Year

sefirah, pl. *sefirot* a fundamental kabbalistic term used to describe the ten stages of emanation that emerged from *Ein Sof; manifestations of God in his various attributes

segulah, pl. *segulot* a kabbalistic protective charm

shaḥarit the morning prayer service

Shemini Atseret (literally, 'the eighth day of solemn assembly') the festival immediately after *Sukkot. *See also* Simhat Torah

shofar, pl. **shofars** ram's horn; normatively blown during the month of Elul, on *Rosh Hashanah, and at the end of *Yom Kippur

Simhat Torah (literally, 'rejoicing of the Torah') the second day of the festival of *Shemini Atseret (in the diaspora); on this day the annual reading of the Torah scroll is completed and immediately begun again

Sitra Ahra the 'other side', i.e. evil in all its various manifestations

Star of David (Heb. *magen david*) a late Jewish symbol incorporating different meanings (magical and messianic); used in *Sabbatian circles

sukkah the booth that becomes a person's 'dwelling' for the week of the *Sukkot festival

Sukkot ('Tabernacles') harvest festival which commemorates the booths (sukkot) in which the Children of Israel dwelt in the wilderness; it takes place five days after *Yom Kippur, in mid-autumn

Targum an Aramaic translation of the Bible. The most authoritative Aramaic translation of the Pentateuch is Targum Onkelos; it is printed in standard Hebrew editions of the Pentateuch alongside the biblical text, together with the classic rabbinic commentary of Rashi

tefilin ('phylacteries') two black leather boxes containing scriptural passages that are bound (or 'laid') on the left hand and on the head using black leather strips, and worn for the morning services on all days of the year except sabbaths and biblically ordained festivals

tikun, pl. *tikunim* kabbalistic corrective prayer or measure

Torah portion according to the annual cycle of readings, the Torah (Pentateuch) is divided into fifty-four portions, one to be read in the synagogue each sabbath. Every portion has a specific name; this name can also be used to refer to the sabbath on which that particular Torah portion is read

Utterances (of Creation) the ten occurrences of 'God said' in the biblical account of Creation in Genesis, as interpreted in Mishnah *Avot* 5: 1, 'With ten utterances the world was created.' Kabbalistic doctrine considered these 'Ten Utterances' to be parallel to the ten *sefirot*

Yom Kippur the Day of Atonement

Zohar the fundamental work of kabbalistic literature, written in Aramaic. Traditionally ascribed to the mishnaic sage Simeon bar Yohai, scholars consider that it dates mainly from the last decades of the thirteenth century and that the principal author was Moses de Leon. The main part of the work, arranged according to weekly *Torah portions, is a kabbalistic commentary on the Torah combined with long expositions, narratives, and legends

BIBLIOGRAPHY

AARON HALEVI OF BARCELONA, *Sefer haḥinukh*. English trans: C. Wengrow, *Sefer haHinnuch: The Book of Mitzvah Education* (Jerusalem, 1992).

ABELSON, J., 'Swedenburg and the Zohar', *The Jewish Chronicle Supplement*, 30 May 1924, VII–VIII.

ABULAFIA, ABRAHAM, 'Epistle' [Igeret], in A. Jellinek, *Philosophie und Kabbala* (Leipzig, 1854), 1–42.

ABULAFIA, TODROS, *Otsar hakavod* (Warsaw, 1879).

ACTON, A., *The Delights of Wisdom: Concerning Conjugal Love* (London, 1970).

ADLER, E. N., *London* (Philadelphia, 1930).

ADLER, H., 'The Baal Shem of London', in *Festschrift zum A. Berliners 70* (Berlin, 1903), 1–9.

——'The Baal Shem of London', *Transactions of the Jewish Historical Society of England (1902–1905)* (1908), 148–73.

ALEXANDER, L., *Memoirs of the Life of Benjamin Goldsmid* (London, 1808).

ALEXANDER, T., 'Design of the Demon Story Genre: Marriages between a Man and a Demon' (Heb.), in Yael Azmon (ed.), *A View into the Lives of Women in Jewish Societies* [Eshnav leḥayeihen shel nashim baḥavarot yehudiyot] (Jerusalem, 1995), 291–308.

ALTMANN, ALEXANDER, *Moses Mendelssohn* (London, 1973).

——'Notes on the Development of Rabbi Menahem Azariah of Fano's Kabbalistic Doctrine' (Heb.), in Joseph Dan and Joseph R. Hacker (eds.), *Studies in Jewish Mysticism Presented to Isaiah Tishby on his Seventy-Fifth Birthday* [Meḥkarim bekabalah mugashim liyeshayah tishby bimlot lo shivim veḥamesh shanim], Jerusalem Studies in Jewish Thought 3/1–2 (Jerusalem, 1984), 241–67.

ARCHENHOLZ, J., *A Picture of England* (London, 1798).

ASHKENAZI, E., *Ta'am zekenim* (Frankfurt am Main, 1854).

AVIVI, Y., 'The Kabbalistic Writings of R. Menahem Azariah of Fano' (Heb.), *Sefunot*, NS 4 (1989), 347–76.

AZMON, YAEL (ed.), *A View into the Lives of Women in Jewish Societies* [Eshnav leḥayeihen shel nashim baḥavarot yehudiyot] (Jerusalem, 1995).

AZULAI, HAYIM JOSEPH DAVID, *Ma'agal tov hashalem* (Berlin, 1921). English trans.: *The Diaries of Rabbi Ha'im Yosef David Azulai ('Ma'agal Tov'—the Good Journey)*, trans. B. Cymerman (Jerusalem, 1997).

BARNETT, A., *The Western Synagogue through Two Centuries (1761–1961)* (London, 1961).

BEINISH, BENJAMIN, *Amtaḥat binyamin* (Wilhelmers, 1716).

BEINISH, BENJAMIN, *Sefer shem tov katan* (Sulzbach, 1706).

BENAYAHU, MEIR, 'The "Holy Brotherhood" of R. Judah Hasid and Their Settlement in Jerusalem' (Heb.), *Sefunot*, 4 (1960), 133–82.

——'The Letters of R. Abraham Cuenque to R. Judah Briel' (Heb.), *Sinai*, 32 (1953), 300–19.

BEN JACOB, YITSHAK, *Otsar hasefarim* (Vilna, 1877–80).

BEN-MENAHEM, N., 'Four Editions of *Mesilat yesharim* Printed at Zolkiew' (Heb.), *Areshet*, 1 (1958), 479–80.

BET-HALEVI, I. D., *History of the Jews of Kalisz* [Toledot yehudei kalish] (Tel Aviv, 1961).

BICK, A., *Rabbi Jacob Emden: The Man and his Thought* [Rav ya'akov emden: ha'ish umishnato] (Jerusalem, 1975).

BOAS, SAMUEL AHARON, *My Ancestors* (privately printed, Givatayim, 1990).

BUDGE, E. A. W., *Amulets and Talismans* (New York, 1970).

CASANOVA, G., *History of My Life*, trans. Willard R. Trask, 12 vols. (New York, 1966).

CAVENDISH, R., *A History of Magic* (London, 1977).

CHETTOUI, W. R., *Cagliostro et Catherine II: Contre le Mage* (Paris, 1947).

DAN, JOSEPH, *The Ancient Jewish Mysticism* [Hamistikah ha'ivrit hakedumah] (Tel Aviv, 1989).

——'Anfiel, Metatron, and the Creator' (Heb.), *Tarbiz*, 52 (1983), 447–57.

——'Demonological Stories in the Writings of R. Judah Hehasid' (Heb.), in id., *Studies in the Literature of Hasidei Ashkenaz*, 9–25.

——*The Esoteric Theology of Hasidei Ashkenaz* [Torat hasod shel ḥasidei ashkenaz] (Jerusalem, 1968).

——'Ḥadrei merkavah' (Heb.), *Tarbiz*, 47 (1978), 49–55.

——'On the History of the *Shevaḥim* Literature' (Heb.), *Jerusalem Studies in Jewish Folklore*, 1 (1981), 82–100.

——'Princes of the Cup and Princes of Thumb' (Heb.), in id., *Studies in the Literature of Hasidei Ashkenaz*, 34–43.

——*Studies in the Literature of Hasidei Ashkenaz* [Iyunim besifrut ḥasidei ashkenaz] (Ramat Gan, 1975).

——(ed.), *Early Jewish Mysticism: Proceedings of the First International Conference on the History of Jewish Mysticism* [Hamistikah hayehudit hakedumah: divrei hakenes habeinle'umi harishon letoledot hamistikah hayehudit], Jerusalem Studies in Jewish Thought 6/1–2 (Jerusalem, 1987).

DAVIS, E., and D. A. FRENKEL, *The Hebrew Amulet* [Hakami'a ha'ivri] (Jerusalem, 1995).

DINUR, B. Z., *Historical Studies* [Bemifneh hadorot] (Jerusalem, 1954).

——'The Origins of Hasidism and its Social and Messianic Foundations' (Heb.), in id., *Historical Studies*, 83–227.

DRUMONT, E., *La France juive* (Paris, 1888).
DUBNOW, SIMON, *The History of Hasidism* [Toledot haḥasidut] (Tel Aviv, 1960).
DUSCHINSKY, D., *The Rabbinate of the Great Synagogue, London from 1786–1842* (London, 1921).
EICHHORN, JACOB, *Sefer afar ya'akov* (Breslau, 1839).
EISENSTEIN, JUDAH DAVID (ed.), *Otsar yisra'el*, 10 vols. (New York, 1951).
ELBAUM, J., *Openness and Insularity: Late Sixteenth-Century Jewish Literature in Poland and Ashkenaz* [Petiḥut vehistagerut: hayetsirah haruḥanit hasifrutit bepolin uve'artsot ashkenaz beshilhei hame'ah hashesh-esreh] (Jerusalem, 1990).
ELITZUR, R., 'Different Readings in R. Menahem Lonzano's *Shetei yadot*, Venice 1618' (Heb.), *Kiryat sefer*, 42 (1966/7), 511.
EMDEN, JACOB, *Megilat sefer* (Warsaw, 1890).
——*Migdal oz* (Lemberg, 1860; Zhitomir, 1874; facsimile of the Zhitomir edn., Jerusalem, 1969).
——*Sefat emet uleshon zehorit* (Altona, 1752).
——*Sefer hitabekut* (Altona, 1762–9; Lvov, 1877).
——*Tsitsim uferaḥim* (Altona, 1768).
ENDELMAN, T. M., *The Jews of Georgian England 1714–1830* (Philadelphia, 1979).
ETKES, IMMANUEL, 'The Role of Magic and *Ba'alei Shem* in Ashkenazi Society in the Late Seventeenth and Early Eighteenth Centuries' (Heb.), *Zion*, 60 (1995), 69–104.
FISHER, H. E. S., 'Jews in England and the 18th-Century English Economy', *Transactions of the Jewish Historical Society of England*, 27 (1982), 156–65.
FLINT, V. I. J., *The Rise of Magic in Early Medieval Europe* (Princeton, 1991).
FRANK, JACOB, *Księga Słów Pańskich* [The Words of the Master], ed. Jan Doktór, 2 vols. (Warsaw, 1997); unpublished Hebrew translation by Fania Scholem.
FREEDMAN, M. (ed.), *A Minority in Britain: Social Studies of the Anglo-Jewish Community* (London, 1955).
GALLICO, SAMUEL, *Asis rimonim*, an abridgement of Cordovero's *Pardes rimonim*, published together with *Pa'amon verimon* (a commentary by Mordecai ben Jacob of Prague on *Pardes rimonim* by Moses Cordovero) and *Pelaḥ harimon* (an abbreviated version of and commentary on the 'Ha'atsilut' section of *Pardes rimonim*, by Menahem Azariah of Fano) as a single volume (Amsterdam, 1708).
GASTER, MOSES (ed.), '*Ḥarba demoshe*', in id. (ed.), *Studies and Texts*, iii.
——*History of the Ancient Synagogue* (London, 1901).
——(ed.), *Studies and Texts in Folklore, Magic, Mediaeval Romance, Hebrew Apocrypha and Samaritan Archaeology*, vol. iii (London, 1928).
GIKATILLA, JOSEPH, *Sha'arei orah*, ed. Y. Ben-Shlomo (Jerusalem, 1971).
GRIES, ZEEV, *Conduct Literature (Regimen Vitae), its History and Place in the Life of the Hasidim of the Ba'al Shem Tov* [Sifrut hanhagot, toledoteiha, umekomah beḥayei ḥasidav shel habesht] (Jerusalem, 1989).

GROT, J. (ed.), *Lettres de Grimm à l'Impératrice Catherine II (Sbornik Imperatorskago Russago Istorichaskago Obscestra)*, 2nd, rev., edn. (St Petersburg, 1884).
GRUENWALD, I., *Apocalyptic and Merkavah Mysticism* (Leiden and Cologne, 1980).
GRUENWALD, I., 'Magic and Myth: Research and Historical Reality' (Heb.), *Eshel be'er sheva*, 4 (1996), 15–28.
——'New Fragments from the *Heikhalot* Literature' (Heb.), *Tarbiz*, 38 (1969), 354–72.
HARKAVY, A., *Teshuvot hage'onim* (New York, 1959).
HEILPRIN, JOEL BEN URI, *Sefer mifalot elohim* (Turka, 1767).
HEYMANN, F., *Der Chevalier, Von Geldern* (Cologne, 1963).
HILLEL, M., *Ba'alei shem* (Jerusalem, 1993).
HILLS, G. P. G., 'Notes on the Rainsford Papers in the British Museum', *Ars Quartor Coronatorum*, 26 (1913), 93–130.
——'Notes on Some Contemporary References to Dr. Falk, the Baal Shem of London, in the Rainsford MSS at the British Museum', *Transactions of the Jewish Historical Society of England*, 8 (1915–17).
HYAMSON, A. M., *The Sepharadim of England: A History of the Spanish and Portuguese Jewish Community, 1492–1951* (London, 1951).
IBN HABIB, JACOB B. SOLOMON, *Ein ya'akov* (Amsterdam, 1725).
IDEL, MOSHE, *The Golem* [Hagolem] (Jerusalem, 1996).
——*Kabbalah: New Perspectives* (New Haven, 1988).
——'The Magical and Neoplatonic Interpretations of the Kabbalah in the Renaissance' (Heb.), *Jerusalem Studies in Jewish Thought*, 1/4 (1982), 60–112.
——*The Mystical Experience in Abraham Abulafia* [Haḥavayah hamistit etsel avraham abulafiyah] (Jerusalem, 1988); English edn.: *The Mystical Experience in Abraham Abulafia*, trans. Jonathan Chipman (Albany, NY, 1988).
——*Studies in Ecstatic Kabbalah* (New York, 1988).
——'The World of Angels in Human Form' (Heb.), in Joseph Dan and Joseph R. Hacker (eds.), *Studies in Jewish Mysticism Presented to Isaiah Tishby on his Seventy-Fifth Birthday* [Meḥkarim bekabalah mugashim liyeshayah tishbi bimlot lo shivim veḥamesh shanim] [= *Jerusalem Studies in Jewish Thought*, 3/1–2] (Jerusalem, 1984), 1–66.
JELLINEK, ADOLF, *Philosophie und Kabbala* (Leipzig, 1854).
——(ed.), 'Midrash konen', in id., *Beit hamidrash* (facsimile edn., Jerusalem, 1967), pt. 2.
KAHANA, D., 'Those in Error and Those Who Lead Astray' (Heb.), *Hashilo'aḥ*, 22 (1899), 55–6.
'Kami'a' (Heb.), in Judah David Eisenstein (ed.), *Otsar yisra'el* (New York, 1951), ix. 193.
KATZ, D. S., *The Jews in the History of England 1485–1850* (Oxford, 1994).
KATZ, J., *Jews and Freemasons in Europe, 1723–1939* (Cambridge, Mass., 1970).
KATZENELLENBOGEN, PINHAS, *Yesh manḥilin*, ed. Y. D. Feld (Jerusalem, 1986), based on Bodleian, MS Mich. 296.

KELLER, E. F., 'Daniel Müller—Ein merkurdiger religioser Schwärmer des achtzehnten Jahrhunderts', *Zeitschrifte für die historische Theologie*, 4 (1834), 39–236.

KIRCHHEIM, RAPHAEL, '*Ketav tamim* by R. Moses Taku' (Heb.), *Otsar neḥmad*, 3 (1860).

KRUPNIK (KARU), B., and A. M. SILBERMANN, *A Dictionary of the Talmud, the Midrash, and the Targum* [Milon shimushi latalmud, lamidrash velatargum] (Tel Aviv, 1970).

LESSING, GOTTHOLD EPHRAIM, *Lessing's Masonic Dialogues (Ernst und Falk)*, trans. A. Cohen (London, 1927).

LEVINE, HILLEL (ed. and trans.), *The Kronika—On Jacob Frank and the Frankist Movement* [Hakeronikah—te'udah letoledot ya'akov frank utenu'ato] (Jerusalem, 1984), Hebrew with English summary.

LEVITA, ELIJAH (BAHUR), *Sefer hatishbi* (Isny, 1541).

LEWIN, B. M., *Otsar hage'onim: ḥagigah* (Jerusalem, 1932).

LIBERMAN, HAIM, *Ohel raḥel* (New York, 1980).

LIEBES, YEHUDA, 'The Author of the Book *Tsadik yesod olam*—the Sabbatian Prophet R. Leibele Prossnitz' (Heb.), in id., *On Sabbatianism and its Belief*, 70–6.

——'Chapters in a Dictionary of the Zohar' (Heb.), Ph.D. diss., Hebrew University of Jerusalem, 1977.

——'Mysticism and Reality: Towards a Portrait of the Martyr and Kabbalist R. Samson Ostropoler' (Heb.), *Tarbiz*, 52 (1983), 83–109.

——'New Sabbatian Kabbalistic Writings from the Circle of R. Jonathan Eybeschuetz' (Heb.), in id., *On Sabbatianism and Its Belief*, 103–97.

——'On a Christian Jewish Sect with Sabbatian Origins' (Heb.), in id., *On Sabbatianism and Its Belief*, 212–37.

——*On Sabbatianism and Its Belief* [Sod ha'emunah hashabeta'it] (Jerusalem, 1995).

LIPSCHUTZ, SHABETAI, *Kitsur segulot yisra'el* [Book of traditional Jewish charms] (Orsova, 1905; expanded edn., Jerusalem, 1993).

MACKAY, C., *Extraordinary Popular Delusions and Madness of Crowds* (1841; London, 1995).

MACKENZIE, K. R. H., *The Royal Masonic Cyclopaedia* (London, 1877; New York, 1987).

MACKEY, ALBERT GALLATIN, *The History of Freemasonry: Its Legendary Origins* (1898; New York, 1990).

MARGOLIOUTH, M., *The History of the Jews in Great Britain* (London, 1851).

MATERS, H., 'A Book of Charms: Customs and Beliefs in Folk Medicine according to the Book *Toledot adam*' (Heb.), Master's thesis, Hebrew University of Jerusalem, 1942.

MAYNIAL, E., *Casanova and His Time*, trans. E. C. Mayne (London, 1911).

MELAMED, E. Z., *Dictionnaire araméen-hébreu* [Milon arami-ivri letalmud bavli] (Jerusalem, 1992).

MENAHEM AZARIAH OF FANO, *Pelaḥ harimon*, a commentary on Moses Cordovero, *Pardes rimonim* (facsimile edn., Jerusalem, 1962).

MICHMAN, J., H. BEEM, and D. MICHMAN (eds.), *Encyclopaedia of Jewish Communities: Holland* [Pinkas hakehilot: holand] (Jerusalem, 1985).

MOSES DE LEON, *Sefer hanefesh hahakhamah* (Basel, 1808; facsimile edn., Jerusalem, 1969).

NAVEH, J., and S. SHAKED, *Amulets and Magic Bowls* (Jerusalem, 1985).

NEUBAUER, A. D., *Catalogue of the Hebrew Manuscripts in the Jews' College, London* (Oxford, 1886).

——'Literary Gleanings', *Jewish Chronicle*, 19 Dec. 1884, 11.

NIGAL, GEDALYAH, 'The Character and Thought of the Ba'al Shem Tov' (Heb.), *Sinai*, 120 (1997), 150–60.

——'*Dybbuk' Tales in Jewish Literature* [Sipurei 'dibuk' besifrut yisra'el] (Jerusalem, 1994).

——*The Hasidic Tale*, trans. Edward Levin (Oxford, 2008).

——*Life Imprisonment for a Ba'al Shem: The Tragic Fate of R. Hirsch Fraenkel* [Ba'al shem lema'asar olam: goralo haterai shel harav hirsh frankel] (Ramat Gan, 1993).

——*Magic, Mysticism, and Hasidism*, trans. E. Levin (Northvale, NJ, 1994).

ORON, MICHAL, 'Dr. Samuel Falk and the Eibeschuetz–Emden Controversy', in K. E. Grozinger and J. Dan (eds.), *Mysticism, Magic, and Kabbalah in Ashkenazi Judaism* (Berlin, 1995).

——'Dream, Vision, and Reality in Hayim Vital's *Sefer hahezyonot*' (Heb.), in Rachel Elior and Yehuda Liebes (eds.), *Lurianic Kabbalah: Proceedings of the Fourth International Conference on the History of Jewish Mysticism* [Kabalat ha'ari: divrei hakenes habeinle'umi harevi'i leheker toledot hamistikah hayehudit], Jerusalem Studies in Jewish Thought 10 (Jerusalem, 1992), 299–309.

——'Mysticism and Magic in Eighteenth-Century London: Samuel Falk, the "London Ba'al Shem"' (Heb.), in R. Tsur and T. Rosen (eds.), *Israel Levin Jubilee Volume: Studies in Hebrew Literature* [Sefer yisra'el levin: kovets mehkarim basifrut ha'ivrit ledoroteiha], vol. ii (Tel Aviv, 1995), 7–20.

——'*Sefer gahalei esh*' (Heb.), in Rachel Elior (ed.), *The Sabbatian Movement and Its Aftermath: Messianism, Sabbatianism and Frankism* [Hahalom veshivro: hatenu'ah hashabeta'it usheluhoteiha: meshihiyut, shabeta'ut, ufrankizm], Jerusalem Studies in Jewish Thought 16–17 (Jerusalem, 2001), 73–93.

PACHTER, MORDECAI, '*Hazut kashah* of Rabbi Moses Alshekh' (Heb.), *Shalem*, 1 (1974), 157–93.

PATAI, R., *The Jewish Alchemists: A History and Source Book* (Princeton, 1994).

PHOIADES, C., *Count Cagliostro*, trans. K. Shelvoanker (London, 1932).

PICCIOTTO, J., *Sketches of Anglo-Jewish History* (London, 1875; new edn., London, 1956).

PIEKARZ, MENDEL, *The Beginning of Hasidism* [Biyemei tsemihat hahasidut] (Jerusalem, 1978).

RANTZOW, J. L. A., *Mémoires du Comte de Rantzow* (Amsterdam, 1762).

ROBERTS, M. M., and H. O. LONDON (eds.), *The Literature of Secret Societies* (New York, 1995).

ROLLESTON, T. W., *Life of Gotthold Ephraim Lessing* (London, 1889).

ROSENTHAL, L., *Heinrich Heines Grossheim, Simon Von Geldern* (Kastellum, 1978).

ROSMAN, MOSHE, *Founder of Hasidism: A Quest for the Historical Ba'al Shem Tov* (Berkeley, Los Angeles, and London, 1968; 2nd edn., Oxford, 2013).

ROTH, CECIL, *Essays and Portraits in Anglo-Jewish History* (Philadelphia, 1962).

—— 'Goldsmid, Aaron' (Heb.), *Ha'entsiklopediyah ha'ivrit* [Encyclopaedia Hebraica], vol. x (Jerusalem, 1969), 388–9.

—— *The History of the Great Synagogue* (London, 1950).

—— *The History of the Great Synagogue in London* (London, 1951).

—— *A History of the Jews in England* (Oxford, 1949).

—— 'The King and the Cabbalist', in id., *Essays and Portraits in Anglo-Jewish History*, 139–64.

—— 'The Membership of the Great Synagogue, London, to 1791', *Jewish Historical Society of England*, Miscellanies 6 (London, 1962), 175–85.

—— *Records of the Western Synagogue, 1761–1932* (London, 1932).

ROTH, I., 'London's Baal Shem, Still a Mystery Man', *The Jewish Week*, 25 Aug. 1985, 21.

RUDERMAN, D. B., *Jewish Enlightenment in an English Key: Anglo-Jewry's Construction of Modern Jewish Thought* (Princeton, 2000).

—— *Kabbalah, Magic and Science* (Cambridge, Mass., 1988).

SCHAEFER, P., *Synopse zur Hekhalot Literatur* (Tübingen, 1981).

SCHECHTER, S., 'The Baalshem—Dr Falk', *Jewish Chronicle*, 9 Mar. 1888, 15–16.

SCHOLEM, GERSHOM, 'Ba'al Shem', *Encyclopaedia Judaica* (Jerusalem, 1971), iv. 5–7.

—— 'Ba'al shem' (Heb.), *Ha'entsiklopediyah ha'ivrit* [Encyclopaedia Hebraica], vol. ix (Jerusalem, 1958), 263–4.

—— 'The Career of a Frankist: Moses Dobruschka and his Reincarnations' (Heb.), in id., *Studies and Texts Concerning the History of Sabbatianism*, 141–209.

—— '*Havdalah derabi akiva*: A Source for the Tradition of Jewish Magic during the Geonic Period' (Heb.), *Tarbiz*, 50 (1981), 243–81.

—— 'Identification of the Book *Magen david* Mentioned in *Pardes rimonim*' (Heb.), *Kiryat sefer*, 9 (1932), 258.

—— *Jewish Gnosticism, Merkabah Mysticism and Talmudic Tradition* (New York, 1965).

—— *Kabbalah* (Jerusalem, 1974).

—— '*Magen david*: The History of a Symbol' (Heb.), in *Lu'aḥ ha'arets* (Tel Aviv, 1949), 148–63.

—— *Major Trends in Jewish Mysticism* (New York, 1942).

—— *The Messianic Idea in Judaism* (New York, 1971).

—— 'Physiognomy and Chiromancy' (Heb.), in U. (M. D.) Cassuto, J. Klausner, and J. Gutmann (eds.), *The Book of Asaf: A Collection of Scholarly Articles Presented to Rabbi Professor Simha Assaf* [Sefer asaf] (Jerusalem, 1953).

SCHOLEM, GERSHOM, 'Reports of Sabbatians in Books by Missionaries in the Eighteenth Century' (Heb.), in id., *Studies and Texts Concerning the History of Sabbatianism*, 609–29.

—— 'The Sabbatian Movement in Poland—Studies in the History of Sabbatianism in Poland' (Heb.), in id., *Studies and Texts Concerning the History of Sabbatianism*, 68–140.

—— *Sabbatianism Studies* [Meḥkerei shabeta'ut], ed. Yehuda Liebes (Tel Aviv, 1995).

—— *Studies and Texts Concerning the History of Sabbatianism and Its Metamorphoses* [Meḥkarim umekorot letoledot hashabeta'ut vegilguleiha] (Jerusalem, 1974).

—— 'The Treatise on the Left Emanation by R. Isaac Hakohen' (Heb.), *Mada'ei hayahadut*, 2 (1926), 82–102.

—— 'The True Author of the Commentary on *Sefer yetsirah* Attributed to Rabad' (Heb.), in id., *Chapters on the History of the Literature of the Kabbalah* [Perakim letoledot sifrut hakabalah] (Jerusalem, 1931), 2–18; repr. from 'Chapters from the History of Kabbalistic Literature' (Heb.), *Kiryat sefer*, 4 (1927/8), 286–302.

SCHUCHARD, MARSHA K., 'Dr. Samuel Jacob Falk: A Sabbatian Adventurer in the Masonic Underground', in M. D. Goldish and R. H. Popkin (eds.), *Millenarianism and Messianism in Early Modern European Culture*, i: *Jewish Messianism in the Early Modern Period* (Dordrecht, 2001), 203–26.

—— 'The Secret Masonic History of Blake's Swedenborg Society', *Blake—An Illustrated Quarterly*, 26/2 (1992), 40–51.

—— 'Yeats and the "Unknown Superiors": Swedenborg, Falk and Cagliostro', in M. M. Roberts and H. Ormsby-Lennon (eds.), *The Literature of Secret Societies* (New York, 1995), 114–68.

Sefer harazim, ed. Mordecai Margalioth (Jerusalem, 1967).

Sefer ḥasidim, ed. Reuben Margaliot (Jerusalem, 1957).

SHALEM, S., 'The Exegetical and Homiletical Method of R. Moses Alshekh's Commentaries on the Bible' (Heb.), *Sefunot*, 5 (1961), 151–206.

—— 'The Life and Works of Rabbi Moses Alshekh' (Heb.), *Sefunot*, 7 (1963), 179–97.

—— 'Thought and Morals in the Commentaries of R. Moses Alshekh' (Heb.), *Sefunot*, 6 (1962), 197–258.

SMITH, W., *Dissertation on the Nerves* (London, 1768).

—— *A Sure Guide in Sickness and Health* (1776).

STORMS, G., *Anglo-Saxon Magic* (The Hague, 1948).

THOMAS, KEITH, *Religion and the Decline of Magic: Studies in Popular Beliefs in Sixteenth- and Seventeenth-Century England* (London, 1991).

TISHBY, ISAIAH, 'Documents Written by the Hand of R. Moses Loanz, the Son of R. Joselmann of Rosheim' (Heb.), in U. (M. D.) Cassuto, J. Klausner, and J. Gutmann (eds.), *The Book of Asaf: A Collection of Scholarly Articles Presented to Rabbi Professor Simha Assaf* [Sefer asaf] (Jerusalem, 1953), 515–28.

——'The Letters of R. Meir Rofe to R. Abraham Rovigo' (Heb.), in id., *Studies in Kabbalah and Its Branches*, 273–332.

——'*Mesilat yesharim*, Zolkiew 1766' (Heb.), *Kiryat sefer*, 45 (1969/70), 300.

——*Studies in Kabbalah and Its Branches* [Ḥekrei kabalah usheluḥoteiha] (Jerusalem, 1993).

TRACHTENBERG, J., *Jewish Magic and Superstition* (New York, 1974).

URBACH, EPHRAIM E., *The Sages: Their Concepts and Beliefs* [Ḥazal: emunot vede'ot] (Jerusalem, 1975).

VAN ZUIDEN, D. S., *Proeve eener genealogie van de Haagsche familie Boas* (The Hague, 1939).

VERMAN, M., *The Book of Contemplations* (New York, 1992).

WALISZEWSKI, K., *The Story of a Throne (Catherine II, of Russia)* (London, 1895).

WALKER, *Spiritual and Demonic Magic: From Ficino to Campanella* (London, 1975).

WEBSTER, N., *Secret Societies* (London, 1921).

WEISS, JOSEPH, 'Beginnings of Hasidism' (Heb.), *Zion*, 15 (1951).

WERSES, SHMUEL, 'Phenomena of Magic and Demonology in the Satirical View of the Galician *Maskilim*' (Heb.), *Meḥkerei yerushalayim befolkelor yehudi*, 17 (1995), 33–62.

WESTCOTT, W. W., *History of the Rosicrucian Societies in Anglia* (London, 1900).

——'The Rosicrucians Past and Present', in R. Gilbert (ed.), *The Magical Mason: Forgotten Hermetic Writings of William Wyn Westcott* (Wellingborough, 1983).

WILENSKY, MORDECAI, 'Notes on the Biography of Rabbi R. E. H. Ricchi' (Heb.), *Kiryat sefer*, 25 (1948/9), 311–14.

WIRSZUBSKI, CHAIM, *Between the Lines* [Bein hashitin] (Jerusalem, 1990).

——'The Kabbalist Moses David of Podhajce' (Heb.), *Zion*, 7 (1942), 73–93; repr. in id., *Between the Lines*, 189–209.

WOLF, L., *Essays in Jewish History* (London, 1934).

WOOLF, M. 'Eighteenth-Century London Jewish Shipowners', *Transactions of the Jewish Historical Society of England*, 24 (1975), 198–204.

YASSIF, ELI, *The Medieval Stories of Ben Sira* [Sipurei ben sira biyemei habeinayim] (Jerusalem, 1985).

YATES, F. A., *The Occult Philosophy in the Elizabethan Age* (London, 1980).

ZFATMAN, S., *The Marriage of a Mortal Man and a She-Demon* [Nisu'ei adam veshedah] (Jerusalem, 1987).

ZIMMER, H., *Philosophies of India* (Princeton, 1974).

INDEX

A
Aaron, Bela 78–9, 84
Aaron ben Abraham of Cardena 267
Aaron Halevi of Barcelona 271
'Aaron Under Reader in my Synagogue' 276, 280
Abraham (child) 99, 134–5
Abraham (teacher of R. Tuvyah) 167–8
Abraham b. David of Posquières (Rabad) 171
Abraham Hakohen 270
Abraham of Hamburg, R. (R. Aberley) 166–7
Abraham of Lissa, R. 141
Abraham Nanshikh (Nancy, Nanzig), R. (aka Abraham b. Solomon Hamburger) 172–3, 176, 235–6, 277, 280
Abulafia, R. Abraham 18n., 42
Abulafia, Todros 18n.
Adler, Herman, Rabbi Dr 47n., 50n., 61, 62–3, 166, 247n.
Alexander, Levy 245–6
Alfalas, Moses 271
Alfandari, Hayim 267, 268
Alkabets, Solomon 271
Alshekh, Moses 186–7, 266, 268, 269
Amsterdam 3–4
amulets:
 activities of *ba'alei shem* 1, 26–7
 container for 120
 description of 27
 Emden's position 23, 27, 41, 263–4
 Falk's activities 8, 27, 30, 38–9, 40, 41, 78, 91, 102–3, 106–7, 109, 116, 117–18, 128, 137, 141
 mentioned in Falk's diary 64, 173, 177, 178, 209–10
 stories of curative powers 23, 30
 stories of writers 17, 18n., 45
 use of 25, 26–7
 writing of 27
Ana bekho'aḥ prayer 94, 99, 172, 186
Archenholz, Johann Wilhelm von 5, 31n., 52
Argas, Dr Abraham Gomez ('Abraham Doctor', aka Dr Philippe de la Cour):
 background 76
 bequest in Falk's will 208, 276, 280
 name 37n., 208, 234
 relationship with Falk 37, 76, 78, 208, 234, 237
Ashkenazi, R. Joseph 171
Austria 209, 243
Ayash, David 271
Azulai, Hayim Joseph David 8, 37–8, 78

B
ba'al shed (possessing or possessed by a demon) 45, 61, 253, 256, 262–3
ba'al shem, ba'alei shem (master(s) of the name):
 amulet-writing 17–18, 26–7
 attitudes to 20–1
 books of charms 25–6
 Falk's status 1, 3, 11, 27, 28–9, 36–7, 45, 47, 54, 57n., 61, 278–9
 first use of term 16
 history 15–20
 magical activities 1, 15–19
 magical uses of holy names 18
 sources for our knowledge of 21–4
 techniques 16, 27, 57n.
 'wonder-workers' 15, 19, 24, 45, 61
Ba'al Shem, R. Joel 22n.
Ba'al Shem Tov 21n., 60
Baer (servant) 176
Bahya b. Asher, R. 27n.
Barbariski, R. Jacob 143, 157
Barbariski, R. Jacob Cohen 100
Barukh, R. 142
Barukh, R. (cantor) 221, 222
Barukhyah Russo b. Judah 56
Behilah, Belah 281
Beinish, R. Benjamin 22
Bendayt of Kalisz, R. 141
Benjamin, Philip 236
Berele, R. 74
Boas, Abraham:
 accounts of Falk's miracles 7, 8
 background 33n., 243
 loan to English royal family 3
 possible reference in Falk's diary 177–8
 relationship with Falk 36n., 206, 211
 signatory for Falk's gold chest 182–4, 208
Boas, Hayim (Abraham) 243
Boas, Samuel Aharon 243n.
Boas, Simeon (Shimon):
 account of Falk's miracles 7, 8
 background 33n., 243–4
 Falk's books at his house in The Hague 187, 212–13
 Falk's will 245
 financial dealings 226
 forest estate 181–2
 Freemasonry 59, 244
 loan to English royal family 3
 possible reference in Falk's diary 177–8
 relationship with Falk 36n., 167, 176, 198, 205–6, 209–11, 215, 225, 244, 245

Boas, Simeon (Shimon) (*cont.*):
  role in Jewish community 243–4
  signatory for Falk's gold chest 182–4, 208
Boas, Tobias (Tuvyah):
  background 3, 33n., 243
  patronage of Falk 3–4
  possible references in Falk's diary 167, 176, 177–8, 181
  relationship with Falk 36n., 205, 211
  signatory for Falk's gold chest 182–4, 208
  son-in-law 183, 184
  sons 3, 7, 8, 243
Boas family:
  background 243
  bank 3, 243
  estate 7
  Falk's visits to The Hague 7
  Freemasons 10
  house in The Hague 205–6, 208, 214
  importance to Falk's career 3–4, 8, 59n., 168
  link with Goldsmid family 3
  link with Prager family 3–4
  marriages 183
  patronage of Falk 3, 7, 33, 244
  possible references in Falk's diary 167, 168, 176, 177–8
books of incantations and charms 19, 22n., 24–6, 161, 188
Boskowitz, Hayim 213
Bozbach, Meyer 75
Braunschweig, duke of 31n., 33, 55n.
Brockmer, John Paul 50
Burley (the coachman) 201, 202
Buzaglo, Shalom ben Moses 271, 272

C
Cagliostro, Count Alessandro di 3, 9–11, 49–50, 52–3, 59
candles, used in Falk's rituals 33, 41–2, 92–3, 94–8, 103, 104, 106–7, 109–13, 117, 122, 139, 144, 146, 148, 184
Cardozo, Jacob ben David Lopez 271
Casanova, Giacomo 3, 10, 11, 52–3, 58, 59
Cassel 3, 4, 30
Castro, Jacob 271
Catherine (maidservant) 81, 82, 85
Catherine the Great, tsarina 53
charms:
  books of 19, 22n., 24–6, 161, 188
  Falk's book 27, 191
  Falk's list 191–3
  Falk's use of 96, 98, 102, 153, 194, 195
  Katzenellenbogen's account 22–3
  made by Eybeschuetz 263n.
  writers of 17–18
  Zevi Hirsch's list 26, 43, 161–3
Chentchin, R. Moses 126
chests:
  arranged for ritual use 116
  extracting powers from 185
  Falk's list of books in 186–8, 212–13, 268–9
  Falk's list of contents of chest in The Hague 211–12
  Falk's list of contents of gold chest 177–81
  Falk's list of five chests sent to Aaron Goldsmid 234–5
  fortune-telling ceremony 194–5
  gold chest buried in Holland 7, 173, 181
  gold chest deposited with Boas family 182, 183, 208
  ordered for ritual use 4, 81, 85
  Torah ark 70
Christianity:
  Falk's rumoured conversion 46–8, 183, 278
  rumours of Jews converting to 45–6
  Sabbatianism and 45–6, 256n.

Clarence, William, duke of (later William IV) 3
Cohen, R. Eliezer 204
Collier family:
  clothes 137
  death of landlord 132, 134, 144
  financial issues 112, 115–16, 134, 145
  house on the Bridge 116, 117, 132, 134, 143–6
  landlord 83, 112
  relationship with the Little One 83
  reports of commotions on the Bridge 117
  son of landlord 144
  widow of landlord 134, 137
Collins family 64, 277
Cologne 3, 29, 108
Coltee, Dr Andrew 273
Cordovero, R. Moses 173, 265, 267, 268
Cour, Philippe de la, *see* Argas
Creation *ex nihilo*, *see* Utterances
Cuenque, Abraham 266n., 268
Czartoryski, Prince 58–9, 209–11, 224–6, 244

D
Dan, Joseph 16–17
Danziger, R. Leib 147
de la Cour, Dr Philippe, *see* Argas
de Lara, Hayim (Hiya) Kohen 271
de Loutherbourg, Philippe Jacques 60n.
demons:
  belief in 23
  blamed for misfortunes 20, 135, 163
  children of 236
  Emden's account of Falk 45, 262
  kabbalist writings 18–19, 135
  pietist writings 16–18
  possession by 7, 137
  protection against 1, 16, 20, 23
  speech of 254
  visions of 37

INDEX

Doctor, R. Abraham, *see* Argas
Doctor, R. Isaac 112
Doctor, R. Leib 208
Donop, Baron von 3, 29–31, 33
Dov Baer, R., of Chmielnik 126
dreams 128, 170–1, 223, 226–7, 248–50

E

Edelstein, Hertz 245
Eichhorn, R. Jacob ben Joseph 278
Eisenstadt, Jacob 'Sofer' ben Eliezer 86–7, 255
Eisenstadt, Meir 86, 255
Eleazar the Great of Worms, Rabbi 18–19
Eliezer, R. 167
Eliezer, R. (in Holland) 176
Emden, Jacob:
  attacks on Falk 24, 40, 44–5, 48, 62, 261–4
  crusade against Sabbatianism 23, 39n., 44–5, 266
  on Falk family history 28n., 29n.
  on Falk's followers 36
  on Falk's link with Eybeschuetz 56, 256n.
  hostility towards *ba'alei shem* 24, 62
  interest in amulets 23, 27
  letter on Falk 261–4
  practical kabbalah 23–4
  publication of Shesnowzi's letter 42n., 45, 251–60, 277
  son 45, 75
  war against Eybeschuetz 23–4, 27, 44, 48, 256n.
Ephraim Solomon ben Aaron of Luntshits 272
Epping Forest 7, 9, 89, 184
Ergas, Joseph 268
Essingen, Samuel 24
Etkes, Immanuel 21
Eybeschuetz, Jonathan:
  amulets 23, 27, 263n.
  Emden's attacks on 23–4, 27, 44–5, 48, 256n., 264

followers 46, 48
link with Falk 45, 256n.
relationship with Müller 51n.
teacher 255n.
Eybeschuetz, Wolf 11n., 44, 46, 51n., 56n., 223
Ezekiel b. Shalom of Zamość, R. 124

F

Falk, Joshua ben Alexander, Rabbi 28
Falk, Joshua ben Judah Leib 268, 272
Falk, Joshua Raphael Falker (Hasefaradi, father of Samuel) 28, 60, 226–7, 250, 253
Falk, Samuel:
  ability to 'move objects' 8, 30–1, 32, 33, 37, 41, 58, 94, 96–7, 107, 153, 262
  accidents 122–3, 128, 140, 146–7
  alchemical and chemical experiments 3, 6, 8, 29, 36, 38–9, 43, 52, 58, 128, 140
  amulets and seals 8, 27, 30, 38–9, 40, 41, 64, 78, 91, 102–3, 106–7, 109, 116, 117–18, 128, 137, 141, 177
  appearance 5, 52, 59–60, 149, 255–6, Plate 1
  arithmetic and calculations 171, 193, 195, 196, 205, 211, 217, 229, 234
  arrival in England 3–4, 33, 136
  attitude to Christianity 30, 46–8, 183, 278
  ba'al shem 1, 3, 11, 27, 28–9, 36–7, 45, 47, 54, 57n., 61, 278–9
  birth and childhood 2, 28
  brandy recipes 214–15, 216
  cake recipes 64, 215–16, 218, 221, 227
  'camp' on the Bridge 40–1, 91–8, 102–3, 106–7, 109–13, 117, 127–8, 136–49, 151, 154, 155–6

'camp' in the forest 171, 184
'camps' 181, 239
career 2–3, 29–30
chamber on London Bridge 5, 7, 36, 58, 72, 91–3, 108, 116, 143
character 5, 35, 44, 57n., 274
charismatic figure 1, 5
charms 191–3, 195
chests, *see* chests
child-rearing and education 83, 86, 88, 99, 114, 134–5
clothing 37, 52, 78, 79, 87, 189, 217–18, 224, 255
death 59
debts 65, 83, 237
debts repaid 70, 201–2, 237
descendants 29n., 277
diary 62–4, 165–239, Plate 6
domain of the camp 92, 94, 96–105, 139
domain in the forest 146, 178, 184–5
domain of *not bayit* 152, 156
dreams 128, 170–1, 223, 226–7, 248–50
family background 28, 29, 33, 37, 226, 253, 261
fasting 92, 103, 117, 142, 154
finances 1, 4–5, 11–12, 35, 37, 80, 88, 114–15, 130–1, 133, 138, 143, 145, 150, 204–6, 245, 262–3, 277–8
fire and explosion 32, 38, 128, 134–5
flying knife 32–3
flying sword 8, 37, 42, 94, 96–7, 107–8, 153
followers 34, 36, 262, 274, 278
fortune-telling 57n., 194–9
geographical scope of social network 7–8
gifts 165, 173, 175, 194, 199, 202–4, 208, 247
grave 60n., 277, 278
healing activities 3, 4, 7, 29, 30, 43, 118, 134–7, 142–3
health 142, 149, 170, 224–5
heirs 275–7

Falk, Samuel (*cont.*):
  house in Prescot Street (Pas) 5, 6, 35–6, 40, 69, 71, 76, 80, 82, 91, 112, 118, 119, 146–9
  house in Wellclose Square 5, 6, 36, 53, 71, 247
  household 35, 85
  library 11, 57n., 186–9, 212–13, 265–72
  life in London 33–4
  lifestyle 11–12
  lists of items 173–5
  lotteries and games of chance 4, 11, 52, 76, 79, 199, 204–5, 217, 224, 238–9, 265
  magical ceremonies 42; *see also* rituals
  magical verbal techniques, *see* magical verbal techniques
  marriage 4, 29, 35, 83, 92, 149, 262
  metal-plating activities 39, 43, 57n., 58, 64, 70, 78, 150, 156
  mother's burial 221–2, 275
  mother's grave 29
  name 28, 206–7, 225, 264n.
  new house on the Bridge 136–40, 143–9, 155, 157
  orthography 64, 206, 207, 221
  patrons 3–5, 7, 10, 12
  plaster recipe 220–1
  pledges 69–71, 129, 145, 150, 200–2, 231–4
  portrait 59–60
  private synagogue 4, 6, 39, 88, 89, 126, 276
  relationship with Cagliostro 9, 49–50, 52–3
  relationship with Casanova 52
  relationship with Christians 3, 4, 5, 8, 9, 11, 30, 44
  relationship with Emden 44–8; *see also* Emden
  relationship with Freemasons 9–11, 36, 44, 46n., 49–56, 58–60, 222, 274
  relationship with Swedenborg 9, 10, 50–3, 56–9
  relationship with wife 35, 83, 92, 149, 150–1, 157, 170, 223, 248–9
  relationship with Zevi Hirsch 64–5, 71, 138–9, 148
  reputation 1, 8, 9, 36–7, 39–40, 44, 57n., 244, 262n., 274
  revealer of lost treasures 29, 262
  revealing gold 32
  rituals, *see* rituals
  rumoured apostasy from Judaism 9–10, 46–8, 56–7, 266, 274, 278
  rumoured conversion to Christianity 46–8, 183, 278
  sale of objects 199–200
  sentenced for sorcery 29, 262
  signature 28n., 206–7, 235, 281
  status in Jewish community 6, 39–40, 44, 59, 89, 126, 222, 274–5, 277–9
  stepson Gedaliah, *see* Gedaliah
  teaching kabbalah 37–8, 44
  tent on the Bridge 149
  tent of East Ham 214
  tent in the forest 178, 211
  tent in The Hague 211–12, 214
  tent in Harderwijk 190, 214
  tent structure 189–91
  tents (dimensions) 214
  tombstone 60–1, Plates 2 and 3
  varnish recipes 219–20
  wife ('the rebbetsin'), *see* Falk's wife
  wife's death 6, 12, 170
  will 12, 29, 48, 59, 62, 172, 203, 245, 246, 273–81, Plate 4
  wine 63–4, 203, 204, 229–30
  wonder-worker 32–3, 41–2, 246n.
  world-view 11
  writings 27, 36, 57n., 69, 191
Falk, son of Abraham Gisa 281
Falk's wife ('the rebbetsin', 'the *rabanit*'):
  burned in explosion 128
  clothing 4
  cooking 35, 83
  death 6, 12, 170, 222, 223
  defended by Zevi Hirsch 76
  dressmaking 93
  finances 4, 35, 74, 108, 117, 118, 119, 123, 130–1, 133, 150
  health 71, 86, 133
  maidservant's story 85
  relationship with husband 35, 83, 92, 149, 150, 157, 248
  separation from husband 149, 150, 155
  slandered by Emden 262
  son, *see* Gedaliah
  speaking French 77
  visitors 77, 116
  watching fireworks 122
Fast of Esther 135
fasting 42, 103, 135
  see also Ninth of Av; Yom Kippur
Firstrag (Pressburg), R. Leib (Lyon) 235
Firstrag (Pressburg), R. Samuel (Baron Lyon de Symons) 5, 235
Fishman, Moses 6, 40, 125, 126
Flanders (pawnbroker) 35, 70, 80
Fleming (Neuhoff's landlord) 128–9
Fleming, Madam ('Flemick') 121
France:
  Boas family contacts 243
  Cosman's reputation 36, 155, 244
  Cosman's travels 148, 203, 236, 245
  Czartoryski's travels 209
  duke of Orléans 247
  Falk's contacts 51, 58
  Falk's financial transactions 116, 204, 205, 206, 207, 245, 277
  Falk's missions to 58
  Falk's will challenged 245, 277
  Jacobite agents 56, 58
  Masonic lodge 37

'servant of the king' 166, 229
see also Paris
Franch, Joseph 87
Frank, Aaron 112
Frank, Jacob 11n., 52, 56n., 279
Frank, Mordecai B. Getz 69
Frankism:
    Falk's relationship with 2,
        28–9, 47, 49, 56n., 266
    sexual teachings 56, 223, 245,
        250n.
Franzmann, Mordecai 69, 79,
    131
Frederick, duke of York 3
Freemasons:
    Cagliostro's career 9, 52–3
    Casanova's career 52
    Cosman Lehman's career 36,
        245
    Falk's relationship with 9–11,
        36, 44, 46n., 49–56, 58–60,
        222, 274
    interest in kabbalah 38, 51–2
    Jewish Freemasons 10
    marquis de Thomé's
        relationship with 37n., 76
    masturbation ritual 223, 250n.
    minister Emmanuel's
        relationship with 166
    Rainsford's relationship with
        203, 245
    relationship with Frankists
        56n.
    Simeon Boas's relationship
        with 244
Froelich, Joseph 88
Fürth 2, 28–9, 221–3, 275, 280

G

Gabbai, Isaac b. Solomon 272
Gabriel, R. 90, 99–100, 102, 115,
    134
Galante, Moses ben Mordecai
    269
Gallena, R. Moses b. Elijah 22n.
Gallico, Samuel 267
Gans, David 270
garments and footwear:
    arba kanfot 189

kitl 93–4, 95, 143–4, 146–7, 149,
    255
Passover 119–20, 137
pawned 76–9, 81, 82, 83–4, 86,
    87–9, 108, 115, 135, 145
purchased 71, 74, 75, 85, 86,
    87–8, 119, 134, 137, 140, 141,
    147, 218
repairs 86, 137
Rosh Hashanah 71
sabbath 189, 211–12
stored in The Hague 189,
    211–12
Gedaliah (stepson of Falk):
    adopted by Falk 29, 262n.
    attendance at the Bridge 103,
        145–9
    attendance in the forest 116
    bequest in Falk's will 262n.,
        276, 280
    bringing money from Cosman
        132–3
    bringing money from von
        Neuhoff 119, 130, 131
    communicating with von
        Neuhoff 121, 125
    errands for Falk 167, 210,
        217–19, 221, 226, 237, 239
    follower of Falk 36n.
    fortune-telling ceremony
        194–5
    meeting with Czartoryski
        224–5
    mission to Flanders 7, 80
    pawnshop visits 72, 81–4,
        86–7, 89, 108, 233–4
    record-keeping 204
    relationship with Falk 203,
        233, 276
    riding accident 121
    sale of objects 199, 201, 223
    stepson of Falk 4, 29
Geldern, Simon von 54, 235
Geller, Uri 262n.
gematriyah (numerology):
    book on 270
    examples 89, 93, 100, 101, 109,
        147, 153, 171, 172, 193, 227
    Falk's use of 57n., 58, 64, 98,

99, 105, 151, 154, 168, 169,
    171–2, 180, 191, 227–8
Genesis, book of 70, 95, 100,
    109, 175, 192
The Gentleman magazine 46, 47
George II, king 50
George III, king 120
George, Prince of Wales (later
    George IV) 3
Germany:
    Cosman's missions 245
    Falk's background and career
        2–3, 8, 28–9, 221, 244, 250,
        278
    Falk's family 275
    Falk's missions to 58, 75
    see also Cassel; Fürth; Leipzig;
        Prussia
Gershom, Rabbenu 77
Gideon, Samson 76
Gikatilla, Joseph 18n., 270
gold:
    alchemical 8, 11, 29, 38, 53, 128
    box 178
    chains 156, 157, 200, 255
    chest 7, 177, 178, 181–3, 185, 208
    coat 37
    coins 126, 166, 208
    discovery 32, 55n.
    embroidery 73, 151
    headdress 255
    ingots 208, 209
    ink 160
    lacquer 220
    lettering 111, 118, 132
    making 11, 29, 38, 100, 128
    objects pawned 4, 70, 72, 74,
        75, 82, 94, 108, 122, 123, 125,
        129, 150, 200, 233
    plating 43, 78, 150, 156
    rings 23, 157, 178
    sale of 87, 150, 171, 199, 223
    seals 108, 210
    staff 179
    stars 4, 70, 72, 74, 108, 180, 181,
        255
    tablets 78, 150, 151, 154–5, 156
    theft of 223–4
    vessel 178

gold (cont.):
    watches 50, 72, 94, 122, 129, 133, 200, 233
Goldsmid, Aaron:
    biographical note 245–6
    daughter's marriage 235
    executor of Falk's will 245, 246, 275, 279, 281
    influence on election of chief rabbi 45
    London home 5
    relationship with Falk 3, 5, 234–6, 246
Goldsmid, Abraham 3, 245–6
Goldsmid, Benjamin 4, 245–6
Goldsmid, Gershom (George) 235, 236, 275, 279
Goldsmid family 3–4, 10, 12, 238, 262n., 275
Gordon, Lord George 93
Goudchaux, Juliette 247
Gries, Zeev 20, 24

H
Haes, David 140
Hagiz, Moses 88, 272
Hague, The:
    Boas family 3, 7–8, 178, 206, 214, 219, 243
    Falk hiding something there 168
    Falk's chest 181, 186–7, 211
    Falk's tent 214
    Falk's visits 3, 7, 184, 189, 223–4
    forest 181
    Jewish community 207
    lottery 217
Hai Gaon 16
Hamburg 23, 54, 56n., 256
Hamburger, Abraham b. Solomon, *see* Abraham Nanshikh
Hamburger, Selig 75
Hannover, Nathan Nata 99
Haparhi, Isaac (Estori) ben Moses 267
Harderwijk 181–2, 190, 208, 214, 236
Hart, Aaron 5, 89

Hart, Moses 83, 112, 246
Hart, R. Zalman 83
Has, David b. Anschel 140
Hasidei Ashkenaz 16–17, 19
Hayim (manservant) 87
Hayim (sick tailor) 239
Hayim (tailor and thief) 217
Hayim, R. 88
Hayim, R. (husband of Hannah) 141
Hayitshari, Matityahu ben Moses 272
Hebrew alphabet:
    chanting 94
    kabbalistic interpretation 270
    letter inversion 252n.
    meditating on 41, 98, 106
    number of letters 41, 106, 172, 211
    numerical value of letters 171, 193
    order and reverse order 162, 166
    sanctifying letters 96
    see also gematriyah; magical verbal techniques
heikhalot literature 15–16
hermetic teachings 56n.–57n.
Hertz, R. (the painter) 149
Hervir (pawnbroker) 79, 80, 82–4
Hesse-Darmstadt, princes of 54
Heymann, Fritz 54
Hills, Gordon 49
Hirsch, Samuel, of Schwersee 71
Hirsch, Zevi, *see* Zevi Hirsch
Hirsch Hazan, R. (possibly Samuel Hirsch of Schwersee):
    daughter 77, 108
    finances 71, 81, 84
    postal communications 72, 77, 90, 92
    son's death 112
Holland:
    Boas family 7, 33, 59n., 176, 182, 219, 243–4, 262n.
    Cosman's missions 203, 245
    Falk's connections 33, 51, 262n.

Falk's gold chest in 7, 173, 181, 182
Falk's missions to 7, 58, 75
Falk's 'tents' 214
Falk's travels 33, 65, 176, 244
financial transactions 238
Jewish community 33, 54n., 76
war with Spain 246
Zevi Hirsch's travels 7, 65, 149
see also Amsterdam; Hague, The
Hoshana Rabba 73, 85, 148, 175
Hurtle (the coachman) 202
Hurwitz, Pinhas Elijah 278n.

I
ibn Dios, Joseph ben Samuel 270
ibn Ezra, Abraham, Rabbi 17
ibn Habib, Jacob b. Solomon 81
ibn Janah, Jonah 270
ibn Tibbon, Judah 270
ibn Tibbon, Samuel 268
ibn Zimra, David 270
Idel, Moshe 24, 52n., 57n.
immersion, ritual 22n., 27, 40, 42, 90, 91, 118, 135, 142, 145, 146
incantations:
    activities of mystics and *ba'alei shem* 16, 18–19
    activities of Zevi Hirsch 90
    books of 22n., 24–6
    Falk's activities 152, 253
    Falk's teachings 8, 37–8
    magical techniques 57n.
    references in Falk's diary 229
Isaac, R. 94–8, 155
Isaac, R., son of R. Ezekiel 124
Isaac, R., son of Hannah 141
Isaac Hakohen, Rabbi 18–19
Isaac Hazan 59, 222
Isaac ben Judah Halevi 270
Isaac ben Samuel Halevi 268
Isaac b. Solomon Gabbai 187
Israel ben Benjamin 269
Itzik of Zamość, R.:
    attendance at Falk's rites 40–1, 92, 94, 100–3, 105, 107, 110–11, 136, 141–4, 146–7

brother 77
at Falk's house 76, 86, 124
finances 87
relationship with Falk 80, 92, 148

J
Jacob (the baby) 83, 86
Jacob, R. (follower of Falk):
  cake recipe 221, 227
  correspondence 198, 209–11
  dealings with Fornis Rafin 225–7
  fortune-telling ceremony 194–5
  relationship with Falk 36n., 194, 225, 226
  wine 203
Jacob (nephew of Cosman) 203
Jacob (*parnas* of Astor) 220
Jacob (pupil of Falk) 86, 88
Jacob (servant):
  cake recipe 215
  dismissal 202–3
  duties 170, 204, 217
  employers 165
  Falk's dream about 217, 249
  finances 169, 176, 202–3, 239
  name 171
Jacob ben Asher 267
Jacob son of Lima Dresden 277, 280
Jacob son of Sazbona 171
Jacob the Sharp, R. 228
Jacob Sofer, R. (Jacob ben Eliezer Eisenstadt) 86–7, 255
Jacob of Zamość, R. 77
Jacob Joshua ben Zevi Hirsch, R. 28
Jacob Saul ben Hananiah 271
Jacobites 50, 53, 129, 179, 185
Jew Bill (1753), repeal 5–6
Johanan, R. 221–3
Jonah of Halberstadt, R. 126
Joseph II, emperor 243
Joseph, R. 76
Joseph della Reina 37
Joseph of Zamość, R. 122

Judah, R. 167
Judah al-Harizi 270
Judah Harofe 272
Judah Hehasid, Rabbi 17, 19n., 37, 149
Judah Leib (Leon), son of Samuel 275, 279

K
kabbalah:
  ba'alei shem 1, 18, 20
  Boas family 3
  Christian interest in 3, 37–8, 44, 53, 265
  eastern Europe 1, 11
  'Egyptian' 53, 56–7n.
  Falk's interest in 11, 28, 57n., 64
  Falk's library 188, 213, 265–9, 271–2
  Falk's teachings 8, 10, 37–8, 58, 265
  Freemasonry 38, 51–2
  Lurianic 24, 99n., 265, 267, 268, 269, 272
  popular literature 19–20
  practical 8, 22, 23, 28, 37–8, 58, 60n., 262
  prayers 91, 94
  Renaissance period 24, 57n.
  Schuchard's claims 10, 56–7
  Zohar, *see* Zohar
  see also Hebrew alphabet; magical verbal techniques
Kahana, David 38, 63
Kalisz 77, 84, 129, 132, 138, 226
Katz, David 63
Katzenellenbogen, Meir b. Hayim, of Eisenstadt 255n.
Katzenellenbogen, Pinhas, Rabbi 21–3
Katzenellenbogen, Saul, Rabbi 22
kavanot, books of 41, 93–6, 98, 99, 101–3, 106, 109, 112, 116–17
Kerem, Moses 238, 239
Kilmallock, Lord ('Milord Kilmachnick') 129
Kimhi, Joseph 272

Kohen de Lara, Hayim (Hiya) 271
Koidonover, Shalom Shakhna ben Nahum 270
Koidonover, Zevi Hirsch ben Aaron Samuel 267
Koppel, Jacob 271n.
Kroka, Levi (Leib Kruka) 185, 276, 280
Krumbold (merchant) 139

L
la Croix, marquise de 8, 37–8
Laniado, Solomon b. Abraham 225
Lazi (Laze, Lazer), *see* Segal, R. Laze, of Hamburg
Lehman, Behrend 244
Lehman, Cosman:
  background 78, 244
  biographical note 244–5
  cake recipe 221, 227
  character 36, 78, 155–6, 244–5
  Falk's dream about 223, 245, 249–50
  Falk's letter to 195–7
  finances 78, 90, 94, 129–33, 135, 136–8, 143, 227, 277
  fortune-telling ceremony 194–5
  Freemasonry 245
  imprisonment 78, 113–14
  journeys to France 138, 141, 148, 229, 236
  lawsuit over Falk's will 245, 277
  list of gifts to 173–4
  missions for Falk 36, 78, 229
  nephew 203
  relationship with Falk 36, 78–80, 93, 115, 129, 136–8, 143, 146, 148, 150–2, 155–7, 209, 227–8, 236, 277
  relationship with Prince Repnin 226
  relationship with von Neuhoff 116–20, 123, 129
  supplying gold tablets 43, 78, 151, 155–6

Lehman, Hertz 244
Leib, David ben Aryeh 266
Leib (Leon), Judah, son of
    Samuel 275, 279
Leib, R., son of R. Eleazar Kann 235
Leib, Samuel 275, 279
Leib, Schwartz 76
Leib, Ze'ev Wolf ben Judah, of Rosni 268
Leib Danziger, R. 147
Leib Kruka (Levi Kroka) 185, 276, 280
Leib Plotzker 148
Leib of Portsmouth 218, 228
Leipzig 84, 88
Lessing, Gotthold Ephraim 50, 54–6, 222
Leszno 72
Levi, Moses 217
Levin, Ber Moses 183
Levin, Zevi Hirschel Levin (Hart Lyon), Rabbi 45
Levy, Benjamin 246
Levy, Elias 6, 40, 71, 126, 132, 246–7
Levy, Isaac, see Segal
Levy, Judith (Hart) 246–7
Levy, Kalman 213
Levy, Simhah, see Segal
Levy of The Hague 223
Levy in Japan 212
Liebes, Yehuda:
    on Eisenstadt 255n.
    on Emden 23
    on Eybeschuetz 256n.
    on Falk 59n., 105, 186, 197, 222
    on Loewe 52n.
    on masturbation ritual 223
    on secret sect of baptized Jews 45–6
Lindo, Elias 93
Lindy, Dr 93
Little One, the:
    dining with Cosman 79–80
    Falk's mystical rites 40–1, 94–7, 104–5, 107–8, 110–11, 128, 132
    finances 71–2, 74, 81–5, 90, 114, 115–16, 119, 131, 134, 138, 140–1
    imprisonment 79, 81, 90, 114, 127, 141
    relationship with Falk 36, 71–2, 90, 115, 119, 127–8, 134, 138, 140–1
    relationship with Zevi Hirsch 83, 87
    synagogue attendance 73
Loanz, Elijah b. Moses 270n.
London:
    Alderney Road Cemetery Plate 8
    Aldgate 72
    Ashkenazi community 6, 12, 39–40, 80, 83, 112, 167, 246, 274–5
    'Bressler' synagogue (Great Synagogue) 39, 89, 126
    chief rabbi 45, 169, 275
    City of 5, 72, 138, 245
    earthquakes 133, 135
    Falk's arrival 33, 136
    Fleet Street 50
    Goodman's Fields 5
    Great Synagogue 6, 8, 64, 71, 89, 126, 246n., 274, 275, 279–81
    hailstorm 139
    Hambro Synagogue 6, 45, 83, 172, 275, 279
    Houndsditch 5, 74, 78–84
    Jewish charitable societies 275, 279–80
    Jewish community 2, 5–6, 12, 33–4, 39, 44, 45, 59, 61, 112, 245, 274–5, 278
    King's Bench prison 9, 39, 127, 131
    Leadenhall Street 53
    London Bridge 5, 7, 36, 58, 72
    Mile End Jewish cemetery 60–1
    New Street 73
    Poultry Counter 90
    Prescot Street (Pas) 5, 6, 35–6, 40, 69, 71, 76, 80, 82, 91, 112, 118, 119, 146–9
    Rampart Street 124
Sephardi community 12, 33, 231, 246, 274–5
Spitalfields 5
Wellclose Square 5, 6, 9, 36, 52, 53, 71, 246–7
Western Synagogue (New Synagogue) 6, 275, 279
Whitechapel 5, 124
lots, casting:
    in book of *kavanot* 94
    for hiding parts of sword 179
    fortune-telling 194
    in Psalms 95, 105, 110
    Sussman Shesnowzi's account 257
lotteries and games of chance:
    buying lottery tickets 4, 79, 199, 217, 238–9, 265
    Falk's enthusiasm for games of chance 52
    Falk's lottery winnings 11, 204–5
    Falk's success at games of chance 204
    Zevi Hirsch's card-playing 76
Louis XV, king of France 50, 166n., 206, 229
Lowenstam, Aryeh Leib ben Shaul, of Kraków 185
Luntshits, Ephraim 187
Luria, Isaac 19n., 187, 213, 267, 270
Luxembourg, Chevalier de 245
Luzzatto, Jacob ben Isaac, of Safed 266, 269
Luzzatto, R. Moses Hayim 51n., 271
Lyon de Symons, see Firstrag

M
McCalman, Iain 9
Maciejko, Paweł 10, 11n.
magic:
    ba'alei shem 1, 15–19
    Jewish attitudes to 15, 18–19, 26–7
    sexual 56–7
    techniques in hermetic writings 57n.

INDEX

magical verbal techniques:
  acronyms 27, 64, 102, 169
  anagrams 153, 154, 228
  books of incantations 24–6
  chanting holy names 16
  chanting letters of alphabet 94
  chanting psalms 41, 94, 95, 97–8, 101, 104, 109–10
  enunciation of letters 101
  esoteric manipulations 102, 153, 184, 195, 197, 198
  gematriyah (numerology), see *gematriyah*
  manipulation of biblical quotations 27, 70, 104, 167, 191–3
  meditating on letters of alphabet 41, 94, 96, 98, 99, 100–1
  meditating on psalms 40–1, 94, 95, 97–100
  notarikon (acrostics) 57n., 96, 102, 105, 168, 270
  permutation of letters 27, 168–9, 171, 209, 229
  sanctifying holy names 113
  sanctifying letters of alphabet 96
  sanctifying sword 178, 179
  temurah (transposition of letters) 58, 153, 196
  used by Falk 42, 191–3, 218
  word permutation 167, 175–6, 198, 229
  writing letters of alphabet 30, 41, 97, 103–6, 111, 112, 195
Maimon, Solomon 7, 8
Maimonides 5 1n., 187, 268, 271
Mann, R. 136, 141–4, 146–8
Margaliot, Jacob Koppel ben Zevi Hirsch 271
masturbation 223, 236, 245, 250
Matityahu ben Moses Hayitshari 272
Meir (R. Meyer), synagogue warden 59, 222
Meir, Wolf, of Prague 271
Meir son of Zelikle 127

Menahem, R. Munish 176, 277
Menahem son of Joshua (servant) 237
Menahem de Lonzano 269
Menahem Azariah of Fano 22, 267, 268
Mendel (cantor) 276, 280
Mendel, R. (follower of Falk, servant):
  bequest in Falk's will 165, 169, 276, 280
  duties 170, 171, 221
  financial transactions 238–9
  follower of Falk 36n.
  fortune-telling ceremony 194–5
  missions for Falk 165, 168, 206, 221, 235
  servant of Falk 165
  travelling with Falk 184
  wages 233, 239
  will 169
Mendelssohn, Moses 54, 55n.
Meshullam Feibush ben Israel 269
Meyer (manservant):
  bequest in Falk's will 276, 280
  leaving Falk's service 203, 204
  missions for Falk 203, 217
  travelling with Falk 184
  wages 203, 204, 233
Meyer, R. (synagogue warden) 59, 222
Michael, R. 90
Mifalot elohim 25
Milper's (pawnbroker) 73–4, 76–84, 89, 115
Monish, Mr, at The Hague 276
Moravian Brethren 50, 126
Mordecai of Dresden (possibly Mordecai the son of Lima Dresden) 157
Mordecai b. Getz Frank 69
Mordecai, son of Hirsch Hazan 112
Mordecai ben Jacob of Prague 267, 268
Mordecai, son of Lima Dresden 277, 280

Moses, Mr ('Priest in the new Synagogue') 276, 280
Moses, R. (ritual slaughterer) 221–2, 223
Moses Chentchin, R. 126
Moses David of Podhajce 24, 28, 45–7, 253, 255, 256, 263, 264
Moses de Leon, R. 18n., 266, 286
Moses ben Menahem Graf of Prague 271
Muelhausen, Yom Tov Lipmann 272
Müller, Johan Daniel 51n.
Mussafia, Benjamin 270

N

Na'amah (she-demon) 236–7
names, holy (divine):
  Abulafia's account 42
  amulets 23, 26–7, 128, 177
  ba'alei shem (masters of the name) 1, 15–16, 27
  carving 42
  chanting 16, 18, 109
  charms 161
  disappearance 108, 132
  Emden's account of Falk 261–2
  Emden's views 23–4
  Falk's use of 1, 40–3, 91–7, 99, 101–3, 105–10, 112–14, 116, 119–24, 126, 128, 132, 134, 139–41, 144–5, 147, 151, 153, 155, 157, 177, 255–7
  formed from initial letters 161
  inscription on tablets 43, 151, 155
  Katzenellenbogen's attitude 22
  knowledge and writing of 27
  letter *heh* 112
  magical uses 16–18, 20
  meditating on 96, 99, 105
  mystical practices 20
  number of letters in 101, 105, 106, 173, 177, 186
  pawned 108
  popular traditions 20

names, holy (divine) (*cont.*):
  pronouncing 17, 42, 101, 147
  reciting 15, 102
  sanctifying 113
  Tetragrammaton 32, 58, 93, 100, 109, 172, 192, 246
  warnings against use of 22
  writing 27, 41, 93–7, 99, 101, 106–7, 110, 112, 113, 134, 147, 151, 154, 173, 177, 186, 209
  written on shofar 92, 180
Nanshikh (Nancy, Nanzig), Abraham, *see* Abraham Nanshikh
Napaha, R. Isaac 167
Nathan of Gaza 56n.
Nathan ben Jehiel of Rome 270
Nehunya b. Hakanah, R. 94, 172, 186
Neta of Zamość, R. 138
Neubauer, Adolf 62, 166
Neuhoff, Theodore Stephen de Stein, Baron von, 'king of Corsica'
  career 38
  country house 120–1, 122–6, 128, 143
  debt problems 128–9, 131
  financing Falk 116–23, 125–6
  gold watch 122, 129, 133
  imprisonment for debt 9, 39, 131, 143
  marriage 129
  meetings with Falk 8–9, 38–9, 116–26
  possible son 52
  relationship with Falk 62–3, 116
  tombstone Plate 7
new moon:
  Falk's calculations 171, 198
  Falk's magical activities 184–5
  immersion before 135
  penitential period 152
  preparation for 87
  Shabat Shekalim 133
  significance to Falk 186, 199, 203, 234
Nicholas (pawnbroker) 35, 72, 74, 75, 82, 94, 123, 125

Nigal, Gedalyah 19, 21
Nina, Moses 79
Ninth of Av 113, 149, 154, 155, 175
Nissim ben Jacob of Kairouan 271
Nordah, Solly 225–6
Nordom, R. Leib 127, 130
notarikon, *see under* magical verbal techniques

O
Obadiah of Bertinoro, R. 187, 272
Obcestva, Colonel Frederick 52
Oppenheim, David 271
Orléans, Louis Philippe Joseph, duke of (Philippe Égalité) 247
Osterer, Moses ben Hillel 272
Ostropoler, Samson ben Pesah 267

P
Paris 8, 37, 50, 119, 138, 169, 244
Passover:
  books 231, 271
  clothing for 119–20, 137
  Falk's expenditure 119–20, 134
  Falk's financial difficulties 4, 87–9
  food for 87, 239
  wine 87, 203–4
pawnbrokers 4, 35, 69, 70, 72, 73, 80, 81
  see also Flanders; Hervir; Milper's; Nicholas; Wyleport
Perles, Aaron ben Moses Meir 269
Piekarz, Mendel 21
Pinchbeck, Christopher 120
Pineira, Lopez 222
plaques 43, 90, 94, 96–7, 139, 209
Plotzker, Leib 148
Podhajce 2, 28, 221, 253, 256
Polack, Isaac 8
Polack, R. Juda 74
Poland:
  Boas family contacts 243

Czartoryski's background 58–9n., 209–10
Falk's birth 2, 11, 28
Falk's family background 28, 221
Falk's reputation 257, 261, 263
postal arrangements 72, 77, 127
Sabbatians 56, 59n., 124
Shesnowzi's letter 251
Tuvyah's travels 130
Zevi Hirsch's background 35, 64
see also Kalisz; Leszno; Podhajce
Pollack, R. Aaron 90
Pollack, Ber 127
Poniatowski, Stanisław August, king of Poland 243
Posner, R. Hertz 134
Posner, R. Meyer 82, 134
postal arrangements:
  Falk's concern about R. Jacob 226
  Green Barg postal company 77, 92, 127, 129
  penny post 131
  role of Jewish community 90, 114–15, 122, 124, 127, 138
  sending money 90, 127, 130, 131
  Zevi Hirsch acting as intermediary 77, 87, 158
  Zevi Hirsch's correspondence with his father 72–3, 77, 84, 90, 92, 114–15, 122, 124, 127, 129, 130, 138
Praeger, Leib 76, 80
Praeger, Wolf 76, 80
Prager, R. Joseph 44n.
Prager, Moses 24
Prager, Yehiel (Israel Levin Salomons) 4, 5
Prager family 3–4, 12
Pressburg, *see* Firstrag
Prossnitz, R. Leibele 255n.
Prussia 50, 52, 58, 127, 209
Psalms:
  casting lots in 40, 95, 105, 110

chanting 41, 94, 95, 97–8, 101, 104, 109–10
  Falk's use of 40–1, 69–70, 91, 95, 99–100, 101–2, 105, 107, 109–10, 144
  meditation on 40–1, 94, 95, 97–100
  mystical meanings 102
  reciting 40, 69–70, 91, 99–102, 104, 144, 162
  Zevi Hirsch on 91, 162–3
Purim 4, 86, 119, 135, 175, 203, 222

R
Rachel (mother of Leib, wife of Meyer) 228, 276, 280
Rafin, Fornas 226
Rainsford, Charles, General 78n., 156n., 203n., 244, 245
Rantzow, Count Alexander Leopold Anton von 3, 29–30
Rantzow, Count Georg Ludwig Albrecht von (son of above) 3, 5, 11, 29–33
Rapoport-Albert, Ada 63n.
remedies and charms 158–63
Renaissance, interest in magic 24, 57n.
Repnin, Prince Nikolai Vasilevich 226
Resona, R. Moses 216
Revesz, R. Zalman 278–9
Ricchi, Raphael Emmanuel Hai 267, 268, 269
Richelieu, Armand de Vignerot du Plessis, duc de 49, 53
rituals:
  accounts of Falk's 6–7, 40–2, 65, 69–70, 91–114, 116–24, 136, 139–57
  'camp' on the Bridge 40–1, 91–8, 102–3, 106–7, 109–13, 117, 127–8, 136–49, 151, 154, 155–6
  'camp' in the forest 171, 184
  candles 33, 41–2, 92–3, 94–8, 103, 104, 106–7, 109–13, 117, 122, 139, 144, 146, 148, 184

candlesticks 4, 70, 79–83, 85, 88, 103, 108, 111, 114, 146, 200, 232, 233
chanting letters of the alphabet 41, 94, 106
chanting psalms 41, 94, 95, 97–8, 101, 104, 109–10
crown 41, 42, 106–7, 111, 113, 177
domain of the camp 92, 94, 96–105, 139
domain in the forest 146, 178, 184–5
domain of *not bayit* 152, 156
Epping forest 7, 9, 89, 184
Falk's experiments 3, 36, 38–9, 43, 52, 58, 128
immersion in ritual bath 22n. 27, 40, 42, 90, 91, 118, 135, 142, 145, 146
knife 32–3, 42
locations 7
London Bridge 5, 7, 36, 58, 72, 91–3, 108, 116, 143
Masonic 10, 223, 250n.
meditating on letters 41, 94, 96, 98, 99, 100–1
meditating on psalms 40–1, 94, 95, 97–100
objects 4, 7, 70, 177–81, 186–7, 211–12
silver egg 4, 70, 74
stars 4, 70, 72, 74, 108, 180–1
sword 8, 37, 41, 42, 89, 92–3, 94, 96–7, 103, 106–8, 113, 144, 147, 152–3, 178–9
tents 149, 178, 189–91, 211–12, 214, 234
writing, *see* writing
Rosh Hashanah:
  Abraham's prayers 175
  candlesticks 80
  clothing for 71
  Falk's financial difficulties 115
  Falk's rituals 96–7, 103
  preparations for 145, 151, 152
  services 129, 207
  shofar 129, 180, 278
  tashlikh ceremony 73
Rosman, Moshe 21

Roth, Cecil 29n., 39n., 47n., 60, 62–3, 277
Roth, Irene 29n., 39n., 62, 277

S
Sabbatai Zevi:
  Barukhyah as successor to 56n.
  claimed allusion in Psalms 105
  Eybeschuetz's amulets 27, 45
  Falk suspected of following 6
  opponents of 279
  reference in Shesnowzi's letter 258n.
  see also Sabbatianism
sabbath:
  cooking 83
  Falk on 168, 185, 197, 228
  festive meal 86
  financial difficulties 80, 84, 87, 114, 115, 133, 150–1, 223
  food for 115, 131, 223
  garments 189, 211–12
  Havdalah ceremony 232
  observance 72, 80, 93, 112, 135, 140, 149, 154, 156–7
  Torah readings 133
Sabbatianism:
  Czartoryski's position 59n.
  Emden's position 23, 44–5
  Falk as crypto-Sabbatian 10, 39, 47, 56–7, 62, 105, 154
  Falk's library 265–6
  Freemasonry 51
  Laze Segal's position 75
  masturbation ritual 245, 250n.
  Moses David's position 28, 45, 256n.
  movement in Podhajce and Fürth 2, 28–9
  movement in Poland 56, 59n., 124
  use of *magen david* symbol 60n.
Saint Priest, Emmanuel 166, 229
Salomons, Israel Levin, *see* Prager (Yehiel)
Samson Hazan of Chentchin 126

Samuel, Edgar 63n.
Samuel of Falaise 270
Samuel Hazan, R. 239
Sasson, Abraham 271
Savalette de Langes, Charles-
  Pierre-Paul, marquis de 49
Schabracg, Joseph 273, 281
Schechter, Solomon 46–7, 62,
  183
Schiff, David Tevele, R. (chief
  rabbi of London) 45, 169
Schneider, Leib 125
Scholem, Gershom 56n., 60n.,
  63
Schuchard, Marsha Keith:
  account of Falk's activities
    9–10, 46–7, 266
  on *ba'al tsafon* 39n.
  on Falk as prince of
    Portuguese Jews in London
    33, 36n.
  on Falk's apostasy from
    Judaism 274
  on Falk's relationship with
    Swedenborg 51–2, 56–7,
    166, 229
  on Falk's ties with Freemasons
    50–3
  on Jesuits 29n.
  on marquis de Thomé 37n.
  on masturbation ritual 223
  on portrait of Falk 60n.
Schuster, Mordecai 88
Sefer haberit (Book of the
  Covenant) 278–9
Sefer hagoralot (Book of
  Fortunes) 36, 57n., 69
Sefer haḥayim (Book of Life) 17
Sefer hasegulot (Book of Charms)
  27
Sefer ḥasidim 18
Sefer hitabekut 45, 251n., 261
Sefer malakhim 149
Sefer segulot vegoralot (Book of
  Charms and Fortunes) 191
Sefer yetsirah 40, 57n., 70, 91, 98,
  100, 102, 110, 171–2, 252, 272
sefirot 57, 57–8n., 70, 98, 102, 152,
  172, 185

Segal, Isaac Eisik, of Kalisz 35,
  163
Segal, R. Laze, of Hamburg:
  background 75
  finances 75, 77, 86–7, 124–5,
    127, 139, 157–8
  imprisonment 84
  relationship with Zevi Hirsch
    75, 77, 86–7, 89, 124–5, 127,
    139, 157–8
  religious views 45
  travels 86, 124–5, 127
Segal, R. Moses 149, 157
Segal, R. Zevi Hirsch 126
Segal (Levy), Isaac (the
  madman) 7, 135–7, 142–3
Segal (Levy), Simhah (the
  madman's father) 7, 135–7,
  142
Sha'arei tsiyon 99, 102
Shapira, Nathan ben Reuben
  David Tevele 270
Sheital, David 202, 208
Sheknopzh, Joseph 276, 280
Sherit (*ba'al muzi*) 79
Shesnowzi, Eliezer Sussman
  17n., 42, 45, 251–60, 261,
  263n., 277
Shimon, R. 167, 176, 215
Shisil 237
Simeon bar Yohai, R. 19n., 256,
  257n., 266
sleeping, restrictions on 40, 91,
  99, 100, 155, 255
Smith, Dr William 9, 50–1, 118,
  121, 123
Solomon ben Israel of Zolkiew
  271
Song of Songs 40, 91, 113, 218,
  266, 272
Spieler, Joseph Teschen 88
Spira, R. Nathan 39n.
Star of David (*magen david*) 27,
  60, 156, 177
Stein, Theodore Stephen de, *see*
  Neuhoff
Suki (maidservant) 202, 204
Sukkot 73–4, 129, 130, 145, 147–8,
  217, 231

Susman, Mr, at Amsterdam 277,
  280
Sweden 50, 55n., 58, 243
Swedenborg, Emmanuel:
  background and career 50
  followers 8, 54n.
  health 9, 50, 118
  in London 9, 50–2
  portrait 60n.
  relationship with Falk 9, 10,
    51–3, 56–9
  Schuchard's work 10, 37n.,
    39n., 46n., 50, 53, 56–7, 166,
    229
Symons, Baron Lyon de, *see*
  Firstrag (R. Samuel)

T
tashlikh ceremony 73
temurah, see under magical verbal
  techniques
Tench, Sir Fisher 124
Tevele, R. David, *see* Schiff
Thomé, marquis de 8, 76, 77–8
Thomé, marquise de 8, 37–8, 76,
  78
Tin, P. de 245
Tuvyah, R. (follower of Falk):
  background 69, 130
  financial matters 84
  participation in Falk's rites
    40–1, 69, 90–8, 100–7,
    109–11, 113–14
  travels 125, 130

U
Utterances (of Creation):
  kabbalistic view of 70
  recital of First Utterance
    103–4
  recital of Second Utterance
    95, 103–4
  recital of Third Utterance
    103–4, 113
  recital of Fourth Utterance
    98, 100
  recital of Fifth Utterance 100,
    101, 110
  recital of Sixth Utterance 70,
    101, 110, 113

recital of seven Utterances 40, 91
recital of Utterance 'In the beginning' 106
writing out Third Utterance 109
writing out Utterance 'In the beginning' 41, 106

V
Vital, R. Hayim 19n., 99, 248, 266, 267

W
Webster, Nesta 47, 49–50, 56n., 247n.
Westphalia 3, 29, 262
Wirszubski, Chaim 45, 256n.
Wodziński, Marcin 71, 127
writing:
　amulets 1, 17, 18n., 26–7, 38–9, 41, 45, 106, 109, 137, 177, 209
　chanting letters of the alphabet 41, 94, 106
　charms 17–18, 25–6, 43, 96, 191, 195
　cryptic language 196
　final letters 40, 64, 69, 99, 100, 105, 106, 167, 192–3, 195, 196–7, 229
　gematriyah (numerology), see *gematriyah*
　gold letters 118, 132, 156
　Hebrew alphabet, *see separate entry*
　holy names 27, 96, 99, 101, 106, 151, 173, 177, 186, 209
　initial letters 96, 99–100, 102, 104, 109, 161, 167, 171, 173, 182, 191–3, 196–8, 229
　letter inversion 252n.
　letters of the alphabet 31–2, 41, 103–6, 111, 112, 195
　letters carved into tent poles 189
　letters inscribed on ring 178
meditating on letters 41, 94, 96, 98, 99, 100–1, 105–7
permutations of letters 27, 168–9, 171, 209, 229
sanctifying letters of alphabet 96,
signatures 28n., 111, 116, 171, 182, 183, 205, 206–7, 235, 239, 281
spellings 64, 69, 251–6nn., 258–9nn., 261n., 263–4nn.
square letters 111, 154
transposition of letters 58, 153, 196
word permutation 167, 175–6, 198, 229
Wyleport (pawnbroker) 77, 81

Y
Yom Kippur:
　Abraham's prayers 175
　ceremonial textiles redeemed from pawnbroker 73
　Falk's rituals 72–3, 146, 204
　fasting 135, 154
　kitl-wearing 93
Yose ben Halafta 270

Z
Zalman, R. (follower of Falk) 69, 86
Zalman (Solomon), Israel Meshullam (son of Jacob Emden) 45
Zamość, R. Moses 124
Zarco, Judah ben Abraham 271
Zelig of Harderwijk 182
Zevi Hirsch:
　background 34n., 35
　career 64, 276
　charms and incantations 90
　clothing 71, 75, 83–90, 115, 119–20, 134, 137–8, 140, 147
　collection of charms 26, 161–3
　collection of remedies 65, 158–61
correspondence with his father 72–3, 77, 84, 90, 92, 114–15, 122, 124, 127, 129, 130, 138
descendants 29n., 64, 277
diary 4, 8, 34, 35–43, 56n., 57n., 62–3, 64–5, 69–163, Plate 5
on Falk's ability to 'move objects' 41, 94, 96–7, 107, 153, 262n.
Falk's bequest 276, 280
on Falk's experiments 38–9, 43
on Falk's finances 4–5, 35, 244
on Falk's healing activities 7, 43, 134–7, 142–3
on Falk's mystical rites 5, 6–7, 40–2, 65, 69–70, 91–114, 116–24, 136, 139–57
on Falk's private synagogue 39–40, 126
on Falk's wife ('the rebbetsin', 'the *rabanit*') 35, 69, 71, 74, 76, 77, 85, 92, 108, 119, 123, 133, 149, 150, 155, 157, 248
father 72–3, 77, 84, 88, 90, 92, 114–15, 122, 124, 126, 127, 129, 130, 138, 148
gambling 76
mission to Holland 7, 65, 149
mother 122, 124
relationship with Falk 64–5, 71, 138–9, 148
sales 171
sister 122, 124, 130
Zohar:
　Falk's library 57n., 188, 213, 265, 266, 269–72
　Katzenellenbogen's library 21n.
　mentioned by Falk 168
　Schuchard's claims 56–7
　sexual symbolism 56–7
　Smith's researches 51n.
　Swedenborg's work 52n.

www.ingramcontent.com/pod-product-compliance
Lightning Source LLC
Chambersburg PA
CBHW080846020526
44114CB00045B/2682